THE NAME DICTIONARY

Modern English and Hebrew Names

by

ALFRED J. KOLATCH

JONATHAN DAVID PUBLISHERS
MIDDLE VILLAGE, N.Y. 11379

TABLE OF CONTENTS

DEDICATED

to the memory of

ANNA *and* SAMUEL RUBIN

PREFACE

Comparatively few books have been written on the general subject of names. On the subject of *Jewish* names an even smaller number exists.

Perhaps there is good reason for this dearth of books dealing with Jewish nomenclature. For one thing, in the years prior to modern times all the average Jew needed was one name—a Hebrew name, and that he found with facility. In the main he was not bothered with the necessity of choosing an additional secular name, as we are today. Only the few who had dealings outside the Jewish world adopted a foreign name in addition to their religious one.

Today, however, the picture has changed. All of us are required to carry a Hebrew and a secular name. This has become a problem to most Jews. How shall these two names be selected? How can we make them harmonize with each other? No recognized method or system is used today that will synchronize these two names for us. It is to help create some semblance of order out of the hodge-podge that this book aims.

The Name Dictionary is an enlargement of a work originally published in 1948 entitled, *These Are the Names*. Because of the increasing number of new personal names that have come into being since that time, particularly Hebrew names, this present work has become mandatory so as to bring the subject up to date.

Special thanks are due to Hagai Lev, a member of The Institute of Contemporary Jewry at the Hebrew University in Jerusalem, for having undertaken research specifically for this book. He extracted several thousand preferred names from a total of almost 100,000 which were later reduced, by careful selection, and were incorporated in this work. The three chief sources of new Hebrew names in *The Name Dictionary* come from the following:

1. From the Registry of Births in Israel, which is under the supervision of the Ministry of the Interior. The complete lists for the years 1956-1961 were checked, covering a total of approximately 80,000 names.

2. A variety of lists of Hebrew University students and faculties, covering a total of 10,000 names, were carefully combed.

3. Lists of Public School and High School students, totaling about 10,000 were studied for new names.

4. The pamphlet issued by the Academy of the Hebrew Language in Israel, which lists proposed names for newborn babies, was also consulted and used to good effect.

Thanks are due to Miss Esther Genuth for typing the manuscript and for her capable assistance in preparing the transliterated name index. Miss Naamah Ki Tov, an Israeli artist, has also contributed immeasurably to the enhancement of this work by her handsome hand-lettering of the Hebrew Index.

ALFRED J. KOLATCH

December 1, 1966

INTRODUCTION

The names in the sections that follow have been selected to guide those searching for the Hebrew equivalents of a particular name. It is a fact that newly chosen Hebrew and English names are generally based upon the name of a close relative, although the original name is not always retained. The arrangement and contents of the name lists have been formulated to meet this basic need. The procedure that has been followed consists of listing Hebrew equivalents consistent in meaning or connotation with the original English name. In addition, Hebrew equivalents of the opposite sex are recorded so as to be of service where the child is not of the same sex as the person after whom he is to be named.

The names listed in this study are all drawn from modern sources, and are names that have, for the most part, been adopted by Jews. A name that occurs very infrequently, such as Bonaparte (which appeared once in the army lists as that of a Jewish person), is not included. To be included, a name had to show sufficient frequency. The chief sources for the names listed were the birth columns of newspapers (primarily *The New York Times*), army lists and school records.

A word should be said about the nature of the English name as compared with the Hebrew. A name is a very accurate gauge of the character of a people. As the culture, character and background of a people differ, to the same extent will the nature of their names be different. Compare, for example, the Teutonic names employed by the early

Germans, Scandinavians and Anglo-Saxons and it will become evident how totally different they are in nature from names of Jewish origin. Whereas Teutonic names point to the occupation of their peoples as hunters for birds and animals in the forests of Totan, and to their aspirations and accomplishments as warriors, the majority of Jewish names have a more spiritual note about them. Teutonic names, in the main, express ideas of courage, power, strength and nobility, and often incorporate more than one of these concepts in a name. Jewish names express hope, salvation, mercy and godliness, with only a sprinkling of these other characteristics. Bearing this one fact in mind, it is evident that many difficulties arise when attempting to correlate these two almost opposite types. A great deal of elasticity therefore had to be employed in translating from one to the other.

Where the English name bore a simple meaning, not alien to Jewish culture, such as Basil or Roy, an equivalent Hebrew name was easily found in the Hebrew Melech or its related forms. Difficulty was encountered, however, with names consisting of more than one element and, especially, where one or all of these elements were foreign to Jewish nomenclature.

In names like Bernard, meaning "bear's heart," or Edgar meaning "happy warrior," it was necessary to divide the two aspects of the name in order to apply a Hebrew name to it. Thus, for example, in the name Edward, meaning "happy or blessed guard or keeper," Hebrew names like Bawruch or Simchaw were suggested to provide for the first element of the name, and names such as Avigdor and Shmaryaw to take care of the second element. Names involving the concepts of war, heroism and mastery, for which there is to be found only a minimum of Hebrew equivalents, were treated on the basis of their connotation, which implied strength, though strictly speaking the "strength" of the English name is not of the same quality as the strength of the Hebrew name. The English name denotes the *personal* strength of the warrior. The Hebrew name as manifested in Hezekiah, Ezekiel, Uzziah, and the like, implied the strength of God. But for the lack of any other exact equivalents, these were chosen and used. Among feminine names, this problem was even greater for, whereas, a great number of the English names conveyed meaning of heroine, battlemaid, strength, and the like, few Hebrew names exist to match them, even in connotation.

In many instances it will be noticed that it might have been possible to suggest additional Hebrew names, but only one was indicated. This was done always in the case where an English name was of biblical origin, and had a direct equivalent. Thus, for example, although there are many names in addition to Sawraw which might have been suggested as equivalents for Sarah, only the one was indicated. By consulting the index, however, other places in the book will be noted where alternate names are to be found.

Names having an unaesthetic or undesirable meaning have often been accorded euphemistic treatment. This is in keeping with an ancient Jewish practice, dating back to talmudic days, termed, "lawshon sageenawhor." In the Talmud a blind man is characterized in euphemistic language as "one who sees light." This procedure has been followed in translating names like Cecil, meaning "blind," and Claudette, meaning "lame."

The Hebrew names listed have been compiled from various sources. A name survey among Hebrew schools scattered through the country accounted for many; names used throughout the centuries in many countries, including modern Israel, accounted for others; original creations for a few more; and the Bible accounted for the majority. We are generally unaware of the reservoir of names that is to be found in the Bible, most of them never used. Twenty-eight hundred different personal names are to be found in the pages of the Bible, of which less than 5% are used today. Many of these Bible names have been included in this section, and although some may appear strange at first because of their novelty, they will in the course of time, if used, become acceptable and desirable because of their favorable meaning and pleasant ring.

Because of the novelty and oddity of many of the new Hebrew names, the first reaction of the reader may be to avoid them. That this may happen is understandable but, nevertheless, unjustifiable. Such a reaction was noted recently when the name Hawgawr was suggested to one rabbi to be used as the Hebrew name of a child who had been named Barbara. "I would never take the responsibility for that," he said. "It would be on my conscience for the rest of my life." Yet, despite its biblical association, the fact is that it is very much in use in Israel today. As a matter of fact practically every Hebrew name in the Hebrew Index is to be found in Jewish sources from biblical to contemporary times. That these names may sound strange to our ears cannot possibly serve as a valid argument against their acceptance. Time and usage will give them greater acceptability.

Although this volume was intended to deal exclusively with Hebrew and English names, a limited number of the more popular Yiddish names have been incorporated. This was necessitated by the fact that a large number of Jews have been known only by a Yiddish name, never having been given a Hebrew name.

To deal with the Yiddish name comprehensively, an independent study in itself is required, for the Yiddish name is complex and confusing. To actually get at the true source of most Yiddish names, the transformations and local influences of many generations and countries must be stripped from the name as it stands today. Most Yiddish names can be traced to a Hebrew origin, but they are often not recognizable because they were all too often completely changed in sound and spelling depending on the country in which they were used. To illustrate, listen to what Joseph Klausner says about the Yiddish name Yachne in his book, *Jesus of Nazareth*: "Johanna is the feminine form of Yochanan and identical with the name Yachne still preserved among the

Lithuanian and Polish Jews, but with no knowledge of its Hebrew origin."

The transliteration method used in this book is original, and does not pretend to be in keeping with any of the "scientific" methods generally employed. The reason for the introduction of this system is obvious to anyone who has tried to read Hebrew from transliterations as presently constituted. If the key to this transliteration (which is to be found on the bottom of each page) is studied and seriously followed, there is no doubt that the reader, unskilled in Hebrew reading, will produce a truer and more exact Ashkenazic pronunciation than under any other system.

For those who have chosen a Hebrew name, but are searching for an English equivalent, the appendix towards the end of the book is provided. Alongside the Hebrew transliterated name will be found listed the pages on which these names are mentioned. A Hebrew vocalized name index is also provided so as to make the correct spelling of each name available.

Masculine Names

AARON, ARON

Aaron, in the biblical narrative, was the older brother of Moses by three years. In the court of Pharaoh he was the spokesman for his people and at the same time head of the priesthood. Today the Hebraic forms Ahron and Aron are used, from time to time, as English names. Aaron has been an extremely popular name throughout the ages. The exact meaning of the name is not agreed upon by all authorities. Based on varying Hebrew roots it has been construed to mean: "teaching, singing, to shine, mountain." Taken as of Arabic origin it would mean "messenger."

The exact Hebrew equivalent is Aharon. Hebrew feminine equivalents: Aharonaw, Aharonis, Mayeeraw, M'eeraw, N'eemaw, Oraw, Reenaw and Sheeraw.

ABBA

From the Arabic or Syrian root meaning "father," and having the connotation of ruler or leader. The name was commonly used among the scholars of the Talmud.

The exact Hebrew equivalent is Abaw. Feminine equivalents: Avee-aylaw, Aveeyaw, Aveega-yil, Aveeshag, B'ulaw and Malkaw.

ABBE, ABBEY, ABBY

Short forms of either Abba or Abbott. These names are also used as feminine forms, usually diminutives of Abigail. They have also been taken as forms of the Hebrew

The key to the transliteration of Hebrew names will be found on the pages that follow.

1

name Abiel. See Abba, Abbott, Abigail and Abiel for definitions.

Hebrew masculine equivalents: Abaw, Awvee, Aveeayl and Avrawhawm. Feminine equivalents: Aveeaylaw, Aveega-yil and Aveeyaw.

ABBOT, ABBOTT
From the Hebrew and Aramaic Ab (Av) and Abba meaning "father." The name became popular in the Middle Ages when the heads of religious orders adopted it. The French form is Abbe.

Hebrew masculine equivalents: Abaw, Awvee, Aveeayl and Avrawhawm. Feminine equivalents: Aveeaylaw, Aveega-yil, and Aveeyaw.

ABE, ABIE
Diminutive forms of Abraham. See Abraham for a full explanation.

ABEL
If taken as a cognate of the Assyrian *abalu*, the meaning is "meadow," and signifies fruitfulness. In the Bible the Hebrew meaning is "breath." Abel was the brother of Cain, and the son of Adam and Eve. Among the monks of Anglo-Saxon England the name was quite popular and often spelled Able.

Exact Hebrew equivalent: Hevel. Feminine Hebrew equivalents: Carmelaw, Ganaw, Nirayl and Zimraw.

ABELARD
From the Teutonic meaning "noble, nobly, resolute, determined."

Hebrew equivalents: Acheerawm, Ameenawdawv, Ishhod, Yehonawdawv and Yisrawayl. Feminine Hebrew equivalents: N'deevaw, Ne'edawraw and Sawraw.

ABIEL, AVIEL
From the Hebrew meaning "God is my father." Aviel is a variant spelling.

Key: *a* as in f*a*ther; *ai* as in *ai*sle; *aw* as in l*aw*; *ay* as in s*ay*; *e* as in b*e*t;

Exact Hebrew equivalent: Aveeayl. Exact feminine Hebrew equivalent: Aveeaylaw.

ABIRI
From the Hebrew meaning, "my strong one," or "my hero."

Exact Hebrew equivalent: Abeeree. Feminine Hebrew equivalents: Abeeraw, Ameetzaw, Aysawnaw and Chaseenaw.

ABNER
Of Hebrew origin, meaning "the father's candle." It bears the connotation of defender (of father's name) or light and brightness. In the Bible Abner ben Ner was the uncle of King Saul and commander of his army.

The exact Hebrew equivalent is Avnayr. Feminine Hebrew equivalents: B'heeraw, M'eeraw, Noga and Oraw.

ABRAHAM
According to the Bible, Abraham was the first Hebrew. He was called a Hebrew because he came from the "other side" (*eber*) of the Euphrates. The original name was Abram meaning "exalted father." It was later changed to Abraham meaning "father of a mighty nation," or "father of a multitude." The Hebrew letter "H" which is the symbol for God, was added (to make Abram Abraham) because of Abraham's acceptance of one God. In the post-Talmudic period (after the year 500), the name became popular. Prior to that time it was not used. Not one rabbi in the Talmud is named Abraham. Early Christians refrained from using the name because of its association with Judaism. Later, however, this bias disappeared, and after the Reformation we find the name being adopted more and more by the Christian community. Among English Jewry of the eleventh and twelfth centuries it was third in popularity. The Persian form of Abraham is Ibrahim while in Arabic it is the familiar Ali Baba. In England and among the Dutch, Bram was often used as a variant form. In 17th

ee as in b*ee*t; *i* as in b*i*t; *o* as in n*o*; *oi* as in v*oi*d; *u* as in r*u*de.

century England Abra gained popularity as a feminine form of Abraham.

The exact Hebrew equivalent is Avrawhawm. Feminine Hebrew equivalents: Aveeyaw, Aveeaylaw, Atawraw, B'ulaw, Layaw, Malkaw and Tz'feeraw.

ABRAM

The original form of Abraham meaning "father of might." It carries the connotation of power, strength. See Abraham for a full explanation.

The exact Hebrew equivalent: Avrawm. Hebrew feminine equivalents: Amtzaw, Areeayl and Awtzmaw. See Abraham for additional suggestions.

ABSALOM

From the Hebrew meaning the "father of peace." Absalom was the third son of King David.

The exact Hebrew equivalent: Avshawlom. Hebrew feminine equivalents: M'nuchaw, Sh'lomis and Shulamis.

ADAIR

From the Celtic meaning "oak-ford." Adair was the name of a place in Scotland.

Hebrew equivalents: Aylaw and Oren. Feminine Hebrew equivalents: Alonaw and Aylaw.

ADAM

In the biblical account, Adam is the name of the first man. A number of meanings have been ascribed to it, but most common is "earth." Some claim that it means *like* (God). These explanations are based on Hebrew roots. Taken of Phoenician or Babylonian origin it means "man," or "mankind."

Adam was not used among Jews until more recent times. Among Christians it was first used in the seventh century by the Irish St. Adamnan (Adam the Little) who was Abbot of Iona. A number of surnames like Adcock, Adams, Adamson, Addison and Atkins are derivatives of Adam. In 19th

Key: *a* as in f*a*ther; *ai* as in *ai*sle; *aw* as in l*aw*; *ay* as in s*ay*; *e* as in b*e*t;

century Scotland Adamina was created as a feminine diminutive form of Adam.

The exact Hebrew equivalent: Awdawm. Hebrew feminine equivalents: Amtzaw, Karmelaw and Yiz'r'elaw.

ADELBERT

Of Teutonic origin. A combination of "athal," and "bertha," meaning "noble," and "illustrious," or "bright all over." With the passage of time the name changed as it was adopted in various countries. Ethelbert, Albert, Albertus and Albrecht are some of the derivative names from Adelbert.

Hebrew equivalents: Aveehud, Avnayr, Nawdawv, Shimshon, Uree, Yisrawayl and Zerach. Feminine Hebrew equivalents: B'heeraw, M'eeraw, N'deevaw, Oraw and Yisr'aylaw.

ADIR

From the Hebrew meaning "lord, noble, majestic."

The exact Hebrew equivalent is Adeer. The exact feminine equivalent is Adeeraw.

ADIV

A Hebrew name derived from the Arabic meaning "pleasant, gently-mannered."

The exact Hebrew equivalent is Awdiv. The exact Hebrew feminine equivalent is Adeevaw.

ADMON

A Hebrew name used in the Middle Ages and, currently, is the name of the red peony flower common in Upper Galilee in Israel.

The exact Hebrew equivalent is Admon. Hebrew feminine equivalent: Odem.

ADOLPH

From the Teutonic meaning "noble helper," or "noble wolf." Dolf, Dolphus and Adolphus are variant forms and diminutives.

Hebrew equivalents: Elee'ezer, Elawzawr, Ezraw and

ee as in b*ee*t; *i* as in b*i*t; *o* as in n*o*; *oi* as in v*oi*d; *u* as in r*u*de.

Nawdawv. Feminine Hebrew equivalents: Aleksandraw, Milkaw, Ne'edawraw and N'deevaw.

ADON
From the Hebrew and Phoenician meaning "lord." In Hebrew literature it is often a synonym for God. In Greek mythology Adonis was a young man of godlike beauty.

Hebrew equivalents: Awdon and Adoneeyaw. Hebrew feminine equivalents: Adeeraw, Malkaw, Sawraw and Yisr'aylaw.

ADRIAN
Adrian, and its Roman form, Hadrian, are the same. It is either a derivative of the Greek meaning "rich," or from the Latin meaning "black." The seaport of Adria (which gave its name to the Adriatic Sea) was known in ancient times for its black sand. Arne is a pet form.

Hebrew equivalents: Hoseer, Hunaw, Yeeshai, and Yisro. Feminine Hebrew equivalents: Bas-shua and Yisraw.

AHARON
The Hebrew word for Aaron. See Aaron for a full explanation.

AKIBA, AKIVA
Famous scholar and teacher of the first century. Of Hebrew derivation, similar to the name Jacob, and interpreted to mean either "supplant, held by the heel, or protect." Kiva and Kiba are pet forms.

The exact Hebrew equivalent is Akeevaw. Feminine Hebrew equivalents: Efraws, Mawgaynaw and Yaakovaw.

AKIM
A Russian short form of the Hebrew "Jehoiakim." See Jehoiakim for a full explanation.

ALAN, ALLAN, ALLEN, ALLYN
In a 1945 survey Alan was very popular as a first name and was the most popular boys' middle name. The exact origin is speculative, but is usually taken from the Celtic

Key: *a* as in *father*; *ai* as in *aisle*; *aw* as in *law*; *ay* as in *say*; *e* as in *bet*;

meaning "harmony, peace," or from the Gaelic meaning "fair, handsome." Alawn was a legendary British poet of the first century C.E.

Hebrew equivalents: Avshawlom, Lawvawn, Naamawn, Shawlom and Shlomo. Feminine Hebrew equivalents: Acheenoam, Naamaw, Nawawmee, Shifraw and Shulamis.

ALASTAIR
From the Greek meaning "the avenger." In Greek mythology Alastor personified revenge. Alastair is also considered a form of Alexander. See Alexander for more information.

ALBERT, ALBRECHT
The original form of these names was Adelbert. See Adelbert for more information.

ALDO, ALDOUS, ALDUS
Of German origin meaning "old." The Anglo-Saxons added the prefix "ald" to many of their names.

Hebrew equivalents: Kadmeeayl, Kaydmaw, Y'sheeshai and Zawkayn. Feminine Hebrew equivalents: Bilhaw, Y'shawnaw and Z'kaynaw.

ALDRED
Derived from the Saxon meaning "all reverent," or "old counsel," or "holy fear." All have the connotation of piety and purity.

Hebrew equivalents: Doayg, Kadish, Y'kuseeayl and Zakai. Feminine Hebrew equivalents: B'ruraw, B'ruryaw and Zakaw.

ALEX, ALEXANDER
Alex is the short form of Alexander, meaning "protector of men." According to the legend, when Macedonian Alexander the Great (356-323 B.C.E.) entered Palestine, all Jewish boys born in that year were named Alexander in his honor. The name was popular among kings and noblemen for centuries. The Italian form is Alessandro while the Scots shortened it to Sandy. The Russians converted

ee as in b*ee*t; *i* as in b*i*t; *o* as in n*o*; *oi* as in v*oi*d; *u* as in r*u*de.

it into Sascha, and the Scots into Sawney. Other variant forms of Alexander are: Alec, Aleck, Alick, Alexis, Alistair, Sander, Sandor and Saunders.

Hebrew equivalents: Aleksandayr, Avigdor, B'tzalayl, Eleefelet, Eltzawfawn and Sh'maryaw. Feminine Hebrew equivalents: Aleksandraw, Areeayl, Chosaw, Migdawlaw, Mawgaynaw and Shimris.

AL, ALF, ALFIE
Al is a short form of many names including: Alan, Albert, Alexander, Alvin and Alfred. Alf and Alfie are pet forms of Alfred.

ALFRED
Derived from the Anglo-Saxon or Teutonic and meaning either "peace," or "keen counsellor," with the connotation of wise, helper. Alfred was among the most common names used by Christians, especially in Northern Europe, prior to the 16th century. Alf and Alfie are pet forms.

Hebrew equivalents: Aleksandayr, Avshawlom, Eflawl, Shawlom and Shlomo. Feminine Hebrew equivalents: Aleksandraw, Bunaw, Milkaw and Shulamis.

ALGER
From the Anglo-Saxon meaning "noble spearman, warrior."

Hebrew equivalents: Aveecha'yil, Ben-Cha'yil, Gawd and Geebor. Feminine Hebrew equivalents: Amtzaw, Gavreelaw, Geeboraw and Tigraw.

ALLISTER
A variant form of Alexander. See Alexander for a full explanation.

ALMON
From the Hebrew meaning "forsaken," or "widower."

Hebrew equivalents: Almon, M'nashe and Yismaw. Feminine Hebrew equivalents: Azuvaw.

Key: *a* as in f*a*ther; *ai* as in *ai*sle; *aw* as in l*aw*; *ay* as in s*ay*; *e* as in b*e*t;

ALON

From the Hebrew meaning "oak tree." It is also a short form of Alphonso meaning "of noble family."

The exact Hebrew equivalent is Alon. The exact feminine equivalent is Alonaw. See Alphonso for additional suggestions.

ALPHONSO

From Old German meaning "of noble family." Alon, Lon and Lonny are pet forms.

Hebrew equivalents: Adoneeyaw, Acheerawm, Ameenawdawv, Cheerom, Nawdawv and Yisrawayl. Feminine Hebrew equivalents: Malkaw, N'deevaw, Ne'edawraw and Yisr'aylaw.

ALSON

From the Teutonic meaning "noble stone," or "the son of Al."

Hebrew equivalents: Eleetzur, Tzur and Tzureeayl. Feminine Hebrew equivalents: Ritzpaw and Tzureeyaw.

ALTER

Among Jews, Alter is a supplementary name given to a critically ill person. Derived either from the Latin meaning "other," or "another," or from the Yiddish meaning "old one." The purpose of the additional name was to confuse the evil spirits or the angel of death, since the sick person was now called by a different name than the person they had set out to visit.

Hebrew equivalents: Kadmeeayl, Shnayor, Yiftawch and (the Yiddish form) Altayr. Feminine Hebrew equivalents: Bilhaw, Z'kaynaw and Y'shawnaw.

ALTON

An old English name meaning "old manor," or "village."

Hebrew equivalents: Chetzron, Mawon, and Z'vulun. Feminine Hebrew equivalents: Leenaw, M'onaw, Teeraw and Z'vulaw.

ee as in beet; *i* as in bit; *o* as in no; *oi* as in void; *u* as in rude.

ALVA
From the Latin meaning "white," and having the connotation of bright.

Hebrew equivalents: Lawvawn and Livnee. Hebrew feminine equivalents: L'vawnaw, L'vonaw and Zawhawraw.

ALVAN, ALVIN
From the Teutonic meaning "everybody's friend," or "beloved by all."

Hebrew equivalents: Achaw, Chovawv, Dawvid, Eldawd and Y'didyaw. Feminine Hebrew equivalents: Ahuvaw, Chaveevaw, Dawveedaw, Dodaw and Yedeedaw.

AMAND
A French form of the Latin Amandus meaning "worthy of love."

Hebrew equivalents: Bildawd, Chovawv, Dawvid and Yedidyaw. Feminine Hebrew equivalents: Ahavaw, Ahuvaw, Chaveevaw and Dawveedaw.

AMBROSE
From the Greek meaning "immortal, divine."

Hebrew equivalent: Netzach. Feminine Hebrew equivalent: Nitzcheeyaw.

AMERY, AMORY
From the Latin meaning "the loving one."

Hebrew equivalents: Bildawd, Chovawv, Dawvid and Yedidyaw. Feminine Hebrew equivalents: Ahavaw, Ahuvaw, Ahudaw, Chaveevaw and Dawveedaw.

AMI
From the Hebrew word meaning "my people."

The exact Hebrew equivalent is Amee. Feminine Hebrew equivalents: Bas-Amee, L'umaw and Umaw.

AMIEL
A current Israeli name of Hebrew origin meaning "God of my people."

The exact Hebrew equivalent is Ameeayl. Feminine Hebrew equivalents: Amee-or, Bas-Amee, L'umaw and Umaw.

Key: *a* as in f*a*ther; *ai* as in *ai*sle; *aw* as in l*aw*; *ay* as in s*ay*; *e* as in b*e*t;

AMITAI

From the Hebrew word meaning "truth." Amitai was the father of Jonah in the Bible.

The exact Hebrew equivalent is Ameetai. Feminine Hebrew equivalents: Amawnaw, Emunaw and Ne'emawnaw.

AMITAN

From the Hebrew meaning "true, faithful."

The exact Hebrew equivalent is Ameesawn. Feminine Hebrew equivalents: Amawnaw, Emunaw and Ne'emawnaw.

AMNON

A popular Hebrew name in Israel meaning "faithful." Amnon in the Bible was the oldest son of David.

The exact Hebrew equivalent is Amnon. Feminine Hebrew equivalents: Amawnaw and Emunaw.

AMOS

From the Hebrew meaning "to be burdened," or "troubled." In the Bible Amos was a prophet of Judean origin in the 8th century B.C.E. He derived his livelihood as a herdsman and a pruner of sycamore trees.

The exact Hebrew equivalent is Awmos. Feminine Hebrew equivalents: Bas-shua and Bilhaw.

AMRAM

Father of Moses in the biblical account. Taken from the Hebrew root it means "a mighty nation," while in the Arabic it means "live, life."

Exact Hebrew equivalent: Amrawm. Hebrew feminine equivalents: Abeeraw, Aveerawmaw, Bas-Amee, Chavaw and Cha'yaw.

ANATOLE

From the Greek meaning "rising of the sun," or "from the east," with the connotation of bright, light.

Hebrew equivalents: Aharon, Kadmeeayl, Kedem, Mayeer, Shimshon, Ureeyaw and Zerach. Feminine Hebrew

ee as in b*ee*t; *i* as in b*i*t; *o* as in n*o*; *oi* as in v*oi*d; *u* as in r*u*de.

equivalents: Chamawneeyaw, Kaydmaw, M'eeraw, Noga, Oraw and Y'eeraw.

ANDREW, ANDY
A favorite among Scandinavians and Scots. From the Greek meaning "manly, valiant, strong, courageous." The forms Andy and Tandy are popular Scottish forms, while in Denmark the derivative name Anders was widely used, hence the surname Anderson. The French André is a form of Andrew. Andy is the favorite short form.

Hebrew equivalents: Aryay, Aveecha'yil, On, Onawn and Gavreeayl. Feminine Hebrew equivalents: Amtzaw, Awtzmaw, Areeayl and Areeaylaw.

ANTHONY, ANTONY
From the Greek meaning "flourishing," or from the Latin meaning "worthy of praise." The diminutive form, Tony, dates back to the seventeenth century.

Hebrew equivalents: Efra'yim, G'dalyaw, Heelayl and Y'hudaw. Feminine Hebrew equivalents: D'voraw, Heelaw, Heelaylaw, Neetzaw and Y'hudis.

ARCHIBALD, ARCHIE, ARCHY
From the Teutonic meaning "very bold," or "holy prince." Archie and Archy are familiar pet forms.

Hebrew equivalents: Aryay, Aveenawdawv, Gavreeayl and Yisrawayl. Feminine Hebrew equivalents: Areeayl, Areeaylaw, Malkaw and Sawraw.

ARDON
A Hebrew name meaning "bronze." In the Bible Ardon was a son of Caleb, of the tribe of Judah.

The exact Hebrew equivalent is Ardon. Feminine Hebrew equivalents: Ardaw and Ardonaw.

AREL, ARELI
From the Hebrew meaning "lion of God," and similar to the name Ariel.

The exact Hebrew equivalent is Arayl. Feminine Hebrew equivalents: Areeayl and Areeaylaw.

Key: *a* as in f*a*ther; *ai* as in *ai*sle; *aw* as in l*aw*; *ay* as in s*ay*; *e* as in b*e*t;

ARI, ARIE

A Hebraic form of Aryay meaning "lion," and having the connotation of strength.

The exact Hebrew equivalent is Aryay. Hebrew feminine equivalents: Areeayl, Areeaylaw, K'feeraw and L'vee-yaw.

ARIO

A variant form of Ari. See Ari for a full explanation.

ARMON, ARMONI

From the Hebrew meaning "castle, palace." Armoni was a son of King Saul in the Bible. When spelled with the Hebrew letter *Ayin*, rather than *Aleph*, the meaning is "a tree in the oak family."

Hebrew equivalents: Armon and Armoni. Feminine Hebrew equivalents: Armonaw, Alonaw, Aylaw, Aylonaw and Migdawlaw.

ARMOND

Most probably a form of the Teutonic Herman, meaning "warrior."

See Herman for masculine and feminine Hebrew equivalents.

ARNE

A short form of Adrian that was popular in the north of England in the Middle Ages. See Adrian for more information.

ARNOLD, ARNO, ARNY

From the Teutonic meaning either "honorable, honest," or "ruler, chief, having the power of an eagle." The connotation is that of strength. Arnold is one of the commonly used Christians names in Northern Europe prior to the 16th century. Arno and Arny are short forms of Arnold.

Hebrew equivalents: Ameetai, Aveecha'yil, Avrawhawm and Melech. Feminine Hebrew equivalents: Atawraw, Layaw, Malkaw and Tawmawr.

---

ee as in b*ee*t; *i* as in b*i*t; *o* as in n*o*; *oi* as in v*oi*d; *u* as in r*u*de.

ARNON
A Hebraic name meaning "roaring stream," and having the connotation of energetic. In the Bible it is a stream on the frontier of Moab that flowed into the Dead Sea. Some authorities claim the root means "roaring, rushing," hence, a mighty, powerful stream.

The exact Hebrew equivalent is Arnon. Feminine Hebrew equivalents: Arnonaw, D'roraw and Miryawm.

ART, ARTIE, ARTY
Popular pet forms of Arthur. See below for a full explanation.

ARTHUR
Taken either from the Celtic and Gaelic with various meanings: "noble, lofty, hill, or bear," and having the connotation of height and strength; or from the Icelandic meaning "a follower of Tur" (Thor was the Norse god of war), and having the connotation of fighter, warrior. Art, Artie and Arty are popular pet forms.

Hebrew equivalents: Aharon, Aveecha'yil, Dov, Hawrawn and Mawrd'chai. Feminine Hebrew equivalents: Areeayl, Areeaylaw, Geeboraw, Sawraw, Yis'r'aylaw.

ARYEH
From the Hebrew meaning "lion," and having the connotation of strength. In the Bible, Aryeh was one of the officers in the army of Pekach. The name Benroy may be a corrupt form of Ben (son of) Aryeh.

The exact Hebrew equivalent is Aryay. Feminine Hebrew equivalents: Areeayl and Areeaylaw.

ASA
From the Hebrew meaning "physician, healer." Asa was a king of Judah.

The exact Hebrew equivalent is Awsaw. Feminine Hebrew equivalents: R'fawaylaw, R'fuaw and Rofee.

ASAEL, ASIEL
From the Hebrew meaning "God has created." Asael was

Key: *a* as in f*a*ther; *ai* as in *ai*sle; *aw* as in l*aw*; *ay* as in s*ay*; *e* as in b*e*t;

a brother of Joab in the Bible; Asiel was a member of the tribe of Simeon.

Exact Hebrew equivalents: Awsawayl and Aseeayl. There are no feminine Hebrew equivalents.

ASHER

From the Hebrew meaning "blessed, fortunate or happy." Asher, the son of Zilpah, was one of the twelve sons of Jacob and the head of one of the tribes.

The exact Hebrew equivalent is Awshayr. Feminine Hebrew equivalents: Ashayraw, B'rawchaw, B'ruchaw and Reena.

ASHLEY

From the Old English meaning "a field of ash trees."

Hebrew equivalent tree names: Armon, Aylaw and Oren. Feminine Hebrew equivalents: Arzaw, Eelawnaw, Ornis and Tirzaw.

ASIR

From the Hebrew meaning "to bind, imprison." Asir was the son of Korah in the Bible.

The exact Hebrew equivalent is Asir. Feminine Hebrew equivalents: Oganyaw and Rivkaw.

AUBREY

From the Teutonic meaning "elf ruler," and having the connotation of rich and powerful. Avery is a variant form.

Hebrew equivalents: Avrawhawm, Kasreeayl, Melech, Rawvaw and Rosh. Feminine Hebrew equivalents: Asheeraw, B'ulaw, Malkaw and N'geedaw.

AUGUST

From the Latin meaning "revered, exalted." Gus and Augie are familiar pet forms. Austin is an English variant.

For Hebrew equivalents see Abraham.

AUREL

From the Latin meaning "gold, golden." Orel is a variant English form.

---

ee as in b*ee*t; *i* as in b*i*t; *o* as in n*o*; *oi* as in v*oi*d; *u* as in r*u*de.

Hebrew equivalents: Eleefaz. Feminine Hebrew equivalents: Ofeeraw, Pazaw and Z'hawvaw.

AUSTIN
An English variant form of August. See August for a full explanation.

AVERELL, AVERIL, AVERILL
From the Anglo-Saxon meaning "to open." These names are associated with the month of April which marks the "opening" of the important spring season. Averell is a variant spelling.

Hebrew equivalents: Awviv, P'sachyaw and Yiftawch. Feminine Hebrew equivalents: Aveevaw, Aveevee and Aveevis.

AVERY
A variant form of Aubrey. See Aubrey for a full explanation.

AVI
From the Hebrew meaning "father." Abba is a popular Aramaic form.

The exact Hebrew equivalent is Awvee. Eemaw, meaning mother, would be an appropriate feminine equivalent.

AVIDAN
From the Hebrew meaning "father of justice," or "God is just."

The exact Hebrew equivalent is Aveedawn. Feminine Hebrew equivalents: Dawnaw, Dawneeaylaw and Dawnis.

AVIDOR
From the Hebrew meaning "father of a generation."

The exact Hebrew equivalent is Aveedor. Feminine Hebrew equivalent: Doris.

AVIGDOR
From the Hebrew meaning "father protector."

Hebrew equivalent: Avigdor. Feminine Hebrew equivalents: Avigdoraw, Efraws, Shimris and Yaakovaw.

Key: *a* as in f*a*ther; *ai* as in *ai*sle; *aw* as in l*aw*; *ay* as in s*ay*; *e* as in b*e*t;

AVINOAM

From the Hebrew meaning "father of delight."

The exact Hebrew equivalent is Aveenoam. Feminine Hebrew equivalents: Acheenoam, Chemdaw, Naamaw and Nawawmee.

AVITAL

From the Hebrew meaning "father of dew." Used as a masculine and feminine name in Israel.

The exact masculine and feminine Hebrew equivalent is Aveetal.

AVIV

From the Hebrew meaning "spring, youthfulness."

The exact Hebrew equivalent is Awviv. The exact feminine Hebrew equivalents are Aveevaw, Aveevee and Aveevis.

AVNIEL

From the Hebrew meaning "God is my rock, or strength."

The exact Hebrew equivalent is Avneeayl. Hebrew feminine equivalents: Abeeraw, Abeeree, Aysawnaw and Tzurayl.

AVNER

A variant form of Abner meaning "father of light." In the Bible Abner was the cousin of King Saul and general of his army.

The exact Hebrew equivalent is Avnayr. Feminine Hebrew equivalents: Oraw, B'heeraw, Nayrlee, N'hawraw and Noga.

AVRAM, AVRUM

A variant form of Abram, which is a short form of Abraham, meaning "father of a mighty nation." See Abraham for a full explanation.

AZRIEL

From the Hebrew meaning "God is my help."

The exact Hebrew equivalent: Azreeayl. Feminine He-

ee as in b*ee*t; *i* as in b*i*t; *o* as in n*o*; *oi* as in v*oi*d; *u* as in r*u*de.

brew equivalents: Ezraw, Ezr'aylaw, Ezreeaylaw and Saadaw.

BALDWIN

A very old English name, particularly common in the 10th century. Variously explained as meaning "bold friend, bold in war," or from the German meaning "swift victory."

Hebrew Equivalents: Bildawd, Binyawmin, Dawvid and Rayee. Feminine Hebrew equivalents: Dawveedaw, Hadasaw, Rus and Y'deedaw.

BALFOUR

The name of Lord Arthur James Balfour (1848-1930), a British statesman who was greatly impressed by Chaim Weizmann. In 1917, as Foreign Secretary, he issued the Balfour Declaration announcing the favorable attitude of England towards the establishment of a Jewish state in Palestine. Balfour's name has been adopted as a personal name in Israel.

The exact Hebrew equivalent is Balfur. The exact Hebrew feminine equivalent is Balfureeyaw.

BANET

A short form of Bennett and Benedict. See Benedict for a full explanation.

BARAK

A Hebrew name meaning "flash of light," and having the connotation of brightness.

The exact Hebrew equivalent is Bawrawk. Hebrew feminine equivalents: Barkawis, Bawrekes, Bawrkas, B'heeraw, M'eeraw and Oraw.

BARAM

A modern Israeli name meaning "son of the nation."

The exact Hebrew equivalent is Barawm. Feminine Hebrew equivalents: Bas-Amee, Bas-Tzeeyon and Umaw.

BARD

From the Celtic meaning "a minstrel, singer or a poet."

Hebrew equivalents: Ameeshawr, Aveeshawr, Ronayn,

Key: *a* as in f*a*ther; *ai* as in *ai*sle; *aw* as in l*aw*; *ay* as in s*ay*; *e* as in b*e*t;

Zemer and Zimraw. Feminine Hebrew equivalents: Leeron, Peeyutaw, Sheeraw, Shirlee and Yawronaw.

BARI, BARRI
Variant spellings of Barrie. See Barrie for a full explanation.

BARNABY
From the Aramaic meaning "speech" or "exhortation."

Hebrew equivalents: Amaryawhu, Divree and Imree. Feminine Hebrew equivalents: Ameeraw, D'voraw and Neevaw.

BARNARD
When the Normans came to England they converted the old Teutonic name Bernard to Barnard. See Bernard for more information.

BARNET, BARNETT
A form of Bernard meaning "bear," and having the connotation of strength. Banet is a variant form, and Barney is a popular pet name. Some authorities believe that Barnaby is the original form of the name.

See Bernard and Barnaby for suggested masculine and feminine Hebrew equivalents.

BARNEY
A pet form of Bernard or Barnaby. See Bernard and Barnaby for full explanations.

BARRIE, BARRY
According to one opinion, these names are derived from the Barry Islands in Wales, which were named after Baruch, a devout man interred there, hence, the connotation of blessedness. Others take it as a Welsh patronymic form of Harry (Ap-Harry and Ab-Harry) meaning "ruler of the home." A third opinion is that Barry is an Old Celtic name meaning "good marksman." Today, both names are also used as pet forms of Baruch.

Hebrew equivalents: Awshayr, Bawruch, Kasreeayl and

ee as in b*ee*t; *i* as in b*i*t; *o* as in n*o*; *oi* as in v*oi*d; *u* as in r*u*de.

Rawvaw. Feminine Hebrew equivalents: B'rawchaw, B'ruchaw and B'ulaw.

BART

A variant spelling of Bard, Bartholemew or Barton. See each of these names for a full explanation.

BARTH

From the Anglo-Saxon meaning "a shelter, dwelling." It may also be a diminutive of Bartholemew.

Hebrew equivalents: Chetzron, Mawon and Z'vulun. Feminine Hebrew equivalents: Leenaw, M'onaw, Teeraw and Z'vulaw.

BARTHOLEMEW

From the Aramaic meaning "son of Talmai." Bartholemew was one of the Twelve Apostles in the New Testament. Talmai has the meaning of "hill, mound," or "furrow."

Hebrew equivalents: Talmai, Talmee, Tayl-Chai and Telem. Feminine Hebrew equivalents: Talmaw and Talmis.

BARTLEY

An Irish form of Bartholemew. See above for a full explanation.

BARTON

From the Anglo-Saxon meaning "barley town" (where the crop was usually housed), and having the connotation of protection. Or, it may be from the Old English meaning "bear town."

Hebrew equivalents: Dov. Feminine Hebrew equivalents: Doobaw and Garnis.

BARUCH

From the Hebrew meaning "blessed," and having the connotation of fortunate, happy. In the Bible, Baruch was the friend and secretary of the prophet Jeremiah. Barrie and Barry are pet forms.

The exact Hebrew equivalent is Bawruch. Feminine Hebrew equivalents: B'rawchaw, B'ruchaw and M'voreches.

Key: *a* as in f*a*ther; *ai* as in *ai*sle; *aw* as in l*aw*; *ay* as in s*ay*; *e* as in b*e*t;

BASIL

From the Greek meaning "kingly," and similar to the Latin "Rex."

Hebrew equivalents: Adoneeyaw, Aveemelech, Kasree-ayl and Melech. Feminine Hebrew equivalents: Atawraw, Malkaw and Yis'r'aylaw.

BARZILAI

From the Hebrew meaning "man of iron," and having the connotation of strength. The name occurs several times in the Bible.

The exact Hebrew equivalent is Barzeelai. Feminine Hebrew equivalents: Amtzaw, Areeayl, Awtzmaw and Geeboraw.

BELLAMY

From the Latin meaning "beautiful friend."

Hebrew equivalents: Aveenoam, Dawvid, Naamawn and Raanawn. Feminine Hebrew equivalents: Acheenoam, Adeenaw, Dawveedaw, Shifraw and Yawfis.

BEN

From the Hebrew meaning "son." Used as an independent name occasionally, but most often is the diminutive form of Benjamin. See Benjamin for a full explanation.

BEN-AMI

From the Hebrew meaning "son of my people."

The exact Hebrew equivalent is Ben-Amee. The exact feminine Hebrew equivalent is Bas-Amee.

BENEDICT

From the Latin meaning "blessed." B'rachyaw, which is the Hebrew form of Benedict, was extremely popular among 12th century Jewry. B'rachyaw Nakdawn, one of the greatest Jewish literary figures, became known as Benedict Le Puncteur. Benito and Benedelto are Italian variants. Banet, Bennet and Bennett are English variants. Ben, Benny, Dix, Dixie and Dixon are short forms.

Hebrew equivalents: Awshayr, Bawruch and B'rachyaw.

ee as in b*ee*t; *i* as in b*i*t; *o* as in n*o*; *oi* as in v*oi*d; *u* as in r*u*de.

Feminine Hebrew equivalents: Awshraw, B'rawchaw and B'ruchaw.

BENJAMIN

From the Hebrew meaning "son of my right hand," and having the connotation of strength. Benjamin was the youngest of Jacob's twelve sons in the Bible. Ben, Benji, Benjy and Benjie are pet forms.

Although biblical in origin, Benjamin did not become popular as a name until the Middle Ages. Benjamin of Tudela, the famous world traveler of the 12th century is the first well known Benjamin. Among Christians, Benjamin came into use after the 16th century.

The exact Hebrew equivalent is Binyawmin. Feminine Hebrew equivalents: Amtzaw, Areeayl, Binyawmeenaw, Geeboraw and Gavreelaw.

BENNET, BENNETT

Variant English forms of the Latin Benedict. See Benedict for a full explanation.

BENROY

Probably a corrupt form of "ben Aryay." See Aryeh for a full explanation.

BENSON

Either a patronymic of Benjamin (meaning son of Ben or Benjamin), and of Scandinavian or English origin, or a short form of Ben Zion. See Benjamin and Ben Zion for a full explanation of each name.

BENZECRY

A corrupt patronymic form meaning "the son of Zechariah." See Zechariah for a full explanation.

BEN ZION, BENZI

From the Hebrew meaning either "excellent son," or "very good." Benzi is a pet form in vogue in Israel.

The exact Hebrew equivalents are: Ben-tzeeyon and Bentzee, which is a diminutive form. Feminine Hebrew equivalents: Bas-tzeeyon, Tovaw and Tzeeyona.

Key: *a* as in f*a*ther; *ai* as in *ai*sle; *aw* as in l*aw*; *ay* as in s*ay*; *e* as in b*e*t;

BERGER
A variant form of Burgess. See Burgess for a full explanation.

BERNARD, BERNI, BERNIE
From the Teutonic meaning "bear," or "bear's heart," and having the connotation of strength. Berni and Bernie are popular pet forms.
Hebrew equivalents: Barzeelai, Binyawmin, Boaz and Dov. Feminine Hebrew equivalents: Areeayl, Awtzmaw, Doobaw, Gavreelaw and Geeboraw.

BERT
A diminutive of either Berthold, Bertol or Bertram. Berthold is from the Teutonic meaning "beloved or bright." Hebrew equivalents: Bildawd, Dawvid, Chovawv and Mayeer. Feminine Hebrew equivalents: B'heeraw, Chaveevaw, Cheebaw and Dawveedaw.

BERTOL
From the Teutonic meaning "superior intellect." Hebrew equivalents: Achbawn, Bunaw, Chanoch, Ish-Sechel and Yawvin. Feminine Hebrew equivalents: Beenaw, Bunaw, Daas and Day'aw.

BERTRAM, BERTREM, BERTRAN, BERTRAND
From the Teutonic meaning "bright, fair or illustrious one." Hebrew equivalents: Bawrawk, G'dalyaw, Heelayl and Shaym-tov. Feminine Hebrew equivalents: B'heeraw, L'vawnaw, Rivkaw, Shifraw and T'heelaw.

BERYL
Either from the Greek meaning "a precious stone," or a Yiddish diminutive of the Teutonic meaning "a bear," and having the connotation of strength. Hebrew equivalents: Binyawmin, Barzeelai, Dov and Yawkawr. Feminine Hebrew equivalents: Gavreelaw, Geeboraw, Margawlis and P'neenaw.

ee as in b*ee*t; *i* as in b*i*t; *o* as in n*o*; *oi* as in v*oi*d; *u* as in r*u*de.

BEVERLEY, BEVERLY

An Old English name meaning "beaver meadow," or "field." Used occasionally as a masculine name, but most often as a feminine form.

Hebrew equivalents: Karmel, Kar'mlee and Yaraw. Feminine Hebrew equivalents: Ganaw, Karmelaw and Nawvaw.

BILDAD

From the Hebrew meaning "beloved." The literal meaning is, "Baal has loved." In the Bible, Bildad was one of the friends of Job.

The exact Hebrew equivalent: Bildad. Feminine Hebrew equivalents: Dawveedaw, Rus and Y'deedaw.

BILGAI, BILGUY

From the Arabic meaning "joy, cheerfulness." Bilgai is the name of a priest in the Book of Nehemiah.

The exact Hebrew equivalent is Bilgai. Feminine Hebrew equivalents: Aveega'yil, Bilgaw, Geelaw and Reenaw.

BILL, BILLIE, BILLY

Diminutive forms of William meaning "warrior and leader." See William for a full explanation.

BLAKE

From the Anglo-Saxon meaning "to whiten, to bleach." Blanchard is an English variant and Blanco is its Spanish counterpart.

Hebrew equivalents: Lawvawn and Livnee. Feminine Hebrew equivalents: L'vawnaw, L'vonaw and Tz'choraw.

BLANCHARD

A variant form of Blake. See Blake for a full explanation.

BOAZ

From the Hebrew meaning "strength and swiftness." Boaz was the second husband of the biblical Ruth.

The exact Hebrew equivalent is Boaz. Feminine Hebrew equivalents: Gavreelaw and Geeboraw.

Key: *a* as in f*a*ther; *ai* as in *ai*sle; *aw* as in l*aw*; *ay* as in s*ay*; *e* as in b*e*t;

BOB, BOBBIE, BOBBY
Diminutive forms of Robert meaning "bright," or "famous counsel." See Robert for a full explanation.

BORIS
From the Slavic meaning "fighting warrior."
Hebrew equivalents: Ben-cha'yil, Gayraw, Mawr'd'chai, Yisrawayl. Feminine Hebrew equivalents: Gavreelaw, Geeboraw and Yis'r'aylaw.

BOYD
From the Slavic meaning "fighting warrior."
Hebrew equivalents: Lawvawn, Livnee, Tzawhuv and Tzochar. Feminine Hebrew equivalents: L'vawnaw, Nawawmee and Z'huvaw.

BRADLEY
From the Old English meaning "a broad lea or meadow."
Hebrew equivalents: Geenas, Karmel and Zimree. Feminine Hebrew equivalents: Ganaw, Karmelaw and Sh'daymaw.

BRAM
A short form of Abraham or Abram. See Abraham and Abram for a full explanation.

BRAND
From the Anglo-Saxon meaning "raven," or "sword," and having the connotation of strength or warrior.
Hebrew equivalents: Barzeelai, Ben-cha'yil, Binyawmin and Orayv. Feminine Hebrew equivalents: Gavreelaw, Geeboraw and Tigraw.

BRET, BRETT
From the Celtic meaning "a Breton," or "a native of Brittany."
There are no Hebrew equivalents.

BRIAN
From the Celtic or Gaelic meaning "strength, nobly born," or "one who is eloquent." Bryan and Bryant are variant English forms.

oo as in b*ee*t: *i* as in b*i*t; *o* as in n*o*; *oi* as in v*oi*d; *u* as in r*u*de.

Hebrew equivalents: Abeer, Awsneeayl, Barzeelai, Ben-Cha'yil, Gavreeayl and Yisrawayl. Feminine Hebrew equivalents: Abeeraw, Gavreelaw, Geeboraw, Sawraw and Yisr'aylaw.

BRIT
A variant form of Bret. See Bret for a full explanation.

BRUCE
A Scottish name of French origin probably meaning "woods," or "thicket."

Hebrew equivalents: Karmel, Kar'mlee and Yaraw. Feminine Hebrew equivalents: Ganaw, Karmelaw and Nawvaw.

BRUNO, BRUNS
From the Teutonic meaning "brown or dark in appearance."

Hebrew equivalents: Ayfai, Kush and Pinchaws. Hebrew feminine equivalents: Chacheelaw and Tzeelaw.

BRYAN, BRYANT
Variant spellings of Brian. See Brian for a full explanation.

BUDD
Taken by some as a pet form of Baldwin. See Baldwin. Others take it from the Old English meaning "messenger." The concensus of opinion, however, is that it is of Cornish, Cymric or Welsh origin meaning "rich," or "victorious."

Hebrew equivalents: Kawlayv, M'vasayr, Yeeshai and Yisro. Feminine Hebrew equivalents: Bas-shua, Dafnaw and Hadasaw.

BUDDY
A pet name for "brother," and having the connotation of friend.

Hebrew equivalents: Achaw, Bildad, Dawvid and Chovawv. Feminine Hebrew equivalents: Ahuvaw, Dawveedaw and Rus.

Key: *a* as in *father*; *ai* as in *aisle*; *aw* as in *law*; *ay* as in *say*; *e* as in *bet*;

BURGESS

In Medieval England a "burgess" was a citizen, a free man, or a townsman. Berger is a variant form.

Hebrew equivalents: Pesach, P'sachyaw and R'chavawm. Feminine Hebrew equivalents: D'roraw, G'ulaw and Rawchawv.

BURLEIGH

An Old English name meaning "a field with prickly, burr covered plants." The pet form is Burl.

See Bruce for Hebrew equivalents.

BURT

Either a form of Burton or taken from the Saxon meaning "bright, clear or excellent."

Hebrew equivalents: Ben-tzeeyon, Mayeer, Tuveeyaw and Uree. Feminine Hebrew equivalents: B'heeraw, Chaveevaw, M'eeraw and Tovaw.

BURTON

An Old English local name meaning "town on a hill," or "borough town." See Alton, to which it is very close in meaning, for equivalents.

BYRON

From the Teutonic meaning "the cottage," with the connotation of dwelling, or from the Old English meaning "a bear."

See Alton and Bernard for equivalents.

CALEB

Variously explained as meaning either "a heart," or "a dog," from the Hebrew; or "priestly, official, a messenger," from the Assyrian; or "bold, brave," from the Arabic.

The exact Hebrew equivalent: Kawlayv. Feminine Hebrew equivalents: Areeayl, Gavreelaw and Geeboraw.

CALVIN

From the Latin meaning "bald."

The exact Hebrew equivalent is Korach. There are no

feminine equivalents. For euphemistic equivalents see Julius.

CAMILLUS
From the Latin meaning "an attendant" (at a sacrifice), or "a messenger," and having the connotation of helper.

Hebrew equivalents: Aharon, Azaryaw, Kawlayv, Malawchee and Ovadyaw. Feminine Hebrew equivalents: Aleksandraw, Ezraw and Saadaw.

CAREY, CARY
From the Welsh or Cornish meaning "stony or rock island."

Hebrew equivalents: Aveeyawm, Tzuree and Tzureeayl. Feminine Hebrew equivalents: Miryawm, Ritzpaw, Tzurayl and Tzureeyaw.

CARL, CAROL, CARROL, CARROLL
Carol, Carrol and Carroll are forms of Carl meaning "strong, stalwart man." Carol and Carrol are primarily feminine names, but occasionally are used as masculine forms.

Hebrew equivalents: Ben-Cha'yil, Chizkeeyaw, Geebor and Kawlayv. Feminine Hebrew equivalents: Amtzaw, Areeayl, Gavreelaw and Geeboraw.

CARLTON
Derived from Carl, and meaning "from Carl's farm." See Carl for a full explanation.

CARMEL, CARMELI, CARMI, CARMIEL
From the Hebrew meaning "vineyard, farm or garden." Carmiel means "vineyard of the Lord."

Hebrew equivalents: Carmel, Carm'lee and Carmeeayl. Feminine Hebrew equivalents: Carmaw, Carmeeyaw and Carmis.

CASPAR
From the Teutonic meaning "imperial."

Hebrew equivalents: Acheemelech, Eleemelech, Kasree-

Key: *a* as in f*a*ther; *ai* as in *ai*sle; *aw* as in l*aw*; *ay* as in s*ay*; *e* as in b*e*t;

yal and Melech. Feminine Hebrew equivalents: Atawraw, Malkaw and Tz'feeraw.

CECIL

From the Latin meaning "blind," or "dim-sighted." Cecil was used in medieval England as a name for both sexes, although until recent times it was primarily used as a girl's name.

Hebrew euphemistic equivalents: Koresh, Mayeer, Shimshon, Ureeayl and Zerach. Feminine Hebrew euphemistic equivalents: M'eeraw, Noga, Oraw and Zawhawraw. Based upon the biblical narrative, Layaw (Leah) would be an appropriate equivalent.

CEDRIC

A Welsh name meaning "bountiful."

Hebrew equivalents: Hoseer, Hunaw, Yeeshai and Yisro. Feminine Hebrew equivalents: Asheeraw, Bas-shua, N'geedaw and Yisraw.

CHAD

From the Celtic meaning "battle or warrior."

Hebrew equivalents: Ben-Cha'yil, Ish-Cha'yil, Gawd, Gidon and Mawrd'chai. Feminine Hebrew equivalents: Amtzaw, Awtzmaw, Gavreelaw and Geeboraw.

CHAIM

A Hebraic name meaning "life." Among Jews it is frequently given to one who is critically ill, with the hope that continued life would be bestowed upon him. French Jews translated Chaim into "Vive." Today, most people named Chaim have as English name Hyman or Charles, but without any etymological basis for it.

The exact Hebrew equivalent is Cha'yim. Feminine Hebrew equivalents: Chavaw, Cha'yaw, Nafsheeyaw and T'cheeyaw.

CHARLES

One of the most common names used by Christians especially in Northern Europe prior to the 16th century. Charles

ee as in b*ee*t; *i* as in b*i*t; *o* as in n*o*; *oi* as in v*oi*d; *u* as in r*u*de.

is of Teutonic origin and is a variant form of Carl meaning "strong." Charlie, Charley, Chick and Chuck are popular pet forms.

Among the many variant forms that Charles has assumed in different countries are the following: In Germany it was Karl; in Sweden, Kalle; in Holland, Karel and Carel; in Slavic countries Karol; in Italy, Carlo and Carlino; in Spain and Portugal, Carlos; in France, Charlot. Charlton is a French-German adaptation.

Hebrew equivalents: Ben-Cha'yil, Chizkee, Chizkeeyaw, Chizkeeyawhu, Geebor, Ish-Cha'yil and Kawlayv. Feminine Hebrew equivalents: Amtzaw, Areeayl, Areeaylaw, Gavreelaw and Geeboraw.

CHARLTON
A French-German name derived from Charles, and meaning "Charles' farm." See Charles for additional information.

CHESTER
From the Latin meaning "fortress or camp," and having the connotation of protection.

Hebrew equivalents: Chosaw, Chupawm, Shmaryaw and Sisree. Feminine Hebrew equivalents: Efraws, Bawtzraw, Tzeelaw and Yaakovaw.

CHRISTOPHER
A name of purely Christian origin meaning, "Christ-bearer." St. Christopher was martyred in 250 C.E. at the hands of the Romans.

There are no Hebrew equivalents.

CLARENCE
From the Latin meaning "illustrious."

Hebrew equivalents: G'dalyaw, Heelayl, Kasreeayl and Melech. Feminine Hebrew equivalents: Malkaw, Sawraw and Yis'r'aylaw.

CLARK
From the Old English meaning "clergyman or learned

Key: *a* as in f*a*ther; *ai* as in *ai*sle; *aw* as in l*aw*; *ay* as in s*ay*; *e* as in b*e*t;

man." A clark, or clerk, was originally a member of a clerical order. The opportunity to study and become a scholar was originally confined, in the main, to members of the clergy.

Hebrew equivalents: Chanoch, Kawlayv, Kohayn and Koheles. Feminine Hebrew equivalents: Beenaw and Bunaw.

CLAUDE

From the Latin meaning "lame."

Hebrew equivalents: Gidon and Pawsayach. Euphemistic Hebrew equivalents: Ayfer, Boaz and Tz'vee. Feminine euphemistic Hebrew equivalents: Awfraw, A'yeles and Tzivyaw.

CLEMENT

From the Latin meaning "merciful or gracious."

Hebrew equivalents: Amee-chayn, Amee-nawdawv, Chawnawn, Chonee, Kalmawn and Yochawnawn. Feminine Hebrew equivalents: Adeevaw, Chanaw, Chaneesaw, Diklaw and Yochawnaw.

CLIFF

Either a short form of Clifford or Clifton, or an independent Old English name meaning "from the cliff or high place."

Hebrew equivalents: Givon, Givson, Talmai, Telem and Tzur. Feminine Hebrew equivalents: Galee, Galis, Givonaw, Talmaw and Tzureeyaw.

CLIFFORD

An English local name meaning the "ford or crossing near the cliff."

Hebrew equivalents: Aharon, Talmai, Telem and Tzureeayl. Feminine Hebrew equivalents: Galee, Migdawlaw, Teemoraw and Yawayl.

CLIFTON

An Old English name meaning "the farm near the cliff."

Hebrew equivalents: Givon, Karmel, Tzuree and Tzureeayl. Feminine Hebrew equivalents: Givonaw, Karmelaw, Ritzpaw, Tzureeyaw and Yizr'elaw.

CLIVE

Originally a place-name in England meaning "cliff, hill, or mountain."

For masculine and feminine Hebrew equivalents see Cliff.

CLYDE

From the Welsh meaning "heard from afar."

Hebrew equivalents: Azanyaw, Shawmaw, Shema, Shimee, Shimon, Shma'yaw, Shma'yawhu, Shmuayl and Yaazanyaw. Feminine Hebrew equivalents: Kashuvaw, Shimaws and Shimonaw.

COLEMAN

From the Latin meaning "dove," or from the Icelandic meaning "head man." It is also taken by some as of occupational origin meaning "charcoal maker," hence, a black or dark man.

Hebrew equivalents: Eleemelech, Kasreeayl, Kush, Melech and Yonaw. Feminine Hebrew equivalents: Chacheelaw, Malkaw, Y'meemaw and Yoneenaw.

COLIN

A diminutive of Nicholas meaning "victory." Colin became popular during World War II as a result of the heroism of air-ace Colin Kelly, although it is known to have been used in 18th century England. In the Celtic Colin means "a cub, whelp, young animal."

Hebrew equivalents: Arayl, Aree, Areeawv, Areeayl, Ben-Guryon, Govayr, K'feer, N'tzeeach and Yatzleeach. Feminine Hebrew equivalents: Areeayl, Areeaylaw, K'feeraw, L'veeyaw, Nitzchaw and Nitzcheeyaw.

CONAN

From the Celtic meaning "chief or king." In Ireland it is a very honored name and carries the added meaning _of "intelligent."

Key: *a* as in f*a*ther; *ai* as in *ai*sle; *aw* as in l*aw*; *ay* as in s*ay*; *e* as in b*e*t;

Hebrew equivalents: Chashmon, Eleemelech, Kasreeayl, Malkeeayl, Melech and Yawvin. Feminine Hebrew equivalents: Alufaw, G'veeraw, Malkaw, N'vonaw and Yis'r'aylaw.

CONRAD
From the Teutonic meaning "able counsellor," and having the connotation of helper, wisdom. In Germanic countries Curt and Kurt are used as variant forms of Conrad.

Hebrew equivalents: Elee'ezer, Aleksandayr, Chachmonee, Ezraw, Haskayl and Pekach. Feminine Hebrew equivalents: Aleksandraw, Bunaw, Chawchmaw, Milkaw and Tusheeyaw.

CORDELL
From the Latin meaning "cord or line."
Hebrew equivalents: Tzur. Feminine Hebrew equivalents: P'seelaw, Rivkaw and Tikvaw.

COREY, CORY
From the Anglo-Saxon meaning "the chosen one."
Hebrew equivalents: Bawchir, Bochayr, Nivchawr and Yivchawr. Feminine Hebrew equivalents: Bawraw, B'cheeraw, B'churaw, Eelaw and Nivcheres.

CORNELIUS, CORNELL
Variously interpreted as meaning a "crow," of Norman-French origin; or from the Latin meaning "horn of the sun," which is a symbol of kingship; or from another Latin root meaning "enduring or long life." According to some authorities Cornelius is derived from the Greek and means "the cornell tree."

Hebrew equivalents: Ameechai, Bar-Yochawee, Cha'yim, Kasreeayl, Melech and Y'cheeayl. Feminine Hebrew equivalents: Chavaw, Cha'yaw, Malkaw, Shikmaw, Shikmonaw, Sh'kaydaw and Y'cheeaylaw.

CRAIG
From the Scottish meaning "from the crag or rugged rocky mass."
Hebrew equivalents: Aveetzur, Avneeayl, Sela, Tz'ror,

ee as in b*ee*t; *i* as in b*i*t; *o* as in n*o*; *oi* as in v*oi*d; *u* as in r*u*de.

Tzur and Tzureeayl. Feminine Hebrew equivalents: Ritzpaw, Tzuris and Tzureeyaw.

CRAWFORD
An Old English local name meaning "the ford or stream where the crows flock."

Hebrew equivalents: Aynawn, B'ayree, Orayv, Peleg and Yuval. Feminine Hebrew equivalents: Chaseedaw, Daleeyaw, D'voraw, Meechal, Miryawm and Tzeeporaw.

CYRIL
From the Greek meaning "lord or lordly."

Hebrew equivalents: Aveemelech, Avrawhawm, Kasreeayl, Nawdawv and Rosh. Feminine Hebrew equivalents: Alufaw, B'ulaw, G'veeraw, Malkaw, N'deevaw and Yis'r'-aylaw.

CYRUS
From the Persian meaning "sun," connoting light and brightness. King Cyrus, in biblical history, was a famous leader.

The exact Hebrew equivalent is Koresh. Feminine Hebrew equivalents: Chamawneeyaw, M'eeraw, Oraw, Orlis, Shimshonaw and Zakaw.

DAGAN
From the Hebrew meaning "corn, grain."

The exact Hebrew is Dawgawn. Feminine Hebrew equivalents: Gawrnaw, Gawrnis, D'gawneeyaw and D'gawnis.

DALE
From the Anglo-Saxon meaning "a dweller in a vale between hills."

Hebrew equivalents: Gai, Gaychazee, Givon and Talmai. Feminine Hebrew equivalents: Bik'aw, Galyaw, Talmaw, Talmis and Teemoraw.

DAN
Dan was one of the twelve sons of Jacob in the Bible and the name of one of the tribes of Israel. Dan is derived from the Hebrew meaning "he judged."

Key: *a* as in father; *ai* as in aisle; *aw* as in law; *ay* as in say; *e* as in bet;

The exact Hebrew equivalent is Dawn. Feminine Hebrew equivalents: Dawnaw, Dawnis, Danyaw and Deenaw.

DANA
The feminine form of the biblical Dan which is used as a name for boys as well as girls. See Dan.

DANI
A modern Israeli name derived from Dan and meaning "my judge."

The exact Hebrew equivalent is Dawnee. Feminine Hebrew equivalents: Dawnaw, Danyaw and Deenaw.

DANIEL
From the Hebrew meaning "God is my judge." Daniel was a famous figure in the Bible during the period of the Babylonian exile and is noted for his escape from the lion's den. Dan and Danny are popular diminutive forms.

The exact Hebrew equivalent is Dawneeayl. The exact feminine Hebrew equivalent is Dawneeaylaw.

DAR
From the Hebrew meaning "pearl or mother-of-pearl." A name used in modern Israel.

The exact Hebrew equivalent is Dar. Feminine Hebrew equivalents: P'neenaw, P'neenee and Margawlis.

DARIAN, DARIEN
These names are probably variant forms of the Persian Darius. See Darius. Darin and Darren are alternate spellings.

DARIN, DARREN
Probably variant forms of the Persian Darius. See Darius. Darian and Darien are alternate spellings.

DARIUS
From the Persian meaning "one who possesses wealth." Darius was a king of Persia mentioned in the Bible. Darian, Darien, Darin, Darren, Dorian, Darrell and Daryl are variant forms.

ee as in b*ee*t; *i* as in b*i*t; *o* as in n*o*; *oi* as in v*oi*d; *u* as in r*u*de.

The exact Hebrew equivalent is Daryawvesh. Feminine Hebrew equivalents: Asheeraw, Bas-shua and N'geedaw.

DARRELL, DARROL, DARYL
From the Anglo-Saxon meaning "darling or dear."

Hebrew equivalents: Chawviv, Dawvid, Dodee, Eldawd and Yedidyaw. Feminine Hebrew equivalents: Ahuvaw, Dawveedaw, Dodaw and Y'deedaw.

DAVI
A short form of the popular name David. See below for a full explanation.

DAVID
King David was a beloved character in biblical history. Although the name was commonly used for many centuries after his time, not one rabbi in the Talmud is named David. It is today among the foremost popular boys' names. David is from the Hebrew meaning "beloved." Dave, Davy and Davi are popular pet forms.

The exact Hebrew equivalent is Dawvid. Feminine Hebrew equivalents: Chaveevaw, Dawveedaw, Dodaw and Y'deedaw.

DEAN
From the Latin meaning "head or leader of a school."

Hebrew equivalents: Chanoch, Rabee, Rosh and Tanaw. Feminine Hebrew equivalents: Moreeyaw, Moreeayl and Moris.

DEKEL
A Hebrew name used in Israel. Derived from the Arabic meaning "palm or date tree."

The exact Hebrew equivalent is Dekel. Feminine Hebrew equivalents: Diklaw and Diklis.

DELANO
Either from the Old French meaning "of the night," or from the Erse meaning "a healthy dark man."

Hebrew equivalents: Adawr, Chachalyaw, Chumee, Kay-

Key: *a* as in f*a*ther; *ai* as in *ai*sle; *aw* as in l*aw*; *ay* as in s*ay*; *e* as in b*e*t;

dawr and Pinchaws. Feminine Hebrew equivalents: Ayfaw, Lailaw, Laylee and Tzeelaw.

DENIS, DENNIS, DENYS
Derived from Dionysius, Greek god of wine and drama. He was originally the god of vegetation and fruitfulness. In 12th century England the name took the form of Dionis. In France it became Diot or Dion, from which evolved the name Dwight.

Hebrew equivalents: Efra'yim, Gefen, Karmel, Puraw and Tzemach. Feminine Hebrew equivalents: Beekuraw, Geetaw, Geetis and Zimraw.

DEREK
An English form of the Gothic name Theodoric meaning "ruler of the people."

Hebrew equivalents: Acheemelech, Adoneeyaw, Elrawd, Kasreeayl, Melech and Nawdawv. Feminine Hebrew equivalents: Atawraw, B'ulaw, G'veeraw, N'deevaw and Yis'r'-aylaw.

DEROR, DERORI
From the Hebrew meaning "freedom or free-flowing," or "a bird (swallow)."

The exact Hebrew equivalents are D'ror and D'roree. Feminine Hebrew equivalents: D'roraw aid D'roris.

DEVIR
A biblical name derived from the Arabic meaning "inner-most room," or "holy place." Devir was king of Eglon in the Bible.

The exact Hebrew equivalent is D'vir. The exact feminine Hebrew equivalent is D'veeraw.

DICK, DICKIE, DICKY
These are some of the more common pet forms of the popular Richard. See Richard for a full explanation.

DIDI
From the Hebrew meaning "beloved." It is used in Israel as a pet form of Jedidiah.

---

ee as in b*ee*t; *i* as in b*i*t; *o* as in n*o*; *oi* as in v*oi*d; *u* as in r*u*de.

Hebrew equivalents: Deedee and Y'didyaw. Feminine Hebrew equivalents: Dawveedaw and Y'deedaw.

DODO

From the Hebrew meaning "beloved," or "his uncle." In the Bible Dodo was a member of the tribe of Issachar.

The exact Hebrew equivalent is Dodo. The exact feminine Hebrew equivalent is Dodaw.

DOMINIC, DOMINICK

From the Latin meaning "belonging to God." Dom is a popular short form.

Hebrew equivalents: Ameeayl, Dawneeayl, D'uayl and Meechawayl. Feminine Hebrew equivalents: Dawneeaylaw, Meechal and Yis'r'aylaw.

DON, DONNIE, DONNY

These are popular pet forms of Donald. Don may also be an independent name derived from the Latin meaning "master." See Donald for a full explanation.

DONALD

From the Celtic or Scottish meaning "proud chief," or "world ruler." Don, Donnie and Donny are popular pet forms.

Hebrew equivalents: Adoneeyaw, Aveenawdawv, Kasreeayl, Melech and Nawdawv. Feminine Hebrew equivalents: Atawraw, B'ulaw, G'veeraw, Layaw, Malkaw and Yis'r'aylaw.

DOR

From the Hebrew meaning "a generation," or "a dwelling."

The exact Hebrew equivalent is Dor. The exact feminine Hebrew equivalent is Doris.

DORE

Probably an abbreviated form of Isidore. See Isidore for a full explanation.

Key: *a* as in f*a*ther; *ai* as in *ai*sle; *aw* as in l*aw*; *ay* as in s*ay*; *e* as in b*e*t;

DORON

From the Hebrew meaning "a gift."

The exact Hebrew equivalent is Doron. Feminine Hebrew equivalents: Doronaw, Doronis, Matawnaw, Migdawnaw and Teshuraw.

DORRIS

Used infrequently as a masculine name. See Doris in feminine section for a full explanation.

DOTHAN, DOTAN

In biblical times Dothan (and its variant form Dotan) was a place in Palestine, north of Samaria. Currently it is used as a personal name in Israel. It is of Hebrew origin meaning "law."

The exact Hebrew equivalent is Dosawn. Feminine Hebrew equivalents: Dawnaw, Dawneeaylaw and Dawnis.

DOUGLAS

Either from the Scottish meaning "dark water," or from the Celtic meaning "dark gray." Doug is a popular pet form.

Hebrew equivalents: Adawr, Aveeyawm, Aynawn, Kaydawr and Peleg. Feminine Hebrew equivalents: D'voraw, Lailaw, Mawrawsaw, Miryawm and Tzeelaw.

DOV

From the Hebrew meaning "a bear," and derived from an Arabic root meaning "to walk gently, leisurely."

The exact Hebrew equivalent is Dov. The feminine Hebrew equivalent is Dubaw.

DOVEV

From the Hebrew meaning "to speak or whisper."

The exact Hebrew equivalent is Dovayv. Feminine Hebrew equivalents: Ameeraw, Dovayvaw, Doveves and Neevaw.

DREW

A diminutive of Andrew. See Andrew for a full explanation.

---

ee as in b*ee*t; *i* as in b*i*t; *o* as in n*o*; *oi* as in v*oi*d; *u* as in r*u*de.

DUDLEY

An Old English name meaning "Duda's meadow," a place in Worcestershire, England.

Hebrew equivalents: Awdawm, Kar'mlee and Shadmon. Feminine Hebrew equivalents: Ganaw, Karmel, Sh'daymaw and Yizra'elaw.

DUFF

From the Celtic meaning "dark or black faced."

Hebrew equivalents: Adawr, Ashchur, Chumee, Kaydawr and Pinchaws. Feminine Hebrew equivalents: Ayfaw, Chacheelaw, Lailaw and Tzeelaw.

DUR

From the Hebrew meaning "to heap, pile up," or "to circle."

The exact Hebrew equivalent is Dur. Feminine Hebrew equivalents: Bas-Galim, Talmis and Yawayl.

DURWARD

From the Persian meaning "a porter, doorkeeper, or guardian."

Hebrew equivalents: Mishmawr, Notzayr, Ovayd, Shmaryawhu and Shotayr. Feminine Hebrew equivalents: Notayraw, Noteres, Shimraw, Shimreeyaw and Shimris.

DURYEA

From the Latin meaning "enduring, lasting."

Hebrew equivalents: Amee-ad, Netzach and Nitzchee. Feminine Hebrew equivalents: Chavaw, Cha'yaw and Nitzcheeyaw.

DWIGHT

Either from the Teutonic meaning "white or fair," or a variant form of Denis.

Hebrew equivalents: Ben-Chur, Churee, Lawvawn, Livnee and L'vawnon. Feminine Hebrew equivalents: L'vawnaw, L'vonaw, Tz'choraw and Zawhawraw.

DYLAN

From the Welsh meaning "the sea."

Key: *a* as in f*a*ther; *ai* as in *ai*sle; *aw* as in l*aw*; *ay* as in s*ay*; *e* as in b*e*t;

Hebrew equivalents: Avee'yawm, Aynawn, Ma'a'yawn, Meechaw and Moshe. Feminine Hebrew equivalents: Meechal, Miryawm, Rus and Tarsheeshaw.

EARL

From the Teutonic meaning "of keen intelligence," and connoting wisdom.

Hebrew equivalents: Achbawn, Bunaw, Chanoch, Maskil, Nawor and Yawvin. Feminine Hebrew equivalents: Beenaw, Milkaw and N'oraw.

EARLE

From the Anglo-Saxon meaning "man," or "noble."

Hebrew equivalents: Adir, Awdawm, Gavreeayl, Gever and Yisrawayl. Feminine Hebrew equivalents: Adeevaw, N'deevaw, Sawraw and Yis'r'aylaw.

ED, EDDIE

Diminutive forms of Edward. See Edward for a full explanation.

EDAN

From the Celtic meaning "fire or flame."

Hebrew equivalents: Lapid, Nur, Nuree, Nureeayl and Reshef. Feminine Hebrew equivalents: Avukaw, Shalheves and Uris.

EDDY

From the Scandinavian meaning "unresting, energetic," and having the connotation of industrious. Sometimes used as a diminutive form of Edward or Edwin.

Hebrew equivalents: Arnon, Yawziz and Zeezaw. Feminine Hebrew equivalents: Chawrutzaw, Tirtzaw and Z'reezaw.

EDGAR

From the Teutonic meaning "happy or blessed warrior," and having the connotation of victorious.

Hebrew equivalents: Bawruch, Gawd, Gid'on, Gayraw and Yatzleeach. Feminine Hebrew equivalents: Aveega'yil, B'rawchaw, Matzleechaw, Gavreelaw, Geeboraw and Geelaw.

---

ee as in b*ee*t; *i* as in b*i*t; *o* as in n*o*; *oi* as in v*oi*d; *u* as in r*u*de.

EDMOND, EDMUND
Variant forms of Edward. See Edward for a full explanation.

EDSEL
From the Teutonic meaning "rich."

Hebrew equivalents: Hoseer, Hunaw, Yeeshai and Yisro. Feminine Hebrew equivalents: Bas-shua and Yisraw.

EDWARD
From the Teutonic meaning "blessed or happy guardian of prosperity." Ed, Eddie and Eddy are popular diminutive forms. Ned is perhaps the oldest pet form.

Hebrew equivalents: Avigdor, Notayr, Mishmawr, Sh'maryawhu, Simchaw, Yachdeeayl and Yitzchawk. Feminine Hebrew equivalents: Efraws, Migdawlaw, Notayraw, Notzeres, Shimraw, Shimreeyaw and Shimris.

EDWIN
From the Teutonic meaning "happy or blessed friend."

Hebrew equivalents: Awshayr, Bawruch, Chovawv, Dawvid, Dodee, Eldawd, Maydawd, Noam and Y'didyaw. Feminine Hebrew equivalents: B'ruchaw, Dawveedaw, Dodaw, Leebaw and Y'deedaw.

EFRAIM, EFREM
One of the sons of Joseph in the biblical narrative. A Hebrew name meaning "fruitful." Efrem and Ephraim are variant spellings.

The exact Hebrew equivalent is Efra'yim. Feminine Hebrew equivalents: Neetzaw, Poraw, Poraws, Poreeyaw, T'nuvaw and Zimraw.

EFRAT
From the Hebrew meaning "honored, distinguished." A member of the tribe of Ephraim in the Bible. Also used as a feminine name in the Bible where it appears as the wife of Caleb.

The exact Hebrew equivalent is Efraws. Feminine Hebrew equivalents: Haduraw, K'vudaw and Nichbawdaw.

Key: *a* as in f*a*ther; *ai* as in *ai*sle; *aw* as in l*aw*; *ay* as in s*ay*; *e* as in b*e*t;

ELAZAR

The son of Aaron in the biblical narrative and one of the most frequently used of biblical names in the Talmud. The Hellenized form, as recorded in the Greek New Testament, is Lazarus. From the Hebrew meaning "God has helped."

The exact Hebrew equivalent is Elawzawr. Feminine Hebrew equivalents: Azreeaylaw, Ezraw, Ezr'aylaw, Ezreeaylaw, Milkaw and Saadaw.

ELDEN, ELDER

From the Anglo-Saxon meaning "older."

Hebrew equivalents: Kadmeeayl, Kedem, Sawvaw, Yiftawch, Y'sheeshai and Zawkayn. Feminine Hebrew equivalents: Bilhaw, Y'sheeshaw and Z'kaynaw.

ELI, ELY

From the Hebrew meaning either "ascend, lifting up, offering," and having the connotation of height, grandeur and prominence. Also a short form of Elijah or Elisha. In the Bible Eli (pronounced Aylee) was a high priest and the last of the Judges in the days of Samuel. Eli (pronounced Eelai) was also the name of one of David's bodyguards in the Bible.

The exact Hebrew equivalent is Aylee. Feminine Hebrew equivalent: Yawayl. For other equivalents see Elijah and Elisha.

ELIAS

The Greek form of either Elijah or Elisha. See Elijah and Elisha for a full explanation.

ELIEZER

From the Hebrew meaning "my God has helped." Eliezer appears in the Bible many times. One Eliezer was Abraham's steward, another was a son of Moses, and a third was a prophet in the day of Jehoshaphat.

The exact Hebrew equivalent is Elee-ezer. Feminine

ee as in beet; i as in bit; o as in no; oi as in void; u as in rude.

Hebrew equivalents: Azreeaylaw, Ezraw, Ezr'aylaw and Ezreeaylaw.

ELIHU

From the Hebrew meaning "He is my God." The young friend of Job in the Bible was named Elihu, as were several other persons. The Hebrew name of the famous prophet Elijah is very similar, but with a slight variation in vocalization.

The exact Hebrew equivalent is Eleehu. For feminine equivalents see Elijah.

ELIJAH

From the Hebrew meaning "the Lord is my God." The name of one of the earliest and most famous of the Hebrew prophets who lived during the reign of Ahab and Jezebel. Variations of the name appear in many languages: In German and Danish it is Elias; in French, Elie; in Italian and German Elia. In England and America Elias, Eliot, Elliot and Ellis are used as variant forms.

The exact Hebrew equivalent is Ayleeyawhu. Feminine Hebrew equivalents: Avee-elaw, Aveeyaw, Eleesheva and Yocheved.

ELIOT, ELLIOT, ELLIOTT

Variant forms of either Elijah or Elisha used in America and England. See Elijah and Elisha for a full explanation.

ELISHA

From the Hebrew meaning "God is my salvation." The prophet Elisha was the student and successor of Elijah. Elias and Eliot are popular variant forms.

The exact Hebrew equivalent is Eleeshaw. Feminine Hebrew equivalents: Aleksandraw, Milkaw, Moshawaw, T'shuaw and Y'shuaw.

ELKAN

From the Hebrew meaning "God bought," and having the connotation of possession.

Key: *a* as in f*a*ther; *ai* as in *ai*sle; *aw* as in l*aw*; *ay* as in s*ay*; *e* as in b*e*t;

Hebrew equivalents: Elkawnaw, Baal, Ka'yin and Kaynawn. Feminine Hebrew equivalent: B'ulaw.

ELLERY

From the Teutonic meaning "from the alder trees," and having the connotation of growth.

Hebrew equivalents: Aylaw, Eelawn, Erez, Luz and Miklos. Feminine Hebrew equivalents: Alonaw, Areezaw, Arnaw, Arnis, Aylaw, Eelawnaw and Eelawnis.

ELMER

From the Teutonic meaning "famous," and having the connotation of exalted.

Hebrew equivalents: G'dalyaw, Heelayl, M'halalayl, M'hulawl, Shevach and Shim'ee. Feminine Hebrew equivalents: Odel'yaw, D'voraw, Heelaw, Heelaylaw, T'heelaw and Y'hudis.

ELRAD

From the Hebrew meaning "God is the ruler."

The exact Hebrew equivalent is Elrawd. Feminine Hebrew equivalents: Alufaw, Atawraw, B'ulaw, Layaw, Malkaw, Miryawm and Tz'feeraw.

ELROY

From the Latin meaning "royal, king." The French form is Leroy.

Hebrew equivalents: Aveemelech, Elrawd, Malkeeayl, Malkeerawm and Malkeetzedek. Feminine Hebrew equivalents: Alufaw, Atawraw, Malkaw and Malkis.

ELVIN

From the Teutonic meaning "godly friend."

Hebrew equivalents: Chawviv, Chovawv, Dawvid, Eldawd and Y'didyaw. Feminine Hebrew equivalents: Ahuvaw, Chaveevaw, Dawveedaw, Dodaw, Leebaw, Rus and Y'deedaw.

EMANUEL, EMMANUEL

From the Hebrew meaning "God is with us," and having the connotation of support and protection.

ee as in b*ee*t; *i* as in b*i*t; *o* as in n*o*; *oi* as in v*oi*d; *u* as in r*u*de.

The exact Hebrew equivalent is Eemawnuayl. Feminine Hebrew equivalents: Ganaw, Eemawnuaylaw, Mawgaynaw, Migdawlaw and Teeraw.

EMIL
From the Teutonic meaning "industrious or energetic."

Hebrew equivalents: Arnon, Yawziz and Zeezaw. Feminine Hebrew equivalents: Charutzaw, Tirtzaw and Z'reezaw.

EMMET, EMMETT
Either from the Hebrew meaning "truth," or from the Anglo-Saxon meaning "an ant," and having the connotation of diligence.

Hebrew equivalents: Ameetai and Haymawn. Feminine Hebrew equivalents: Tamaw, Tawmawr and T'meemaw.

ENOCH
From the Hebrew meaning "educated or dedicated." In the Bible Enoch was the son born to Cain after Cain killed Abel.

The exact Hebrew equivalent is Chanoch. Feminine Hebrew equivalents: Beenaw, Bunaw, Chanukaw and N'oraw.

EPHRAIM
An alternate spelling for Efraim. See Efraim for a full explanation.

ERIC, ERIK
From the Teutonic and Anglo-Saxon meaning "ever kingly, brave or powerful." Rickie is a popular pet form.

Hebrew equivalents: Amatzyaw, Aveecha'yil, Chizkee, Kasreeayl, Malkawm and Melech. Feminine Hebrew equivalents: Atawraw, Gavreelaw, Geeboraw, Malkaw and Tz'feeraw.

ERNEST, ERNST, ERNIE
From the Teutonic meaning "earnest or serious-minded." Erno is a variant form. Ernie and Ern are used as diminutive forms.

Hebrew equivalents: Ameetai, Amnon, Aveeshur and Konanyawhu. Feminine Hebrew equivalents: B'ruraw, Tawmawr and T'meemaw.

ERNO
A variant form of Ernest commonly used in Hungary. See Ernest for a full explanation.

ERROL
From the Latin meaning "wanderer," and having the connotation of exiled, stranger.

Hebrew equivalents: Gawlyas, Gayrshom, Gayrshon and Z'rubawvel. Feminine Hebrew equivalents: Aveeshag and Hawgawr.

ERWIN
A variant form of Irvin and of Irving meaning "handsome." See Irvin for a full explanation.

ESHKOL
From the Hebrew meaning "a cluster of grapes." In Hebrew literature it is a word signifying a group of great scholars. Presently used in Israel as a personal name as well as a surname. Levi Eshkol, a Prime Minister of Israel, adopted it as a surname.

The exact Hebrew equivalent is Eshkol. Feminine Hebrew equivalents: Gafnaw, Gefen, Karmelaw and Karmis.

ESMOND, ESMUND
From the Anglo-Saxon meaning "gracious protector." Esmond became popular after the publication of Thackeray's historical novel, *Henry Esmond,* dealing with 18th century life and politics. Esmund is a variant form.

Hebrew equivalents: Armonee, Eleefelet, Lot, Lotawn, Saadyaw and Zimree. Feminine Hebrew equivalents: Chasyaw, Chosaw, Mawgaynaw, Shimraw and Shimreeyaw.

ETAN, ETHAN
From the Hebrew meaning "permanent, firm, strong." Ethan became popular in America in honor of the revolutionary war soldier, Ethan Allen.

ee as in b*ee*t; *i* as in b*i*t; *o* as in n*o*; *oi* as in v*oi*d; *u* as in r*u*de.

The exact Hebrew equivalent is Aysawn. Feminine Hebrew equivalents: Amtzaw, Awtzmaw, Aysawnaw, Azaw, Azeezaw and Chaseenaw.

EUGENE

From the Greek meaning "well born, born lucky," or "one of noble descent." Eugen and Eugine are variant spellings. Gene is a popular pet form.

Hebrew equivalents: Ameenawdawv, Cheeraw, Mazawl-Tov, Nawdawv, Y'honawdawv, Y'horawm and Yisrawayl. Feminine Hebrew equivalents: Malkaw, Mazawl, N'deevaw, N'seechaw and Yis'r'aylaw.

EVAN, EVANS, EVANDER

From the Celtic meaning "young warrior," or a Welsh form of John, meaning "gracious." Owen is a variant form.

Hebrew equivalents: Aveecha'yil, Ben-Cha'yil, Gawd, Geebor, Gidon and Yochawnawn. Feminine Hebrew equivalents: Amtzaw, Chanaw, Gavreelaw, Geeboraw and Yochawnaw.

EVELYN

Used occasionally as a masculine name, as in the case of author Evelyn Waugh, and polar explorer Richard Evelyn Byrd. The name was first used as a masculine name by Evelyn Pierrepont, Duke of Kingston (born in 1665). Evelyn was his mother's maiden name. See Evelyn in feminine section for explanation and definitions.

EVERETT

Either from the Anglo-Saxon meaning "a boar," or from the Norse meaning "a warrior."

Hebrew equivalents: Aveecha'yil, Ben-Cha'yil, Gawd, Gayraw, Gid'on, Naftawlee and Mawr'd'chai. Feminine Hebrew equivalents: Awtzmaw, Gavreelaw, Geeboraw and Tigraw.

EZEKIEL

From the Hebrew meaning "God will strengthen." One

ee as in b*ee*t; *i* as in b*i*t; *o* as in n*o*; *oi* as in v*oi*d; *u* as in r*u*de.

of the better known biblical prophets towards the end of
First Temple days (6th century B.C.E.).

The exact Hebrew equivalent is Y'chezkayl. The exact
feminine Hebrew equivalent is Y'chezkaylaw.

EZER

From the Hebrew meaning "help." Many biblical names
are derived from this word including Ezra, Azariah, Ezri,
Azur and Azrikam. Ezer is used as a personal name in
Israel.

See Ezra for masculine and feminine Hebrew equivalents.

EZRA, EZRI

From the Hebrew meaning "help." Ezra was a leader
of the Jews after the destruction of the First Temple. The
Yemenites, it has been noted, never name their sons Ezra.
They claim that when Ezra took the Jews out of Babylonia
he did not take the Yemenites along. Ezri is mentioned in
the Book of Chronicles. Ezra is also used as a feminine
name in Israel.

The exact Hebrew equivalents are Ezraw and Ezree.
Feminine Hebrew equivalents: Azreeaylaw, Ezraw, Ezr'aylaw, Ezreeaylay, Milkaw, Moshawaw and T'shuaw.

FABIAN

From the Latin meaning "bean farmer."

Hebrew equivalents: Awdawm, Karmel, Kar'mlee, Yiz'-
r'ayl. Feminine Hebrew equivalents: Karmelaw, Nawvaw
and Yiz'r'elaw.

FEIBUSH

A Yiddish name which is a variant form of Feivel. See
Feivel for a full explanation.

FEIVEL, FEIWEL

A Yiddish form of Phoebus, the goddess of light in
Greek mythology.

Hebrew equivalents: Mayeer, Shimshon, Shimshai, Uree

ee as in b*ee*t; *i* as in b*i*t; *o* as in n*o*; *oi* as in v*oi*d; *u* as in r*u*de.

and Ureeyaw. Feminine Hebrew equivalents: B'heeraw, M'eeraw, Noga, Shimshonaw and Zawhawraw.

FELIX
From the Latin meaning "happy, fortunate, prosperous."
Hebrew equivalents: Awshayr, Bawruch, Simchaw, Yawgil and Yitzchawk. Feminine Hebrew equivalents: Aleezaw, B'rawchaw, Geelaw, Reenaw and Seesaw.

FERD
A short form of Ferdinand. Also used as an independent name. See Ferdinand for a full explanation.

FERDINAND
From the Teutonic meaning "brave, strong." Ferd is a popular pet form. Fern is a feminine form of Ferdinand.
Hebrew equivalents: Amatzyaw, Awmotz, Kawlayv, Uzeeayl and Uzeeyaw. Feminine Hebrew equivalents: Amtzaw, Areeayl, Gavreelaw and Geeboraw.

FISHKE
A Yiddish name derived from the Old German meaning "fish." See Fisk.

FISK, FISKE
From the Scandinavian meaning "fish."
According to one scholar, Nun is a Hebrew name meaning fish. Joshua son of Nun was the successor of Moses. There are no feminine Hebrew equivalents.

FLORENCE
Used occasionally as a masculine name, spelled Florence, Florenz or Florentz. Fiorello is an Italian variant form. See Florence in feminine section for interpretation and definitions.

FLOYD
A corrupt form of Lloyd. See Lloyd for a full explanation.

FORREST
From the Latin meaning "out-of-doors, woods."

Key: *a* as in f*a*ther; *ai* as in *ai*sle; *aw* as in l*aw*; *ay* as in s*ay*; *e* as in b*e*t;

Hebrew equivalents: Karmel, Kar'm'lee, Yaraw and Yaaree. Feminine Hebrew equivalents: Ganaw, Karmelaw, Kar'm'lee and Yaraw.

FRANCIS, FRANK, FRANKIE

Frank and Frankie are forms of Francis meaning "free born, liberal," in the Teutonic. Frances, spelled with an "e," is a feminine form.

Hebrew equivalents: Aveed'ror, Chayrus, P'sachyaw, Pesach, R'chavyaw and R'chavawm. Feminine Hebrew equivalents: D'voraw, D'roraw, D'roris, G'ulaw, Lee-d'ror and Rawchawv.

FRANKLIN

From the Old English meaning "free-holder," and having the connotation of ownership, possession.

Hebrew equivalents: Baal, Elkawnaw, Pesach, P'sachyaw and R'chavawm. Feminine Hebrew equivalents: B'ulaw, D'voraw, G'ulaw and Rawchawv.

FRED, FREDDIE, FREDDY

Popular pet forms of Frederic or Frederick. See below for a full explanation.

FREDERIC, FREDERICK, FREDRIC, FREDRICK

Frederick and its various forms are from the Teutonic meaning "peaceful ruler."

Hebrew equivalents: Avshawlom, Ish-Shawlom, Kasreeayl, Margoa, Mclech, Shaanawn, Shawlom and Shlomo. Feminine Hebrew equivalents: M'nuchaw, Rivkaw, Shaannanaw, Shlomis, Shulamis and Za'yis.

FRITZ

Fritz is the German form of Frederick. See Frederick.

GABE

A popular short form of Gabriel. See Gabriel for a full explanation.

GABI

An Israeli name, derived by shortening Gabriel. Pronounced: Gabee. See Gabriel for a full explanation.

---

ee as in b*ee*t; *i* as in b*i*t; *o* as in n*o*; *oi* as in v*oi*d; *u* as in r*u*de.

GABRIEL

From the Hebrew meaning "God is my strength." In the Bible Gabriel was the angel seen by Daniel in a vision. Gabe and Gabby are popular pet forms. In Israel, Gabi, a short form of Gabriel, is used as an independent name.

The exact Hebrew equivalent is Gavreeayl. Gabee is a short form of Gavreeayl. Feminine Hebrew equivalents: Ameetzaw, Areeayl, Aysawnaw, Azeezaw, Gavreeaylaw, Gavreelaw and Geeboraw.

GAD

From the Hebrew and Arabic meaning "happy, fortunate," or "a troop, a warrior." One of the sons of Jacob in the Bible.

The exact Hebrew equivalent is Gawd. Feminine Hebrew equivalents: Ashayraw, Gadaw, Gadis, Gavreelaw, Mazawl and Tigraw.

GADI

A modern Hebrew name derived from the Arabic meaning "goat, kid," or "my fortune." In the Bible, Gadi is mentioned as a member of the tribe of Manasseh.

The exact Hebrew equivalent is Gawdee. Feminine Hebrew equivalents: Gadaw, Gadis, Yaalis, Yawayl, and Y'aylaw.

GADIEL

From the Hebrew meaning "God is my fortune or blessing." Gadiel, in the Bible, was a member of the tribe of Zebulun.

The exact Hebrew equivalent is Gadeeayl. See Gad for additional equivalents.

GAL, GALI

From the Hebrew meaning "a wave" or "a mountain, a heap." Gali is the first person possessive form of the name (i.e. my mountain). Both names are also used as feminine names in Israel.

The exact Hebrew equivalents are Gal and Galee.

Key: *a* as in father; *ai* as in *ai*sle; *aw* as in l*aw*; *ay* as in s*ay*; *e* as in b*e*t;

GAMALIEL, GAMLIEL

From the Hebrew meaning "God is my reward," and having the connotation of blessing.

The exact Hebrew equivalent is Gamleeayl. Feminine Hebrew equivalents: Ashayraw, B'rawchaw, Gamleeaylaw, Gamleeaylis and G'mulaw.

GARDEN, GARDENER

From the Old High German meaning "a garden."

Hebrew equivalents: Awdaw, Geenas, Ginson, Karmel and Kar'mlee. Feminine Hebrew equivalents: Ganaw, Ganis, Karmelaw and Nawvaw.

GARNET

From the Latin meaning "a grain." The dark, red seed of the pomegranate resembled the precious jewel in color and shape, hence the name Garnet for the deep-red colored jewel.

Hebrew equivalents: Admon, Almog, Gunee, P'rudaw and Zohar. Feminine Hebrew equivalents: Garnis, Gawrnaw, Puaw, S'gulaw and Yakeeraw.

GAVIN

An Old Welsh name meaning "little hawk." It is a very popular name in Scotland.

Hebrew equivalent bird names: Gozawl, Orayv and Tzeepor. Feminine Hebrew equivalents: Chawglaw, Efronaw, Gozawlaw, Tzeeporaw and Yawayn.

GARY, GARRY

A diminutive of Gerard or Gerald meaning "warrior-like, brave."

See Gerald for Hebrew equivalents.

GEDALIA, GEDALIAH, GEDALIAHU

From the Hebrew meaning "God is great." In the Bible Gedaliah was the governor of Judea appointed by Nebuchadnezzar. Gedaliahu is a variant form of Gedalia and Gedaliah.

Hebrew equivalents: G'dalyaw and G'dalyawhu. Feminine Hebrew equivalents: Asalyaw and G'dulaw.

ee as in b*ee*t; *i* as in b*i*t; *o* as in n*o*; *oi* as in v*oi*d; *u* as in r*u*de.

GEFANIA, GEPHANIA
From the Hebrew meaning "wine or vineyard of the Lord." A name currently used in Israel.

The exact Hebrew equivalent is G'fanyaw. The exact feminine Hebrew equivalent is Gafnaw.

GEOFFREY
From the Anglo-Saxon meaning "gift of peace." Jeffery and Jeffrey are variant forms. The surname Jefferson (a derivative of Jeffery or Geoffrey) became popular as a personal name after Thomas Jefferson's election in 1801.

Hebrew equivalents: Avshawlom, Magdeeayl, N'sanayl, Shawlom and Shlomo. Feminine Hebrew equivalents: Migdawnaw, M'nuchaw, Shlomis, Shulamis and Za'yis.

GEORGE
From the Greek meaning, "a farmer."

Hebrew equivalents: Awdawm, Geenas, Karmel, Kar'mlee, Notaya, Shadmon and Yiz'r'ayl. Feminine Hebrew equivalents: Ganaw, Karmelaw, Nawvaw, Sh'daymaw and Yiz'r'elaw.

GERALD, GERARD, GERHART
From the Teutonic meaning "warrior-like, brave heart, spear-bearer, warrior." Gerry and Jerry are the more popular of the many short forms for these names. Gary and Jarry have been used for pet forms of Gerard, in particular. Some of the short forms have also been adopted as feminine names in recent years.

Hebrew equivalents: Aveecha'yil, Ben-Cha'yil, Chaltzon, Chizkeeyaw, Ish-Cha'yil, Gawd, Gayraw, Gid'on, Kawlayv, Y'chezkayl and Y'hoawsh. Feminine Hebrew equivalents: Awtzmaw, Azaw, Azeezaw, Chaseenaw, Gavreelaw, Geeboraw and Tigraw.

GEROME, GERRY
Gerry is a diminutive form of Gerome meaning "of holy fame," or "sacred name," in the Greek. Jerome is a popular variant spelling. Gerry is a variant pet form.

Key: *a* as in *father*; *ai* as in *aisle*; *aw* as in *law*; *ay* as in *say*; *e* as in *bet*;

Hebrew equivalents: G'dalyaw, Heelayl, Kadish, M'hu-lawl, Shaym-Tov, Shmuayl, and Yishbach. Feminine Hebrew equivalents: D'voraw, Heelaw, Heelaylaw, Ode'l'yaw, T'heelaw, Y'hudis and Zimraw.

GERSHOM, GERSHON, GERSON
From the Hebrew meaning "stranger." In the Bible Gershom was a son of Moses. Gershon was a son of Levi in the Book of Genesis.

The exact Hebrew equivalents: Gayrshom and Gayrshon. The exact Feminine Hebrew equivalent is Gayrshonaw.

GEVA
From the Hebrew meaning "a hill." In the Bible it is the name of a place, but is currently used as a personal name in Israel.

The exact Hebrew equivalent is Geva. Feminine Hebrew equivalents: Gal, Galee, Galis, Givaw and Givonaw.

GIBOR
From the Hebrew meaning "strong."

The exact Hebrew equivalent is Geebor. The exact feminine Hebrew equivalent is Geeboraw.

GIDEON, GIDI
From the Hebrew meaning either "maimed" or "a mighty warrior." Gideon was one of the Judges in the Bible who helped conquer Palestine. He is most famous as the warrior-hero who defeated the Midianites. Gidi is currently used in Israel as a pet form of Gideon.

The exact Hebrew equivalents are Gidon and Geedee. Feminine Hebrew equivalents: Adeeraw, Ameetzaw, Aysawnaw, Gavreelaw, Geeboraw, Gidonaw, Odaydaw and Tigraw.

GIL, GILL, GILI, GILLI
From the Hebrew meaning "joy." Gili means "my joy." Gil and Gili are used in Israel as both feminine and masculine names. Gil is also a short form of Gilbert. See Gilbert for explanation.

---

ee as in b*ee*t; *i* as in b*i*t; *o* as in n*o*; *oi* as in v*oi*d; *u* as in r*u*de.

The exact Hebrew equivalents are Gil and Geelee. Feminine Hebrew equivalents: Geel, Geelee, Geeleeyaw and Geelis.

GILAD, GILEAD, GILADI
Popular names in Israel, probably derived from the Arabic meaning "hump of a camel," and having the connotation of height. Gilad (or Gilead) was a mountain range and hilly country east of the Jordan river, referred to quite often in the Bible. Giladi means "a man from Gilad."

The exact Hebrew equivalents are: Gilawd and Gilawdee. Feminine Hebrew equivalents: Gal, Galee, Gilawdaw, Talmaw and Talmis.

GILBERT
From the Teutonic meaning either "light of many," or "a bright pledge," or "a sword."

Hebrew equivalents: Barkai, Bawrawk, Eleeor, Mayeer, Nayreeyaw, Shimshon, Shragai, Shragaw, Ureeayl and Zohar. Feminine Hebrew equivalents: B'heeraw, Eleeoraw, M'eeraw, Noga, Oraw, Orlee, Orlis and Zakaw.

GINSON, GINTON
From the Hebrew meaning "a garden, orchard." In the Bible it is the name of a priest who returned with the Babylonian exiles to Palestine. Currently used in Israel. Ginton is the Israeli pronunciation of Ginson.

The exact Hebrew equivalent is Ginson. Feminine Hebrew equivalents: Ganaw, Ganis, Geenas and Geenaw.

GIRARD
A variant spelling of Gerard which is a form of Gerald. See Gerald for a full explanation.

GITI, GITAI
From the Hebrew meaning "one who presses grapes." Both are popular names in Israel.

The exact Hebrew equivalents are Geetai and Geetee. Feminine Hebrew equivalents: Gas, Geetaw and Geetis.

Key: *a* as in f*a*ther; *ai* as in *ai*sle; *aw* as in l*aw*; *ay* as in s*ay*; *e* as in b*e*t;

GIVON
From the Hebrew meaning "hill or heights." Givon is a place-name in the Bible.

The exact Hebrew equivalent is Givon. The exact feminine Hebrew equivalent is Givonaw.

GLEN, GLENN
From the Celtic meaning "a dale," or "a small secluded woody valley."

Hebrew equivalents: Gai, Gaychazee, Ginson, Karmel and Yaaree. Feminine Hebrew equivalents: Ganaw, Ganis, Geenas, Geenaw, Karmelaw and Karmeeyaw.

GODFREY
From the Teutonic meaning "God's peace," or "divinely peaceful."

Hebrew equivalents: Avshawlom, Ish-Shawlom, Margoa, Mawnoach, Shawlom and Shlomee. Feminine Hebrew equivalents: Margayaw, M'nuchaw, M'shulemes, Shlomis and Shulamis.

GOEL
From the Hebrew meaning "the redeemer." A name current in Israel.

The exact Hebrew equivalent is Goayl. Feminine Hebrew equivalents: G'alyaw, Goeles, G'ulaw and Y'gawawlaw.

GOLIATH
From the Hebrew meaning "exiled, stranger." Goliath, the victim of David in the Bible, was famous for his great strength and size.

The exact Hebrew equivalent is Gawlyas. Feminine Hebrew equivalents: Aveeshag and Hawgawr.

GORDON
Of doubtful derivation, but probably from the Gaelic meaning "hero, strongman." Gordon is the name of a place in England.

Hebrew equivalents: Aryay, Dawsawn, Gavreeayl, Gee-

ee as in b*ee*t; *i* as in b*i*t; *o* as in n*o*; *oi* as in v*oi*d; *u* as in r*u*de.

bor and Y'chezkayl. Feminine Hebrew equivalents: Areeayl, Gavreelaw, Geeboraw, Odaydaw, Tigraw and Y'chezkaylaw.

GOVER
From the Hebrew meaning "victorious."

The exact Hebrew equivalent is Govayr. Feminine Hebrew equivalents: Dafnaw, Hadasaw, Nitzchaw and Nitzcheeyaw.

GOZAL
From the Hebrew meaning "a bird."

The exact Hebrew equivalent is Gozawl. The exact feminine Hebrew equivalent is Gozawlaw.

GRAHAM
From the Teutonic meaning "from the gray home or dwelling."

Hebrew equivalents: Dur, Y'shawvawm, Y'shevawv, Z'vul and Z'vulun. Feminine Hebrew equivalents: Keres, M'onaw, Leenaw and Teeraw.

GRANT
From the Old French meaning "to give, grant or assure."

Hebrew equivalents: Aveeshai, Doron, Elnawsawn, Matanyaw, Matawn, Matisyawhu, Nawsawn and Y'honawsawn. Feminine Hebrew equivalents: Matawnaw, Migdawnaw, Minchaw, N'seenaw, T'rumaw and T'shuraw.

GREGORY
From the Greek meaning "vigilant, to awaken, or watchman." Greg and Gregor are variant forms.

Hebrew equivalents: Avigdor, Geenas and Sh'maryawhu. Feminine Hebrew equivalents: Avigdoraw, Bawtzraw, Ganaw, Teeraw and Yaakovaw.

GRIFFIN, GRIFFITH
From the Welsh and Cymric origin meaning "strong in faith."

Hebrew equivalents: Ameetai, Amnon, Bukee, Haymawn

Key: *a* as in f*a*ther; *ai* as in *ai*sle; *aw* as in l*aw*; *ay* as in s*ay*; *e* as in b*e*t;

and Y'kuseeayl. Feminine Hebrew equivalents: Bitchaw, B'ruraw, Emunaw, Gavreelaw, Geeboraw and Tikvaw.

GUNI
A Hebrew biblical name derived from the Arabic meaning "reddish-black."

The exact Hebrew equivalent is Gunee. Feminine Hebrew equivalents: Ayfaw, Chacheelaw, Lailaw and Tzeelaw.

GUNTHER
Either from the Saxon meaning "warrior," or from the Welsh meaning "plainsman."

Hebrew equivalents: Ish-Cha'yil, Ben-Cha'yil, Geebor, Chavakuk, Gawd, Gayraw and Gidon. Feminine Hebrew equivalents: Ameetzaw, Amtzaw, Gavreelaw, Geeboraw and Tigraw.

GUR
From the Hebrew meaning "a young lion."

The exact Hebrew equivalent is Gur. Feminine Hebrew equivalents: Areeayl, Areeaylaw, Guris, K'feeraw and L'veeaw.

GURI
From the Hebrew meaning "my young lion."

The exact Hebrew equivalent is Guree. Feminine Hebrew equivalents: Areeayl, Areeaylaw, Guris, K'feeraw and L'veeaw.

GURIEL
From the Hebrew meaning "God is my lion," or "God is my refuge or protection."

The exact Hebrew equivalent is Gureeayl. Feminine Hebrew equivalents: Areeayl, Areeaylaw, Ganaw, Guris, Mawgaynaw, K'feeraw and L'veeaw.

GURION
From the Hebrew meaning "a lion" or "strength." David Ben-Gurion, whose name was originally David Gruen, assumed this name after settling in Palestine.

ee as in b*ee*t; *i* as in b*i*t; *o* as in n*o*; *oi* as in v*oi*d; *u* as in r*u*de.

The exact Hebrew equivalent is Guryon. Feminine Hebrew equivalents: Areeayl, Areeaylaw, Guris, K'feeraw and L'veeaw.

GUS, GUSTAVE

From the Swedish meaning "war." Gus is a diminutive form of Gustave.

Hebrew equivalents: Ben-Cha'yil, Gawd, Gayraw, Gidon, Mawrd'chai and Yisrawayl. Feminine Hebrew equivalents: Gavreelaw, Geeboraw, Tigraw and Yisr'aylaw.

GUY

From the Old French meaning "a guide," or "a rope that guides," and having the connotation of instructor, leader. It may also be taken from the Hebrew meaning "valley."

Hebrew equivalents: Chanoch, Guy, Gaychazee, Rosh and Tzur. Feminine Hebrew equivalents: G'veeraw, Malkaw, P'seelaw, Rivkaw and Tz'feeraw.

HADAR

From the Hebrew meaning "adornment, glory or majesty." In the Bible Hadar was a king of Edom. Currently a popular masculine and feminine name used in Israel.

The exact Hebrew equivalent is Hadar and Hawdawr. Feminine Hebrew equivalents: Hadawr, Hadawraw and Hadawris.

HADRIAN

From the Greek meaning "rich." A variant form of Adrian.

Hebrew equivalents: Hoseer, Hunaw, Yeeshai and Yisro. Feminine Hebrew equivalents: Bas-Shua and Yisraw.

HAIM, HAYM

Forms of Chaim meaning "life." See Chaim for more information.

Key: *a* as in f*a*ther; *ai* as in *ai*sle; *aw* as in l*aw*; *ay* as in s*ay*; *e* as in b*e*t;

HAL
A pet form of Harold or Haley. See Harold and Haley for more information.

HALEY, HALLEY
From the Anglo-Saxon meaning "holy or healthy." Hale is a pet form.

Hebrew equivalents: Awsaw, D'vir, Kadish, R'fawayl and Y'kuseeayl. Feminine Hebrew equivalents: R'fuaw, Rofee and T'rufaw.

HANAN
From the Hebrew meaning "grace, gracious." Hanan is a short form of Johanan from which John is derived.

The exact Hebrew equivalent is Chawnawn. Feminine Hebrew equivalents: Adeevaw, Avee-Chayn, Chanaw, Chaneesaw and Yochawnaw.

HANS, HANSEL
The Dutch, German and Swedish forms of John. Hansel is also a Bavarian form. See John for a full explanation.

HAREL
From the Hebrew meaning "mountain of God." In the Bible Harel is a place-name. Currently used in Israel as a personal name.

The exact Hebrew equivalent is Harayl. The exact feminine Hebrew equivalent is Haraylaw.

HARLAN, HARLEY, HARLIN
Teutonic names meaning "warrior," or "from the frost land."

Hebrew equivalents: Ish-Cha'yil, Ben-Cha'yil, Bered, Gayraw, Geebor and Korach. Feminine Hebrew equivalents: Ameetzaw, Amtzaw, Gavreelaw, Geeboraw, Shalgis, Shalgeeyaw and Tigraw.

HARMAN
From the Old English meaning "a keeper or guardian of hares or deers."

ee as in b*ee*t; *i* as in b*i*t; *o* as in n*o*; *oi* as in v*oi*d; *u* as in r*u*de.

Hebrew equivalents: Hertzayl, Ovadyaw, Ovayd, Mishmawr, Notzar, Nitron and Tz'vee. Feminine Hebrew equivalents: A'yawlaw, A'yeles, Tzivyaw, Shimris and Shomayraw.

HARMON
From the Greek meaning "peace, harmony."

Hebrew equivalents: Avshawlom, Ish-Shawlom, Shaanawn, Shawlom, Shlomo and Zaysawn. Feminine Hebrew equivalents: M'nuchaw, M'shulemes, Shlomis and Shulamis.

HAROLD
From the Teutonic meaning "warrior, strength." A very popular name in the 10th and 11th centuries. It lost popularity for several hundred years and was revived in the 19th century.

Hebrew equivalents: Aryay, Aveecha'yil, Barzeelai, Chizkeeyawhu, Helem, La-yish and Y'chezk'ayl. Feminine Hebrew equivalents: Ameetzaw, Areeayl, Chaseenaw, Gavreelaw, Geeboraw and Tigraw.

HARRIS
A variant form of Harry. See Harry for an explanation.

HARRY
From the Teutonic meaning "ruler of the home, rich lord or mighty lord." Harry was once a very popular name, but has declined greatly in past years. The English kings named Henry were called Harry by their subjects. Harris is a patronymic form meaning "Harry's son."

Hebrew equivalents: Avrawhawm, Chashmon, Chashmonawee, Kasreeayl, Rav, Rawvaw, Rosh and Yisrawayl. Feminine Hebrew equivalents: Alufaw, Atawraw, Malkaw, Miryawm, Sawraw and Yisr'aylaw.

HARTLEY
A variant form of Harley. See Harley for a full explanation.

Key: *a* as in f*a*ther; *ai* as in *ai*sle; *aw* as in l*aw*; *ay* as in s*ay*; *e* as in b*e*t;

HARVEY

From the Celtic meaning "progressive," and having the connotation of flourishing, liberal. According to some linguists Harvey also has the meaning of "battle-worthy."

Hebrew equivalents: Efra'yim, Poraws, P'rachyaw, Puraw and R'chavawm. Feminine Hebrew equivalents: Neetzaw, Porachas, Poraw, Poreeyaw and Rawchawv.

HASKEL, HASKELL

Probably a corrupt Yiddish form of Ezekiel meaning "strength." See Ezekiel. Some take it as an Old English name meaning "powerful leader or chief." Haskel has become popular in Israel, and is generally assumed to be a derivative of the Hebrew word meaning "wisdom, understanding."

Hebrew equivalents: Achbawn, Acheemelech, Chachmonee, Chanoch, Haskayl, Kasreeayl, Pekach and Yawvin. Feminine Hebrew equivalents: Beenaw, Bunaw, Chochmaw, Milkaw, N'veeaw and Tusheeyaw.

HAVELOCK

From the Teutonic meaning "a haven or dwelling by the lake."

Hebrew equivalents: Dur, Y'shevawv, Z'vul and Z'vulun. Feminine Hebrew equivalents: Keres, Leenaw, M'onaw and Teeraw.

HAYYIM

A variant spelling of Haim and Chaim. See Chaim for a full explanation.

HECTOR

From the Greek meaning "anchor," and having the connotation of keeper, protector.

Hebrew equivalents: Avigdor, Chetzron, Geenas, R'fawayl, Saadyaw, Sh'maryawhu and Yachmai. Feminine Hebrew equivalents: Bawtzraw, Chasyaw, Chosaw, Shimris, Teeraw and Yaakovaw.

---

ee as in b*ee*t; *i* as in b*i*t; *o* as in n*o*; *oi* as in v*oi*d; *u* as in r*u*de.

HEIMAN
Either a form of Hyman meaning "a dweller on heights," (see Hyman), or a form of Herman meaning "warrior" (see Herman).

HEINRICH
The German form of Henry. See Henry for explanation.

HELEM
From the Hebrew meaning "a hammer" or "to strike down." In the Bible Helem was a member of the tribe of Asher.

The exact Hebrew equivalent is Helem. Feminine Hebrew equivalent: Makabis.

HEMAN
From the Hebrew meaning "faithful." The name occurs several times in the Bible.

The exact Hebrew equivalent is Haymawn. Feminine Hebrew equivalents: Amawnaw, Emunaw, Ne'emawnaw, Tamaw, Tawmawr, and T'meemaw.

HENRY
From the Teutonic meaning "ruler of the home, rich lord, or mighty lord." In France the name was Henri, and it came to be pronounced Harry in an attempt to give it an authentic French sound. As a result, Harry became a nickname for Henry. All English kings named Henry were called Harry. Heinrich is a German form of Henry, and Hank is a popular pet form.

Hebrew equivalents: Adoneeyaw, Avrawhawm, Hunaw, Chashmon, Chashmonawee, Yisrawayl and Yisro. Feminine Hebrew equivalents: Atawraw, Geeboraw, Layaw, Malkaw, Sawraw, Tz'feeraw and Yisr'aylaw.

HERBERT
From the Teutonic meaning "bright or excellent lord, ruler, soldier." Herb and Herbie are short forms of Herbert.

Hebrew equivalents: Adoneeyaw, Avrawhawm, Has-

Key: *a* as in father; *ai* as in *ai*sle; *aw* as in l*aw*; *ay* as in s*ay*; *e* as in b*e*t;

kayl, Kasreeayl, Melech and Nawdawv. Feminine Hebrew
equivalents: Atawraw, Gavreelaw, Malkaw and Yisr'aylaw.

HERMAN
From the Saxon meaning "soldier, man of the army."
Hebrew equivalents: Gayraw, Mawr'd'chai, Yawriv and
Yisrawayl. Feminine Hebrew equivalents: Gavreelaw, Gee-
boraw, Tigraw and Yisr'aylaw.

HERSCH, HERSH
From the Yiddish meaning "a deer," and having the
connotation of swiftness. Hirsch, Hirsh, Herzel, Heschel
and Heshel are variant forms.
Hebrew equivalents: A'yawl, A'yawlon, Efron, Hersh,
Hertzayl, Ofer, Tz'vee and Tzivyon. Feminine Hebrew
equivalents: Awfraw, A'yawlaw, A'yeles, Hertzaylaw, Tzivyaw, Yaalis and Yawaylaw.

HERSCHEL, HERSHEL
A diminutive form of Hersch. See Hersch for a full
explanation.

HERZL
A diminutive form of Hirsch. From the Yiddish meaning "a deer." The name became popular as a result of the
activity of Theodor Herzl (1860-1904) in behalf of the
establishment of a Jewish state. His first and middle names,
Benjamin Ze'ev, also became popular as personal names
in Israel, and elsewhere.
The exact Hebrew equivalent is Hertzayl. The exact
feminine Hebrew equivalents are Hertzaylaw and Hertz'leeyaw.

HESCHEL, HESHEL
Variant forms of Hersch and Herschel. See Hersch for
a full explanation.

HEVEL
From the Hebrew meaning "breath, vapor," or from the

ee as in b*ee*t; *i* as in b*i*t; *o* as in n*o*; *oi* as in v*oi*d; *u* as in r*u*de.

Assyrian meaning "son." Hevel is the Hebrew name of Abel, son of Adam and Eve.

The exact Hebrew equivalent is Hevel. Feminine Hebrew equivalents: Basyaw and Sh'eefaw.

HEYWOOD

From the Teutonic meaning "from the dark forest."

Hebrew equivalents: Ayfaw, Karmel, Kaydawr, Pinchaws and Yaaree. Feminine Hebrew equivalents: Ayfaw, Chacheelaw, Karmelaw, Lailaw, Tzeelaw and Yaaraw.

HILARY, HILLARY

From the Teutonic meaning "guardian in war, protector." These names may also be derived from the Greek meaning "cheerful." They are used as feminine as well as masculine names. Hillard and Hilliard are variant forms.

Hebrew equivalents: Avigdor, Awgil, Chuseeayl, Shmaryawhu, Semach, Simchon and Yachmai. Feminine Hebrew equivalents: Aveega'yil, Avigdoraw, Bawtzraw, Chedvaw, Geelaw, Shimris and Yaakovaw.

HILL

From the Anglo-Saxon meaning "hill, high place." Hill is also a diminutive form of Hillary, Hillard and Hilliard.

Hebrew equivalents: Aharon, Geva, Givon, Harayl, Mawrom and Talmai. Feminine Hebrew equivalents: Gal, Galee, Gilawdaw, Haraylaw, M'romaw, Talmaw and Talmis.

HILLARD, HILLIARD

Variant forms and spellings of Hilary and Hillary. See Hilary for a full explanation.

HILLEL

From the Hebrew meaning "praised or famous." Although the name appears as the father of a Hebrew judge in the Bible, it did not become popular until used by the renowned Jewish scholar who was born in Babylonia about 75 B.C., and who was the founder of a great academy.

The exact Hebrew equivalent is Heelayl. Feminine Hebrew equivalents: Heelaw, Heelaylaw, T'heelaw and Y'hudis.

Key: *a* as in f*a*ther; *ai* as in *ai*sle; *aw* as in l*aw*; *ay* as in s*ay*; *e* as in b*e*t;

HIRAM
From the Hebrew meaning "noble born," or "exalted brother."

The exact Hebrew equivalent is Cheerawm. Feminine Hebrew equivalents: Asalyaw, B'rawchaw, Malkaw and Sawraw.

HIRSCH, HIRSH
Variant spellings of Hersch and Hersh. See Hersch for a full explanation.

HOD
From the Hebrew meaning "splendor, vigor." In the Bible Hod was a member of the tribe of Asher.

The exact Hebrew equivalent is Hod. Feminine Hebrew equivalents: Azeezaw, Azaw, Hodeeyaw, Odaydaw, Sawraw and Uzis.

HODIYA
A biblical name derived from the Hebrew meaning "God is my splendor." Used as a masculine and feminine name in Israel.

The exact Hebrew equivalent is Hodeeyaw.

HOLLIS
A variant form of Haley and Halley. See Haley for a full explanation.

HOMER
From the Greek meaning "blind."

Hebrew euphemistic equivalents: Koresh, Shimshon, Uree, Ureeayl and Zerach. Feminine Hebrew equivalents: Noga, Oraw and Zawhawraw.

HONI
From the Hebrew meaning "gracious." Derived from the same root as the names Johanan (John) and Hannah.

The exact Hebrew equivalent is Chonee. Feminine Hebrew equivalents: Adeevaw, Chanaw and Yochawnaw.

---

ee as in b*ee*t; *i* as in b*i*t; *o* as in n*o*; *oi* as in v*oi*d; *u* as in r*u*de.

HORACE

From the Greek meaning "to see, to behold." Horatio is a derivative of Horace.

Hebrew equivalents: Achazyaw, N'vawt and R'uvayn. Feminine Hebrew equivalents: Ro'aw, R'uvaynaw, Tzofee, Tzofeeyaw and Tzofis.

HORATIO

A derivative of Horace. See Horace for an explanation.

HOWARD

From the Saxon meaning "watchman, guardian of the army," and having the connotation of protector.

Hebrew equivalents: Avigdor, Chetzron, Geenaw, R'fawayl, Saadyaw and Shmaryawhu. Feminine Hebrew equivalents: Bawtzraw, Chasyaw, Chosaw, Shimris, Teeraw and Yaakovaw.

HUBERT

A variant form of Herbert. Hugh and Hugo are diminutive forms. See Herbert for an explanation.

HUGH

A diminutive form of Herbert. See Herbert. Hugh is also used as an independent name derived from the Old German meaning "of bright mind, intelligent."

In addition to the equivalents listed under Herbert the following equivalents may be added. Masculine Hebrew equivalents: Bunaw, Chanoch, Haskayl, Maskil and Yawvin. Feminine Hebrew equivalents: Beenaw, Chanukaw, N'vonaw and N'oraw.

HUGO

A diminutive form of Herbert. Hugo is a Latinized form. See Herbert for a full explanation.

HYMAN

From the Teutonic meaning "dweller on a high place." Some authorities believe it is related to the Hebrew Chaim or Hayyim, but this is doubtful.

Key: *a* as in father; *ai* as in aisle; *aw* as in law; *ay* as in say; *e* as in bet;

Hebrew equivalents: Aharon, Givon, Harayl, Hawrawn, Rawm, Talmai and Yishpaw. Feminine Hebrew equivalents: Gal, Galee, Gilawdaw, Haraylaw, Talmaw and Talmis.

HUMPHREY
Either from the Anglo-Saxon meaning "protector of the home," or from Old German meaning "man of peace."

Hebrew equivalents: Avshawlom, Ish-Shawlom, Mishmawr, M'shulam, Shawlom, Shlomee, Shlomeeayl and Shmaryawhu. Feminine Hebrew equivalents: M'nuchaw, Shimris, Shlomis, Shomayraw and Shulamis.

IAN
The Scotch form of John. See John for a full explanation.

IKE
A short form of Isaac meaning "laughter." See Isaac for a full explanation.

IMANUEL
A variant spelling of Emanuel. See Emanuel for a full explanation.

IRA
From the Hebrew meaning "descendants."

Hebrew equivalents: Aveedor, Yered and Yardayn. Feminine Hebrew equivalents: Tz'leelaw and Yardaynaw.

IRVIN, IRVINE, IRVING
From the Gaelic meaning "beautiful, handsome, fair." One of the most popular names a generation ago, but rarely used today. Irvin is the original form of these names. Some authorities contend that Irving is of Anglo-Saxon origin meaning "sea friend," and that Marvin and Mervin are variant forms.

Hebrew equivalents: Aveenoam, Chemdawn, Naamawn, Raanawn and Yawfe. Feminine Hebrew equivalents: Acheenoam, Adeenaw, Naamaw, Raananaw and Rivkaw.

---

ee as in b*ee*t; *i* as in b*i*t; *o* as in n*o*; *oi* as in v*oi*d; *u* as in r*u*de.

IRWIN

A variant spelling of Irvin. See Irvin for a full explanation.

ISA

A diminutive form of Isaiah. See Isaiah for a full explanation.

ISAAC

From the Hebrew meaning "he will laugh." Isaac, the second of the three patriarchs, is one of the most frequently used biblical names in the Talmud. Although Abraham was not acceptable to the early Christians, Isaac left a deep impression and the name was commonly used. Statistics show that among English Jewry of the 12th century Isaac was the most popular name. Among the present generation it is rarely bestowed upon children. Isak, Itzik and Yischak are variant spellings.

The exact Hebrew equivalent is Yitzchawk. Feminine Hebrew equivalents: Aleezaw, Aveega'yil, Chedvaw, Deetzaw, Geelaw, R'nawnaw and Seesaw.

ISADOR, ISADORE

Variant spellings of Isidor and Isidore. See Isidore for a full explanation.

ISAIAH

From the Hebrew meaning "God is salvation," and having the connotation of helper. One of the most famous of the Hebrew prophets, he prophesied in Jerusalem from 740-701 B.C.E. Isa is a diminutive form.

The exact Hebrew equivalents are Y'sha'yaw and Y'sha'yawhu. Feminine Hebrew equivalents: Aleksandraw, Milkaw, Yishaw and Y'shuaw.

ISHMAEL

From the Hebrew meaning "God will hear."

The exact Hebrew equivalent is Yishmawayl. Feminine Hebrew equivalent: Shimaws, Shimonaw and Shmuaylaw.

Key: *a* as in *father*; *ai* as in *aisle*; *aw* as in *law*; *ay* as in *say*; *e* as in *bet*;

ISIDOR, ISIDORE

From the Greek meaning "gift of Isis." Isis was the Egyptian moon goddess. Isador and Isadore are later spellings.

Hebrew equivalents: Elnawsawn, Elzawvawd, Aveeshai, Matisyawhu, Nawsawn, N'sanayl, Y'honawsawn, Zavdee and Zawvawd. Feminine Hebrew equivalents: Matawnaw, Migdawnaw, N'sanyaw, N'saneeaylaw, N'seenaw, Z'veedaw and Z'vudaw.

ISRAEL

The later name given to Jacob, the third of the three patriarchs. From the Hebrew meaning either "prince of God," or "wrestled with God," and having the connotation of fighter or ruler.

The exact Hebrew equivalent is Yisrawayl. The exact feminine Hebrew equivalents are Yis'r'aylaw and Yis'r'-aylis.

ISSACHAR

In the Bible Issachar was the son of Jacob and Leah. He was the head of one of the twelve tribes of Israel. Derived from the Hebrew meaning "there is a reward."

The exact Hebrew equivalent is Yisawchawr. Feminine Hebrew equivalents: Ashayraw and B'rawchaw.

ITAI, ITTAI

From the Hebrew meaning "friendly, companionable." In the Bible Itai was one of David's mighty warriors. Ittai is a variant spelling.

The exact Hebrew equivalent is Eetai. Feminine Hebrew equivalents: Ahuvaw, Ameesaw, Chaveevaw, Dawveedaw and Tirtzaw. Eetai is also used as a feminine name.

ITIEL

From the Hebrew meaning "God is with me." In the Bible Itiel was a member of the tribe of Benjamin.

The exact Hebrew equivalent is Eeseeayl. Feminine Hebrew equivalents: Eleeanaw, Elee-ezraw and Eleeoraw.

ee as in b*ee*t; *i* as in b*i*t; *o* as in n*o*; *oi* as in v*oi*d; *u* as in r*u*de.

ITTAMAR

From the Hebrew meaning "island of palm," and having the connotation of uprightness, grace.

The exact Hebrew equivalent is Eesawmawr. Feminine Hebrew equivalents: Chanaw, Diklaw, Tawmar, Teemoraw and Y'shawraw.

IVAN

The Russian form of John meaning "grace." See John for more information.

JACK, JACKIE

Diminutive forms of Jacob. See Jacob for a full explanation. Jack has also been used as a nickname for John.

JACOB

From the Hebrew meaning "held by the heel, supplanter, or protected." The third of the three patriarchs and the father of the twelve sons who were founders of the tribes of Israel. The Book of Genesis describes Jacob's encounter with an angel and how he was given the name Israel, in addition to his original name. Jacob has been a popular name for many centuries. Among the many variations of the name that have developed throughout the centuries James and Jacques are the most popular. Jake, Jack and Jackie are popular pet forms.

The exact Hebrew equivalent is Yaakov. Feminine Hebrew equivalents: Mawgaynaw, Migdawlaw, Tzeelaw and Yaakovaw. Yaakovaw is also used as a masculine name in the Bible.

JACQUES

The French form of Jacob. See Jacob for a full explanation.

JAMES

The English form of the Hebrew Jacob, meaning "held by the heel, supplanter, or protected." Jim, Jimmie, Jimmy

Key: *a* as in f*a*ther; *ai* as in *ai*sle; *aw* as in l*aw*; *ay* as in s*ay*; *e* as in b*e*t;

and Jamie are popular pet forms. Variant forms of James occur in many languages.

The exact Hebrew equivalent is Yaakov. Feminine Hebrew equivalents: Mawgaynaw, Migdawlaw, Tzeelaw and Yaakovaw.

JAN

Either a form of John (see John) or a diminutive form of James (see James).

JANUS, JANNY

Janus is a form of the Latin Janarius meaning "in the beginning," from which the month January is derived. Janarius was the Roman god of the sun and the year.

Hebrew equivalents: Rabaw, Rawvaw, Rav, Rosh and Shimshon. Feminine Hebrew equivalents: Reeshonaw and Shimshonaw.

JAPHET

From the Hebrew meaning either "spacious, youthful, or beautiful." In the Bible Japhet was one of the sons of Noah.

The exact Hebrew equivalent is Yefes. Feminine Hebrew equivalents: Adeenaw, Aveevaw, Yawfaw and Y'neekaw.

JARDINE

From the Teutonic and French meaning "a garden."

Hebrew equivalents: Bust'nai, Geenas, Ginson, Karmel and Tzemach. Feminine Hebrew equivalents: Ganaw, Karmaw, Karmelaw and Karmis.

JARON

From the Hebrew meaning "to sing or cry out."

The exact Hebrew equivalent is Yawron. Feminine Hebrew equivalents: N'eemaw, Reenaw, Sheeraw, T'heelaw and Yawronaw.

JARVIS, JARY

Jarvis and its diminutive Jary are from the Old English

ee as in b*ee*t; *i* as in b*i*t; *o* as in n*o*; *oi* as in v*oi*d; *u* as in r*u*de.

meaning "a driver," or from Teutonic meaning "sharp spear."

Hebrew equivalents: Kaneeayl and Raychawv. Feminine Hebrew equivalents: Chaneesaw, Chanis and Cheenis.

JASON

From the Greek meaning "healer." Jaeson is a variant spelling. Jason, whose name was also Joshua, was a famous High Priest in the second century B.C.E.

Hebrew equivalents: Awsaw, Marpay, Rawfaw, Rawfu and R'fawayl. Feminine Hebrew equivalents: R'fawaylaw, R'fuaw, Rofee and T'rufaw.

JASPAR, JASPER

Either from the Greek meaning a "semi-precious stone," or from the Persian meaning "a treasured secret." Kaspar is a variant form used in Germany.

Hebrew equivalents: Shoham, Shovai, Tz'fanyaw and Yawkawr. Feminine Hebrew equivalents: Margawlis, P'neenaw, S'gulaw and Tz'feeraw.

JAY

From the Teutonic meaning "happy."

Hebrew equivalents: Yachdeeayl, Yawgil, Yawron and Yitzchawk. Feminine Hebrew equivalents: Aleezaw, Aveega'yil, Deetzaw, Reenaw and R'nawnaw.

JED

From the Arabic meaning "hand."

Hebrew equivalents: Binyawmin, Chawfnee and Y'da'-yaw. There are no feminine Hebrew equivalents.

JEFF, JEFFERY, JEFFEREY

Forms of Geoffrey meaning "gift of peace." See Geoffrey for a full explanation.

JEHIEL

From the Hebrew meaning "may God live." Yehiel is a variant spelling.

The exact Hebrew equivalent is Y'cheeayl. Feminine

Hebrew equivalents: Chavaw, Cha'yaw, T'cheeyaw and Y'cheeaylaw.

JEHOIAKIM

From the Hebrew meaning "God will establish."

The exact Hebrew equivalent is Y'ho'yawkim. Feminine Hebrew equivalent: Bonaw and Yavn'aylaw.

JEPHTHAH, JEPHTAH

From the Hebrew meaning "he will open," and connoting the first-born or the oldest.

The exact Hebrew equivalent is Yiftawch. Feminine Hebrew equivalents: B'choraw, Bilhaw, Reeshonaw, Y'shawnaw and Z'kaynaw.

JEREMIAH, JEREMIAS, JEREMY

From the Hebrew meaning "God will loosen (the bonds)" or "God will uplift." Jeremiah is one of the six Hebrew prophets whose name is mentioned as a personal name in the Talmud. He belonged to a family of priests living near Jerusalem and began to prophecy in 625 B.C.E. The Greek New Testament records Jeremiah as Jeremias. Jeremy is a pet form.

The exact Hebrew equivalents are Yirmeeyaw and Yirmeeyawhu. Feminine Hebrew equivalents: Romaw, Romaymaw, Romeeyaw, Romis and Rom'mis.

JEROLD, JERROLD

Variant forms of Jeremiah and Jeremias. See above for a full explanation.

JEROME

A form of Gerome meaning "of holy fame," or "sacred name." See Gerome for full explanation.

JESS, JESSE

From the Hebrew meaning "wealthy," or "a gift." Jesse was the father of David in the Bible. Jess is a pet form.

The exact Hebrew equivalent is Yeeshai. Feminine He-

ee as in b*ee*t; *i* as in b*i*t; *o* as in n*o*; *oi* as in v*oi*d; *u* as in r*u*de.

brew equivalents: Bas-Shua, Matawnaw, Minchaw, N'see-naw, Z'veedaw and Yisraw.

JETHRO
From the Hebrew meaning "abundance, riches." Jethro was the father-in-law of Moses in the Bible.

The exact Hebrew equivalent is Yisro. Feminine Hebrew equivalents: Bas-Shua and Yisraw.

JIM, JIMMIE, JIMMY
Diminutive of James, which is a form of Jacob. For a full explanation see James and Jacob.

JOAB
From the Hebrew meaning "willing," or "God is father," and connoting a ruler or leader.

The exact Hebrew equivalent is Yoawv. Feminine Hebrew equivalents: Alufaw, Malkaw, N'deevaw, Tirtzaw and Yis'r'aylaw.

JOB
From the Hebrew meaning "hated and oppressed." Job in the Bible was noted for his patience and faith in God.

The exact Hebrew equivalent is Eeeyov. Feminine Hebrew equivalent: Bas-Shua.

JOCHANAN, JOHANAN
From the Hebrew meaning "God is gracious, merciful." Jochanan was extremely popular in talmudic times. More than fifty-two different persons in the Talmud are named Jochanan. John is derived from Jochanan.

The exact Hebrew equivalent is Yochawnawn. Feminine Hebrew equivalents: Chanaw, Chanunaw, Chayn, Cheenaw and Yochawnaw.

JOE, JOEY
Diminutive forms of Joseph. See Joseph for a full explanation.

JOEL
From the Hebrew meaning "God is willing." Joel was

Key: *a* as in f*a*ther; *ai* as in *ai*sle; *aw* as in l*aw*; *ay* as in s*ay*; *e* as in b*e*t;

one of the twelve Minor Prophets whose works are included in the Bible.

The exact Hebrew equivalent is Yoayl. Feminine Hebrew equivalents: Yo'aylaw and Yo'aylis.

JOHN, JOHNNIE, JOHNNY

John is a contraction of Jochanan. Derived from the Hebrew meaning "God is gracious or merciful." Variant forms of John appear in many languages: Ivan, Sean, Jan, Hans and Ian are among the most popular. Johnnie and Johnny are diminutive forms as are Jon and Jonny.

Hebrew equivalents: Chananayl, Chananyaw, Chawnawn and Yochawnawn. Feminine Hebrew equivalents: Chanaw, Chanunaw, Chayn, Cheenaw, Diklaw, Tawmar and Yochawnaw.

JON, JONNY

Diminutives of either John or Jonathan. See John and Jonathan for a full explanation.

JONAH

From the Hebrew meaning "a dove." Jonah was one of the prophets mentioned in the Bible who gained fame after being swallowed by a big fish.

The exact Hebrew equivalent is Yonaw. Feminine Hebrew equivalents: Y'meemaw and Yoneenaw.

JONAS

In the Greek New Testament Jonah is recorded Jonas. See Jonah for a full explanation.

JONATHAN

From the Hebrew meaning "God has given," or "gift of God." The first Jonathan in history was the son of King Saul. Jonathan's friendship with David is one of the most moving stories in the Bible. Jon and Jonny are pet forms.

The exact Hebrew equivalents are: Y'honawsawn and Yonawsawn. Feminine Hebrew equivalents: Matawnaw, Migdawnaw, Minchaw, Yawhawvaw, Z'veedaw and Z'vudaw.

ee as in b*ee*t; *i* as in b*i*t; *o* as in n*o*; *oi* as in v*oi*d; *u* as in r*u*de.

JORDAN, JORI, JORY
From the Hebrew meaning "descend, descendant," and "flowing down."

The exact Hebrew equivalent is Yardayn. The exact feminine Hebrew equivalent is Yardaynaw.

JOSE
A variant form of Joseph. It was a popular name in talmudic times (from 2nd to 6th centuries) and is popular today in Spanish-speaking countries. See Joseph for a full explanation.

The exact Hebrew equivalent is Yosee. Feminine Hebrew equivalents: Yosayfaw and Yoseefaw.

JOSEPH
From the Hebrew meaning "He (God) will add or increase." Joseph was Jacob's son in the Bible. Almost 25% of the Book of Genesis is devoted to his life-story. Joseph was an extremely popular name throughout the ages and has appeared in many languages in variant forms. In the talmudic period (from the second to the sixth century) it appears often either as Joseph or Jose. Among 12th century Jewry in England it appeared often in its French form, Josce. Many church leaders and saints were named Joseph in honor of Joseph, father of Jesus. In Arabic countries the variant form, Yussuf, is used; in Italy Giuseppe, Beppo and Peppo are common; in Spanish and Portuguese-speaking countries Jose, Pepe and Pepito are popular; and in Slavic countries Josko and Joska are variant forms derived from Joseph. Jo, Joe and Joey are the most popular American pet forms.

The exact Hebrew equivalent is Yosayf. Yosee is a variant form. The exact feminine Hebrew equivalents are Yosayfaw and Yoseefaw.

JOSEPHUS
The Latin form of Joseph. Josephus was a famous Jewish soldier and historian who lived in the first century

Key: *a* as in f*a*ther; *ai* as in *ai*sle; *aw* as in l*aw*; *ay* as in s*ay*; *e* as in b*e*t;

(circa 30-100). His full name was Flavius Josephus. In Hebrew he was known as Yosayf ben Matisyawhu Ha-Kohayn. For more information see Joseph.

The exact Hebrew equivalent is Yoseefus. The exact feminine Hebrew equivalent is Yoseefaw.

JOSH

A pet form of Joshua. See Joshua for a full explanation.

JOSHUA

From the Hebrew meaning "the Lord is my salvation." Joshua in the Bible was the successor to Moses who led the children of Israel into the Promised Land. His original name was Hoshea. The prefix *Yah* was added later by Moses. In the post-biblical period Joshua was probably one of the most commonly used biblical names. During the Greek period, Jews in the upper strata of society who were called Joshua used the name Jason. This was true of many of the High Priests. The name Jesus is a variant form of Joshua. Today, Josh is a very popular pet form.

The exact Hebrew equivalent is Y'hoshua. Feminine Hebrew equivalents: Aleksandraw, Milkaw, Moshawaw, T'shuaw and Y'shuaw.

JOSIAH

From the Hebrew meaning "fire of the Lord," or from the Arabic meaning "God has supported or protected." In the Bible Josiah was a king of Judah (637-608 B.C.E.), who ascended the throne at the age of eight, upon the murder of his father Amon.

The exact Hebrew equivalent is Yosheeyaw or Yosheeyawhu. Feminine Hebrew equivalents: Efraws, Meeraw, Oraw, Shimris, Udeeyaw and Yaakovaw.

JOSLYN

A common form of the Latin Justin. See Justin for a full explanation.

---

ee as in b*ee*t; *i* as in b*i*t; *o* as in n*o*; *oi* as in v*oi*d; *u* as in r*u*de.

JOTHAM
From the Hebrew meaning "God is perfect." Jotham in the Bible was the youngest of Gideon's seventy sons. Another Jotham was king of Judah from 751-735 B.C.E. His father was King Uzziah.

The exact Hebrew equivalent is Yosawm. Feminine Hebrew equivalents: K'leelaw, Shlomis, Shulamis and T'meemaw.

JUDAH
Judah is among the most frequently occurring biblical names used in the Talmud. The name makes its first appearance in the book of Genesis where Judah is the fourth son of Jacob. It is derived from the Hebrew meaning "praise." Judd is a variant form, as is Jude, Juda and Judas. The surname Judson means "son of Judah."

The exact Hebrew equivalent is Y'hudaw. The exact feminine Hebrew equivalent is Y'hudis.

JUDD
A variant form of Judah. See Judah for a full explanation.

JULES
A variant form of Julian or Julius. See Julian for a full explanation.

JULIAN, JULIUS
From the Greek meaning "soft-haired, mossy-bearded," and having the symbolic meaning of "youth." Jules is a variant form and Jule is a diminutive form.

Hebrew equivalents: Awviv, Aylawm, S'orim and Yefes. Feminine Hebrew equivalents: Almaw, Aveevaw, D'leelaw, Neemaw, Tz'eeraw, Y'neekaw and Zilpaw.

JUNIUS
From the Latin meaning "the young lion." The name Junior may be a variant form of Junius.

Hebrew equivalents: Aree, Aryay, Geeoraw, Gur, Guree

Key: *a* as in *father*; *ai* as in *aisle*; *aw* as in *law*; *ay* as in *say*; *e* as in *bet*;

and Lawvee. Feminine Hebrew equivalents: Areeayal, Aree-aylaw, K'feeraw and L'veeaw.

JUSTIN, JUSTUS

From the Latin meaning "just or honest."

Hebrew equivalents: Amnon, Dawn, Dawneeayl, Eetaw-mawr, Tzawdok, Tzidkeeyaw, Yehoshawfawt, and Y'ho-tzawdawk. Feminine Hebrew equivalents: Danyaw, Dawnee-aylaw, Diklaw, Tawmawr and Y'shawraw.

KADMIEL

From the Hebrew meaning "God is the ancient One." In the Bible it is the name of a Levite.

The exact Hebrew equivalent is Kadmeeayl. Feminine Hebrew equivalents: Bilhaw and Z'kaynaw.

KAILIL

In the Talmud Kailil was the father of the scholar Abaye. See Kalil for a full explanation.

KALIL

From the Hebrew meaning "a crown, a wreath." Kalila is the feminine form. Kailil is a variant spelling.

The exact Hebrew equivalent is Kawlil. Feminine Hebrew equivalents: Aturaw, K'leelaw, Livyaw and Malkaw.

KALMAN

A short form of Kalonymos, which is a diminutive of the Latin Clement meaning "merciful or gracious."

The exact Hebrew equivalent is Kalmawn. Feminine Hebrew equivalents: Chanaw, Chaneesaw, Diklaw and Yochawnaw.

KALONYMOS

A variant form of the Latin Clement meaning "merciful or gracious." The name became popular in the 14th century after the death of the famous author and translator Kalonymos ben Kalonymos who lived in France and Italy and translated many Arabic works into Hebrew and Latin for King Robert of Naples.

---

ee as in b*ee*t; *i* as in b*i*t; *o* as in n*o*; *oi* as in v*oi*d; *u* as in r*u*de.

The exact Hebrew equivalent is Klonimos. Feminine Hebrew equivalents: Chanaw, Chaneesaw, Diklaw and Yochawnaw.

KANIEL
From the Hebrew meaning "a reed, a stalk," or from the Arabic meaning "a spear," and having the connotation of strength.

The exact Hebrew equivalent is Kaneeayl. Feminine Hebrew equivalents: Chaneesaw, Chaseenaw, Cheenis, Gavreelaw and Geeboraw.

KARL
A variant spelling for Carl. See Carl for a full explanation.

KARMEL, KARMELI, KARMI, KARMIEL
Variant spellings for names popular in Israel. See Carmel for full information about each.

KATRIEL
From the Hebrew meaning "crown of the Lord."

The exact Hebrew equivalent is Kasreeayl. Feminine Hebrew equivalents: Atawraw, Aturaw, K'leelaw, K'lulaw and Malkaw.

KAUFMAN
From the German meaning "a buyer," and having the connotation of owner, or possession.

Hebrew equivalents: Baal and Elkawnaw. Feminine Hebrew equivalents: Achuzaw, B'ulaw and S'gulaw.

KAY
Either from the Greek meaning "rejoicing," or from the Teutonic meaning "a fortified place," or "a warden, a keeper." Kay may also be derived from the Latin meaning "gay" and was popularized by the Welsh who converted it into Kai. Caius (or Gaius) was the first name, or praenomen, of Julius Caesar.

Hebrew equivalents: Akeevaw, Armonee, Eleefelet, Yaa-

Key: *a* as in f*a*ther; *ai* as in *ai*sle; *aw* as in l*aw*; *ay* as in s*ay*; *e* as in b*e*t;

kov and Yitzchawk. Feminine Hebrew equivalents: Aleezaw, Aveega'yil, Mawgaynaw, Shimris and Yaakovaw.

KEDEM

From the Hebrew meaning "old, ancient" or "from the east."

The exact Hebrew equivalent is Kedem. Feminine Hebrew equivalents: Bilhaw, Kaydmaw and Z'kaynaw.

KEITH

A popular name in Scotland. It is similar to the Old Gaelic word for "wood," although some authorities claim it means "wind."

Hebrew equivalent: Yaaree. Feminine Hebrew equivalent: Yaaraw.

KEN

A short form of Kenneth. See Kenneth for an explanation. In addition, it is used as an independent name derived from the Scotch and meaning either "to know," or "a chief, a champion."

Hebrew equivalents: D'uayl, Elyawdaw, Maskil, Melech, Y'deeayl, Y'hoyawdaw. Feminine Hebrew equivalents: Alufaw, Day'aw, Malkaw, Sawraw and Yis'r'aylaw.

KENNETH

From the Celtic and Scotch meaning "comely, handsome." Ken, Kent, Kemp and Camp are variant forms. The surname Mackenzie means "son of Kenneth."

Hebrew equivalents: Aveenoam, Chemdawn, Nawam, Naamawn, Shapir and Yawfe. Feminine Hebrew equivalents: Acheenoam, K'leelaw, K'lulaw, Naamaw, Nawawmee, Shifraw, Tirtzaw and Rivkaw.

KENT

A variant form of Kenneth. See Kenneth for a full explanation.

KEVIN

From the Gaelic meaning "handsome, beautiful."

ee as in b*ee*t; *i* as in b*i*t; *o* as in n*o*; *oi* as in v*oi*d; *u* as in r*u*de.

Hebrew equivalents: Aveenoam, Chemdawn, Naamawn, Nawve. Raanawn and Shapir. Feminine Hebrew equivalents: Acheenoam, Haduraw, K'leelaw, K'lulaw, Nawawmee, Nawvis and Yawfis.

KIRK

From the Old Norse meaning "a church," symbolizing a holy place.

Hebrew equivalents: Chagai, D'vir, Kadish and Y'kuseeayl. Feminine Hebrew equivalents: Chageeyaw and Chagis.

KITRON

From the Hebrew meaning "crown."

The exact Hebrew equivalent is Kisron. Feminine Hebrew equivalents: Atawraw, Aturaw, K'leelaw, K'lulaw and Malkaw.

KIVI

A short form of Akiba or Yaakov used today in Israel. See Jacob and Akiba for a full explanation.

The exact Hebrew equivalent used in Israel is Keevee. See Akiba and Jacob for feminine equivalents.

KONRAD

A variant spelling of Conrad. See Conrad for a full explanation.

KORAH, KORACH

From the Hebrew meaning "bald." In the Bible Korah was a Levite who was related to Moses. He led a rebellion against the leadership of Moses and Aaron, but failed when the earth opened up and swallowed him and his group of 250 rebels.

Hebrew equivalent is Korach. For euphemistic interpretation and further equivalents see Julius.

KURT

Kurt is the familiar form of Konrad which is a variant form of Conrad. See Conrad for a full explanation.

Key: *a* as in father; *ai* as in aisle; *aw* as in law; *ay* as in say; *e* as in bet;

LABAN

From the Hebrew meaning "white." In the Bible Laban, a resident of Aram Naharaim, was the brother of Rebekah, father of Leah and Rachel. In Jewish folklore Laban, the Aramean, is synonymous with "deceiver."

The exact Hebrew equivalent is Lawvawn. Feminine Hebrew equivalents: L'vawnaw, L'vonaw, Tz'choraw and Tz'choris.

LABEL

A Yiddish diminutive form of Leib meaning "lion." See Leo for a full explanation.

LAMBERT

From the Teutonic meaning "country's brightness," and having the connotation of great fame.

Hebrew equivalents: Avnayr, Heelayl, Lapeedos, Mayeer, Uree, Ureeyaw and Y'hudaw. Feminine Hebrew equivalents: Heelaw, Heelaylaw, L'vawnaw, M'eeraw, Noga, Y'hudis and Zawhawraw.

LANCE, LANCELOT

From the Latin meaning "servant or helper." Lance is the diminutive form of Lancelot. Twelfth century Sir Lancelot of the Round Table was the first to have this name as a personal name.

Hebrew equivalents: Avdee, Malawchee, Maluchee, Ovadyaw and Ovayd. Feminine Hebrew equivalents: Aleksandraw, Ezr'aylaw, Eemawnuaylaw and Saadaw.

LARRY

A popular pet form of Laurence and Lawrence. See Lawrence for a full explanation.

LAURENCE

A variant spelling of Lawrence. See Lawrence for a full explanation.

LAWRENCE

From the Latin meaning "crowned with laurel," which

ee as in be*e*t; *i* as in b*i*t; *o* as in n*o*; *oi* as in v*oi*d; *u* as in r*u*de.

is the symbol of victory. Laurence, Lawrance, Lorence and
Lorenz are variant spellings. Larry and Laurie are popular
pet forms.

Hebrew equivalents: Govayr, Matzleeach, N'tzeeach and
Yatzleeach. Feminine Hebrew equivalents: Dafnaw, Dafnis,
Hadasaw, Nitzchaw and Nitzcheeyaw.

LAVI
From the Hebrew meaning "a lion."

The exact Hebrew equivalent is Lawvee. Feminine Hebrew equivalents: Areeayl, Areeaylaw, K'feeraw, La'yish
and L'veeyaw.

LAZAR, LAZARUS
Greek forms of the Hebrew biblical names, Elazar and
Eliezer. See Elazar and Eliezer for a full explanation.

LEE
Either a diminutive form of Leo, Leon, or Leslie, or
derived from the Anglo-Saxon meaning "field, meadow."
In Israel Lee is used as an independent name meaning "to
me, mine."

Hebrew equivalents: Awdawm, Bust'nai, Karmel, Notaya and Yizr'ayl. Feminine Hebrew equivalents: Ganaw,
Karmelaw, Sh'daymaw and Yizr'elaw. See Leo for additional equivalents.

LEIB, LEIBEL
Yiddish names of Germanic origin meaning "lion." See
Leo for more information.

LEIF, LIEF
From the Teutonic meaning "love." Lief is a variant
spelling of Leif. The German form of Lief is Lieb. Liebe,
Lipman, Layb and Lev are derivative Yiddish forms of the
same name.

Hebrew equivalents: Eldawd, Bildawd, Chavivayl, Dawvid, Dodee, Nilbawv and Y'didyaw. Feminine Hebrew equivalents: Ahuvaw, Chaveevaw, Cheebaw, Dawveedaw, Leebaw
and Y'deedaw.

Key: *a* as in f*a*ther; *ai* as in *ai*sle; *aw* as in l*aw*; *ay* as in s*ay*; *e* as in b*e*t;

LENNIE

A popular pet form of Leonard. See Leonard for a full explanation.

LEO, LEON

Leon is derived from the Greek meaning "lion," or "of the lion's nature," and has the connotation of strength. Leo is the Latin form. It was the Greeks who called the lion the king of the beasts. Leib and Leibel and Label are variant Yiddish forms.

Hebrew equivalents: Aree, Areeayl, Aryay, La'yish, Lawvee and Uzeeayl. Feminine Hebrew equivalents: Amtzaw, Areeaylaw, Gavreelaw, Geeboraw and L'veeyaw.

LEONARD

A Teutonic form of Leo and Leon. Lennie is the pet form of Leonard. See Leo for a full explanation.

LEOPOLD

From the Teutonic meaning "defender of the people, protector."

Hebrew equivalents: Avigdor, Chosaw, Sh'maryaw, Sh'maryawhu and Zimree. Feminine Hebrew equivalents: Avigdoraw, Efraws, Migdawlaw, Shimris, Tzeelaw and Yaakovaw.

LEOR

From the Hebrew meaning "I have light." In Israel it is used as a masculine and feminine name.

The exact Hebrew equivalent is Leeor.

LEROY

An Old French name of Latin origin meaning "the king" or "royalty."

Hebrew equivalents: Aveemelech, Eleemelech, Kasreeayl and Melech. Feminine Hebrew equivalents: Atawraw, Layaw, Malkaw, and Yis'r'aylaw.

LESHEM

From the Hebrew meaning "a precious stone." In the

---

ee as in b*ee*t; *i* as in b*i*t; *o* as in n*o*; *oi* as in v*oi*d; *u* as in r*u*de.

Bible *leshem* was an amber stone that the High Priest wore in his breastplate.

The exact Hebrew equivalent is Leshem. Feminine Hebrew equivalents: Yahalomaw, Yakeeraw and Y'kawraw.

LESLIE

From the Anglo-Saxon meaning "meadow lands." Lee is a popular pet form. Leslie is used as a feminine name as well as a masculine name.

Hebrew equivalents: Karmel, Kar'mlee and Yaaree. Feminine Hebrew equivalents: Ganaw, Karmelaw, Nawvaw, and Yaaraw.

LESSER

A form of either Elazar or Eliezer. See both names for a full explanation.

LESTER

An English name of Latin origin meaning "camp of legion," and having the connotation of protection.

Hebrew equivalents: Avigdor, Chosaw, Shmaryaw, Sh'maryawhu and Zimree. Feminine Hebrew equivalents: Avigdoraw, Efraws, G'dayraw, Shimris, Tzeelaw and Yaakovaw.

LEV

Either from the Hebrew meaning "a heart," or from the Yiddish meaning "a lion." In Israel Lev is also used as a pet form of Levi.

The exact Hebrew equivalent is Layv. Feminine Hebrew equivalents: Areeayl, K'feeraw, Leebaw and L'veeyaw.

LEVI

From the Hebrew meaning "joined to," or "attendant upon," and having the connotation of devotion, friendship. Levi in the Bible was the third of Jacob's twelve sons. His mother was Leah. The descendants of Levi were the Priests and Levites who served in the Temple of Jerusalem. Levic is a variant form.

Key: *a* as in father; *ai* as in aisle; *aw* as in law; *ay* as in say; *e* as in bet;

The exact Hebrew equivalent is Layvee. Feminine Hebrew equivalents: Ahuvaw, Aveevaw, Dawveedaw and Rus.

LEWIS
An English form of the French Louis. See Louis for a full explanation.

LINCOLN
Either from the Teutonic meaning "from the linden (tree) hill," or a Celtic-Latin name meaning "from the place by the pool."

Hebrew equivalents: Aylaw, Miklos, Oren and Peleg. Feminine Hebrew equivalents: Eelawnaw, Miryawm, Tz'-ruyaw and Tirzaw.

LINDSEY
From the Teutonic and probably meaning "from the linden tree by the sea."

See Lincoln, which is very similar in meaning, for equivalents.

LION, LIONEL, LYONEL
Forms of Leon. See Leon for a full explanation. Lyonel is an uncommon spelling.

LIPMAN
A corrupt form of the German Liebman meaning "lover of man." See Leif for a full explanation.

LIRON, LYRON
A Hebraic form of the word "lyric or lyrical," used in Israel today. Liron in Hebrew means "song is mine." It is also used as a feminine name. Leron is a variant spelling.

The exact Hebrew equivalent is Leeron. Feminine Hebrew equivalents: Leeris, Leeron, Sheeree, Sheerlee and Yawronaw.

LLEWELLYN
From the Welsh meaning "in the likeness of a lion."

Hebrew equivalents: Aree, Areeayl, La'yish and Law-

ee as in b*ee*t; *i* as in b*i*t; *o* as in n*o*; *oi* as in v*oi*d; *u* as in r*u*de.

vee. Feminine Hebrew equivalents: Areeaylaw, K'feeraw and L'veeyaw. See Leo for additional equivalents.

LLOYD

From the Celtic or Welsh meaning "grey or brown," or "a person with a dark complexion."

Hebrew equivalents: Adawr, Kaydawr, Pinchaws and Tzilsai. Feminine Hebrew equivalents: Ayfaw, Chacheelaw, Lailaw and Tzeelaw.

LON, LONNY

Diminutive forms of Alphonso, derived from the Old German, and meaning "of noble family."

For Hebrew equivalents see Alphonso.

LORENCE

A form of Lawrence meaning "crowned with laurel." See Lawrence for a full explanation.

LOTAN

From the Hebrew meaning "to envelop," and signifying protection. Lotan is a biblical name currently used in Israel.

The exact Hebrew equivalent is Lotawn. Feminine Hebrew equivalent: Efraws.

LOUIS

From the Teutonic meaning "hero or refuge of the people," or "warrior, prince." Lou and Louie are popular pet forms. The original spelling of the name was Lewis, as was common in England. The name became very popular in France and the French pronunciation which is Louie became the acceptable form even in America.

Hebrew equivalents: Aveecha'yil, Ben-Cha'yil, La'yish, Naftawlee, Shmaryawhu and Yisrawayl. Feminine Hebrew equivalents: Gavreelaw, Sawraw, Tigraw and Yis'r'aylaw.

LOTHAR, LOTHER

From the Teutonic meaning "noted warrior," or "hero of the people." Lothar was the name of a Saxon king. Luther is a variant form.

Key: *a* as in f*a*ther; *ai* as in *ai*sle; *aw* as in l*aw*; *ay* as in s*ay*; *e* as in b*e*t;

Hebrew equivalents: Ish-Cha'yil, Ben-Cha'yil, Gawd, Gidon and Naftawlee. Feminine Hebrew equivalents: Gavreelaw, Geeboraw, Tigraw and Yis'r'aylaw.

LOWELL, LOVELL

From the Old English meaning "beloved."

Hebrew equivalents: Bildawd, Eldawd, Dawvid, Dodee, Nilbawv, Yawdid and Y'didyaw. Feminine Hebrew equivalents: Ahuvaw, Chaveevaw, Dawveedaw, Leebaw, Nilbawvaw, Nilbeves and Y'deedaw.

LUCAS, LUCIUS

From the Latin meaning "light." Lucas is a variant Latin form of Lucius. Luce is a French variant and Lukas is the German spelling for Lucas.

Hebrew equivalents: Avnayr, Bawrawk, Eleeor, Lawvawn, Mayeer and Shragaw. Feminine Hebrew equivalents: B'heeraw, M'eeraw, Oraw, Oris, Orlee and Tz'feeraw.

LUDWIG

A Germanic form of Louis. See Louis for a full explanation.

LUTHER

A variant form of Lothar. Luther became popular because of the famous German theologian and reformer. See Lothar for a full explanation.

LYLE

A French name of Latin origin meaning "from the island." Lyle is also a Scotch name meaning "little."

Hebrew equivalents: Arnon, Aynawn, Kawtawn, Moshe and Peleg. Feminine Hebrew equivalents: D'voraw, Galee, K'tanaw, Mawraw and Miryawm.

LYNN

From the Welsh meaning "cataract or lake."

Hebrew equivalents: Arnon, Aynawn, Moshe and Peleg. Feminine Hebrew equivalents: D'voraw, Galeeyaw, Maraw and Miryawm.

---

ee as in b*ee*t; *i* as in b*i*t; *o* as in n*o*; *oi* as in v*oi*d; *u* as in r*u*de.

MAC, MACK

From the Gaelic meaning "son of." Mc and Mac were used as Gaelic and Irish prefixes to personal names, thus creating a surname. McDonald and MacDonald mean "the son of Donald."

Hebrew equivalents: Ben, Binyawmin, Ibn and Moshe. Feminine Hebrew equivalents: Basyaw, B'sulaw and Naaraw.

MACEY, MACY

Either a French pet name for Matthew (see Matthew for a full explanation), or from the Old English meaning "a mace (club) bearer," and having the connotation of a warrior. In recent years Macey has been used as a variant form of the Hebrew Moshe (Moses).

Hebrew equivalents: Matan, Matanyaw, Matisyawhu, Mawrd'chai, M'dawn, Midyawn and Moshe. Feminine Hebrew equivalents: Amtzaw, Awtzmaw, Matawnaw and Migdawnaw.

MAGEN

From the Hebrew meaning "protection or protector."

The exact Hebrew equivalent is Mawgayn. The exact feminine Hebrew equivalent is Mawgaynaw.

MAGNUS

From the Latin meaning "great." Manus is a variant form used in Ireland.

Hebrew equivalents: G'dalyaw, Geedayl, Rav, Rawvaw and Yigdalyawhu. Feminine Hebrew equivalents: Asalyaw, G'dulaw and Rawchawv.

MAHIR

From the Hebrew meaning "industrious, excellent, expert."

The exact Hebrew equivalent is Mawheer. The exact feminine Hebrew equivalent is M'heeraw.

MAIMON, MAIMUN

From the Arabic meaning "luck, good fortune." The

Key: *a* as in f*a*ther; *ai* as in *ai*sle; *aw* as in l*aw*; *ay* as in s*ay*; *e* as in b*e*t;

most famous personality with the name Maimon was Moses ben Maimon (also called, Maimonides), a Jewish philosopher who lived from 1135-1204. Maimun is a variant spelling.

The exact Hebrew equivalent is Maimon. Feminine Hebrew equivalents: B'rawchaw, B'ruchaw, Gadaw and Mazawl.

MAKS

A modern variant spelling of Max. See Max and Maxwell for a full explanation.

MALACHAI, MALACHI

From the Hebrew meaning "my messenger, minister, or my servant." Malachai was the last of the Hebrew prophets. His period of most intense activity was from 460-450 B.C.E.

The exact Hebrew equivalent is Malawchee. Feminine Hebrew equivalents: Aleksandraw, Malawch, Milkaw and Saadaw.

MALCOLM

Either from the Arabic meaning "a dove," or from the Gaelic meaning "servant of St. Columba." Until recent times Malcolm was used primarily in Scotland where it was a favorite name. There is a biblical name meaning "their king," which is pronounced Malkawm in Hebrew. Mal is a common pet form of Malcolm.

Hebrew equivalents: Avdee, Malawchee, Ovadyaw, Ovayd and Yonaw. Feminine Hebrew equivalents: Malkaw, Malkis, Milkaw, Saadaw, Y'meemaw and Yoneenaw.

MANASSEH

A variant spelling of Menasseh. See Menasseh for a full explanation.

MANFRED

From the Teutonic meaning "man of peace."
Hebrew equivalents: Avshawlom, Shawlom and Shlomo.

ee as in b*ee*t; *i* as in b*i*t; *o* as in n*o*; *oi* as in v*oi*d; *u* as in r*u*de.

Feminine Hebrew equivalents: M'nuchaw, M'shulemes, Shlomis and Shulamis.

MANN, MANNES
Forms of Menachem. See Menachem for more information.

MANNY, MANUEL
Forms of Emanuel. See Emanuel for more information.

MANUS
A variant form of Magnus popular in Ireland. See Magnus for a full explanation.

MARC, MARCUS
The Latin Marc and its forms are related to Mars, the Roman god of war. Marc has been defined to mean "hammer, martial, warlike." Marc is commonly used in French while Marcus is used in various languages including Danish, Dutch and German. Markos is a popular Greek form. Mark is a variant spelling.

Hebrew equivalents: Ish-Cha'yil, Ben-Cha'yil, Gawd, Gidon, Mawr'd'chai, M'dawn and Midyawn. Feminine Hebrew equivalents: Amtzaw, Awtzmaw, Gavreelaw, Geeboraw and Yis'r'aylaw.

MARCEL
A name derived from Marcus and meaning "little Marc.'" Marcel is commonly used in France. The Italian variant form is Marcello. See Marc for a full explanation.

MARIUS
A variant form of Marc and Marcus. See Marc for a full explanation.

MARK
A variant spelling of Marc. See Marc for a full explanation.

MARNIN
From the Hebrew meaning "one who creates joy," or "one who sings." A name currently used in Israel.

Key: *a* as in f*a*ther; *ai* as in *ai*sle; *aw* as in l*aw*; *ay* as in s*ay*; *e* as in b*e*t;

The exact Hebrew equivalent is Marnin. The exact feminine Hebrew equivalent is Marneenaw.

MARSHAL, MARSHALL
From the Old English meaning "a high officer or official."

Hebrew equivalents: Acheemelech, Eleemelech, Kawlayv, Melech and Malkawm. Feminine Hebrew equivalents: Atawraw, G'veeraw, Malkaw, Malkis, Tz'feeraw and Yis'r'aylaw.

MARSHE
Either a variant of Marc or a form of Marshal. See Marc and Marshal for a full explanation.

MARTIN
Like Marc, Mark and Marius, Martin is related to Mars, meaning "warlike." Marten and Martyn are modern variant spellings. Marty and Martie are common short forms. For a full explanation see Marc.

MARVIN
Either from the Celtic meaning "white sea or lake," or from the Gaelic meaning "rich of hills, mountainous." Marvin may also be derived from the Anglo-Saxon meaning "famous friend."

Hebrew equivalents: Aharon, Aveeyawm, Giv'aw, Hawrawn, Maydawd, R'uayl, Talmai, Talmee, Tayl-Chai and Telem. Feminine Hebrew equivalents: Ameesaw, Dawveedaw, Mawrawsaw, Migdawlaw, Miryawm, Talmaw, Talmis and Yawayl.

MASKIL
From the Hebrew meaning "enlightened, educated." Used currently in Israel.

The exact Hebrew equivalent is Maskeel. Feminine Hebrew equivalents: Beenaw, Bunaw, Chanukaw, Daas and Day'aw.

MASON
A French-Teutonic name meaning "a mason, a worker in stone."

ee as in b*ee*t; *i* as in b*i*t; *o* as in n*o*; *oi* as in v*oi*d; *u* as in r*u*de.

Hebrew equivalents: Eleetzur, Shawmir, Tz'ror, Tzur and Tzureeayl. Feminine Hebrew equivalents: Ritzpaw, Tzurayl, Tzureeyaw and Tzuris.

MATIA, MATIAH

An independent Hebrew name used in Israel which is probably a short form of Mattathias. See Mattathias for a full explanation.

The exact Hebrew equivalent is Matee and Masyaw. See Mattathias for feminine equivalents.

MATTATHIAS

From the Hebrew meaning "gift from God." The first Mattathias was a Jewish patriot and priest who died about 167 B.C.E. He was the father of the five famous Hasmonean brothers, Judah the Maccabee being the most famous. The Greek form is Matthias and the Latin form is Matthaeus. In France it took the form of Mathieu. Matthew is the English form. Some authorities believe Macey is derived from Matthew. Matty is the most popular short form.

The exact Hebrew equivalent is Matisyawhu. Feminine Hebrew equivalents: Matawnaw, Mataws, Migdawnaw, Minchaw, N'seenaw, Z'veedaw and Z'vudaw.

MATTHEW

An English variant form of the Hebrew Mattathias. See Mattathias for a full explanation.

MATMON

From the Hebrew meaning "treasure, wealth, riches." A name currently used in Israel.

The exact Hebrew equivalent is Matmon. The exact feminine Hebrew equivalent is Matmonaw.

MATOK

From the Hebrew meaning "sweet."

The exact Hebrew equivalent is Mawsok. The exact feminine Hebrew equivalents: Acheenoam, M'sukaw and Nawawmee.

Key: *a* as in f*a*ther; *ai* as in *ai*sle; *aw* as in l*aw*; *ay* as in s*ay*; *e* as in b*e*t;

MATTY

A popular short form of Mattathias and Matthew. See Mattathias for a full explanation.

MAURICE

From the Latin meaning "moorish or dark-skinned." Morus is an Old Welsh variation of Maurice. The English used the name Seymour as a variant form of Maurice, which according to some authorities is derived from the French abbey, Saint Maur. Maur is a form of the Latin meaning "a moor."

Hebrew equivalents: Adawr, Ayfai, Chawm, Kaydawr and Pinchaws. Feminine Hebrew equivalents: Ayfaw, Chacheelaw, Sh'choraw and Tzeelaw.

MAUREY

A form of Murray or Maurice. See Murray and Maurice for a full explanation.

MAX, MAXIM

Max and Maxim are short forms of Maximilian. Max is the pet form of Maxwell.

MAXIMILIAN

From the Latin meaning "great or famous." Maxwell is derived from Maximilian. Max, Maxie, Maxey and Maxy are pet forms.

Hebrew equivalents: G'dalyaw, Geedayl, Heelayl, Rabaw, Rav and Rawvaw. Feminine Hebrew equivalents: T'heelaw, Asalyaw, G'dulaw, Yawayl, Y'hudis and Zimraw.

MAXWELL

An English form of the Latin Maximilian. See above for a full explanation.

MAYER

Either from the Hebrew meaning "one who brightens, shines," or from the German meaning "overseer, farmer."

Hebrew equivalents: Awdawm, Mayeer, Shimshon,

ee as in be*e*t; *i* as in b*i*t; *o* as in n*o*; *oi* as in v*oi*d; *u* as in r*u*de.

Sh'maryaw and Zimree. Feminine Hebrew equivalents: B'heeraw, Karmelaw, M'eeraw, Nawvaw and Yiz'r'elaw.

MAYNARD

Either from the French-Latin meaning "a hand," or from the Teutonic meaning "strong."

Hebrew equivalents: Aryay, Awmotz, Binyawmin, Chawfnee and Y'da'yaw. Feminine Hebrew equivalents: Amtzaw, Areeayl, Awtzmaw and Geeboraw.

MAZAL-TOV

A name used by Jews in the Middle Ages. Derived from the Hebrew meaning "good luck or lucky star."

The exact Hebrew equivalent is Mazawl-Tov. The feminine Hebrew equivalent is Mazawl.

MEGED

From the Hebrew meaning "goodness, sweetness, excellence."

The exact Hebrew equivalent is Meged. Feminine Hebrew equivalents: Adeenaw, M'sukaw, Nawawmee, Tovaw and Tovis.

MEIR, MEIRI

From the Hebrew meaning "one who brightens or shines."

The exact Hebrew equivalents are Mayeer and M'eeree. Feminine Hebrew equivalents: B'heeraw, Mazheeraw, M'eeraw, M'oraw, Noga and Oraw.

MELTON

A variant form of Milton. See Milton for a full explanation.

MELVIN

From the Celtic meaning "leader or chief." Some authorities claim that Melvin is from the Anglo-Saxon meaning "friendly toiler," or "famous friend."

Hebrew equivalents: Awmis, G'dalyaw, Maydawd, Ovadyaw, Ovayd, Rav, Rawvaw and Y'hudaw. Feminine Hebrew equivalents: Ameesaw, Atawraw, Malkaw, Y'hudis and Yis'r'aylaw.

For equivalents of the Anglo-Saxon interpretation see David.

MELVYN

Either a form of Marvin or Melvin. See Marvin and Melvin for a full explanation.

MENACHEM, MENAHEM

From the Hebrew meaning "comforter." The Hellenized form of Menachem during the Greek period was Manelaus. The latter name was used mostly by Jews in the upper strata of society including the High Priests. Among Italian Jewry it was common to translate Menachem into Tranquillus. During the Middle Ages it was customary to name boys born on the 9th day of Awv (a day of national mourning for the Temple), Menachem. In the Bible Menachem was a king of Israel (c. 744-735 B.C.E.) who was notorious for his cruelty. Menahem is a variant spelling of Menachem.

The exact Hebrew equivalent is M'nachaym. The exact feminine Hebrew equivalent is M'nachaymaw.

MENASSEH

From the Hebrew meaning "causing to forget." In the Bible Menasseh, which is also spelled Manasseh, was the oldest son of Joseph. His brother was Ephraim.

The exact Hebrew equivalent is M'nashe. There are no other equivalents for this name, unless we accept the Irish definition which associates the name with Magnus meaning "the great," in Latin. For equivalents of this latter definition see Magnus.

MENDEL

Derived either from the Latin meaning "of the mind," or it is a Yiddish variant form of Menachem.

Hebrew equivalents: Menachaym, Mendel, Nawchum

---

ee as in b*ee*t; *i* as in b*i*t; *o* as in n*o*; *oi* as in v*oi*d; *u* as in r*u*de.

and Nachman. Feminine Hebrew equivalents: Daas, Day'-aw, Nechawmaw and Ruchawmaw.

MEREDITH

An Anglo-Saxon name meaning either "sea-dew," or "sea defender." If taken as of Welsh origin it means "great chief or defender."

Hebrew equivalents: Arnon, Aveeyawm, Aynawn, G'dal-yaw, Ovayd and Peleg. Feminine Hebrew equivalents: Ataw-raw, Malkaw, Mawraw, Mawrawsaw and Miryawm.

MERON

From the Hebrew meaning "army troops."

The exact Hebrew equivalent is Mayron. Feminine Hebrew equivalents: Amtzaw, Gadaw, Gavreelaw, Geeboraw and Tigraw.

MERRILL

From the Teutonic meaning "famous."

Hebrew equivalents: G'dalyaw, Heelayl, M'halalayl, M'hulawl, Shamai, Shim'ee and Shaym-Tov. Feminine Hebrew equivalents: Heelaw, Heelaylaw, T'heelaw, Yawayl, Y'hudis and Zimraw.

MERTON

From the Anglo-Saxon meaning "from the farm by the sea."

Hebrew equivalents: Aveeyawm, Awdaw, Aynawn, Karmel, Meechaw and Peleg. Feminine Hebrew equivalents: Dalyaw, D'roraw, Galvaw, Mawrawsaw, Meechal, Miryawm and Sh'daymaw.

MERVIN, MERVYN

Either a form of Melvin or the Welsh form of Marvin. See Melvin and Marvin for a full explanation.

MEYER, MYER

Variant spellings of Meir. See Meir for a full explanation.

Key: *a* as in father; *ai* as in aisle; *aw* as in law; *ay* as in say; *e* as in bet;

MICAH

From the Hebrew meaning "who is like God." It is a variant short form of Michael, and has the same meaning. In the Bible Micah was a prophet in Judah during the latter part of the 8th century.

The exact Hebrew equivalent is Meechaw. The exact feminine Hebrew equivalent is Meechal.

MICHAEL

From the Hebrew meaning "who is like God." Micah is a derivative short form of Michael which appears early in the Bible, in the Book of Numbers, as a member of the tribe of Asher. According to the Book of Daniel, Michael was the prince of the Angels—the archangel closest to God, and the chief divine messenger who carries out God's judgments. Michael was adopted as a popular name in England in the 12th century, having been imported from France where it was spelled Michel. Mitchel and Mitchell are variant English forms. In France Michon was used in addition to Michel. In Italy Michele was a popular form and in Spanish-speaking countries Miquel was common. The Russian Misha is also a variant form of Michael. Mike, Mick, Mickey and Mitch are popular pet forms.

The exact Hebrew equivalent is Meechawayl. The exact feminine Hebrew equivalent is Meechawaylaw.

MICKEY, MIKE

Popular diminutive forms of Michael. See Michael for a full explanation.

MILES, MYLES

From the Greek and Latin meaning "a warrior, a soldier." In England both names were used as short forms of Michael. In addition to the Latin derivation, some authorities believe Miles and Myles are derived from the Old German meaning "beloved."

Hebrew equivalents: Dawvid, Gawd, Gidon, Mawrd'chai, M'dawn, Midyawn and Y'didyaw. Feminine Hebrew equiva-

ee as in beet; i as in bit; o as in no; oi as in void; u as in rude.

lents: Ahuvaw, Amtzaw, Awtzmaw, Dawveedaw, Gavreelaw, Geeboraw and Y'deedaw.

MILTON
An Old English name of Teutonic origin meaning "from
the mill, farmstead, or mill-town." Melton is a variant form.
Mily and Milty are pet forms.

Hebrew equivalents: Awdawm, Karmel, Kar'mlee, Shadmon and Yizr'ayl. Feminine Hebrew equivalents: Karmelis,
Nawvaw, Sh'daymaw and Yiz'r'elaw.

MISHA
The Russian variant form of Michael. See Michael for
a full explanation.

MITCHEL, MITCHELL
Either a form of Michael, or from the Old English
meaning "great."

See Michael and Magnus for masculine and feminine
equivalents.

MOE, MOISE
Moe is the diminutive of Moses, and Moise is the French
and Italian form of Moses. See Moses for a full explanation.

MONROE, MUNROE
From the Celtic meaning "red marsh." In Ireland they
refer to the "mouth (mun) of the river Roe."

Hebrew equivalents: Arnon, Aveeyawm, Moshe and
Peleg. Feminine Hebrew equivalents: Mawraw, Mawrawsaw and Miryawm.

MONTAGUE
The French form of the Latin meaning "from the
pointed mountain." Montgomery is an English variant.
Monte and Monty are diminutive forms.

Hebrew equivalents: Aharon, Awmir, Gal, Galee, Harayl, Hawrawn and Mawrom. Feminine Hebrew equivalents:
Galeeyaw, Gilawdaw, Givonaw, Talmaw and Talmis.

Key: *a* as in father; *ai* as in aisle; *aw* as in law; *ay* as in say; *e* as in bet;

MONTE, MONTY
Diminutive forms of Montague and Montgomery. See Montague for a full explanation.

MONTGOMERY
The English variant of the French name Montague. See Montague for a full explanation.

MORDECAI, MORDECHAI
Derived from the Persian and meaning "warrior, war-like." The Persian god Marduke was the god of war. In the Bible, Mordecai, the cousin of Queen Esther was instrumental in saving the Jewish people who were threatened with extermination by Haman, Prime Minister of King Ahasueros. The Jewish holiday, Purim, grew out of the victory over Haman. In the Middle Ages it was cutomary to name Jewish boys born on Purim, Mordecai. Mordy and Morty are diminutive forms.

The exact Hebrew equivalent is Mawrd'chai. Feminine Hebrew equivalents: Amtzaw, Awtzmaw, Gavreelaw, Geeboraw and Tigraw.

MORDY, MORTY
Diminutive forms of Mordecai. See Mordecai for a full explanation. Morty is also a form of Morton (see Morton).

MOREY, MORIE, MORRIE, MORREY, MORRY
Forms of Morris or Murray. See Morris and Murray for a full explanation.

MORRIS
Either a variant form of the Latin Maurice meaning "moorish, dark-skinned," or derived from the Gaelic meaning "great warrior."

Hebrew equivalents: Adawr, Ayfai, Chawm, Dawvid, Gawd, Gidon, Kaydawr, Mawrd'chai, M'dawn, Midyawn and Pinchaws. Feminine Hebrew equivalents: Amtzaw, Awtzmaw, Ayfaw, Chacheelaw, Gavreelaw, Geeboraw and Tzeelaw.

---

ee as in b*ee*t; *i* as in b*i*t; *o* as in n*o*; *oi* as in v*oi*d; *u* as in r*u*de.

MORTIMER

A French-Latin name meaning "dweller by the still water." Morty is a common pet form.

Hebrew equivalents: Arnon, Aveeyawm, Moshe and Peleg. Feminine Hebrew equivalents: Mawraw, Mawrawsaw and Miryawm.

MORTON

An Old English name meaning "from the farm or field on the moor."

Hebrew equivalents: Awdawm, Chetzron, Mawon and Z'vulun. Feminine Hebrew equivalents: Karmelaw, Nawvaw and Yiz'r'elaw.

MOSES

The name of the great biblical figure who led the children of Israel out of Egypt after centuries of bondage. The name is derived either from the Hebrew meaning "drawn out or saved (from the water)," or from the Egyptian meaning "son, child." Although the name was rarely used in the post-biblical era (not one rabbi in the Talmud is named Moses), it became an extremely popular name in later centuries. Moshe is the exact Hebrew form of Moses while Moss, Moy, Moyes and Moyse are English forms. In the Domesday Book of England Moses appeared as Moyses.

The exact Hebrew equivalent is Moshe. Feminine Hebrew equivalents: Basyaw, B'sulaw, Dawleeyaw, Matzeelaw, Miryawm and Moshawaw.

MOSHA

From the Hebrew meaning "salvation," similar to the name Joshua. Used currently in Israel.

The exact Hebrew equivalent is Moshaw. Feminine Hebrew equivalents: Matzeelaw, Moshawaw and T'shuaw.

MOSHE

Moshe is the exact Hebrew form of Moses. See Moses for a full explanation.

MOSS

An English variant form of Moses. See Moses for a full explanation.

MOY, MOYSE

English variant forms of Moses. See Moses for a full explanation.

MURRAY, MURRY

From the Celtic meaning "seaman." There was an old Scottish clan that used the name Moray and Murray. Murry is a variant spelling of Murray.

Hebrew equivalents: Arnon, Aveeyawm, Moshe and Peleg. Feminine Hebrew equivalents: Mawraw, Mawrawsaw and Miryawm.

MYRON

From the Greek meaning "fragrant, sweet, pleasant."

Hebrew equivalents: Acheenoam, Aveenoam, Magdeeayl, Mawsok, Meged, M'hudawr, Naaman and Nawam. Feminine Hebrew equivalents: Acheenoam, D'vawshaw, M'sukaw, Naamaw, Naamawnaw, Nawawmee, Tirtzaw and Yawtvaw.

NAAMAN

From the Hebrew meaning "sweet, beautiful, pleasant and good." In the Bible Naaman was the general of the Army of Aram (c. 9th century B.C.E.) who went to the prophet, Elisha, to be cured of his leprosy.

The exact Hebrew equivalent is Nawdiv. The exact fem-Hebrew equivalents: Acheenoam, Dawvshaw, M'sukaw and Nawawmee.

NADIV

From the Hebrew meaning "prince, noble."

The exact Hebrew equivalent is Nawdiv. The exact feminine Hebrew equivalent is N'deevaw.

---

ee as in b*ee*t; *i* as in b*i*t; *o* as in n*o*; *oi* as in v*oi*d; *u* as in r*u*de.

NAFTALI, NAFTALIE

Variant spellings of Naphtali. See Naphtali for a full explanation.

NAGID

From the Hebrew meaning "ruler, prince."

The exact Hebrew equivalent is Nawgid. The exact feminine Hebrew equivalent is N'geedaw.

NAHIR

From the Aramaic meaning "light."

The exact Hebrew equivalent is Nawhir. The exact feminine Hebrew equivalent is N'heeraw or N'horaw.

NAHUM

The name of one of the minor prophets who lived in the 7th century B.C.E. He foretold the fall of Nineveh. Derived from the Hebrew meaning "comforted."

The exact Hebrew equivalent is Nawchum. Feminine Hebrew equivalents: Nechawmaw and Ruchawmaw.

NAMIR

From the Hebrew meaning "leopard," and having the connotation of swiftness and strength. Currently used in Israel.

The exact Hebrew equivalent is Nawmir. Feminine Hebrew equivalents: Dawaw, Da'yaw, Gavreelaw, Geeboraw and N'mayraw.

NAPHTALI, NAPHTHALI

From the Hebrew meaning "to wrestle." In the Bible Naphtali was the sixth son of Jacob, the second by his wife Bilhah.

The exact Hebrew equivalent is Naftawlee. Feminine Hebrew equivalents: Amtzaw, Awtzmaw, Gavreelaw, Geeboraw and Yaakovaw.

NATHAN

From the Hebrew meaning "he gave," and implying a gift of God. Nathan was the prophet in the Bible during

Key: *a* as in f*a*ther; *ai* as in *ai*sle; *aw* as in l*aw*; *ay* as in s*ay*; *e* as in b*e*t;

the 11th and 12th centuries B.C.E. who pronounced that the dynasty of King David would be perpetually established, but at the same time he reprimanded David for his unfair treatment of Uriah the Hittite.

The exact Hebrew equivalent is Nawsawn. Feminine Hebrew equivalents: Matawnaw, Migdawnaw, Minchaw, N'sanayl and N'sanyaw.

NATHANIEL

From the Hebrew meaning "a gift of God." The name appears many times in the Bible. One Nathaniel was the fourth son of Jesse, a brother of David.

The exact Hebrew equivalent is N'sanayl. Feminine Hebrew equivalents: Matawnaw, Migdawnaw, Minchaw, N'sanaylaw and N'sanyaw.

NEAL, NEALE, NEIL

From the Gaelic meaning either "dark complexioned one," or "courageous." These names are also used as pet forms of Nathaniel.

Hebrew equivalents: Awsneeayl, Aysawn, Binyawmin, Chawm and Pinchaws. Feminine Hebrew equivalents: Amtzaw, Areeayl, Ayfaw, Chacheelaw and Tzeelaw.

NED, NEDDY

Diminutive forms of Edmond and Edward. See Edmond and Edward for a full explanation.

NEGEV

From the Hebrew meaning "south, southerly." Currently used in Israel.

The exact Hebrew equivalent is Negev. Feminine Hebrew equivalent is D'romis.

NEHEMIAH

From the Hebrew meaning "comforted of the Lord." During the fifth century B.C.E., Nehemiah, a contemporary of Ezra in the Bible, served as governor of Judah. He had previously been cupbearer of the Persian king, Artaxerxes I.

ee as in b*ee*t; *i* as in b*i*t; *o* as in n*o*; *oi* as in v*oi*d; *u* as in r*u*de.

The exact Hebrew equivalent is N'chemyaw. Feminine Hebrew equivalents: Nechawmaw and Ruchawmaw.

NELSON
Taken as either a form of Neal or Cornelius. See Neal and Cornelius for a full explanation.

NEVILLE
Of French origin meaning "new town." Nevil and Nevile are variant spellings.

Hebrew equivalents: Chetzron, Dur, Yawshawvawm, Y'shevawv, Z'vul and Z'vulun. Feminine Hebrew equivalents: Keres, Leenaw, Shafreeraw and Teeraw.

NEWTON
An Old English name meaning "from the new estate or farmstead."

Hebrew equivalents: Awdawm, Karmel, Karm'lee, Shadmon and Yiz'r'ayl. Feminine Hebrew equivalents: Karmelaw, Nawvaw, Sh'daymaw and Yiz'r'elaw.

NICHOLAS, NICOLAS
From the Greek meaning "victory." The short forms Nick, Nicol and Colin, as well as the German Klaus or Claus, are derivative forms. The Russian Nikita is likewise a form of Nicholas.

Hebrew equivalents: Govayr, N'tzeeach and Yatzleeach. Feminine Hebrew equivalents: Dafnaw, Hadasaw, Nitzchaw and Nitzcheeyaw.

NILI
An abbreviation of the Hebrew words in I Samuel 15:29: "The glory (or eternity) of Israel will not lie." Nili was the name of a pro-British and anti-Turkish Jewish underground organization in Palestine during World War I. Used also as a feminine name in Israel.

The exact Hebrew equivalent is Neelee.

NIR, NIREL, NIRIA, NIRIEL
From the Hebrew meaning "a plow or plowed field."

Key: *a* as in father; *ai* as in aisle; *aw* as in law; *ay* as in say; *e* as in bet;

Nirel, Niria and Niriel means "the plowed land of the Lord." All these names are current in Israel.

The exact Hebrew equivalents are Nir, Nirayl, Nireeyaw and Nireeayl. Feminine Hebrew equivalents: Nawvaw, Nawvis, Nofeeyaw and No'yaw.

NISI, NISSI

From the Hebrew meaning "my sign or emblem." A variant form of Nissan or Nissim used in Israel. See Nissan and Nissim for a full explanation.

The exact Hebrew equivalent is Neesee.

NISSAN

From the Hebrew meaning "flight" or "standard, emblem." Nissan is the name of the Hebrew month in which the Passover holiday occurs.

The exact Hebrew equivalent is Neesawn. Feminine Hebrew equivalent: Hawgawr.

NISSIM

From the Hebrew meaning "signs or miracles." It is derived from the same Hebrew root as Nissan. See Nissan for a full explanation.

The exact Hebrew equivalent is Neesim.

NIV

From the Aramaic and Arabic meaning "speech, expression." Currently used in Israel.

The exact Hebrew equivalent is Niv. Feminine Hebrew equivalents: Ameeraw, D'voraw and Neevaw.

NOAH

From the Hebrew meaning "rest, quiet peace." In the Bible Noah was the main character in the story of the flood.

The exact Hebrew equivalent is Noach. Feminine Hebrew equivalents: M'nuchaw, M'shulemes, Nachas, Nawchaw, Nechaw, Shlomis and Shulamis.

NOAM

From the Hebrew meaning "sweetness or friendship."

ee as in b*ee*t; *i* as in b*i*t; *o* as in n*o*; *oi* as in v*oi*d; *u* as in r*u*de.

The exact Hebrew equivalent is Noam. Feminine Hebrew equivalents: Naamaw, Nawawmee, Naamis, Tirtzaw and Yawtvaw.

NODA

From the Hebrew meaning "famous, well-known."

The exact Hebrew equivalent is Nodaw. Feminine Hebrew equivalents: D'voraw, Heelaylaw, Tishbawchaw and Y'hudis.

NOEL

A French-Latin name meaning "Christmas, Christmas-born, Christmas carol or song." The original Latin form was Natalis (compare, Natalie) meaning "birthday."

Hebrew equivalents: Aharon, Ameerawn, Ameeron, Anaw, Leeron, Ron, Ronee and Ronayl. Feminine Hebrew equivalents: Leeris, Leeron, Mangeenaw, Reenaw, Sheeraw, Sheerlee and Yawronaw.

NOGA

From the Hebrew meaning "light or bright." In the Bible Noga was a son of King David. In Israel today it is also used as a feminine name.

The exact Hebrew equivalent is Noga. Feminine Hebrew equivalents: B'heeraw, N'hawraw, M'eeraw, Noga and Zawhawraw.

NOLAN, NOLAND

From the Celtic meaning "noble or famous."

Hebrew equivalents: Aveenawdawv, Heelayl, Nawdawv, Nodaw, Shim'ee and Y'hudaw. Feminine Hebrew equivalents: N'deevaw, Sawraw, T'heelaw, Y'hudis and Yis'r'aylaw.

NORBERT

From the Teutonic meaning "divine brightness."

Hebrew equivalents: Mayeer, Shimshon, Z'rachyaw, Uree and Ureeyaw. Feminine Hebrew equivalents: B'heeraw, M'eeraw, Noga, Oraw and Ureeaylaw.

Key: *a* as in f*a*ther; *ai* as in *ai*sle; *aw* as in l*aw*; *ay* as in s*ay*; *e* as in b*e*t;

NORMAN
Pertaining to the "north." Norman means "a man from Normandie" (in the northern part of France). Nor, Norm and Normie are pet forms.

Hebrew equivalents: Tz'fanyaw and Tz'fanyawhu. Feminine Hebrew equivalent: Tzawfonaw.

NORTON
Like Norman, Norton pertains to the North. It refers specifically to the northern town of Yorkshire.

See Norman for masculine and feminine equivalents.

NORRIS
Either from the Teutonic meaning "a man from the north," (see Norman), or a French-Latin name meaning "caretaker," and having the connotation of protector.

Hebrew equivalents: Avdee, Ovadyaw and Ovayd. Feminine Hebrew equivalents: Ganaw, Mawgaynaw and Teeraw. See Norman for additional equivalents.

NOY
From the Hebrew meaning "beauty."

The exact Hebrew equivalent is Noy. Feminine Hebrew equivalents: Naamaw, Nawawmee, Nawvaw, Nofeeyaw and Raananaw.

NUR, NURI, NURIA, NURIAH, NURIEL
Variant forms of Hebrew names of Aramaic origin meaning "fire" or "fire of the Lord." The ia, iah, and iel suffix mean "of the Lord," in Hebrew. All these names are currently used in Israel.

Hebrew equivalents: Nur, Nuree, Nureeyaw and Nureeayl. Feminine Hebrew equivalents: Avukaw, Shalheves, Udeeyaw and Uris.

OBADIAH
From the Hebrew meaning "servant of God." In the Bible Obadiah was the fourth of the twelve minor prophets. He lived in the 6th century B.C.E. The entire Book of Obadiah in the Bible consists of only one chapter.

---

ee as in b*ee*t; *i* as in b*i*t; *o* as in n*o*; *oi* as in v*oi*d; *u* as in r*u*de.

The exact Hebrew equivalent is Ovadyaw. Feminine Hebrew equivalents: Ganaw, Mawgaynaw and Teeraw.

OFER
From the Hebrew meaning "a young deer."
The exact Hebrew equivalent is Ofer. Feminine Hebrew equivalents: Awfraw, A'yawlaw, A'yeles, Tzivyaw and Yaalis.

OLIVER, OLIVIER
From the Latin meaning "man of peace." The name is derived from the olive tree, which is the symbol of peace. Olivier is a variant form of Oliver used in the Middle Ages. Some authorities maintain that Havelock is a Welsh form of Oliver.
Hebrew equivalents: Mawnoach, Noach, Shawlom, Shlomo and Zaysawn. Feminine Hebrew equivalents: M'shulemes, Shlomis, Shulamis and Za'yis.

OMRI
From the Arabic meaning "to live, to live long," or "worship, worshipper." In the Bible Omri was a king of Israel (887-876 B.C.E.) and the founder of a dynasty.
The exact Hebrew equivalent is Awmree. Feminine Hebrew equivalents: Chavaw, Cha'yaw, Cheeyusaw and Y'cheeaylaw.

OPHER
A variant spelling of Ofer. See Ofer for a full explanation.

OREN
From the Hebrew meaning "a tree (cedar or fir)." In the Bible Oren was a descendant of Judah. Orin, Orrin and Oron are variant forms.
The exact Hebrew equivalent is Oren. Feminine Hebrew equivalents: Areezaw, Armonaw, Arzaw, Aylaw, Eelawnaw, Eelawnis and Tz'ruyaw.

Key: *a* as in f*a*ther; *ai* as in *ai*sle; *aw* as in l*aw*; *ay* as in s*ay*; *e* as in b*e*t;

ORIN, ORRIN, ORON
Variant forms of Oren. See Oren for a full explanation.

ORSON
From the Latin meaning "a bear."
Hebrew equivalents: Dov and Dubee. Feminine Hebrew equivalent: Dubaw.

OSCAR
Either from the Celtic meaning "leaping warrior," or "god-spear," or from the Anglo-Saxon meaning "power of godliness."
Hebrew equivalents: Gawd, Gidon, Kaneeayl, Mawrd'-chai, M'dawn and Midyawn. Feminine Hebrew equivalents: Amtzaw, Awtzmaw, Chaneesaw, Cheenis, Gavreelaw and Geeboraw.

OSWALD
Taken by some authorities to be the common form of Oscar. Others take it from the Teutonic meaning "house ruler or steward," and having the connotation of helper. Still others contend that Oswald is of Welsh origin meaning "god-power." Ozzie and Ozzy are pet forms.
Hebrew equivalents: Aveemelech, Avdee, Melech, Ovad-yaw, Ovayd and Rozayn. Feminine Hebrew equivalents: Aleksandraw, Ameetzaw, Amtzaw, Gavreelaw and Geeboraw.

OTTO
From the Teutonic meaning "prosperous, or wealthy."
Hebrew equivalents: Hoseer, Hunaw, Yeeshai and Yisro. Feminine Hebrew equivalents: Bas-Shua, Matzleechaw and Yisraw.

OWEN
From the Welsh meaning "young," or "young warrior." It may also be a derivative of the Latin Eugenius meaning "well-born."
Hebrew equivalents: Aveecha'yil, Aveenawdawv, Ben-Cha'yil, Ish-Hod, Nawdawv, Nawdiv and Yisrawayl. Femi-

ee as in b*ee*t; *i* as in b*i*t; *o* as in n*o*; *oi* as in v*oi*d; *u* as in r*u*de.

nine Hebrew equivalents: Amtzaw, Gavreelaw, Malkaw, N'deevaw, Sawraw and Yis'r'aylaw.

OZ, OZNI

From the Hebrew meaning "my ear or my hearing." Ozni in the Bible was a son of Gad, grandson of Jacob. Oz is a pet form of Ozni and of Oswald.

The exact Hebrew equivalent is Awznee. Feminine Hebrew equivalents: Kashuvaw, Shimaws and Shimonaw.

PALTI, PALTIEL, PILTAI

These names are from the same Hebrew root meaning "my escape or deliverance." In the Bible Palti was the second husband of Michal, the daughter of King Saul. Piltai was a member of a priestly family. Paltiel was a prince of the tribe of Isaachar and the name means "god is my savior."

The exact Hebrew equivalents are Paltee, Palteeayl and Piltai. Feminine Hebrew equivalents: Moshawaw, Sawrid, T'shuaw and Y'shuaw.

PAT

A popular diminutive form of Patrick. Also used as a pet form of Patricia. See Patrick for a full explanation.

PATRICK

From the Latin meaning "a patrician," or "one of noble descent." Pat is a popular pet form.

Hebrew equivalents: Aveenawdawv, Cheerom, Nawdawv and Yisrawayl. Feminine Hebrew equivalents: N'deevaw, Sawraw and Yis'r'aylaw.

PAUL

From the Latin meaning "small." First used by New Testament Saul of Tarsus who dropped his Old Testament name, which symbolized his rejection of Judaism. Paul is used in different forms in different countries: In Russia it is Pavel; in Spain Pablo; in Italy Paola.

Hebrew equivalents: Kawtawn, Tzuawr, Vawfsee and

Key: *a* as in father; *ai* as in aisle; *aw* as in law; *ay* as in say; *e* as in bet;

Z'ayraw. Feminine Hebrew equivalents: D'leelaw and K'tanaw.

PENINI
From the Hebrew meaning "pearl or precious stone."
The exact Hebrew equivalent is P'neenee. Feminine Hebrew equivalents: Margawlis, P'neenaw and P'neenis.

PERETZ, PEREZ
From the Hebrew meaning "burst forth."
The exact Hebrew equivalent is Peretz. Feminine Hebrew equivalents: Neetzaw and Neetzawnaw.

PERRY, PETE
Perry is the French form of Peter. Pete is a popular pet form of Peter. See Peter for a full explanation.

PESACH
From the Hebrew meaning "to pass or skip over." It is the Hebrew name used in the Bible for the Passover holiday, the holiday of freedom, commemorating the exodus from Egypt and the saving of the first-born Israelites during the last of the ten plagues.
The exact Hebrew equivalent is Pesach. Feminine Hebrew equivalents: D'roraw, D'roris, G'ulaw, Lee-d'ror and Rawchawv.

PETER
From the Greek meaning "rock." In the New Testament Jesus gave Simon bar Jonah the nickname *Cephas* which means "rock" in Aramaic. Perry is the French form of Peter, according to some authorities, while others take it to be a variant of the Welsh, Parry, meaning "the son of Harry." Among the Welsh and Spanish Peter was also Pedro. Aside from Perry, the French used Pierre for Peter. Pete is a popular diminutive form.
Hebrew equivalents: Acheetzur, Aveetzur, Avneeayl, Sela, Shawmir, Tz'ror, Tzur and Tzureeayl. Feminine Hebrew equivalents: Ritzpaw, Tzureeyaw and Tzuris.

---

ee as in b*ee*t; *i* as in b*i*t; *o* as in n*o*; *oi* as in v*oi*d; *u* as in r*u*de.

PHILLIP, PHILIP

From the Greek meaning "lover of horses," and having the connotation of a warrior. Phil is a common short form. Dickens, in his *Great Expectations*, was probably the first to use Pip as a short form of Philip.

Hebrew equivalents: Ben-Cha'yil, Gidon, Mawr'd'chai, Naftawlee, Peresh and Susee. Feminine Hebrew equivalents: Amtzaw, Awtzmaw, Gavreelaw and Geeboraw.

PHINEAS

From the Egyptian meaning "negro, dark-complexioned." In the Bible Phineas was a priest who was the grandson of Aaron.

The exact Hebrew equivalent is Pinchaws. Feminine Hebrew equivalents: Ayfaw, Chacheelaw, Sh'chorah and Tzeelaw.

PHOEBUS

The god of light and sun in Greek mythology. Pheobe is the feminine form.

Hebrew equivalents: Mayeer, Shimshon, Shimshai, Uree and Ureeyaw. Feminine Hebrew equivalents: B'heeraw, M'eeraw, Noga, Shimshonaw and Zawhawraw.

PIERCE

A form of Peter meaning "rock." See Peter for a full explanation.

PIERRE

A French variant form of Peter. See Peter for a full explanation.

PINCHAS, PINCUS, PINKAS

Pinchas and its variant spellings are the original forms of Phineas as found in the Hebrew Bible. See Phineas for a full explanation.

PRESTON

An Old English name meaning "priest's town."

Hebrew equivalents: Kadish, Kawlayv, Kohayn and

Y'kuseeayl. Feminine Hebrew equivalents: Beenaw and Bunaw.

QUENTIN
From the Latin meaning "the fifth." This name was sometimes given in Roman times to the fifth son in a family, just as the seventh was called Septimus and the eighth, Octavius.

There are no Hebrew equivalents.

RAANAN
From the Hebrew meaning "fresh, luxuriant, beautiful."

The exact Hebrew equivalent is Raanawn. The exact feminine Hebrew equivalent is Raananaw.

RALEIGH
From the Old English meaning "the roe or deer meadow."

Hebrew equivalents: Ayfer, Karmel, Kar'mlee and Tz'vee. Feminine Hebrew equivalents: Ganaw, Karmelaw, Nawvaw and Tzivyaw.

RALPH
From the Teutonic meaning "help, counsel, or wolf-counsel." Ralph is considered a short form of Randolph although, in the opinion of some scholars, it is probably the original form. Rolf and Rolfe are variant Germanic forms.

Hebrew equivalents: Aleksandayr, Azaryaw, Azreeayl, Elee-ezer and Z'ayv. Feminine Hebrew equivalents: Aleksandraw, Beenaw, Bunaw and Milkaw.

RANDAL, RANDALL, RANDI, RANDY
Variant forms of Randolph. See Randolph for a full explanation.

RANDOLPH
A Teutonic name meaning "help, counsel, or wolf-counsel." Many variant names have been developed from Randolph including, Ralph, Randall, Raoul and Rolf. In Medieval England Rowl and Rawl were variant forms which

ee as in b*ee*t; *i* as in b*i*t; *o* as in n*o*; *oi* as in v*oi*d; *u* as in r*u*de.

gave rise to surnames like Rowlett and Rawlings. Rollo is another variant form which was introduced by the early Normans into France.

Hebrew equivalents: Aleksandayr, Azaryaw, Azreeayl, Elee-ezer and Z'ayv. Feminine Hebrew equivalents: Aleksandraw, Beenaw, Bunaw and Milkaw.

RANEN, RANON

Modern names recently introduced in Israel. From the Hebrew meaning "to sing, to be joyous."

The exact Hebrew equivalents are Ranayn and Rawnon. Feminine Hebrew equivalents: Rawneesaw, Roneeyaw, Ronis, Sheeraw and Simchonaw.

RAOUL

A French variant form of the Teutonic Randolph or Ralph. See Randolph for a full explanation.

RAPHAEL

From the Hebrew meaning "God has healed." Raphael was the archangel and divine messenger mentioned in the apocryphal books of Enoch and Tobit, although the name does appear in the Bible as one of the Levites. Raff and Rafe are short forms used in England.

The exact Hebrew equivalent is R'fawayl. Feminine Hebrew equivalents: Rofee, R'fawaylaw, R'fuaw and T'rufaw.

RAVID

From the Hebrew meaning "ornament or jewelry."

The exact Hebrew equivalent is Rawvid. Feminine Hebrew equivalents: Adee, Adeenaw, Adeeyaw, Awdaw and Ednaw.

RAVIV

From the Hebrew meaning "rain or dew."

The exact Hebrew equivalent is Rawviv. The exact feminine Hebrew equivalent is R'veevaw.

Key: *a* as in father; *ai* as in *ai*sle; *aw* as in l*aw*; *ay* as in s*ay*; *e* as in b*e*t;

RAY

Either a diminutive form of Raymond (see Raymond), or a variant of Rey and Roy (see Roy), or from the Celtic meaning "grace."

See Raymond, Roy and John for Hebrew equivalents.

RAYMOND

Either from the German meaning "quiet, peace," or from the Saxon meaning "mighty protector." Ray is a popular pet form.

Hebrew equivalents: Avigdor, Shawlom, Shlomo and Shmaryawhu. Feminine Hebrew equivalents: Bawtzraw, Efraws, Shlomis, Shulamis and Teeraw.

RAZ, RAZI, RAZIEL

Popular names in Israel derived from the Aramaic meaning "secret, my secret, or secret of the Lord." Raz and Razi are also used as feminine names.

The exact Hebrew equivalents are: Rawz, Rawzee and Rawzeeayl. Feminine Hebrew equivalents: Leerawz, Rawz, Rawzee and Rawzeeaylaw.

REGEM

A biblical name used in Israel today. Derived from the Arabic meaning "a friend."

The exact Hebrew equivalent is Regem. Feminine Hebrew equivalents: Ahuvaw, Ameesaw, Dawveedaw, Naamaw and Nawawmee.

REGINALD

From the Teutonic meaning "a mighty or powerful ruler." Rex, which is an independent name, derived from the Latin meaning "king," is also a pet form of Reginald. Reynold is a variant French form.

Hebrew equivalents: Barzeelai, Gavreeayl, Kasreeayl, Melech, Rawzin, Rozayn and Y'chezkayl. Feminine Hebrew equivalents: Atawraw, G'veeraw, Malkaw and Yis'r'aylaw.

ee as in b*ee*t; *i* as in b*i*t; *o* as in n*o*; *oi* as in v*oi*d; *u* as in r*u*de.

REUBEN

From the Hebrew meaning "behold—a son!" In the Bible Reuben was Jacob's first-born son from his wife Leah. Ruben, Rubin and Ruvane are variant forms.

The exact Hebrew equivalent is R'uvayn. The exact feminine Hebrew equivalents are R'uvas and R'uvaynaw.

REX

From the Latin meaning "a king."

Hebrew equivalents: Aveemelech, Eleemelech, Malkawm, Melech, Rawzin and Rozayn. Feminine Hebrew equivalents: Atawraw, Malkaw, Malkis and Tz'feeraw.

REYNARD

From Old High German meaning "strong in counsel."

Hebrew equivalents: Avee-ezer, Eflawl, Ezraw, Pawlawl and Y'utz. Feminine Hebrew equivalents: Beenaw, Bunaw, Ezr'aylaw, Ezreeaylaw and Milkaw.

REYNOLD

A variant French form of Reginald. In Scotland it took the form of Ronald and was quite popular. Rex, Reg and Reggie are pet forms. See Reginald for a full explanation.

RICARDO, RICCARDO

Variant forms of Richard. See below for a full explanation.

RICHARD, RICHARDO

From the Teutonic meaning "powerful, valiant rider," or "treasurer of the kingdom." Richard is one of the most popular names used in America today. Richardo, Riccardo and Ricardo are Spanish, Portugese and Italian variant forms. Dick, Rici, Ricci, Rick, Ricki, Richie and Rickie are common pet forms.

Hebrew equivalents: Barzeelai, Chizkeeyaw, Gavreeayl, Hunaw, Kasreeayl, Matmon and Melech. Feminine Hebrew equivalents: Amtzaw, Areeayl, Asheeraw, Gavreeaylaw, Gavreelaw, Otzawraw and S'gulaw.

Key: *a* as in f*a*ther; *ai* as in *ai*sle; *aw* as in l*aw*; *ay* as in s*ay*; *e* as in b*e*t;

RICI, RICCI, RICHIE, RICKI, RICKIE
Diminutive forms of Richard and Richardo. See above for a full explanation.

RIMON
From the Hebrew meaning "pomegranate." A biblical name used in Israel today.

The exact Hebrew equivalent is Reemon. The exact feminine Hebrew equivalent is Reemonaw.

ROBERT
One of the most popular names of the last generation. From the Teutonic meaning "bright or famous counsel." Rob, Robbie, Robin and Bob are diminutive forms.

Hebrew equivalents: Azreeayl, Elee-ezer, Ezraw, Heelayl and Mayeer. Feminine Hebrew equivalents: Aleksandraw, Ezr'aylaw, Milkaw, M'eeraw and Y'hudis.

ROBIN
A variant form of Robert popular in France. See Robert for a full explanation.

RODERICK
From the Old German meaning "famous ruler." It has assumed different forms in different countries over the centuries. The most famous is the popular Irish version, Rory.

Hebrew equivalents: Aveemelech, Rabaw, Rawvaw, Rosh and Yisrawayl. Feminine Hebrew equivalents: Atawraw, Malkaw, Sawraw and Tz'feeraw.

RODGER
A variant spelling of Roger. See Roger for a full explanation.

RODNEY
From the Teutonic meaning "famous."

Hebrew equivalents: G'dalyaw, Heelayl, Shevach, Shim'ee and Y'hudaw. Feminine Hebrew equivalents: Ahudaw, Heelaw, Heelaylaw, Y'hudis and Yocheved.

---

ee as in b*ee*t; *i* as in b*i*t; *o* as in n*o*; *oi* as in v*oi*d; *u* as in r*u*de.

ROGER
From the Teutonic meaning either "spear of fame," and having the connotation of war-hero, or "a man of his word, honest."

Hebrew equivalents: Ameetai, Aveecha'yil and Gayraw. Feminine equivalents: Tigraw, Y'hudis and Y'shawraw.

ROLAND, ROLLAND
From the Teutonic meaning "fame of the land."

Hebrew equivalents: Awdawm, G'dalyaw, Heelayl and Y'hudaw. Feminine Hebrew equivalents: Heelaw, Heelaylaw and Y'hudis.

ROLF, ROLFE
Variant forms of Ralph and Randolph. See Ralph for a full explanation.

ROLLO
A variant form of Rudolph or Roland introduced into France by the early Normans. See Rudolph and Roland for a full explanation of each name.

RON, RONEL, RONI, RONLI
Variant forms derived from the Hebrew meaning "joy or song." Ronel means "joy, or song, of the Lord"; Roni means "my song, or my joy"; Ronli means "joy, or song, is mine."

The exact Hebrew equivalents are: Ron, Ronayl, Ronee and Ronlee. Feminine Hebrew equivalents: Reenaw, Sheeraw, Sheeree, Sheerlee, T'heelaw and Zimraw.

RONALD, RONNIE
Ronald and its diminutive Ronnie are contracted forms of Reginald. See Reginald for a full explanation.

RORY
Either the Irish form of Roderick (see Roderick) or from the Celtic meaning "the ruddy one."

Hebrew equivalents: Admon, Almog, Gunee and Tzochar. See Roderick for additional equivalents.

Key: *a* as in f*a*ther; *ai* as in *ai*sle; *aw* as in l*aw*; *ay* as in s*ay*; *e* as in b*e*t;

ROSCOE

From the Teutonic meaning "a swift horse." Ross is sometimes used as a diminutive form.

Hebrew equivalents: Ben-Cha'yil, Ish-Cha'yil, Peresh, Rechev and Susee. Feminine Hebrew equivalent: Avee-Cha'yil.

ROSS

From the Anglo-Saxon meaning "woods or meadow." Ross may also be a form of Roscoe (see Roscoe).

Hebrew equivalents: Karmel, Kar'mlee and Yaraw. Feminine Hebrew equivalents: Ganaw, Karmelaw, Nawvaw and Yaaree.

ROY, ROYE

From the Old French meaning "king." Some authorities believe that Roy may also be derived from the Gaelic meaning "red."

Hebrew equivalents: Aveemelech, Eleemelech, Kasree-ayl and Melech. Feminine Hebrew equivalents: Atawraw, Gavreelaw, Malkaw and Yis'r'aylaw.

RUBEN, RUBIN

Variant spellings of Reuben. Surnames like Rubens and Rabinowitz are derivative forms. See Reuben for a full explanation.

RUBY

Either a diminutive form of Reuben (see Reuben for a full explanation), or a French name derived from the Latin meaning "a red, precious stone."

Hebrew equivalents: Shoham, Shovai and Yawkawr. Feminine Hebrew equivalents: Margawlis, S'gulaw, P'nee-naw and Tz'feeraw.

RUDOLPH, RUDULPH

Variant forms of Randolph and Ralph. See Randolph for a full explanation.

---

ee as in b*ee*t; *i* as in b*i*t; *o* as in n*o*; *oi* as in v*oi*d; *u* as in r*u*de.

RUFUS
From the Latin meaning "red, red-haired."
Hebrew equivalents: Admon, Almog, Gunee and Tzochar. Feminine Hebrew equivalents: D'leelaw and Neemaw.

RUSSEL
Either from the Latin meaning "rusty-haired," or from the Anglo-Saxon meaning "a horse." In medieval England a red fox was known as a "russel." Rusty is a popular short form.
Hebrew equivalents: Admon, Almog, Gunee, Ish-Cha'yil, and Sussee. Feminine Hebrew equivalents: Avee-Chayil and Puaw.

RUVANE
The Hebrew form of Reuben. See Reuben for a full explanation.

SALVADORE, SALVATORE
From the Latin meaning "to save, to help." Sal is a popular short form.
Hebrew equivalents: Eleeshaw, Eleeshua, Hoshaya, Moshaw, Moshe and Y 'hoshua. Feminine Hebrew equivalents: Moshawaw, Y'shuaw and T'shuaw.

SAADIAH, SAADYAH
From the Hebrew meaning "God's helper," and having the connotation of protection. Saadiah ben Joseph was a famous Egyptian-born Jewish scholar who lived from 882 to 942.
The exact Hebrew equivalent is Saadyaw. Feminine Hebrew equivalents: Bawtzraw, Efraws, Saadaw, Tzeelaw, Yaakovaw and Y'shuaw.

SAGI
From the Hebrew and Aramaic meaning "strong, mighty."
The exact Hebrew equivalent is Sagee. Feminine Hebrew equivalents: Ameetzaw, Aysawnaw, Azaw, Azeezaw and Geeboraw.

Key: *a* as in f*a*ther; *ai* as in *ai*sle; *aw* as in l*aw*; *ay* as in s*ay*; *e* as in b*e*t;

SALMON, SALO, SALOMAN

Variant spellings of Solomon. See Solomon for a full explanation.

SAMSON, SAMPSON

From the Hebrew meaning "sun." In the Bible Samson was an Israelite judge from the tribe of Dan. He was noted for his strength and courage, and his success in battling the Philistines, until he was betrayed by Delilah. In literature Samson has become a synonym for "strong man." Sampson is a variant spelling.

The exact Hebrew equivalent is Shimshon. The exact feminine Hebrew equivalent is Shimshonaw.

SAMUEL

A famous biblical figure who lived during the 11th century B.C.E. He was the prophet and judge in Israel who anointed Saul as the first king. The name is derived from a Hebrew root, and has been interpreted to mean either "His name is God," or "God has heard," or "God has anointed or dedicated." Sam and Sammy are popular diminutive forms.

The exact Hebrew equivalent is Shmuayl. The exact feminine Hebrew equivalent is Shmuaylaw.

SANDER, SANDERS, SANDY

Abbreviated forms of Alexander. See Alexander for a full explanation. Sandy is also a short form of Sanford (see Sanford).

SANFORD

From the Teutonic meaning "peaceful counsel."

Hebrew equivalents: Avshawlom, Pawlawl, Shawlom, Shlomo and Y'utz. Feminine Hebrew equivalents: Aleksandraw, Beenaw, Bunaw and Shulamis.

SAPIR, SAPHIR

A name used in Israel derived from the Greek meaning "a precious stone, a sapphire." Saphir is a variant form.

---

ee as in b*ee*t; *i* as in b*i*t; *o* as in n*o*; *oi* as in v*oi*d; *u* as in r*u*de.

The exact Hebrew equivalents are Safir and Sapir. Feminine Hebrew equivalents: Sapeeraw, Sapeeris, S'gulaw, Y'kawraw and Yakeeraw.

SAUL
From the Hebrew meaning "asked or borrowed." In the Bible Saul was the first king to rule over Israel (11th century B.C.E.). He was the son of Kish from the tribe of Benjamin. Samuel, the prophet, anointed him king only because of the clamor of the populace, and despite his own better judgment. Saul of Tarsus in the New Testament adopted the name Paul after his conversion to Christianity.

The exact Hebrew equivalent is Shawul. The exact feminine Hebrew equivalent is Shawulaw.

SCOTT
A very popular name today. It is a late Latin form for "Scotchman," the meaning of which may be "the tatooed one."

Tatooing was contrary to biblical law which may account for the fact that no Hebrew names with this meaning have been adopted.

SEAN
A popular variant Gaelic form of John. See John for a full explanation.

SEGEL
From the Hebrew meaning "treasure." It is a derivative of the biblical concept of *Am Segulah,* "a treasured people," as Israel is often referred to.

The exact Hebrew equivalent is Segel. The exact feminine Hebrew equivalent is S'gulaw.

SEGEV
From the Hebrew meaning "glory, majesty, exalted."

The exact Hebrew equivalent is Segev. Feminine Hebrew equivalents: Asalyaw, Atawraw, Malkaw and Sawraw.

Key: *a* as in f*a*ther; *ai* as in *ai*sle; *aw* as in l*aw*; *ay* as in s*ay*; *e* as in b*e*t;

SELIG

From the Teutonic meaning "blessed." It has become a popular Yiddish name meaning "blessed soul."

Hebrew equivalents: Awshayr, Bawruch and M'vorawch. Feminine Hebrew equivalents: Awshraw, Brawchaw and Bruchaw.

SELDEN, SELDON

Either from the Anglo-Saxon meaning "rare," and having the connotation of precious, or from the Teutonic meaning "from the manor valley."

Hebrew equivalents: Gai, Shoham, Shovai and Yawkawr. Feminine Hebrew equivalents: Bik'aw, B'rawchaw, Margawlis, P'neenaw, S'gulaw and Y'kawraw.

SELWYN

From the Anglo-Saxon meaning "palace friend," or "friend at court."

Hebrew equivalents: Bildawd, Dawvid, Eldawd and Rayee. Feminine Hebrew equivalents: Ahuvaw, Chaveevaw, Rus and Y'deedaw.

SENDER

A variant spelling of Sander which is a form of Alexander. See Alexander for a full explanation.

The exact Hebrew equivalent is Sender. See Alexander for additional equivalents.

SENIOR

From the Latin meaning "the elder."

Hebrew equivalents: Kadmeeayl, Y'sheeshai and Zawkayn. Feminine Hebrew equivalents: Bilhaw, Y'shawnaw and Z'kaynaw.

SERGE

From the Latin meaning "to serve."

Hebrew equivalents: Eved, Malachee, Ovayd and Ovadyaw. Feminine Hebrew equivalents: Ezraw and Ezreeaylaw.

ee as in b*ee*t; *i* as in b*i*t; *o* as in n*o*; *oi* as in v*oi*d; *u* as in r*u*de.

SETH

Either from the Hebrew meaning "garment," or "appointed," or from the Syriac meaning "appearance." Seth, in the Bible, was a son of Adam who was born after the death of Abel. Adam called him Seth, for he said, "God hath appointed me another seed instead of Abel."

The exact Hebrew equivalent is Shays. Feminine Hebrew equivalent: Shmuaylaw.

SEYMOUR, SEYMORE

From the Teutonic meaning either "famed at sea," or "the sower," and having the connotation of farmer. Some authorities believe that Seymour is derived from the Latin root from which the name Maurice is derived. See Maurice for a further explanation.

Hebrew equivalents: Aveeyawm, Aynawn, Karmel, Yiz'r'ayl and Peleg. Feminine Hebrew equivalents: Karmelaw, Miryawm, Nawvaw and Yiz'r'elaw.

SHALOM, SHLOMO, SHOLOM

Independent names with a common root. From the Hebrew meaning "peace." Shlomo is the Hebrew name corresponding to Solomon.

Exact Hebrew equivalents: Shawlom and Shlomo. Feminine Hebrew equivalents: M'shulemes, Shlomis, Shulamis and Za'yis.

SHAMIR

From the Hebrew meaning "a very strong, rock-like substance," capable of cutting through metal. It is referred to in the Bible in the Book of Ezekiel. According to talmudic legend it was created on Sabbath eve, at twilight.

The exact Hebrew equivalent is Shawmir. Feminine Hebrew equivalents: Ritzpaw, Tzur-ayl, Tzureeyaw and Tzuris.

SHAMMAI

A first century Palestinian scholar and leader who was the founder of an important school of learning. From the

Key: *a* as in f*a*ther; *ai* as in *ai*sle; *aw* as in l*aw*; *ay* as in s*ay*; *e* as in b*e*t;

Hebrew and Aramaic meaning "name," and having the connotation of reputation.

The exact Hebrew equivalent is Shamai. Feminine Hebrew equivalents: Shimaws, Shimonaw, Shmuaylaw, T'heelaw, Y'hudis and Zimraw.

SHANE, SHAUN, SHAWN

These names are variant forms of the Gaelic Sean used prominently in Ireland. The original form of these names is John. See John for a full explanation.

SHANAN, SHAANAN, SHANON

From the Hebrew meaning "peaceful, secure." Shanon, a variant spelling of Shanan, may also be a variant form of Shawn or Sean which are forms of John.

The exact Hebrew equivalent is Shaanawn. The exact feminine Hebrew equivalent is Shaananaw.

SHAPIR

From the Aramaic meaning "beautiful." The surname Shapiro is derived from this personal name.

The exact Hebrew equivalent is Shapeer. The exact feminine Hebrew equivalent is Shifraw.

SHEFER

From the Hebrew meaning "pleasant, beautiful." Derived from the same root as the name Shapir.

The exact Hebrew equivalent is Shefer. The exact feminine Hebrew equivalent is Shifraw.

SHELDON

From the Old English meaning "shepherd's hut," or "hut on a hill," and having the connotation of protection.

Hebrew equivalents: Aharon, Avigdor, Chosaw, Shmaryaw and Talmai. Feminine Hebrew equivalents: Bawtzraw, Migdawlaw, Shimris and Teeraw.

SHELLEY

From the Teutonic meaning "shell island, shell water." Hebrew equivalents: Aveeyawm, Aynawn and Peleg.

ee as in b*ee*t; *i* as in b*i*t; *o* as in n*o*; *oi* as in v*oi*d; *u* as in r*u*de.

Feminine Hebrew equivalents: D'roraw, Mawrawsaw and Miryawm.

SHELOMI, SHELOMO

Variant forms of Shlomo which is the Hebrew form of Solomon. See Solomon for a full explanation. Shelomi, sometimes spelled Shlomi, is an independent biblical name.

SHEM

From the Hebrew meaning "name," and having the connotation of "good reputation." In the Bible Shem was the oldest of the three sons of Noah.

The exact Hebrew equivalent is Shaym. Feminine Hebrew equivalents: Bas-shaym, Heelaw, Heelaylaw, T'heelaw and Y'hudis.

SHEPARD, SHEPHERD

From the Anglo-Saxon meaning "a shepherd," and having the connotation of protection.

Hebrew equivalents: Roee, Shmaryaw, Shmaryawhu, and Yaakov. Feminine Hebrew equivalents: Bawtzraw, Mawgaynaw, Migdawlaw, Rawchayl, Tzeelaw and Yaakovaw.

SHERAGA, SHRAGA, SHERAGAI, SHRAGAI

These names are variant forms derived from the Aramaic meaning "light." In Yiddish, the hybrid name Shraga-Feivel is commonly used, Feivel being a variant form of Phoebus, the goddess of light in Greek mythology.

The exact Hebrew equivalents are Shragaw and Shragai. Feminine Hebrew equivalents: B'heeraw, M'eeraw, N'hawraw, Noga, Oraw and Zawhawraw.

SHERIRA

From the Aramaic meaning "strong." The first important personage to have this name was a Babylonian scholar, the head of an academy in Pumbedita in the 10th century.

The exact Hebrew equivalent is Shreeraw. Feminine Hebrew equivalents: Abeeraw, Ameetzaw, Azeezaw, Chaseenaw and Gavreelaw.

Key: *a* as in f*a*ther; *ai* as in *ai*sle; *aw* as in l*aw*; *ay* as in s*ay*; *e* as in b*e*t;

SHERMAN
From the Anglo-Saxon meaning "one who shears or cuts."

Hebrew equivalent: Gid'on. There are no feminine equivalents.

SHERWIN
Either from the Anglo-Saxon meaning "one who shears the wind," or from Old English meaning "shining friend."

Hebrew equivalents: Awmis, Dawvid, Eetai, Rayee and Regem. Feminine Hebrew equivalents: Ahuvaw, Ameesaw, Rus and Tirtzaw.

SHERWOOD
From the Anglo-Saxon meaning "a forest."

Hebrew equivalents: Karmel, Kar'mlee and Yaaree. Feminine Hebrew equivalents: Ganaw, Karmelaw, Nawvaw and Yaraw.

SHIMON
The Hebraic form of Simon or Simeon. See Simon for a full explanation.

SHLOMI, SHLOMO
Variant spellings of Shelomi and Shelomo which are forms of Solomon. See Solomon for a full explanation.

SHNEUR
A Yiddish name derived from the Latin, Senior, meaning "the elder." See Senior for a full explanation.

SHUSHAN
From the Hebrew meaning "a flower or a lily." Shushan appears first in the Bible as the name of the capital city of Persia.

The exact Hebrew equivalent is Shushan. The exact feminine Hebrew equivalent is Shoshawn and Shoshanaw.

SIDNEY, SYDNEY
Contracted forms of Saint Denys. The original form of Denys or Denis was Dionysius, the Greek god of wine,

ee as in b*ee*t; *i* as in b*i*t; *o* as in n*o*; *oi* as in v*oi*d; *u* as in r*u*de.

drama and fruitfulness. According to some authorities the original form of Sidney is from a Phonecian root meaning "charming," or "the enchanter." Sid and Syd are popular pet forms. Sydney is also used as a feminine name.

Hebrew equivalents: Efra'yim, Kar'm'lee, Maksim, Poraws and Puraw. Feminine Hebrew equivalents: Beekuraw, Makseemaw, Neetzaw and Zimraw.

SIEGFRIED
From the Teutonic meaning "victorious peace."

Hebrew equivalents: Avshawlom, N'tzeeach, Shlomo and Yatzleeach. Feminine Hebrew equivalents: Dafnaw, Hadasaw, Shlomis and Shulamis.

SIGMOND, SIGMUND
From the Teutonic meaning "protecting conqueror."

Hebrew equivalents: Avigdor, Chosaw, Shmaryawhu and Yatzleeach. Feminine Hebrew equivalents: Efraws, Mawgaynaw, Shimris and Tzeelaw.

SILAS
The English form of Sylvester. See Sylvester for a full explanation.

SILVESTER
A variant spelling of Sylvester. See Sylvester for a full explanation.

SIMCHA, SIMHA
From the Hebrew meaning "joy, or joyous occasion."

The exact Hebrew equivalent is Simchaw. Simchaw is also used as a feminine Hebrew name. S'maychaw is a variant form of the same name.

SIMEON, SIMON
From the Hebrew meaning "to hear," or "to be heard." In the Bible Simeon is the second son of Jacob and Leah. Simon is a Greek form. Si or Sy as well as Simi, Simie and Simmie are pet forms of Simeon or Simon.

Key: *a* as in f*a*ther; *ai* as in *ai*sle; *aw* as in l*aw*; *ay* as in s*ay*; *e* as in b*e*t;

The exact Hebrew equivalent is Shimon. The exact feminine Hebrew equivalent is Shimonaw.

SIMI, SIMIE, SIMMIE
These are diminutive forms of Simeon and Simon. See above for a full explanation.

SINCLAIR
From the Latin meaning "shining" or "sanctified." Some authorities maintain that it is a contracted form of St. Claire.

Hebrew equivalents: Aharon, Chagai, D'vir, Kawdosh, Ziv, Zerach and Z'rachyaw. Feminine Hebrew equivalents: B'heeraw, M'eeraw, Noga, Zawhawree, Z'horis and Zoheres.

SISI, SISSI
From the Hebrew meaning "my joy."

The exact Hebrew equivalent is Seesee. Feminine Hebrew equivalents: Aleesaw, Aleetzaw, Reenaw, Ronee, Roneeyaw and Seesaw.

SIVAN
Sivan is the ninth month after the Jewish New Year, corresponding to May-June. In the Zodiac its sign is Gemini ("twins").

The exact Hebrew equivalent is Seevawn. The exact feminine Hebrew equivalent is Seevawnaw.

SKELTON
A variant form of Sheldon. See Sheldon for a full explanation.

SOL
Normally, Sol is the diminutive form of Solomon (see below), although it may be taken as a Latin name meaning "sun." Apollo, the sun god, is frequently referred to as Sol.

In addition to Solomon, see Feivel or Phoebus for equivalents.

ee as in b*ee*t; *i* as in b*i*t; *o* as in n*o*; *oi* as in v*oi*d; *u* as in r*u*de.

SOLOMON

From the Hebrew meaning "peace." Solomon, in the Bible, was the son of David. He built the Temple in Jerusalem and was noted for his great wisdom. Sol is a popular short form.

The exact Hebrew equivalent is Shlomo. Feminine Hebrew equivalents: Shlomis and Shulamis.

SPENCER

From the Anglo-Saxon meaning "steward, administrator, or guardian."

Hebrew equivalents: Avdee, Avigdor, Ovayd and Shmaryawhu. Feminine Hebrew equivalents: Efraws, Teeraw, Tzeelaw and Yaakovaw.

STACEY, STACY

From the Latin meaning "firmly established."

Hebrew equivalents: Elyawkum, Konayn, Yawchin and Y'hoyawkim. Feminine Hebrew equivalent: Ameetzaw and Kanaw.

STANFORD

From the Old English meaning "from the stone, or paved ford."

Hebrew equivalents: Acheetzur, Aveetzur, Avneeayl, Eleetzur, Shawmir and Tzur. Feminine Hebrew equivalents: Tzur-ayl, Tzureeyaw and Tzuris.

STANLEY

From the Old English meaning "from the stony field."

Hebrew equivalents: Acheetzur, Aveetzur, Avneeayl, Eleetzur, Shawmir and Tzur. Feminine Hebrew equivalents: Tzur-ayl, Tzureeyaw and Tzuris.

STEFAN, STEPHAN, STEVAN

Russian and Germanic variant forms of Stephen. See below.

STEPHEN

From the Greek meaning "a crown." An old name pop-

Key: *a* as in f*a*ther; *ai* as in *ai*sle; *aw* as in l*aw*; *ay* as in s*ay*; *e* as in b*e*t;

ular among Christian saints and monarchs in various European countries. A variety of names developed from Stephen including, Steven, Stefan, Stephan, Stevan, Steffen, Stefano and Stepka. Surnames like Stevenson and Steffens are derivative forms. Steve and Stevie are popular pet forms.

Hebrew equivalents: Aveemelech, Avrawhawm, Eleemelech, Kasreeayl, Kisron, Malkawm and Melech. Feminine Hebrew equivalents: Atawraw, Ateres, Kleelaw, K'lulaw, Tzfeeraw and Tagaw.

STEVEN
An English variant form of Stephen. See above.

STEWART, STUART
From the Teutonic meaning "an administrator, guardian, or keeper of the estate." Stewart has been a popular name in Scotland for centuries. Stuart is the variant form used in England as well as America. Stu is a popular pet form.

Hebrew equivalents: Avdee, Avigdor, Ovayd and Shmaryaw. Feminine Hebrew equivalents: Efraws, Teeraw, Tzeelaw and Yaakovaw.

SY
A diminutive of either Seymour or Sylvan. See Seymour and Sylvan for a full explanation.

SYLVAN
A variant form of Sylvester. See below.

SYLVESTER
From the Latin meaning "a forest," or "one who dwells in the woods." In Roman mythology Sylvanus was the god of the forest. Silas, Sylvan, Silvester, Silva, Silvan are variant forms and spellings of Sylvester. Si, Sy and Sil are diminutive forms. The girls' name, Sylvia, is a derivative form.

Hebrew equivalents: Karmel, Kar'm'lee and Yaraw. Feminine Hebrew equivalents: Ganaw, Karmelaw and Nawvaw.

ee as in b*ee*t; *i* as in b*i*t; *o* as in n*o*; *oi* as in v*oi*d; *u* as in r*u*de.

SYSHE

From the Yiddish meaning "sweet." Zushe, Zusye and Zisya are variant forms.

Hebrew equivalents: Aveenoam, Magdeeayl, Mawsok, Meged, Naamawn and Nawam. Feminine Hebrew equivalents: Acheenoam, M'sukaw, Naamaw, and Nawawmee.

SUMNER

An Old French-Latin name meaning "one who summons, a messenger."

Hebrew equivalents: Aharon, Kawlayv, Malawchee, M'vasayr and M'vasayr-tov. Feminine Hebrew equivalents: Erelaw and Malawch.

TABBAI

From the Aramaic meaning "good."

The exact Hebrew equivalent is Tabai. Feminine Hebrew equivalents: Tovaw and Tovis.

TAD

A variant pet form of Thaddeus which, in turn, is a form of Timothy, derived from the Greek meaning "to honor or fear God."

Hebrew equivalents: Hadar, Hadarawm, Hadarezer, Hawdur, M'chubawd and Mokeer. Feminine Hebrew equivalents: Hadawr, Hadawris, Haduraw, K'vudaw and Nichbawdaw.

TAL

From the Hebrew meaning "dew or rain." Used as a masculine and feminine form in Israel.

The exact Hebrew equivalent for both masculine and feminine forms is Tal.

TALIA

From the Aramaic meaning "a young lamb." Used also as a feminine name in Israel.

The exact Hebrew equivalent is Talyaw for both masculine and feminine forms.

Key: *a* as in f*a*ther; *ai* as in *ai*sle; *aw* as in l*aw*; *ay* as in s*ay*; *e* as in b*e*t;

TALMAI, TALMI
From the Hebrew meaning either a "furrow" or "a mound." In the Bible, Talmai was king of Geshur, and father-in-law of King David.

The exact Hebrew equivalents are Talmai and Talmee. Feminine Hebrew equivalents: Givonaw, Odayraw, Talmaw and Talmis.

TALMAN, TALMON
Hebraic names derived from the Aramaic meaning "to oppress or injure."

The exact Hebrew equivalent is Talmon. Feminine Hebrew equivalents: Bas-Shua and Bilhaw.

TALOR
From the Hebrew meaning "dew of the morning."

The exact Hebrew equivalent is Talor. Feminine Hebrew equivalents: Aveetal, Taloraw and Talyaw.

TAMIR
From the Hebrew meaning either "a hidden or sacred vessel," or "tall and stately like the palm tree."

The exact Hebrew equivalent is Tawmir. Feminine Hebrew equivalents: Tawmar and Teemoraw.

TATE
From the Anglo-Saxon meaning "to be cheerful."

Hebrew equivalents: Awgil, Chusheeayl, Ditz, Gil, Yachdeeayl and Yawgil. Feminine Hebrew equivalents: Aleezaw, Chedvaw, Deetzaw, Simchonaw and Tzawhawlaw.

TAVI
From the Aramaic meaning "good."

The exact Hebrew equivalent is Tawvee. Feminine Hebrew equivalents: Shapeeraw, Tovaw and Tovis.

TED, TEDDY
Popular diminutive forms of Theodore. See Theodore for a full explanation.

ee as in b*ee*t; *i* as in b*i*t; *o* as in n*o*; *oi* as in v*oi*d; *u* as in r*u*de.

TELEM

A Hebraic name derived from the same Hebrew root as Talmai. See Talmai for a full explanation.

TEMAN, TEMANI

Derived from the Hebrew meaning "right side," and denoting the south. (The south is to the right of a person as he faces east, towards Jerusalem.) Temani, meaning "a man from Teman," is used in Israel, and refers, primarily, to those new settlers who came from Yemen (Teman).

The exact Hebrew equivalents are Taymawn and Taymawnee. Feminine Hebrew equivalent: D'romis.

TERENCE, TERRENCE, TERRY

From the Latin meaning "tender, good, gracious." Terry is a diminutive form.

Hebrew equuivalents: Chawnawn, Naamawn, Tuveeyaw and Yochawnawn. Feminine Hebrew equivalents: Chanaw, Nawawmee, Tovaw and Tzeeyonaw.

THEODOR, THEODORE

From the Greek meaning "divine gift." Theodore has appeared in many forms and many lands over the centuries. In Wales it took the form of Tudor, in Russia, Fyodor, in Spain and Italy Teodoro, in Portugal Theodoro, in Poland Feodore, etc. . . . Ted and Teddy are popular pet forms.

Hebrew equivalents: Elnawsawn, Matanyaw, Matisyawhu, N'sanayl, Y'honawsawn, Yawhawv and Yozawvawd. Feminine Hebrew equivalents: Doronis, Matawnaw, Migdawnaw, N'seenaw, T'shuraw, Z'veedaw, Z'vudaw and Yawhawvaw.

THOMAS

Either from the Hebrew and Aramaic meaning "a twin," or from the Phonecian meaning "sun god," and having the connotation of light, bright. Tom and Tommy are popular short forms. Tami and Tammy are feminine variants.

Hebrew equivalents: Acheenayr, Aharon, Eleeor, May-

Key: *a* as in father; *ai* as in *ai*sle; *aw* as in l*aw*; *ay* as in s*ay*; *e* as in b*e*t;

eer, Seevawn, T'om, Uree, Ureeyaw and Ureeayl. Feminine
Hebrew equivalents: Ameeor, B'heeraw, Oraw, Oris, Orlee,
Seevawnaw and Y'eeraw.

TIBON, TIVON

From the Hebrew meaning "a naturalist, a student of
nature."

The exact Hebrew equivalent is Tivon. The exact feminine Hebrew equivalent is Tivonaw.

TIGER

From the Greek, Latin and Old French meaning "a
tiger." Used in recent times in America.

The exact Hebrew equivalent is Nawmayr. The exact
feminine Hebrew equivalent is N'mayraw.

TIMOTHY

From the Greek meaning "to honor or fear God." Tim,
Timmy and Tad are diminutive forms. Thaddeus is an old
Greek variant.

Hebrew equivalents: Hadar, Hadarawm, Hadarezer,
Hawdur, M'chubawd and Mokeer. Feminine Hebrew equivalents: Haduraw, K'vudaw and Nichbawdaw.

TIMUR

From the Hebrew meaning "tall, stately." Derived from
the word Tamar meaning "a palm tree."

The exact Hebrew equivalent is Teemur. The exact feminine Hebrew equivalent is Teemoraw.

TOBIAH, TOBIAS

From the Hebrew meaning "the Lord is my good." Tobiah is the original form, and Tobias is a Greek adaptation
of the name. Toby is a diminutive form that is extremely
popular in Ireland.

The exact Hebrew equivalent is Tuveeyaw. Feminine
Hebrew equivalents: Bas-tzeeyon, Tovaw, Tovis, Yawtvaw,
and Tzeeyonaw.

---

ee as in b*ee*t; *i* as in b*i*t; *o* as in n*o*; *oi* as in v*oi*d; *u* as in r*u*de.

TOD, TODD
From the Old English meaning "a thicket," or from the Scottish and Norse meaning "a fox."

Hebrew equivalents: Eelawn, Shuawl and Yaaree. Feminine Hebrew equivalents: Eelawnaw and Yaraw.

TOM, TOMMY
Diminutive forms of Thomas. See Thomas for a full explanation.

TONI, TONY
Diminutive forms of Anthony. See Anthony for a full explanation.

TOV, TOVI
From the Hebrew meaning "good." Tovi means "my good." These names are related to Tobiah and Tobias.

The exact Hebrew equivalents are Tov and Tovee. Feminine Hebrew equivalents: Tovaw and Tovis.

TRACEY, TRACY
From the Old French meaning "path or road." It was a popular name in England where it was used for boys and girls.

Hebrew equivalent: Nawsiv. Feminine Hebrew equivalent: N'seevaw.

TYRON, TYRONE
From the Greek meaning "lord or ruler."

Hebrew equivalents: Avrawhawm, Kasreeayl, Malkeerawm, Melech and Yisrawayl. Feminine Hebrew equivalents: Atawraw, B'ulaw, G'veeraw and Sawraw.

TZEVI, TZVI
From the Hebrew meaning "a deer."

The exact Hebrew equivalent is Tz'vee. The exact feminine Hebrew equivalent is Tzivyaw.

URI, URIAH, URIEL
All three are independent names, but of a common root —from the Hebrew meaning "light." Uri means "my light."

Key: *a* as in f*a*ther; *ai* as in *ai*sle; *aw* as in l*aw*; *ay* as in s*ay*; *e* as in b*e*t;

Uriah and Uriel mean "God is my light." Uriah the Hittite, in the Bible, was one of David's warriors whose wife, Bathsheba, later became David's wife. Uriel, according to ancient Jewish legend, was one of the four angels who ministered in God's Presence.

The exact Hebrew equivalents are Uree, Ureeyaw and Ureeayl respectively. Feminine Hebrew equivalents: Ameeor, M'eeraw, N'heeraw, Oraw, Oris, Orlee, Orlis, Tz'feeraw, Ureeaylaw, Uris and Zawhawraw.

VAL

An abbreviated form of the feminine Valentine which is derived from the Latin meaning "strong or healthy." Valentine was popular in the Middle Ages. The masculine form, Val, developed much later.

Hebrew equivalents: Abeer, Abeeree, Awmotz, Gever, La'yish, Uzee and Uzeeyaw. Feminine Hebrew equivalents: Ameetzaw, Azaw, Azeezaw, Chaseenaw, Gavreelaw and Geeboraw.

VERED

From the Hebrew meaning "a rose."

The exact Hebrew equivalent is Vered. The exact feminine Hebrew equivalent is Vardaw.

VIC, VICKIE

Diminutive forms of Victor. See Victor for a full explanation.

VICTOR

From the Latin meaning "victor, conqueror." Vic and Vickie are pet forms.

Hebrew equivalents: Govayr, N'tzeeach and Yatzleeach. Feminine Hebrew equivalents: Atawraw, Ateres, Dafnaw, Dafnis, G'veeraw and Hadasaw.

VINCENT, VINICENT

From the Latin meaning "victor or conqueror." Vin, Vince and Vinnie are pet forms.

---

ee as in be*e*t; *i* as in b*i*t; *o* as in n*o*; *oi* as in v*oi*d; *u* as in r*u*de.

See Victor for masculine and feminine Hebrew equivalents.

VIVIAN, VYVYAN

Used only occasionally as masculine names. See Vivian in feminine section for an explanation.

WAL, WALLIE, WALT, WALLY

Short forms of either Walter or Wallace. See Walter and Wallace for a full explanation.

WALLACE

From the Latin meaning "a foreigner, stranger."

Hebrew equivalents: Gayrshom and Gayrshon. Feminine Hebrew equivalents: Aveeshag, G'rushaw and Hawgawr.

WALLIS

A variant spelling of Wallace. See above for a full explanation.

WALTER

Either a Welsh-Latin name meaning "pilgrim, stranger," or from the Teutonic meaning "ruler, general," or from the Old English meaning "woodmaster, master of the forest."

Hebrew equivalents: Gawlyas, Gayrshon, Chashmon, Malkeeayl, Melech, Yamlaych, Yisrawayl and Yoawv. Feminine Hebrew equivalents: Aveeshag, G'rushaw, Hawgawr, Malkaw, N'deevaw and Sawraw.

WARNER

A variant form of Warren used in England. See Warren below.

WARREN

From the Teutonic meaning "enclosure or park," and having the connotation of protection, or protector. Warner and Werner are variant forms of Warren.

Hebrew equivalents: Chupawm, Geenaw, Karmel, Kar'-m'lee. Feminine Hebrew equivalents: Ganaw, Karmelaw, Mawgaynaw and Teeraw.

Key: *a* as in f*a*ther; *ai* as in *ai*sle; *aw* as in l*aw*; *ay* as in s*ay*; *e* as in b*e*t;

WAYNE
An English variant of the Teutonic Wainwright meaning "a maker of wagons (wains)."

Hebrew equivalent: Eglon. Feminine Hebrew equivalent: Agawlaw.

WENDEL, WENDELL
From the Teutonic meaning "a wanderer, a stranger."

Hebrew equivalents: Gayrshom and Gayrshon. Feminine Hebrew equivalents: Aveeshag, G'rushaw and Hawgawr.

WERNER
A variant form of Warren. See Warren for a full explanation.

WHITNEY
From the Anglo-Saxon meaning "a white palace."

Hebrew equivalents: Armon, Armonee, Beesawn and Lawvawn. Feminine Hebrew equivalents: Armonaw, Beeraw and L'vawnaw.

WILBERT, WILBUR
From the Teutonic meaning "bright resolve."

Hebrew equivalents: Mayeer, Shimshon, Uree and Z'rachyaw. Feminine Hebrew equivalents: M'eeraw, Noga, Zakaw and Zawhawraw.

WILFRED
From the Teutonic meaning "much peace."

Hebrew equivalents: Shabsai, Shawlayv, Shawlom and Shlomo. Feminine Hebrew equivalents: M'nuchaw, M'shulemes, Shlomis and Shulamis.

WILHELM
The German form of William. See below for a full explanation.

WILLIAM
From the Teutonic meaning "a resolute warrior or defender and leader of many." Willie, Willy, Bill, Billie and

ee as in beet; i as in bit; o as in no; oi as in void; u as in rude.

Billy are common pet forms. Wilmot is an English variant, and Wilhelm is a German form.

Hebrew equivalents: Gawd, Kasreeayl, Melech, Rawvaw, Rosh and Yisrawayl. Feminine Hebrew equivalents: Awtzmaw, Malkaw, Tz'feeraw and Yis'r'aylaw.

WILL, WILLIE, WILLY
Popular pet forms of William. See above for a full explanation.

WILLOUGHBY
From the Teutonic meaning "a place by the willows."

Hebrew equivalent: Eelawn. Feminine Hebrew equivalent: Eelawnaw.

WILTON
From the Old English meaning "from the farmstead by the spring."

Hebrew equivalents: Aveeyawm, Aynawn and Peleg. Feminine Hebrew equivalents: D'roraw, Mawrawsaw and Miryawm.

WINSTON
From the Old English meaning "firm friend, or a friend firm like a stone."

Hebrew equivalents: Acheetzur, Avneeayl, Awmis, Noam, Shawmir and Tzur. Feminine Hebrew equivalents: Ameesaw, Dawveedaw, Nawawmee, Tirtzaw and Tzuris.

WINTHROP
From the Teutonic meaning "friendly village."

Hebrew equivalents: Awch, Bildawd, Maydawd, Noam, Rayee and Regem. Feminine Hebrew equivalents: Ahuvaw, Chaveevaw, Dawveedaw, Naamaw and Rus.

WOLF, WOLFE
From the Teutonic meaning "a wolf," and having the connotation of strength.

Hebrew equivalents: Ben-Cha'yil, Binyawmin, Y'chezk'ayl, Z'ayv and Z'ayvee. Feminine Hebrew equivalents: Amtzaw, Areeayl, Gavreelaw and Geeboraw.

Key: *a* as in f*a*ther; *ai* as in *ai*sle; *aw* as in l*aw*; *ay* as in s*ay*; *e* as in b*e*t;

WOOD, WOODY
From the Anglo-Saxon meaning "from the wooded area or forest."

Hebrew equivalents: Eelawn, Karmel and Yaaree. Feminine Hebrew equivalents: Eelawnaw, Karmelaw and Yaraw.

WOODROW
From the Anglo-Saxon meaning "wooded hedge."

Hebrew equivalents: Eelawn, Karmel and Yaaree. Feminine Hebrew equivalents: Eelawnaw, Karmelaw and Yaraw.

XAVIER
From the Arabic meaning "bright." A favorite name throughout the Christian world which became popular in honor of the missionary Saint Francis Xavier.

Hebrew equivalents: Bawheer, Zawhur, Z'haryaw and Zohar. Feminine Hebrew equivalents: B'heeraw, Zawhawraw, Z'heeraw and Z'horis.

YAACOV, YAAKOV
The Hebraic form of Jacob. See Jacob for a full explanation.

YADID
From the Hebrew meaning "beloved," or "friend."

The exact Hebrew equivalent is Yawdid. The exact feminine Hebrew equivalent is Y'deedaw.

YADIN, YADON
From the Hebrew meaning "he will judge." Yadon is a biblical name.

The exact Hebrew equivalents are Yawdin and Yawdon. Feminine Hebrew equivalents: Danyaw, Dawneeaylaw, Dawnis and Nawdin.

YAGEL
From the Hebrew meaning "to reveal, to uncover."

---

ee as in b*ee*t; *i* as in b*i*t; *o* as in n*o*; *oi* as in v*oi*d; *u* as in r*u*de.

The exact Hebrew equivalent is Yawgayl. Feminine Hebrew equivalent: Geelaw.

YAGIL

From the Hebrew meaning "to rejoice."

The exact Hebrew equivalent is Yawgil. Feminine Hebrew equivalents: Geelaw, Geelee, Geeleeyaw, Gilis and Ronlee.

YAKIR

From the Hebrew meaning "dear, beloved, honorable."

The exact Hebrew equivalent is Yakir. Feminine Hebrew equivalents: Ahuvaw, Chaveevaw, Dawveedaw, Leebaw and Y'deedaw.

YALE

From the Teutonic meaning "one who pays or yields."

Hebrew equivalents: Efra'yim, Haymawn, Poraws and Puraw. Feminine Hebrew equivalents: Beekuraw, Poraws, Poreeyaw, T'nuvaw and Zimraw.

YANCY

A corruption of the French word for "Englishman," which later became "Yankee," and was transferred to Americans. Or, Yancy may be a variant form of the Danish Jan, which is a form of John.

Hebrew equivalents: Chawnawn, Chonee, Chonyo and Yochawnawn. Feminine Hebrew equivalents: Chaneesaw, Chanaw and Yochawnaw.

YARKON

From the Hebrew meaning "green." The name of a bird of greenish-yellow color that inhabits Israel in the summertime and migrates to Egypt in the fall. Yarkon is a name used primarily in Israel.

The exact Hebrew equivalent is Yarkon. The exact feminine Hebrew equivalent is Yarkonaw.

Key: *a* as in f*a*ther; *ai* as in *ai*sle; *aw* as in l*aw*; *ay* as in s*ay*; *e* as in b*e*t;

YASHAR, YESHER
From the Hebrew meaning "upright, honest." Yesher is a biblical name, the son of Caleb.

The exact Hebrew equivalents are Yawshawr and Yesher. The exact feminine Hebrew equivalent is Y'shawraw.

YAVIN
From the Hebrew meaning "to understand." In the Bible Yavin (or Jabin, as it is spelled in its English form) was a Canaanite king in the days of Deborah.

The exact Hebrew equivalent is Yawvin. Feminine Hebrew equivalents: Beenaw and Bunaw.

YAVNIEL
From the Hebrew meaning "God will build."

The exact Hebrew equivalent is Yavneeayl. The exact feminine Hebrew equivalent is Bonaw.

YEDIEL
From the Hebrew meaning "knowing the Lord." The name occurs in the Bible several times in a variant form as Yedia-el.

The exact Hebrew equivalent is Y'deeayl. Feminine Hebrew equivalents: Beenaw and Bunaw.

YEHUDA, YEHUDAH
From the Hebrew meaning "praise." The exact English form is Judah. Judah was the fourth son of Jacob and Leah in the Bible, and was the founder of one of the twelve tribes. After the division of King David's dynasty, part of the Jewish nation that lived in the South became known as Judah, and a citizen of Yehuda (or Judah) was called Yehudi. Eventually the northern kingdom consisting of the ten tribes disappeared and all Jews, in subsequent generations, became known by the appelation Yehudi.

The exact Hebrew equivalent is Y'hudaw. The exact feminine Hebrew equivalent is Y'hudis.

---

ee as in b*ee*t; *i* as in b*i*t; *o* as in n*o*; *oi* as in v*oi*d; *u* as in r*u*de.

YEHUDI
From the Hebrew meaning "praise." Although this name appears in the Bible as an officer of King Jehoiakim, it is better known because of its association with the name Yehuda. See Yehuda for more information.

YEHIEL, YEHIELI
From the Hebrew meaning "may God live." Yehiel, which occurs several times in the Bible, was one of King David's chief musicians.

The exact Hebrew equivalents are Y'cheeayl and Y'chee-aylee. The exact feminine Hebrew equivalent is Y'chee-aylaw.

YESHURUN
A poetic appelation used in the Bible to designate the Hebrew nation. Yeshurun means "upright one."

The exact Hebrew equivalent is Y'shurun. Feminine Hebrew equivalents: Y'hudis, Yisr'aylaw and Y'shawraw.

YIGAL
From the Hebrew meaning "he will redeem." The name appears several times in the Bible. Igal is a variant form.

The exact Hebrew equivalent is Yeegal. Feminine Hebrew equivalents: G'alyaw, G'ulaw, P'duyaw, Podaw and Y'gawawlaw.

YIGDAL
From the Hebrew meaning "large," or "to grow."

The exact Hebrew equivalent is Yigdal. Feminine Hebrew equivalents: G'dulaw, Poraw, Poreeyaw, Romaw and Romeeyaw.

YOAV
From the Hebrew meaning "God is father." In the Bible Yoav (English spelling: Joab) was David's sister's son and captain of his army.

The exact Hebrew equivalent is Yoawv. Feminine Hebrew equivalent: Avee, Avee-elaw, Aveeyaw and Eemaw.

Key: *a* as in f*a*ther; *ai* as in *ai*sle; *aw* as in l*aw*; *ay* as in s*ay*; *e* as in b*e*t;

YOEL

The Hebraic name of the prophet Joel, meaning "God is willing."

The exact Hebrew equivalent is Yoayl. The exact feminine Hebrew equivalents are Yo'aylaw and Yo'aylis.

YORA

A biblical name, from the Hebrew meaning "to teach."

The exact Hebrew equivalent is Yoraw. Feminine Hebrew equivalents: Moreeayl, Moreeyaw and Moris.

YORAM

From the Hebrew meaning "God is exalted." This is a biblical name which also appears as Joram and Jehoram.

The exact Hebrew equivalent is Yorawm. Feminine Hebrew equivalents: Asalyaw, Malkaw, Romaw, Romeeyaw and Sawraw.

YUDAN

From the Hebrew meaning "to judge, to be judged."

The exact Hebrew equivalent is Yudawn. Feminine Hebrew equivalents: Danyaw, Dawneeaylaw and Deenaw.

ZACHARIAH, ZACHARY

Variant spellings of Zechariah. See Zechariah for a full explanation.

ZAK

Either a short form of Isaac (see Isaac for an explanation), or a pet form of Zechariah and Zachary (see above).

ZAKKAI

From the Hebrew meaning "pure, clean, innocent." In the Bible Zakkai was the head of a family thaat returned from the Babylonian exile. Zakkai is well known in talmudic literature because of the great scholar Johanan ben Zakkai. Some scholars consider it to be a form of Zechariah.

The exact Hebrew equivalent is Zakai. The exact feminine Hebrew equivalent is Zakaw.

ee as in b*ee*t; *i* as in b*i*t; *o* as in n*o*; *oi* as in v*oi*d; *u* as in r*u*de.

ZAMIR

From the Hebrew meaning "a song" or "a bird" (nightingale). Currently used in Israel.

The exact Hebrew equivalent is Zawmir. The exact feminine Hebrew equivalent is Zimraw.

ZAVDI, ZAVDIEL

From the Hebrew meaning "my gift," or "my gift is God." In the Bible it is the name of the father of one of David's officers.

The exact Hebrew equivalents are Zavdee and Zavdeeayl. Feminine Hebrew equivalent: Z'vudaw.

ZEBULUN, ZEVULUN

From the Hebrew meaning "to exalt, honor," or "a lofty house." In the Bible Zebulun was the sixth son of Jacob and Leah. Zevulun is a variant Hebrew spelling.

The exact Hebrew equivalent is Z'vulun. The exact feminine Hebrew equivalent is Z'vulaw.

ZECHARIAH

From the Hebrew meaning "the memory or the remembrance of the Lord." Zachariah and Zachary are variant forms of Zechariah. The most famous Zechariah was the prophet who lived during the first half of the 6th century B.C.E., during the period of the return of the Babylonian exiles. Another Zechariah was the king of Israel, the son of Jeroboam the second in the 8th century B.C.E.

The exact Hebrew equivalent is Z'charyaw. Feminine Hebrew equivalent: Zichronaw.

ZEDEKIAH

From the Hebrew meaning "God is righteousness." In the Bible Zedekiah was king of Judah from 597 to 586 B.C.E. His original name was Mattaniah, but he adopted the name Zedekiah when he was appointed king by Nebuchadnezzar of Babylonia to succeed the exiled Jehoiakin.

The exact Hebrew equivalents are Tzidkeeyaw and Tzidkeeyawhu. Feminine Hebrew equivalents: Diklaw, Taw-mawr, Tz'dawkaw and Y'shawraw.

ZEHAVI
From the Hebrew meaning "gold." Used as a masculine and feminine name in Israel.

The exact Hebrew equivalent is Zawhawvee. Feminine Hebrew equivalents: Zawhawvaw, Zawhawvee, Zehawvaw, Z'hawvis and Z'huvaw.

ZEKE
A short form of Zechariah meaning "the memory or remembrance of the Lord," or possibly from the Aramaic meaning "a spark," or from the Arabic meaning "a shooting star."

Hebrew equivalents: Orawn, Kochav, Kochvaw, Z'char-yaw and Zik. Feminine Hebrew equivalents: Estayr, Koch-awvaw, Kochawvis, Kocheves and Mazal.

ZELIG
A variant form of Selig. See Selig for a full explanation.

ZEMARIA
From the Hebrew meaning "song, melody of God."

The exact Hebrew equivalent is Z'maryaw. The exact feminine Hebrew equivalent is Zimraw.

ZEMER
From the Hebrew meaning "a song." Currently used in Israel.

The exact Hebrew equivalent is Zemer. The exact feminine Hebrew equivalent is Zimraw.

ZEMIRA
An old biblical name meaning "song, melody."

The exact Hebrew equivalent is Z'meeraw. The exact feminine Hebrew equivalent is Zimraw.

---

ee as in b*ee*t; *i* as in b*i*t; *o* as in n*o*; *oi* as in v*oi*d; *u* as in r*u*de.

ZEPHANIAH

From the Hebrew meaning "God has treasured." Zephaniah was a 7th century prophet, a member of a noble family of Judah.

The exact Hebrew equivalent is Tz'fanyaw or Tz'fanyawhu. Feminine Hebrew equivalents: Otzawraw, Seemaw and S'gulaw.

ZERA, ZEIRA, ZERO

From the Aramaic meaning "small."

The exact Hebrew equivalents are Zayraw and Z'eeraw. Feminine Hebrew equivalents: D'leelaw and K'tanaw.

ZETAN

From the Hebrew meaning "olive tree." In the Bible, Zetan was a member of the tribe of Benjamin.

The exact Hebrew equivalent is Zaysawn. The exact feminine Hebrew equivalent is Zaysawnaw.

ZEV, ZEVI, ZEVIEL

Variant forms of the Hebrew name, Tz'vee, meaning "a deer." Zev also has the meaning of "wolf." Zeviel means "gazelle of the Lord."

The exact Hebrew equivalents are Z'ayv, Tz'vee and Tz'veeayl. The exact feminine Hebrew equivalent is Tzivyaw.

ZEVADIA

From the Hebrew meaning "gift of the Lord," or "God has bestowed." The name appears several times in the Bible.

The exact Hebrew equivalent is Z'vadyaw. The exact feminine Hebrew equivalents are Z'veedaw and Z'vudaw.

ZEVULUN

The original Hebrew spelling for Zebulun. See Zebulun for a full explanation.

Key: *a* as in f*a*ther; *ai* as in *ai*sle; *aw* as in l*aw*; *ay* as in s*ay*; *e* as in b*e*t;

ZIMRAN

Derived from the Hebrew, and similar in meaning to Zimri. In the Bible Zimran was the son of Abraham and Keturah. See Zimri for a full explanation.

ZIMRI

From the Hebrew meaning "mountain-sheep, goat" or "protected, sacred thing," or "my vine, my branch." Used originally as a biblical name. Zimri was a member of the tribe of Simeon.

The exact Hebrew equivalent is Zimree. Feminine Hebrew equivalents: Chosaw, Ganaw, Shimris, Yawayl and Z'heeraw.

ZION

From the Hebrew meaning "excellent" or "a sign." In the Bible Zion is used as the name of a place as well as an appelation for the Hebrew people.

The exact Hebrew equivalent is Tzeeyon. The exact feminine Hebrew equivalent is Tzeeyonaw.

ZIV, ZIVI

From the Hebrew meaning "to shine, brilliance." Ziv is also an early Hebrew synonym for the Hebrew spring-month, Iyar.

The exact Hebrew equivalents are Ziv and Zeevee. Feminine Hebrew equivalents: B'heeraw, M'eeraw, Noga, Oraw, Zawhawraw and Zakaw.

ZOHAR

From the Hebrew meaning "light, brilliance." Used more frequently as a feminine name.

The exact Hebrew equivalent is Zohar. The exact feminine Hebrew equivalents are: Zawhawraw, Zawhawree, Zohar, Zahawraw and Zoheres.

ZVI

A variant spelling of Zevi. See Zevi for a full explanation.

---

ee as in b*ee*t; *i* as in b*i*t; *o* as in n*o*; *oi* as in v*oi*d; *u* as in r*u*de.

Feminine Names

ABBE, ABBEY, ABBY

Popular diminutive forms of Abigail. See Abigail for a full explanation.

ABELA

From the Latin meaning "beautiful."

Hebrew equivalents: Acheenoam, Adeenaw, Rivkaw, Shifraw, Tirtzaw and Yawfis. Masculine Hebrew equivalents: Aveenoam, Chemdawn, Naamawn, Raanawn and Shapir.

AIBA, ABIBI, ABIBICE, ABIBIT

Variant Anglicized spellings of the Hebraic names Aviva, Avivi, Avivice and Avivit. See Aviva for a full explanation.

ABIGAIL

Of Arabic and Hebrew origin meaning "father's joy," or "my father is joy." In the Bible Abigail became the wife of King David after the death of her husband, Nabal. Abbe, Abbey, Abby and Gail are a few of the many pet forms of Abigail.

The exact Hebrew equivalent is Aveega'yil. Masculine Hebrew equivalents: Abaw, Abawhu, Avuyaw, Awgil, Bilgai, Elez, Gil, Geelawn, Geelon, Yachdeeayl, Yawgil and Yitzchawk.

ABIELA, ABIELLA

From the Hebrew meaning "God is my father."

The exact Hebrew equivalent is Aveeaylaw. Masculine Hebrew equivalents: Aveeayl, Aveeyaw, Aveehu, Awvee and Yoawv.

155

ABIRA
From the Hebrew meaning "strong." A popular name in Israel.

The exact Hebrew equivalent is Abeeraw. Masculine Hebrew equivalents: Abeer, Abeeree, Amitz, Aveerawm and Eleerawm.

ABITAL
From the Hebrew meaning "father of dew," or "my father is the dew." In the Bible Abital was a wife of King David. Avital is a variant spelling. In Israel Abital is used as masculine and feminine name.

The exact Hebrew equivalent is Aveetal.

ABRA
A short feminine form of Abraham used in 17th century England where it attained a degree of popularity. See Abraham in masculine section for a full explanation of the name.

ADA
Either from the Teutonic meaning "happy," or from the Latin meaning "of noble birth." In the Bible two persons with the name Ada are mentioned: one was the wife of Lamech; the other was the wife of Esau. The biblical Ada is derived from the Hebrew meaning "an ornament."

Hebrew equivalents: Adeenaw, Awdaw, Malkaw, N'deevaw and Sawraw. Masculine Hebrew equivalents: Ameenawdawv, Avrawhawm, Nawdawv, Yawgayl and Yisrawayl.

ADALINE
From the Teutonic meaning "of noble birth."

Hebrew equivalents: Ne'edawraw, N'deevaw, Sawraw and Yisr'aylaw. Masculine Hebrew equivalents: Adir, Avrawhawm, Awdiv, Ish-Hod, Nawdawv and Y'honawdawv.

ADAMINA
A name coined in 19th century Scotland which is the diminutive form of Adam and was used as a feminine form. See Adam in masculine section a full explanation.

Key: *a* as in f*a*ther; *ai* as in *ai*sle; *aw* as in l*aw*; *ay* as in s*ay*; *e* as in b*e*t;

ADDA, ADDIE
Diminutive forms of Adelaide and Adeline. See below for a full explanation.

ADELAIDE
From the Teutonic meaning "of noble birth." The name was first popularized in Germany in 931 by Queen Adelaide. The name has many variant forms including Adda, Addie, Adelia, Elsie, Helsa, Ilsa, Alisa, Adelina and Adeline.

Hebrew equivalents: Adeenaw Malkaw, Ne'edawraw, N'deevaw, N'seechaw, Sawraw and Yis'r'aylaw. Masculine Hebrew equivalents: Adawr, Adoneeyaw, Ameenawdawv, Aveehud, Cheerawm, Cheerom, Nawdawv and Y'honawdawv.

ADELA, ADELIA, ADELE, ADELLE
These names all popular in Germany, mean "of noble birth." See Adelaide for full information.

ADELINA, ADELINE
Variant forms of Adele and Adelaide. See Adelaide for a full explanation.

ADENA, ADINA
From the Hebrew and Greek meaning, "noble, desired, adorned or voluptuous." It also has the meaning of "delicate."

The exact Hebrew equivalent is Adeenaw. Masculine Hebrew equivalents: Adeeayl, Adoneeyaw, Aveehud, Hadar, Hawdur, Nawdawv, Y'honawdawv and Yochawnawn.

ADERES, ADERET
From the Hebrew meaning "a cape, an outer garment."

The exact Hebrew equivalent is Aderes. Masculine Hebrew equivalent: Shays.

ADIE, ADIELLA
From the Hebrew meaning "ornament." Adiella means "ornament of the Lord." Adie is sometimes used as a pet form of Adele, Adeline or Adelaide.

The exact Hebrew equivalents are Adee and Adeeaylaw. The exact masculine Hebrew form is Adeeayl.

ee as in b*ee*t; *i* as in b*i*t; *o* as in n*o*; *oi* as in v*oi*d; *u* as in r*u*de.

ADIONA, ADONIAH

The feminine form of the Greek Adonis, and meaning "beautiful lady." In the Bible the same name is a masculine form meaning "my Lord is God."

Hebrew equivalents: Adeenaw, Adeevaw, Acheenoam, No'yaw, Yawfaw and Yawfis. Masculine Hebrew equivalents: Adoneeyaw, Adoneeyawhu, Aveenoam, Naamawn, Raanawn, Yawfe and Shefer.

ADIRA

From the Hebrew meaning "mighty, strong."

The exact Hebrew equivalent is Adeeraw. The exact masculine Hebrew form is Adeer.

ADIVA

From the Arabic meaning "gracious, pleasant."

The exact Hebrew equivalent is Adeeva. The exact masculine Hebrew equivalent is Awdiv.

ADORNA

From the Anglo-Saxon meaning "to adorn."

Hebrew equivalents: Adeeayl, Adeenaw, Hawdawraw, Hadawris and Y'hoadawn. Masculine Hebrew equivalents: Adeeayl, Hod, Hodeeyaw, M'udawn and R'malyawhu.

ADRIA, ADRIAN, ADRIENNE

Adrian is a form of Hadrian meaning "rich," and is more popular as a masculine name. Adrienne, a French form of the Greek is at times taken to mean "girl from (the Latin city) Adria."

Hebrew equivalents: Asheeraw, Bas-Shua, N'geedaw and Yisraw. Masculine Hebrew equivalents: Hoseer, Hunaw, Yeeshai and Yisro.

ADVA

From the Aramaic meaning, "a wave, a ripple."

The exact Hebrew equivalent is Advaw. Masculine Hebrew equivalents: Aveeyawm, Aynawn, B'ayree and Moshe.

Key: *a* as in f*a*ther; *ai* as in *ai*sle; *aw* as in l*aw*; *ay* as in s*ay*; *e* as in b*e*t;

AFRA

From the Hebrew meaning "a young female deer."

The exact Hebrew equivalent is Awfraw. The exact Masculine Hebrew equivalent is Ayfer.

AGATHA

From the Greek meaning "good."

Hebrew equivalents: Bas-Tzeeyon, Shifraw, Tovaw and Yawtvaw. Masculine Hebrew equivalents: Acheetuv, Ben-Tzeeyon, Naamawn, Tov, Tuveeyaw and Shapir.

AGNES

From the Greek and Latin meaning "lamb," symbolizing purity and chastity. In the Middle Ages Annis, Annice and Annes were popular forms of Agnes. Inez is a Portuguese variant.

Hebrew equivalents: B'ruraw, Rawchayl, Talyaw, T'lee and Zakaw. Masculine Hebrew equivalents: Ameetai, Amnon, Tzawdok and Yesher.

AHARONA, AHARONICE, AHARONIT

Hebrew variant feminine forms of the masculine Aharon or Aaron. See Aaron for a full explanation.

The exact Hebrew equivalents are Aharonaw and Aharonis. The masculine equivalent is Aharon.

AHAVA, AHUVA

From the Hebrew meaning "love or beloved."

The exact Hebrew equivalents are Ahavaw and Ahuvaw. The exact masculine Hebrew equivalents are Ahuveeyaw and Awhuv.

AHUDA

From the Hebrew meaning "beloved."

The exact Hebrew equivalent is Ahudaw. The exact masculine Hebrew equivalent is Ohad or Ohayd.

AIMEE

Aimee is the French form of the Latin Amy meaning "I love," or "beloved." Amy is a variant spelling.

---

ee as in b*ee*t; *i* as in b*i*t; *o* as in n*o*; *oi* as in v*oi*d; *u* as in r*u*de.

Hebrew equivalents: Ahuvaw, Chaveevaw, Dawveedaw and Y'deedaw. Masculine Hebrew equivalents: Eldawd, Dawvid, Chavivayl, Chovawv and Y'didyaw.

ALBERTA
The feminine form of the masculine Albert. See Albert in masculine section for a full explanation.

ALDA
From the German meaning "rich."

Hebrew equivalents: Asheeraw, N'geedaw and Y'israw. Masculine Hebrew equivalents: Hoseer, Hunaw, Yeeshai and Yisro.

ALDORA
From the Anglo-Saxon meaning "noble gift."

For Hebrew equivalents see Alda.

ALEEZA
From the Hebrew meaning "joy or joyous one." Aliza is a variant spelling.

The exact Hebrew equivalent is Aleezaw. Masculine Hebrew equivalents: Alis, Alitz, Aliz, Eles and Eletz.

ALENE
Either a variant form of Arlene or Eileen. See Arlene and Eileen for a full explanation.

ALETTA
From the Latin meaning "the winged one."

Hebrew equivalents: A'yaw, Dawaw, Da'yaw, Snunis and Tzeeporaw. Masculine Hebrew equivalents: Orayv, Gozawl and Tzeepor.

ALEXANDRA
The feminine form of the Greek Alexander meaning "helper of mankind." Queen Salome Alexandra, ruler of Judea from 76-67 B.C.E., was one of the early, prominent personalities to use this name. Sandra, Alexa and Alexia are common pet forms.

Key: *a* as in f*a*ther; *ai* as in *ai*sle; *aw* as in l*aw*; *ay* as in s*ay*; *e* as in b*e*t;

The exact Hebrew equivalent is Aleksandraw. The exact masculine Hebrew equivalent is Aleksandayr.

ALFREDA
The feminine form of the masculine Alfred meaning "all peace," or "keen counsellor."

Hebrew equivalents: Aleksandraw, Binaw, Bunaw, Shlomis and Shulamis. Masculine Hebrew equivalents: Avshawlom, Eflawl, Shawlom and Shlomo.

ALICE, ALICIA, ALYSE
Alice is of Teutonic origin meaning "noble or noble cheer," although according to some authorities it is of Greek origin meaning "truth." Alicia, Alyse, Alyce, Alissa, Alecia are some of its variant forms and spellings. Alison and Allison are surnames that have evolved from Alice.

Hebrew equivalents: Malkaw, Matawnaw, Masays, Mataws, N'deevaw, N'sanyaw and Sawraw. Masculine Hebrew equivalents: Adawr, Adoneeyaw, Eleenawsawn, Elnawsawn, Elzawvawd, N'sanayl, Yasneeayl and Yisrawayl.

ALINA, ALINE, ALYNA
These names are shortened forms of Adeline. Alina may also be derived from the Celtic meaning "fair, the fair one." See Adeline for a full explanation.

ALISON, ALLISON
Forms of Alice which are also used as surnames. See Alice for a full explanation.

ALISA, ALISSA
Variant forms of Alice. See Alice for a full explanation.

ALIYA, ALIYAH
From the Hebrew meaning "to ascend, to go up."
The exact Hebrew equivalent is Aleeyaw. Masculine Hebrew equivalents: Aharon, Aylee and Yaal.

ALIZA, ALIZAH, ALITZA, ALITZAH
From the Hebrew meaning "joy or joyous one." Aleeza is a variant spelling.

ee as in b*ee*t; *i* as in b*i*t; *o* as in n*o*; *oi* as in v*oi*d; *u* as in r*u*de.

The exact Hebrew equivalent is Aleezaw. Masculine Hebrew equivalents: Alis, Aliz, Alitz, Eles, Eletz, Sawson and Yachdeeayl.

ALLEN, ALLYN
These names are occasionally used as feminine names, but are primarily masculine names. Consult the masculine section for further information.

ALMA
From the Hebrew meaning "young woman, maiden." Also, it may be a derivative of the Latin meaning "fair or kind." In Italian and Spanish Alma means "the soul."

The exact Hebrew equivalent is Almaw. Masculine Hebrew equivalents: Aylawm, Cha'yim, Nawam and Naaman.

ALONA
From the Hebrew meaning "oak tree." It is the feminine form of Alon.

The exact Hebrew equivalent is Alonaw. The exact masculine Hebrew equivalent is Alon.

ALTHEA
From the Greek meaning "the healed" or "healthy, wholesome."

Hebrew equivalents: R'fuaw, Rofee and T'rufaw. Masculine Hebrew equivalents: Awsaw, Marpay, Rawfaw, Rawfu and R'fawayl.

ALUFA, ALUPHA
From the Hebrew meaning "leader, ruler, princess."

The exact Hebrew equivalent is Alufaw. The exact masculine Hebrew equivalent is Aluf.

ALUMA, ALUMICE, ALUMIT
From the Hebrew meaning either "girl, maiden" or "hidden, secret." Alumice and Alumit are variant forms, as is Alma.

The exact Hebrew equivalents are Alumaw and Alumis.

Key: *a* as in f*a*ther; *ai* as in *ai*sle; *aw* as in l*aw*; *ay* as in s*ay*; *e* as in b*e*t;

Masculine Hebrew equivalents: Aylawm, Bawchur, Naarai and Naaryaw.

AMALIA, AMALIAH
From the Hebrew meaning "the work of the Lord," or "industrious."

The exact Hebrew equivalent is Amalyaw. Masculine Hebrew equivalents: Awmayl, Bashaw, Ovayd, and Ovadyaw.

AMALIE
A German variant form of Amelia. See Amelia for a full explanation.

AMANA
From the Hebrew meaning "faithful."

The exact Hebrew equivalent is Amawnaw. Masculine Hebrew equivalents: Ameesawn, Ameetai, Amnon, Haymawn and Neemawn.

AMANDA
From the Latin meaning "to love." Mandy is often used as a pet form.

Hebrew equivalents: Ahadaw, Ahavaw, Ahudaw, Chaveevaw, Cheebaw, and M'labeves. Masculine Hebrew equivalents: Ahuveeyaw, Awhuv, Chovayv, Chubaw and Nilbawv.

AMBER
From the Arabic meaning "amber or brownish-yellow."

Hebrew equivalents: Ofeeraw, Pazaw, Pazeeyaw, Zawhawvaw and Z'hawvis. Masculine Hebrew equivalents: Elefaz, Pawz, Upawz and Zahawvee.

AMELIA
From the Latin meaning "to work, industrious." Amalie is a German variant form and Emily is a popular English version. Millie and Milly are common pet forms.

Hebrew equivalents: Amalyaw, Tirtzaw and Z'reezaw.

ee as in b*ee*t; *i* as in b*i*t; *o* as in n*o*; *oi* as in v*oi*d; *u* as in r*u*de.

Masculine Hebrew equivalents: Arnon, Awmayl, Ovayd, Ovadyaw and Yawziz.

AMINTA
From the Latin meaning "to protect."

Hebrew equivalents: Chasyaw, Chosaw, Mawgaynaw, Shimris, Tzeenaw and Z'heeraw. Masculine Hebrew equivalents: Eleefelet, Eleetzawfawn, Lotawn, Mivtachyawhu, Mivtawch and Tachan.

AMIRA
From the Hebrew meaning "speech, utterance."

The exact Hebrew equivalent is Ameeraw. Masculine Hebrew equivalents: Amaryaw, Awmir, Dovayv, Imree, Niv and Yawniv.

AMISA, AMISSA
From the Hebrew meaning "friend or associate." When used in its variant form, Amita, it also has the meaning of "truth." See below.

The exact Hebrew equivalent is Ameesaw. The exact Masculine Hebrew equivalent is Awmis.

AMITA
From the Hebrew meaning "truth or axiomatic."

The exact Hebrew equivalent is Ameesaw. The exact masculine Hebrew equivalent is Ameetai.

AMIZA, AMITZA
From the Hebrew meaning "strong, courageous."

The exact Hebrew equivalent is Ameetzaw. The exact masculine Hebrew equivalent is Awmotz.

AMY
The American form of the French Aimee. See Aimee for a full explanation.

ANDRA
From the Old Norse meaning "a breath."

Hebrew equivalents: Chavaw and Sh'eefaw. Masculine Hebrew equivalents: Hevel and Terach.

Key: *a* as in f*a*ther; *ai* as in *ai*sle; *aw* as in l*aw*; *ay* as in s*ay*; *e* as in b*e*t;

ANDREA
The feminine form of the Greek Andrew meaning "valiant, strong, courageous."

Hebrew equivalents: Ameetzaw, Amtzaw, Aysawnaw, Azaw and Odaydaw. Masculine Hebrew equivalent: Abeer, Abeeree, Awmotz, Awsneeayl, Chawson, Dawsawn and Uzeeayl.

ANGELA
From the Latin meaning "angel," or from the Greek meaning "messenger." Angie, Angelina, Angeline, Angela and Angelica are forms of Angela.

Hebrew equivalents: Erelaw and Malawch. Masculine Hebrew equivalents: Aharon, Kawlayv, Malawchee and M'vasayr-Tov.

ANN, ANNA, ANNE, ANNETTE, ANNIE, ANITA
All forms of the Hebrew Chanaw (Hannah) meaning "gracious, merciful." Anna is a Hellenized form recorded in the Greek New Testament. It is very commonly coupled with Judith, Barbara and Patricia. Nan, Nance, Nancy, Nanette, Hanita, Hanette, Nanine, Nanna and Nita are but a few of the many variant and pet forms of Ann and Hannah.

The exact Hebrew equivalent is Chanaw. Masculine Hebrew equivalents: Avee-Chayn, Chawnawn, Chonayn, Chonyo, Elchawnawn and Yochawnawn.

ANNABEL
It is generally assumed that Annabel means "Anna the beautiful." Another theory is that it is a variant form of the Latin Amabel meaning "lovable," which may be the origin of Mabel.

Hebrew equivalents: Ahuvaw, Chanaw, Haduraw, Nofeeyaw, Tifawraw and Tiferes. Masculine Hebrew equivalents: Awhuv, Bildawd, Eldawd, Nechmawd, Noy and Shifron.

---

ee as in b*ee*t; *i* as in b*i*t; *o* as in n*o*; *oi* as in v*oi*d; *u* as in r*u*de.

ANTOINETTE, ANTONIA

From the Greek and Latin meaning "of high esteem, revered." Toni and Tonia are pet forms.

Hebrew equivalents: Asalyaw, Ahudaw, Malkaw, Odel'-yaw, Shawvchaw and Tishbawchaw. Masculine Hebrew equivalents: Adoneeyaw, Ameenawdawv, G'dalyaw, Heelayl, M'hulawl and Yishbach.

APHRA

A variant spelling for Afra. See Afra for a full explanation.

ARDITH

A variant Anglo-Saxon form of Edith. See Edith for a full explanation. Some have used this name basing it on a combination of *Ar*thur and E*dith*.

ARDRA

From the Celtic meaning "high, the high one."

Hebrew equivalents: Galee, Galis, Givonaw, M'romaw and Talmaw. Masculine Hebrew equivalents: Awmir, Givon, Mawrom and Talmai.

ARIANA

From the Latin meaning "a song." Ariana was a princess in Greek mythology.

Hebrew equivalents: Mangeenaw, Leeron, N'eemaw, Reenaw and Yawronaw. Masculine Hebrew equivalents: Aharon, Ameerawn, Anaw, Yawron, Zimrawn and Z'mar-yaw.

ARELA, ARELLA

From the Hebrew meaning an "angel or messenger."

The exact Hebrew equivalent is Arelaw. Masculine Hebrew equivalents: Arayl, Araylee, Malawch and Malawchee.

ARIEL, ARIELA, ARIELLA

From the Hebrew meaning "lioness of God," and having the connotation of strength.

The exact Hebrew equivalents are Areeayl and Areeaylaw. Masculine Hebrew equivalents: Arayl, Araylee and Aryay.

ARIZA
From the Hebrew meaning "cedar panels."

The exact Hebrew equivalent is Areezaw. Masculine Hebrew equivalents: Arzee and Erez.

ARLANA
See Arlene and Arline. It may be a form of either name.

ARLENE, ARLEYNE
From the Teutonic or Celtic meaning "a pledge, an oath."

Hebrew equivalents: Bas-Sheva and Eleesheva. Masculine Hebrew equivalent: Sheva.

ARLINE, ARLYNE
From the Teutonic meaning "girl," or a form of Adeline.

Hebrew equivalents: Almaw, B'sulaw, Naaraw and Tz'eeraw. Masculine Hebrew equivalents: Moshe, Naarai, Naaryaw and Nun. See Adeline for additional information.

ARMONA, ARMONICE, ARMONIT
From the Hebrew meaning "a castle, a palace." It also has the meaning, in Hebrew, of "a tree in the oak family."

The exact Hebrew equivalents are Armonaw and Armonis. The exact masculine Hebrew equivalent is Armon.

ARNA
From the Hebrew meaning "a cedar tree."

The exact Hebrew equivalent is Awrnaw. The exact masculine Hebrew equivalent is Oren.

ARNICE, ARNIT
Variant forms of Arna meaning "a cedar tree."

The exact Hebrew equivalent is Arnis. The exact masculine Hebrew equivalent is Oren.

ARNI, ARNINA, ARNICE, ARNINIT
Forms of Arona or Aharona, which are currently used in Israel. They are feminine variants of the masculine name

ee as in b*ee*t; *i* as in b*i*t; *o* as in n*o*; *oi* as in v*oi*d; *u* as in r*u*de.

Aaron. See Aaron in masculine section for a full explanation.

Hebrew equivalents: Arnee, Arneenaw and Arneenis. The exact masculine Hebrew equivalent is Aharon.

ARNOLDINE

A French variant of the Teutonic masculine name, Arnold, meaning "eagle rule," and signifying strength and power. Arnolde is another French form of the same name.

Hebrew equivalents: Abeeraw, Adeeraw, Ameetzaw, Aysawnaw and Odaydaw. Masculine Hebrew equivalents: Abeer, Areeayl, Atzmon, Aysawn, Chaltzon and Uzeeayl.

ARNONA, ARNONICE, ARNONIT

From the Hebrew meaning "a stream or a roaring stream." These names are derived from the masculine Arnon. See Arnon in masculine section for more information.

The exact Hebrew equivalents are Arnonaw and Arnonis. The exact masculine Hebrew equivalent is Arnon.

ARONA

A variant spelling of Aharona which is the feminine form of Aharon or Aaron. See Aharona for a full explanation.

ARVA

From the Danish meaning "the eagle," signifying strength.

Hebrew equivalents: Abeeraw, Adeeraw, Ameetzaw and Aysawnaw. Masculine Hebrew equivalents: Abeer, Areeayl, Atzmon, Aysawn and Sagee.

ARZA

From the Hebrew meaning "cedar beams or panels."

The exact Hebrew equivalent is Arzaw. Masculine Hebrew equivalents: Arzee, Erez and Oren.

Key: *a* as in f*a*ther; *ai* as in *ai*sle; *aw* as in l*aw*; *ay* as in s*ay*; *e* as in b*e*t;

ARZICE, ARZIT
Variant forms of Arza meaning "cedar beams or panels."

The exact Hebrew equivalent is Arzis. Masculine Hebrew equivalents: Arzee, Erez and Oren.

ASHIRA
From the Hebrew meaning "wealthy."

The exact Hebrew equivalent is Asheeraw. Masculine Hebrew equivalents: Hunaw and Yisro.

ASISA
From the Hebrew meaning "juicy, ripe."

The exact Hebrew equivalent is Aseesaw. Masculine Hebrew equivalents: Efra'yim and Puraw.

ASTA
In Greek Asta means "a star," similar to the Persian Esther. See Astera, below for a full explanation.

ASTERA, ASTERIA
Hebraic names used in Israel derived from the Aster flower. In Persian the name Esther means "star." Because of its star-shaped leaves, the Aster flower has been called the "star-flower." Hence, the names Astera and Esther are closely related.

The exact Hebrew equivalent is Estayr. Masculine Hebrew equivalents: Bar-Kochvaw, Kochawv, Kochvaw, Mazawl, Orawn and Zik.

ATARA
From the Hebrew meaning "a crown."

The exact Hebrew equivalent is Atawraw. Masculine Hebrew equivalents: Kasreeayl, Kisron, Melech, Tzofar and Zayraw.

ATERET
From the Hebrew meaning "a crown or covering."

The exact Hebrew equivalent is Ateres. Masculine Hebrew equivalents: Kasreeayl, Kisron, Melech, Tzofar and Zayraw.

---

ee as in b*ee*t; *i* as in b*i*t; *o* as in n*o*; *oi* as in v*oi*d; *u* as in r*u*de.

ATHALIA
From the Hebrew meaning "God is exalted." In the Bible Athaliah was Queen of Judah from 842 to 836 B.C.E., and was the daughter of Ahab and Jezebel.

The exact Hebrew equivalent is Asalyaw. Masculine Hebrew equivalents: Acheerawm, Aylee, Rom, Romaym, Segev, S'guv and Z'vulun.

ATIDA
From the Hebrew meaning "the future."

The exact feminine Hebrew equivalent is Aseedaw.

ATIRA
From the Hebrew meaning "a prayer."

The exact Hebrew equivalent is Ateeraw. Masculine Hebrew equivalents: Eflawl and Pawlawl.

ATURA
From the Hebrew meaning "ornamented, adorned with crown or wreath."

The exact Hebrew equivalent is Aturaw. Masculine Hebrew equivalents: Atir, Awtur, Eter, Melech, M'udawn and Rawvid.

AUDREY
From the Teutonic meaning "noble, noble strength."

Hebrew equivalents: Abeeraw, Areeayl, Malkaw, N'deevaw and N'seechaw. Masculine Hebrew equivalents: Adeer, Adoneeyaw, Awdiv, Cheerom, Y'honawdawv and Y'horawm.

AUGUSTA, AUGUSTINE
From the Latin meaning "revered or sacred." Augustine is a French variant. Gussie is a popular diminutive form.

Hebrew equivalents: Asalyaw, B'ruchaw, Chermonaw and Sawraw. Masculine Hebrew equivalents: Aveerawm, Chermon, G'dalyawhu, Kadish and Yirmeeyahu.

AURELIA
A feminine form of the Latin Aurelius meaning "gold." Oriana is a Celtic variant meaning "golden girl."

Key: *a* as in f*a*ther; *ai* as in *ai*sle; *aw* as in l*aw*; *ay* as in s*ay*; *e* as in b*e*t;

Hebrew equivalents: Ofeeraw, Pazaw, Pazeeyaw, Pazis, Tz'huvaw and Z'huvis. Masculine Hebrew equivalents: Eleefawz, Pawz, Upawz and Zawhawvee.

AURORA
From the Latin meaning "dawn." Zora and Zorica are Slavic variant forms.

Hebrew equivalents: Shachar, Shacharis and Tz'feeraw. Masculine Hebrew equivalents: Ben-Shachar and Shachar-yaw.

AURY
A diminutive form of Aurelia. See Aurelia for a full explanation.

AVA
From the Latin meaning "a bird." According to some authorities it is a variant form of the German Eva.

Hebrew equivalents: A'yaw, Chaseedaw, D'roraw, Tzee-poraw and Yawayn. Masculine Hebrew equivalents: Gozawl, Orayv and Tzeepor.

AVELINE
From the French meaning "hazel nut." See Hazel for a full explanation.

AVI
From the Hebrew meaning "my father," or "my lord." Used as masculine and feminine name.

The exact Hebrew equivalent is Awvee.

AVIELLA
A variant spelling of Abiela. See Abiela for a full explanation.

AVIRICE, AVIRIT
From the Hebrew meaning "air, atmosphere."

The exact Hebrew equivalent is Aveeris. Masculine Hebrew equivalents: Hevel and Or-Cha'yim.

---

ee as in b*ee*t; *i* as in b*i*t; *o* as in n*o*; *oi* as in v*oi*d; *u* as in r*u*de.

AVIS

An Old Germanic name meaning "refuge in war," or "fortress." It may also be derived from the Latin meaning "bird."

Hebrew equivalents: Armonaw, Migdawlaw, M'tzawdaw and Tzeenaw. Masculine Hebrew equivalents: Armonee, Betzer, Beetzawron, Mivtawch, Luz and Yosheeyaw.

AVITAL

A variant spelling of Abital. See Abital for a full explanation.

AVIVA, AVIVAH

From the Hebrew meaning "springtime," and connoting youthfulness, freshness.

The exact Hebrew equivalent is Aveevaw. The exact masculine Hebrew equivalent is Awviv.

AVIVI, AVIVICE, AVIVIT

From the Hebrew meaning "spring-like." These forms are related to Aviva.

The exact Hebrew equivalents are Aveevee and Aveevis. The exact masculine Hebrew equivalent is Awviv.

AVUKA, AVUKAH

From the Hebrew meaning "torch, flame."

The exact Hebrew equivalent is Avukaw. Masculine Hebrew equivalents: Lapid, Lapeedos, Nur, Nuree, Nureeyaw, Nureeayl, Ud and Udee.

AYALA, AYALAH

From the Hebrew meaning "a deer a gazelle."

The exact Hebrew equivalent is A'yawlaw. Masculine Hebrew equivalents: A'yawl, A'yawlon, Tzivyon, Tz'vee and Tz'veeayl.

AYELET

From the Hebrew meaning "a deer, a gazelle."

The exact Hebrew equivalent is A'yeles. Masculine Hebrew equivalents: A'yawl, A'yawlon, Tzivyon, Tz'vee, and Tz'veeayl.

Key: *a* as in f*a*ther; *ai* as in *ai*sle; *aw* as in l*aw*; *ay* as in s*ay*; *e* as in b*e*t;

AYLA
From the Hebrew meaning "a terebinth tree or an oak tree."

The exact Hebrew equivalent is Aylaw. The exact masculine Hebrew equivalent is Alon.

AZA
From the Hebrew meaning "strong."

The exact Hebrew equivalent is Azaw. Masculine Hebrew equivalents: Az, Azai, Azawn, Oz, Uzee and Uzeeyaw.

AZIZA, AZIZAH
From the Hebrew meaning "strong."

The exact Hebrew equivalent is Azeezaw. Masculine Hebrew equivalents: Az, Azai, Azawn, Oz, Uzee, Uzeeayl and Uzeeyaw.

BAB, BABS, BABETTE
Bab and Babs are short forms of Babette which, in turn, is a diminutive form of Barbara. See Barbara for a full explanation.

BAILA, BAYLE, BEYLAH
These names are either variant Yiddish forms of the Hebrew Bilhaw (Bilhah) meaning "troubled, weak, old," or they are derived from the Slavic meaning "white."

Hebrew equivalents: Bilhaw, Layaw, L'vawnaw, Tz'choraw, Tz'choris, Y'sheeshaw and Z'kaynaw. Masculine Hebrew equivalents: Altayr, Gawlyas, Gayrshon, Kedem, Sawvaw, Yawshish and Y'sheeshai.

BALFOURIA
The feminine form of the masculine Balfour. Balfour was created as a name in honor of Lord Arthur James Balfour, the British statesman and philosopher (1848-1930) who, as Foreign Secretary of England, issued the Balfour Declaration paving the way for the establishment of the State of Israel. Balfour and Balfouria are names used primarily in Israel.

---

ee as in b*ee*t; *i* as in b*i*t; *o* as in n*o*; *oi* as in v*oi*d; *u* as in r*u*de.

The exact Hebrew equivalent is Balfureeyaw. The exact masculine Hebrew equivalent is Balfur.

BAMBI
The diminutive form of the Italian Bambalina meaning "boy."

Hebrew equivalents: Alumaw, Alumis, Bas-Tzeeyon and Reevaw. Masculine Hebrew equivalents: Ben, Ben-Tzeeyon, Naarai and Naaryaw.

BARA
From the Hebrew meaning "to choose."

The exact Hebrew equivalent is Bawraw. Masculine Hebrew equivalents: Bawchir, Bochayr, Nivchawr and Yivchawr.

BARBARA
From the Greek meaning "strange or stranger." The ancient Greeks applied the term "barbaros" to all strangers. Babs, Bab, Babette, Bobs, Bobbi and Bobby are common pet forms.

Hebrew equivalents: Aveeshag and Hawgawr. Masculine Hebrew equivalents: Gawlyas, Gayrshom, Gayrshon and Z'rubawvel.

BARI, BARRIE
A feminine form of the masculine Barrie. See Barrie in masculine section for a full explanation.

BATHSHEBA, BATSHEVA
Batsheva is the modern Israeli form of Bathsheba which is derived from the Hebrew meaning "daughter of an oath." In the Bible Bathsheba was the wife of King David. In order to marry her, David planned the death of her husband Uriah the Hittite by sending him off to the battle-front. The prophet, Nathan, rebuked David severely for this offense. Solomon, who later became king, was the second son of David and Bathsheba.

The exact Hebrew equivalent is Bas-Sheva or Batsheva,

Key: *a* as in f*a*ther; *ai* as in *ai*sle; *aw* as in l*aw*; *ay* as in s*ay*; *e* as in b*e*t;

according to Sephardic pronunciation. Masculine Hebrew equivalents: Amaryaw, Aylaw and Sheva.

BATHSHUA, BATSHUA
A biblical name generally taken as a variant spelling of Bas-Sheva (Bathsheba), or meaning either "daughter of opulence, rich, noble," or "daughter of crying, woe." In the Bible (I Chronicles 3:5) Bathshua is referred to as the wife of King David and the mother of King Solomon. It is, therefore, probable that Bathshua is a variant spelling of Bathsheba. Batshua is the Sephardic pronunciation of Bathshua.

The exact Hebrew equivalent is Bas-Shua. Masculine Hebrew equivalents: Eeyov, Hunaw, Shua and Yisro.

BATYA, BASYA
From the Hebrew meaning "daughter of God." In the Bible, Bitya (English spelling: Bithia) was a daughter of Pharaoh who married Mered, a member of the tribe of Judah. Batya is a modern Sephardic pronunciation.

The exact Hebrew equivalent is Basyaw. Masculine Hebrew equivalents: Ben-Tzeeyon, Binyawmin and Moshe.

BEATRICE
From the Latin meaning "a blessing." In its earliest form the name was Beatrix. Bea, Beatie, Beatty, Trix and Trixie are some of its diminutive forms.

Hebrew equivalents: Awshraw, B'rawchaw and B'ruchaw. Masculine Hebrew equivalents: Awshayr, Bawruch, B'rachya, B'rechyaw, Gadeeayl, M'vorawch and Y'vorawch.

BECKIE, BECKY
Popular pet forms of Rebecca. See Rebecca for a full explanation.

BEHIRA
From the Hebrew meaning "light, clear, brilliance."

The exact Hebrew equivalent is B'heeraw. Masculine Hebrew equivalents: Barkai, Bawhir, Bawrawk, Bawrekes, Nayreeyaw, Pekach and Shragaw.

ee as in b*ee*t; *i* as in b*i*t; *o* as in n*o*; *oi* as in v*oi*d; *u* as in r*u*de.

BELA, BELLA, BELLE

Either a form of Isabella meaning "God's oath," or from the Hungarian meaning "nobly bright," or from the Latin meaning "beautiful one." Belle is a French form.

Hebrew equivalents: Acheenoam, B'heeraw, Eleesheva, M'eeraw, Rivkaw and Shifraw. Masculine Hebrew equivalents: Aveenoam, Bawhir, Bawrawk, Mayeer and Ureeayl.

BELINDA

An Old Germanic name derived from the Latin meaning "beautiful serpent," having the connotation of wise, shrewd. Snakes were once regarded as sacred animals.

Hebrew equivalents: Beenaw, Bunaw, Rivkaw and Yawfaw. Masculine Hebrew equivalents: Achbawn, Chemdawn, Yawvin and Y'utz.

BENEDICTA

A feminine form derived from the masculine Benedict meaning "blessed," in the Latin. Dixie is sometimes used as a pet form.

Hebrew equivalents: Ashayraw, B'rawchaw and B'ruchaw. Masculine Hebrew equivalents: Awshayr, Bawruch, B'rachyaw and B'rechyaw.

BENJAMINA

A modern variant form of Benjamin used in Israel. See Benjamin in masculine section for a full explanation.

The exact Hebrew equivalent is Binyawmeenaw. The exact masculine Hebrew equivalent is Binyawmin.

BERENICE, BERNICE, BERNITA

Bernice, the most common of the three names, is a telescoped form of Berenince meaning "bringer of victory," in the Greek. Bernita and Bunny are diminutive forms.

Hebrew equivalents: Dafnaw, Dafnis, Hadasaw, Nitzchaw and Nitzcheeyaw. Masculine Hebrew equivalents: Govayr, N'tzeeach and Yatzleeach.

Key: *a* as in father; *ai* as in aisle; *aw* as in law; *ay* as in say; *e* as in bet;

BERTHA, BERTA

From the Teutonic meaning "bright," or "beautiful," or "famous." Bert, Bertie, and Birdie are diminutive forms. Berta is a variant spelling.

Hebrew equivalents: B'heeraw, M'eeraw, Zakaw and Zawhawraw. Masculine Hebrew equivalents: Aveenoam, Avnayr, Bawhir, Naamawn, Raanawn and Shevach.

BERURA, BERURIA

From the Hebrew meaning "pure, clean." In Aramaic the same word means "pious, kind, honest," and in Assyrian it has the meaning of "shining." Beruria was the saintly and scholarly wife of the talmudic scholar Rabbi Meir who lived in the second century. She is the only woman mentioned in the Talmud who participated in legal discussions. Berura is a modern name used in Israel.

The exact Hebrew equivalents are B'ruraw and B'ruryaw. Masculine Hebrew equivalents: Bawrur, Tzach, Tzachai and Zakai.

BERYL, BERYLLA

From the Greek and also the Sanskrit meaning "a precious stone." In Persian and Arabic the meaning is "crystal or crystal clear." Berylla is a variant spelling. Beryl is also used as a masculine name.

Hebrew equivalents: Awdaw, Bahat, Margawlis, Pit'-daw, Tarsheeshaw and Yakeeraw. Masculine Hebrew equivalents: Bahawt, Leshem, Nofach, Sapir, Shoham and Yahalom.

BESS, BESSIE

Short, popular form of Elizabeth. See Elizabeth for a full explanation.

BETH, BETSEY, BETSY

Beth is a short form of Elizabeth. Betsey and Betsy are forms of Beth. See Elizabeth for a full explanation. According to some authorities Beth is a short form of Bethia. See below.

ee as in b*ee*t; *i* as in b*i*t; *o* as in n*o*; *oi* as in v*oi*d; *u* as in r*u*de.

BETHIA
The English form of Batya. See Batya for a full explanation.

BETTE, BETTY
These names are diminutive forms of Beth and Elizabeth. See Elizabeth for a full explanation.

BETULA
From the Hebrew meaning "maiden, girl."
The exact Hebrew equivalent is B'sulaw. Masculine Hebrew equivalents: Bawchur, Naarai and Naaryaw.

BEULAH
From the Hebrew meaning "married," or "ruled over."
The exact Hebrew equivalent is B'ulaw. Masculine Hebrew equivalents: Aveemelech, Baal, Rav and Rabaw.

BEVERLEY, BEVERLY
Used as masculine as well as feminine names. Derived from the Old English meaning "a field, a meadow."
Hebrew equivalents: Ganaw, Karmelaw, Nawvaw and Nirayl. Masculine Hebrew equivalents: Karmel, Karm'lee, Yaaree and Zimree.

BILHAH
The maid-servant of Jacob's wife, Rachel, in the Bible. Bilhah was the mother of Dan and Naphtali. From the Hebrew meaning "weak, troubled, old."
The exact Hebrew equivalent is Bilhaw. Masculine Hebrew equivalents: Eeyov, Kaydmaw, Yiftawch and Zawkayn.

BINA, BUNA
Hebraic names meaning "understanding, intelligence, wisdom."
Exact Hebrew equivalents are Beenaw and Bunaw. Exact masculine Hebrew equivalents: Beenaw and Bunaw (which are masculine as well as feminine names) and Achbawn, Utz, Yawvin and Y'utz.

Key: *a* as in f*a*ther; *ai* as in *ai*sle; *aw* as in l*aw*; *ay* as in s*ay*; *e* as in b*e*t;

BIRA
From the Hebrew meaning "fortress, capital."
The exact Hebrew equivalent is Beeraw. Masculine Hebrew equivalents: Armon, and Armonee.

BIRD, BYRD, BIRDIE, BYRDIE
From the English meaning "a bird." These names have also been used as diminutive forms of Bertha.
Hebrew equivalents: A'yaw, Efronaw, Snunis, Tzeepawrtaw, Tzeeporah, Tzifreeyaw and Yawayn. Masculine Hebrew equivalents: Gozawl, Orayv and Tzeepor.

BLANCHE
Either from the Italian and French meaning "white, fair," or of Late Latin origin meaning "pure, unsullied."
Hebrew equivalents: L'vawnaw, Nawawmee, Yawfaw, Zakaw and Zawhawraw. Masculine Hebrew equivalents: Chemdawn, Lawvawn, Livnee, Raanawn and Zakai.

BLOSSOM
From Old English meaning "a blooming flower."
Hebrew equivalents: Neeris, Neetzaw, Ofris, Perach, Pircheeyaw, Pirchis, Shoshanaw, Tifrachas, Tifrawchaw and Y'neekaw. Masculine Hebrew equivalents: Efra'yim, Neetzawn, Perach, P'rachyaw, Puraw, Savyon and Shoshan.

BLUMA
An anglicized Yiddish name meaning "flower," derived from the German.
See Blosson for Hebrew equivalents.

BOB, BOBBIE, BOBBY
See Barbara and Roberta, of which these are diminutive forms.

BONA
From the Hebrew meaning "a builder."
The exact Hebrew equivalent is Bonaw. Masculine Hebrew equivalents: B'nawyaw, B'nawyawhu and Yavneeayl.

ee as in beet; i as in bit; o as in no; oi as in void; u as in rude.

BONITA, BONNIE, BONNY

From the Latin and Gaelic meaning "good," or "pretty."

Hebrew equivalents: Naamaw, Nawawmee, Nofeeyaw, Tovaw, Yawfaw and Yawtvaw. Masculine Hebrew equivalents: Acheetuv, Ben-Tzeeyon, Naamawn, Nawam, Shefer, Shifron and Tuveeyaw.

BRENDA

From the Celtic meaning "dark-haired."

Hebrew equivalents: Ayfaw, Chacheelaw, Dalaw, D'leelaw and Tzeelaw. Masculine Hebrew equivalents: Adawr, Ayfai, Kaydawr, Kush and Pinchaws.

BRIAN, BRINE, BRINY

From the Celtic or Gaelic meaning "strength," or "nobly-born," or "one who is eloquent." Also used as masculine names.

Hebrew equivalents: Abeeraw, Gavreelaw, Geeboraw, Sawraw, and Yis'r'aylaw. Masculine Hebrew equivalents: Abeer, Awsneeayl, Barzeelai, Ben-Cha'yil, Gavreeayl and Yisrawayl.

BRIDGET, BRIDGIT, BRIGIT

From the Celtic meaning "strength." Bridget and its various forms are very popular in Ireland and their usage has spread to other countries.

Hebrew equivalents: Abeeraw, Adeeraw, Ameetzaw, Gavreelaw, Geeboraw and Uzis. Masculine Hebrew equivalents: Abeer, Abeeree, Barzeelai, Ben-Cha'yil, Binyawmin, Gever, Noawz and Uzeeyaw.

CAASI, CASY, CASSIE

A diminutive form of Catherine. See Catherine for a full explanation.

CAMILLA, CAMILLE

From the Latin meaning "a servant or a helper at a sacrifice."

Hebrew equivalents: Aleksandraw, Ezraw, Ezr'aylaw

Key: *a* as in *father*; *ai* as in *aisle*; *aw* as in *law*; *ay* as in *say*; *e* as in *bet*;

and Ezreeaylaw. Masculine Hebrew equivalents: Eved, Ezraw, Malawchee, Ovayd and Ovadyaw.

CANDACE, CANDICE, CANDIDA, CANDIDE, CANDY

From the Greek meaning "the fire-white or incandescent," or from the Latin meaning "pure, unsullied." Candy is a diminutive form which is gaining in popularity. Candide is a French form.

Hebrew equivalents: Avukaw, L'vawnaw, Oraw, Shalheves, Udeeyaw, Uris and Zakaw. Masculine Hebrew equivalents: Amee-Zakai, Bawrur, Lapeedos, Lawvawn, Nuree, Tzach, Tzachai, Ud, Uree and Zakai.

CARA, CARLA, CARLOTTA

See Caroline, of which these are shortened forms.

CAREN, CARON

Also spelled Karen. See Catherine, of which these are short forms.

CARMA, CARMEL, CARMELA, CARMELIT, CARMEN, CARMIA, CARMIELA, CARMINE, CARMIS, CARMIT, CARMIYA

Either of Hebrew origin meaning "vineyard, park," or from the Arabic meaning "field of fruit." Carmen is the Spanish form of Carmel, while Carmine is an Italian form. Carmia, Carmiya and Carmiela mean "vineyard of the Lord." Each of these names is also spelled with a "K."

Hebrew equivalents: Karmaw, Karmeeyaw, Karmelaw, Karmis, Nureesaw. Masculine Hebrew equivalents: Karmee, Karmeeayl, Karmel, Karmelis, Karm'lee and Kerem.

CARNA, CARNIS, CARNIT

From the Hebrew meaning "horn." These names, also spelled with a "K," symbolize "strength."

The exact Hebrew equivalents are Karnaw, and Karnis. Masculine Hebrew equivalents: Keren and Karneeayl.

ee as in b*ee*t; *i* as in b*i*t; *o* as in n*o*; *oi* as in v*oi*d; *u* as in r*u*de.

CARNIELA, CARNIELLA
From the Hebrew meaning "the horn of the Lord." These names, also spelled with a "K," are forms of Carna.

The exact Hebrew equivalent is Karneeaylaw. Masculine Hebrew equivalents: Keren and Karneeayl.

CAROL, CAROLA, CAROLE
Either from the Gaelic meaning "melody, song," or diminutive forms of Caroline.

Hebrew equivalents: Reenaw, Sheeraw, T'heelaw and Yawronaw. Masculine Hebrew equivalents: Aharon, Anaw, Ronayn, Ronlee and Yawron. See Caroline for additional equivalents.

CAROLINE, CAROLINA, CAROLYN, CARRIE, CARROLL, CARRY, CARY, CARYL
Caroline, like few other names, has given rise to a variety of shortened forms and diminutives. It is of Teutonic origin meaning "valiant, virile, strong." The original form of these names is the Latin Carl.

Hebrew equivalents: Amtzaw, Areeayl, Awtzmaw, Gavreelaw and Geeboraw. Masculine Hebrew equivalents: Aveecha'yil, Barzeelai, Chizkeeyaw, Kawlayv and Y'chezkayl.

CATHERINE, CATHLEEN, CATHY
Cathleen and Cathy are forms of Catherine meaning "pure, purity," in Greek, and having the connotation of righteous, truthful. Katherine is a variant spelling for Catherine.

Hebrew equivalents: B'ruraw, Diklaw, Rawchayl, Tawmawr and Zakaw. Masculine Hebrew equivalents: Ameetai, Amnon, Eetawmawr, Konanyawhu, Yesher and Y'shurun.

CECELIA, CECILE, CECILLE, CECILY
From the Latin meaning "blind," or "dim-sighted." The original form is Cecil, used primarily as a masculine name. In ancient Rome there was a famous family named Caecilii whose founder was said to have been blind. Ciss and Cissy are pet forms.

Key: *a* as in *father*; *ai* as in *aisle*; *aw* as in *law*; *ay* as in *say*; *e* as in *bet*;

Hebrew euphemistic equivalents: M'eeraw, Noga, Oraw and Zawharaw. Based upon the biblical narrative Layaw would also be an appropriate equivalent. Masculine euphemistic Hebrew equivalents: Koresh, Mayeer, Shimshon, Ureeayl and Zerach.

CELESTE
From the Latin meaning "heavenly."

Hebrew equivalents: Estayr, Kochawvaw, Kochawvis, Kocheves and L'vawnaw. Hebrew masculine equivalents: Bar-Kochvaw, Kochawv, Kochvaw and Shimshon.

CELIA, CELE
Either a form of Cecilia (see above), or from the Latin meaning "heavens, heavenly."

Hebrew equivalents: Estayr, Kochawvaw, Kochawvis and L'vawnaw. Masculine Hebrew equivalents: Bar-Kochvaw, Kochawv, Kochvaw and Shimshon. See Cecilia for additional equivalents.

CHANA, CHANAH
Hebraic forms of Hana or Hannah. See Hannah for a full explanation.

CHARITY
From the Latin meaning "love, affection."

Hebrew equivalents: Ahuvaw, Chaveevaw, Dawveedaw, Tz'dawkaw and Y'deedaw. Masculine Hebrew equivalents: Bildawd, Chovawv, Dawvid, Tzadik, Tzadkeeayl, Tzawdok, Tzidkeeyaw and Tzidkeeyawhu.

CHARLENE, CHARLET, CHARLOT, CHARLOTTE
Variant forms of Caroline derived from the Teutonic meaning "strong, valiant." Hebrew equivalents: Azaw, Azeezaw, Gavreelaw, Geeboraw and Uzis. Masculine Hebrew equivalents: Az, Gavreeayl, Geebor, Gever, G'varawm, G'varyaw and Uzee.

CHAYA
From the Hebrew meaning "life, living."

ee as in be*e*t; *i* as in b*i*t; *o* as in 'n*o*; *oi* as in v*oi*d; *u* as in r*u*de.

The exact Hebrew equivalent is Chayaw. The exact masculine Hebrew equivalent is Cha'yim.

CHERI, CHERIE, CHERYL

From the French meaning "dear, beloved, sweetheart." Cheryl is also a variant spelling of Sheryl. See Sheryl.

Hebrew equivalents: Ahuvaw, Chaveevaw, Cheebaw and Y'deedaw. Masculine Hebrew equivalents: Eldawd, Bildawd, Chovawv and Y'didyaw.

CHESNA

A Slavic name meaning "peaceful."

Hebrew equivalents: M'shulemes, Shlomis and Shulamis. Masculine Hebrew equivalents: Ish-Shawlom, Shabsai, Shlomee and Shlomo.

CHRISTINA, CHRISTINE

A purely Christian name derived from Christ, meaning "anoint, or the anointed one" in Greek.

CINDY

Usually used as a diminutive form of Cynthia. See Cynthia for a full explanation.

CISS, CISSY

See Cecelia of which these are diminutives.

CIVIA

A form of the Hebrew Tzivyaw, meaning "deer," and having the connotation of swiftness.

The exact Hebrew equivalent is Tzivyaw. Masculine Hebrew equivalents: Awfree, Ayfer, Efron, Tzivyon, Tz'vee and Tz'veeayl.

CLAIRE, CLARA, CLARABELLA, CLARABELLE, CLARE, CLARISSE

From the Latin meaning "fair, bright, clear." Clare is used occasionally as a masculine name. Clarice and Clarette are French forms.

Hebrew equivalents: B'heeraw, M'eeraw, Noga and

Key: *a* as in f*a*ther; *ai* as in *ai*sle; *aw* as in l*aw*; *ay* as in s*ay*; *e* as in b*e*t;

Zakaw. Masculine Hebrew equivalents: Bawrawk, Koresh, Nayreeyaw, Shimshon and Z'rachyaw.

CLAUDETTE, CLAUDIA, CLAUDINE
From the Latin meaning "lame." A euphemistic interpretation would give these names the connotation of "swiftness." Claude is the masculine form of these names. In Wales, Gladys is considered the Welsh form of Claudia. Claudette and Claudine are French pet forms of Claudia.

Hebrew equivalents: Awfraw, A'yeles, M'heeraw and Tzivyaw. Masculine Hebrew equivalents: Ayfer, Boaz, Gidon, Maharee, Mahayr, Mawhir, Pawsayach and Tz'vee.

CLEMENTINE
From the Latin meaning "merciful." The masculine form is Clement.

Hebrew equivalents: Chanaw, Chaneesaw, Chanunaw and Ruchawmaw. Masculine Hebrew equivalents: Ben-Chesed, Rachmeeayl, Y'rachmeeayl, Y'rochawm and Y'ruchawm.

CONNIE, CONSTANCE
Connie is a diminutive of Constance meaning "constant, firm, faithful," in the Latin.

Hebrew equivalents: Bitchaw, Emunaw, Tamaw and T'meemaw. Masculine Hebrew equivalents: Ameetai, Amnon, Haymawn, Konanyawhu and Nawchon.

CORA, CORI, CORINNE, CORINNA
From the Greek meaning "maiden." Cora may also be a form of Corey. See below.

Hebrew equivalents: Almaw, Alumaw, B'sulaw, Naaraw and Tz'eeraw. Masculine Hebrew equivalents: Bawchur, Naarai and Naaryaw.

COREY, CORIE, CORREY, CORRIE, CORRY, CORY
From the Gaelic meaning "a ravine, a deep hollow."

Hebrew equivalents: Bik'aw and B'rawchaw. Masculine Hebrew equivalents: Gai and Gaychazee.

---

ee as in b*ee*t; *i* as in b*i*t; *o* as in n*o*; *oi* as in v*oi*d; *u* as in r*u*de.

CORINNE
From the Greek meaning "a humming bird." Corinne may also be a variant form of Corey or Cory. See above.

CORNELIA
The feminine form of Cornelius. See Cornelius in the masculine section for a full explanation.

Hebrew equivalents: Chaseedaw, Chawglaw and Tzeeporaw. Masculine Hebrew equivalents: Orayv and Tzeepor.

CYMA
From the Greek meaning "sprout, grow, flourish."

Hebrew equivalents: Karmel, Neetzaw, Shoshanaw and Vardaw. Masculine Hebrew equivalents: Efra'yim, Pekach, P'rachyaw and Tzemach.

CYNTHIA
The Greek goddess of the moon which is also known as Phoebe. Cindy and Sindy are diminutive forms.

Hebrew equivalents: Chodesh, L'vawnaw, M'eeraw, Oraw, Saharaw and Zakaw. Masculine Hebrew equivalents: Mayeer, Nayreeyaw, Shragaw, Yerach and Z'rachyaw.

DAFNA, DAFNE, DAFNICE, DAFNIT
Variant spellings and forms of the Greek Daphne. See Daphne for a full explanation.

DAGANIA, DAGANYA
From the Hebrew meaning "corn, or the grain of cereals." Dagan is the masculine form of the name.

The exact Hebrew equivalent is D'gawneeyaw. The exact masculine Hebrew equivalent is Dawgawn.

DAGMAR
From the Danish meaning "the glory of the Danes."
There are no Hebrew equivalents.

DAHLIA
A variant spelling for Dalia. See Dalia for a full explanation.

Key: *a* as in f*a*ther; *ai* as in *ai*sle; *aw* as in l*aw*; *ay* as in s*ay*; *e* as in b*e*t;

DAISY

Usually taken as a nickname for Margaret and derived from St. Margherita of Italy who took the daisy (flower) as her symbol. Daisy may also be a derivative of the Anglo-Saxon meaning "day's eye," symbolic of the dawn.

Hebrew equivalents: B'heeraw, M'eeraw, Noga, Oraw, Shachareeyaw, Shacharis and Zawhawraw. Masculine Hebrew equivalents: Ben-Shachar, Avnayr, Mayeer, Shachar, Shimshon, Zerach and Z'rachyaw.

DALE

This name is more commonly used as a masculine name. From the Anglo-Saxon meaning "a dweller in a vale between hills."

Hebrew equivalents: Bik'aw, Galyaw, Talmis and Teemoraw. Masculine Hebrew equivalents: Gai, Gaychazee, Givon and Talmai.

DALIA

From the Hebrew meaning either "a branch, a bough," or "to draw water."

The exact Hebrew equivalent is Dalyaw or Daleeyaw. Masculine Hebrew equivalents: Moshe, Naytzer and Sawrig.

DALICE, DALIT

From the Hebrew meaning either "to draw water," or "a bough, a branch."

The exact Hebrew equivalent is Dawlis. Masculine Hebrew equivalents: D'lawyaw, Moshe, Naytzer and Sawrig.

DAMA, DAMITA

From the Latin meaning "a lady." Damita is a diminutive form.

Hebrew equivalents: Basyaw, Bisyaw, B'suayl, B'sulaw and G'veeraw. Masculine Hebrew equivalents: Ben-Gever, Gavreeayl, Gever and G'varyaw.

DANA

From the Latin meaning "bright, pure as day," or from

ee as in beet; i as in bit; o as in no; oi as in void; u as in rude.

the Hebrew meaning "to judge." In Israel Dana is used as the feminine form of Dan.

The exact Hebrew equivalent is Dawnaw. The exact masculine Hebrew equivalent is Dawn.

DANIA, DANYA, DANICE, DANIT
Variant forms of the masculine name Dan which is derived from the Hebrew meaning "to judge." Dania and Danya mean "judgment of the Lord."

The exact Hebrew equivalents are Dawneeyaw and Dawnis. The exact masculine Hebrew equivalents are Dawn and Dawneeayl.

DANIELA, DANIELLA, DANIELE, DANIELLE
Feminine forms of the masculine name Daniel which is derived from the Hebrew meaning "God is my judge."

The exact Hebrew equivalent is Dawneeaylaw. The exact masculine Hebrew equivalent is Dawneeayl.

DAPHNA, DAPHNE, DAPHNICE, DAPHNIT
From the Greek meaning "a bay-tree or a laurel," the symbol of victory. In Greek mythology Daphne was a nymph who, pursued by Apollo, managed to escape capture by turning into a laurel tree. Laurel leaves were worn by victors in honor of Apollo. Daphna, Daphnice and Daphnit (also spelled with a "f" instead of "ph") are variant forms.

The exact Hebrew equivalent is Dafnaw. Masculine Hebrew equivalents: Govayr, N'tzeeach and Yatzleeach.

DARCIE
From the Celtic meaning "dark." The masculine form is Darcy.

Hebrew equivalents: Ayfaw, Chacheelaw, Lailaw and Tzeelaw. Masculine Hebrew equivalents: Adawr, Ashchur, Ayfai, Chachalyaw and Pinchaws.

DARIA
The feminine form of the Persian Darius meaning "wealth."

Key: *a* as in f*a*ther; *ai* as in *ai*sle; *aw* as in l*aw*; *ay* as in s*ay*; *e* as in b*e*t;

Hebrew equivalents: Asheeraw, Bas-Shua, N'geedaw and Yisraw. Masculine Hebrew equivalents: Hoseer, Hunaw, Yeeshai and Yisro.

DASI, DASSI
Diminutive forms of Hadassah. See Hadassah for a full explanation.

The exact Hebrew equivalent used in Israel is Dasee. See Hadassah for additional equivalents.

DASIA, DATIA
From the Hebrew meaning "law of the Lord," or "faith in God."

The exact Hebrew equivalent is Dasyaw. Masculine Hebrew equivalents: Dawsawn, Deenai and Dosawn.

DAVENE, DAVI, DAVIDA, DAVITA
Feminine forms of David meaning "beloved, friend," in the Hebrew.

The exact Hebrew equivalent is Dawveedaw. The exact masculine Hebrew equivalent is Dawvid.

DAWN
The translation of the Greek *aurora* is "dawn." Aurora was the Roman goddess of day-break or dawn. Orrie and Rora are used as pet forms of Aurora and Dawn.

Hebrew equivalents: Barkawis, Bawrekes, Bawrkas, Bas-Shachar, Tzafraw, Tzafreeraw and Tzafreeris. Masculine Hebrew equivalents: Aveeshachar, Tzafreer, Tzafreerce and Tzofar.

DAYA
From the Hebrew meaning "a bird." It is usually taken to be "a kite, a bird of prey."

The exact Hebrew equivalent is Da'yaw. Masculine Hebrew equivalents: Gozawl, Orayv and Tzeepor.

DEAN, DEANE
These names are used more commonly as masculine names. See Dean in masculine section.

---

ee as in b*ee*t; *i* as in b*i*t; *o* as in n*o*; *oi* as in v*oi*d; *u* as in r*u*de.

DEANNA, DEANNE
Variant spellings of Diane or of Dinah. See Diane and Dinah for a full explanation.

DEBBI, DEBBY
Pet forms of Deborah. See Deborah for a full explanation.

DEBORAH, DEBRA
From the Hebrew meaning either "a swarm of bees," or "to speak kind words." In the Bible two charming characters were known by this name: 1) Deborah, the nurse of Rebekah, and 2) the prophetess-judge, the wife of Lapidos, who lived about 1150 B.C.E., and led the revolt against the Canaanite king and his general, Sisera. Her victory song, known as the "Song of Deborah," is one of the oldest poems preserved in Hebrew. Debra, Devora, Dobra and Devra are variant forms. Debbi and Debby are variant forms and popular pet names.

The exact Hebrew equivalent is D'voraw. Masculine Hebrew equivalents: Amaryaw, Chaveelaw, Divree, Dovayv, Imree, Niv and Omer.

DEENA, DENA, DENNA
Variant Hebraic forms of the biblical Dinah meaning "judgment." Dena is also derived from the Anglo-Saxon meaning "from the valley." Dee is used as a short form.

See Dinah, and also Dale, for feminine and masculine equivalents.

DEGANIA, DEGANYA
Variant spellings of Dagania. See Dagania for a full explanation.

DEGULA
From the Hebrew meaning "excellent or famous."

The exact Hebrew equivalent is D'gulaw. Masculine Hebrew equivalents: Acheetuv, Aveetuv, Ben-Tzeeyon, Mishbawch, M'shubawch and Tzeeyon.

Key: *a* as in f*a*ther; *ai* as in *ai*sle; *aw* as in l*aw*; *ay* as in s*ay*; *e* as in b*e*t;

DELILA, DELILAH

From the Hebrew meaning either "poor" or "hair." In the Bible Delilah was a Philistine woman, the mistress of Samson. When she learned that the secret of Samson's strength was in his hair, she had his locks cut off and betrayed him to the Philistines.

The exact Hebrew equivalent is D'leelaw. Masculine Hebrew equivalents: Meechaw and S'orim.

DELL, DELLA

Pet forms of Adele and Adeline. See Adela and Adeline for a full explanation.

DENIS, DENISE, DENYSE

Feminine forms of the masculine Denis which is derived from Dionysius, the Greek god of wine and drama. Dione and Dionetta are variant forms. See Denis in masculine section for a full explanation.

DERORA, DERORICE, DERORIT

From the Hebrew meaning either "a flowing stream," or a "bird (a swallow)," or "freedom, liberty."

The exact Hebrew equivalents are D'roraw and D'roris. The exact masculine Hebrew equivalents are D'ror and D'roree.

DEVORA, DEVORAH, DEVRA

Variant Hebraic forms of Deborah. See Deborah for a full explanation.

DIANA, DIANE, DIANNE

From the Latin meaning "bright, pure as day." Diana was the moon goddess in Roman mythology.

Hebrew equivalents: B'heeraw, L'vawnaw, M'eeraw, Noga and Zakaw. Masculine Hebrew equivalents: Aharon, Bawheer, Lawvawn, Nayreeyaw, Shimshon and Shragaw.

DICKLA, DIKLA, DIKLICE, DIKLIT

The Aramaic form of the Arabic word meaning "a palm or date tree." In the Bible Dikla is also used as a masculine

ee as in beet; *i* as in bit; *o* as in no; *oi* as in void; *u* as in rude.

name. In Israel it is used as a feminine form along with its variant forms.

The exact Hebrew equivalents are Diklaw and Diklis. Masculine Hebrew equivalents: Dekel, Diklaw, Eetawmar and Miklos.

DINAH

From the Hebrew meaning "judgment." In the Bible Dinah was the daughter of Jacob and Leah. Dena, Dina and Deena are variant spellings. Dinah is not to be confused with Diana.

The exact Hebrew equivalent is Deenaw. Masculine Hebrew equivalents: Ameedawn, Aveedawn, Dawn and Dawneeayl.

DIZA, DITZA, DITZAH

From the Hebrew meaning "joy."

The exact Hebrew equivalent is Deetzaw. The exact masculine Hebrew equivalent is Ditz.

DOBRA

A variant spelling of Deborah. See Deborah for a full explanation.

DODA, DODI, DODIE

From the Hebrew meaning "beloved." The names David and Davida are derived from the same Hebrew root. The literal meaning of Doda is "an aunt," and the literal meaning of Dodi is "my uncle." Dodi is also used as a short form of Dorothy.

The exact Hebrew equivalents are Dodaw and Dodee. Masculine Hebrew equivalents: Awhud, Dawvid, Dodai, Dodo, Ohayd and Yawdid.

DOLLY

Dolly is either a variant form of Dorothy meaning "gift of God" in Greek, or is an independent name, from the Old English meaning "doll."

Hebrew equivalents: Bubaw, Matawnaw, Migdawnaw,

Key: *a* as in f*a*ther; *ai* as in *ai*sle; *aw* as in l*aw*; *ay* as in s*ay*; *e* as in b*e*t;

T'rumaw and T'shuraw. Masculine Hebrew equivalents: Doron, Magdeeayl, Matanyaw, Matisyawhu, Nawsawn, Yawhawv and Yozawvawd.

DOLORES

Originally a purely Christian name from the Latin, meaning "lady of sorrows." A very popular name in Spain, and among Spanish speaking people.

Hebrew equivalents: Mawraw, Miryawm and Tzawraw. Masculine Hebrew equivalents: Awmos and Eeyov. For a euphemistic interpretation and its equivalents, see Abigail.

DONNA

From the Latin and Italian meaning "lady of nobility."

Hebrew equivalents: Adeeraw, Adeevaw, N'deevaw, Needawraw, N'seechaw and Sawraw. Masculine Hebrew equivalents: Adeer, Awdiv, Ish-Hod, Nawdawv, Nawdiv, Yisrawayl and Yonawdawv.

DORA, DOREEEN, DORENE

Dora is a pet form of Dorothy. Doreen and Dorene are diminutive forms of Dora. All are derived from the Greek meaning "gift of God."

Hebrew equivalents: Doronis, Mataws, Migdawnaw, Minchaw, Z'veedaw and Z'vudaw. Masculine Hebrew equivalents: Doron, Doronee, Matawn, Matisyawhu, Matnai, Tesher and Yawhawv.

DORCIA

From the Greek meaning "a gazelle."

Hebrew equivalents: Awfraw, A'yawlaw, A'yeles, Tzivyaw, Yaalis and Y'aylaw. Masculine Hebrew equivalents: A'yawl, A'yawlon, Efron, Ofer, Tzivyon and Tz'vee.

DORICE, DORIT

A name used in Israel with many possible meanings. It may be from the Greek meaning "to heap, to pile," or "a dwelling place." It may also be of Hebrew origin meaning "a generation."

ee as in b*ee*t; *i* as in b*i*t; *o* as in n*o*; *oi* as in v*oi*d; *u* as in r*u*de.

The exact Hebrew equivalent is Doris. Massculine Hebrew equivalents: Aveedor, Dor, Doron, Doronee, Gal, Galee and Harayl.

DORIS, DORRIS

From the Greek meaning "a sacrificial knife," or a mythological character, the wife of Nereus, "mother of sea gods." Some authorities claim Doris means "bountiful," one who is blessed with many good gifts.

Hebrew equivalents: Doronis, D'roraw, Galeeyaw, Maraw and Miryawm. Masculine Hebrew equivalents: Arnon, Aynawn, Doron, Doronee, Matawn, Matisyawhu and Y'honawsawn.

DORONICE, DORONIT

From the Aramaic meaning "a gift."

The exact Hebrew equivalent is Doronis. The exact masculine Hebrew equivalent is Doron.

DOROTHEA

A variant form of Dorothy. See below for a full explanation.

DOROTHY

From the Greek meaning "gift of God." The original form of the name is Theodora. Among the many variant forms are: Dorothea, Dora, Dorita, Theodora, Doreen and Dore. Dot, Dottie, Dollie, Dolly, Dodo and Dodi are common pet forms.

Hebrew equivalents: Doronis, Matawnaw, Mataws, Migdawnaw, Minchaw, N'saneeaylaw, N'sanyaw, T'rumaw, T'shuraw, Z'veedaw and Z'vudaw. Masculine Hebrew equivalents: Aveeshai, Doron, Doronee, Eleenawsawn, Elnawsawn, Elzawvawd, Zawvawd, Zavdee and Zavdeeayl.

DUBA

From the Hebrew meaning "a bear."

The exact Hebrew equivalent is Doobaw. The exact masculine Hebrew equivalent is Dov.

Key: *a* as in father; *ai* as in aisle; *aw* as in law; *ay* as in say; *e* as in bet;

DULCIE
From the Latin meaning "charming, sweet."

Hebrew equivalents: Acheenoam, M'sukaw, Naamaw and Nawawmee. Masculine Hebrew equivalents: Aveenoam, Magdeeayl, Mawsok, Meged, Naamawn and Noam.

DURENE
From the Latin meaning "enduring, lasting."

Hebrew equivalents: Chavaw, Cha'yaw and Nitzchee-yaw. Masculine Hebrew equivalents: Ameead, Cha'yim, Netzach and Nitzchee.

EDDA
From the Icelandic meaning "poetic," or "a composer or singer of songs."

Hebrew equivalents: Leeris, N'eemaw, Reenaw, Sheeree, Sheerlee and Zimraw. Masculine Hebrew equivalents: Aharon, Ameerawn, Ameeshawr, Anaw, Leeron, Yawron, Zimrawn and Z'maryaw.

EDGA
Feminine form of Edgar. See Edgar in masculine section for a full explanation.

EDIA, EDYA, EDYAH
From the Hebrew meaning "adornment of the Lord."

The exact Hebrew equivalent is Edyaw. Masculine Hebrew equivalents: Adeeayl, Hawdawr, Hawdur and M'udawn.

EDIE
A popular Scottish diminutive form of Edith. See Edith for a full explanation.

EDINA
From the Teutonic meaning "rich friend."

Hebrew equivalents: Ahuvaw, Bas-Shua, Chaveevaw, Rus and Y'deedaw. Masculine Hebrew equivalents: Aveeshai, Dawwid, Tz'fanyaw, Y'didyaw and Yeeshai.

ee as in b*ee*t; *i* as in b*i*t; *o* as in n*o*; *oi* as in v*oi*d; *u* as in r*u*de.

EDITH, EDYTHE
Either from the Anglo-Saxon meaning "happiness," or from the Teutonic meaning "rich gift." Edythe is a modern spelling.

Hebrew equivalents: Aleezaw, Aveega'yil, Bas-Shua, Deetzaw, Migdawnaw, Reenaw and Z'vudaw. Masculine Hebrew equivalents: Elnawsawn, Nawsawn, N'sanayl, Simchaw, Yachdeeayl and Yawgil.

EDNA, EDNAH
From the Hebrew meaning "delight, desired, adorned, voluptuous." It may also be a contracted form of the Anglo-Saxon name Edwina meaning "rich friend." Edna occurs first as a name in the Apocrypha, in the Book of Tobit. Adena and Adina are forms similar to Edna.

Hebrew equivalents: Adeenaw, Adis, Ednaw, Nawawmee and Tirtzaw. Masculine Hebrew equivalents: Aveenoam, Chemdawn, Nawam, Yoawv and Yoayl.

EDWARDA
The feminine form of Edward. See Edward in masculine section for a full explanation.

EDWINA
The feminine form of Edwin. See Edwin in masculine section for a full explanation.

EFRATA
From the Hebrew meaning "honored, distinguished." In the Bible it is the name of the wife of Caleb. The masculine form is Efrat which is also used in the Bible.

The exact Hebrew equivalent is Efrawsaw. The exact masculine Hebrew equivalent is Efraws.

EFRONA
From the Hebrew meaning "a bird" (of a species that sings well).

The exact Hebrew equivalent is Efronaw. The exact masculine Hebrew equivalent is Efron.

Key: *a* as in father; *ai* as in aisle; *aw* as in law; *ay* as in say; *e* as in bet;

EILEEN

In Ireland Eileen is a popular substitute for Helen and its related names. See Elaine and Helen for more information.

ELAIN, ELAINE, ELANE, ELAYNE

Elaine is a French version of Helen meaning "light" in the Greek. Eileen is an Irish version. Elane, Elain and Elayne are variant spellings. Some authorities claim that Elain and its various forms are derived from the Welsh meaning "a fawn, a young hind."

Hebrew equivalents: B'heeraw, M'eeraw, Noga, Oraw, Or-Lee, Orlis, Tzivyaw and Zawhawraw. Masculine Hebrew equivalents: Mayeer, Nayreeyaw, Or, Oron, Shimshon, Tz'vee and Z'rachyaw.

ELANA

A variant spelling of Ilana meaning "a tree" in Hebrew.

See Ilana for feminine and masculine Hebrew equivalents.

ELEANOR, ELEANORE, ELENOR, ELINOR

Either variant forms of Helen which means "light" in the Greek, or from the Teutonic meaning "fruitful." Eleonora and Leonora are Italian forms of Eleanor while Eleonore and Lenore are German variants. Ellie is a popular diminutive form.

Hebrew equivalents: B'heeraw, M'eeraw, Neetzaw, Noga, Oraw, Shoshanaw, Vardaw and Zawhawraw. Masculine Hebrew equivalents: Efra'yim, Mayeer, Nayreeyaw, P'rachyaw, Shoshan, Tzemach and Z'rachyaw.

ELIANA, ELIANNA

From the Hebrew meaning "God has answered me."

The exact Hebrew equivalent is Eleenaw. Masculine Hebrew equivalents: Amaryaw, Imree and Omer.

ELIN, ELYN, ELYNN

Variant spellings of Ellen, which is a form of Helen. See Helen for a full explanation.

---

ee as in b*ee*t; *i* as in b*i*t; *o* as in n*o*; *oi* as in v*oi*d; *u* as in r*u*de.

ELINOAR
From the Hebrew meaning "God is my youth," or "God of my youth."

The exact Hebrew equivalent is Eleenoar. Masculine Hebrew equivalents: Awviv, Aylawm, Naarai and Naaryaw.

ELIORA, ELEORA
From the Hebrew meaning "God is my light."

The exact Hebrew equivalent is Eleeanaw. Masculine masculine Hebrew equivalent is Eleeor.

ELISA, ELISSA, ELIZA, ELIZE
These are some of the many variant forms which have been derived from Elisabeth and Elizabeth. See below.

ELISABETH, ELIZABETH
From the Hebrew meaning "God's oath," or "God is an oath." The original Hebrew form is Elisheva. In the Bible Elisheva (also spelled: Elisheba) was the wife of Aaron who was the brother of Moses. Elisabeth was the way in which the Greek translation of the Bible rendered Elisheva. Elizabeth, spelled with a "z" is the more common English spelling. Few names have produced more variant forms than Elisabeth. Among these are: Babette, Bess, Bessie, Bessy, Bet, Beth, Bettina, Betsie, Betsey, Betta, Bette, Eliza, Elsie, Elspeth, Isabel, Ilse, Libby, Lilibet, Lilla, Lillah, Lisa, Lisbet, Lisbeth, Liz, Liza, Lizzie, Tetsy and Tetty.

The exact Hebrew equivalent is Eleesheva. Masculine Hebrew equivalents: Amaryaw, Aylaw and Sheva.

ELISHEVA
From the Hebrew meaning "God is my oath." This is the exact Hebrew form of the name Elizabeth. See Elizabeth for a full explanation.

ELLA
Although some claim Ella is derived from an old Ger-

man word meaning "all," it is most probably a variant form of Eleanor which, in turn, is derived from Helen meaning "light" in the Greek.

See Helen for feminine and masculine Hebrew equivalents.

ELLEN, ELLIN, ELLYN, ELYN
Variant forms of Eleanor. See Eleanor for a full explanation.

ELOISE
A variant form of Louise which is derived from the masculine Louis meaning "hero or refuge of the people, a warrior, a prince."

Hebrew equivalents: Gavreelaw, Geeboraw, Sawraw, Tigraw, and Yis'r'aylaw. Masculine Hebrew equivalents: Aveecha'yil, Ben-Cha'yil, La'yish, Naftawlee, Sh'maryawhu and Yisrawayl.

ELSA
From the Anglo-Saxon meaning "a swan." The figurative meaning is poet or singer.

Hebrew equivalents: Leeris, N'eemaw, Reenaw, Sheeree, Sheerlee and Zimraw. Masculine Hebrew equivalents: Aharron, Ameerawn, Ameeshawr, Anaw, Yawron and Z'maryaw.

ELSE
From the Teutonic meaning "of noble lineage."

Hebrew equivalents: N'deevaw, Needawraw, N'seechaw, Malkaw and Saraw. Masculine Hebrew equivalents: Aveenawdawv, Cheerawm, Nawdawv and Yisrawayl.

ELSIE
Taken either as a form of Adelaide or Elisabeth. See Adelaide and Elisabeth for a full explanation.

ELYSA, ELYSE, ELYSSA
Variant forms of Elisabeth. See Elisabeth for a full explanation.

Hebrew equivalents: Aleezaw, Awshraw, B'rawchaw,

ee as in b*ee*t; *i* as in b*i*t; *o* as in n*o*; *oi* as in v*oi*d; *u* as in r*u*de.

B'ruchaw, Geelaw and Seesaw. Masculine Hebrew equivalents: Awshayr, Baruch, Yawgil and Yitzchawk.

ELZA
From the Hebrew meaning "God is my joy."

Hebrew equivalents: Aleesaw, Aleezaw, Elzaw, Reenaw, Ronaw and R'nawnaw. Masculine Hebrew equivalents: Alis, Aliz, Eles, Eletz, Gil, Geelee and Simchonee.

EMANUELA, EMANUELLA
The feminine form of Emanuel meaning "God is with us."

The exact Hebrew equivalent is Eemawnuaylaw. The exact masculine Hebrew equivalent is Eemawnuayl.

EMILIE
From the Teutonic meaning "a flatterer," and connoting one facile of speech. Emilie may also be a variant form of Emily (see below), with Amelia being the German form.

Hebrew equivalents: D'voraw, Neevaw, Y'hudis and Zimraw. Masculine Hebrew equivalents: Dovayv, Heelayl, M'halalayl, Shevach and Y'hudaw.

EMILY
From the Latin meaning "industrious."

Hebrew equivalents: Chawrutzaw, Tirtzaw and Z'reezaw. Masculine Hebrew equivalents: Awmayl, Mawhir, Meretz, Yawziz, Zeeruz and Zeezaw.

EMMA
From the Teutonic meaning "the big one," or "grandmother." Emma has appeared in a variety of forms over the centuries including Ymma, Imma and Eme. In the 12th century it appeared as Em. Emmie is a popular pet form.

Hebrew equivalents: Asalyaw, Eemaw, G'dulaw and Rawchawv. Masculine Hebrew equivalents: Abaw, G'dalyaw, Geedayl, Rabaw, Rawvaw and Sawvaw.

EMUNA, EMUNAH
From the Hebrew meaning "faithful." Used in the middle ages and currently in Israel.

Key: *a* as in f*a*ther; *ai* as in *ai*sle; *aw* as in l*aw*; *ay* as in s*ay*; *e* as in b*e*t;

The exact Hebrew equivalent is Emunaw. Masculine Hebrew equivalents: Ameesawn, Ameetai, Amnon and Ne'emawn.

ENA

A variant spelling or Ina or a pet form of Eugenia. See Eugenia for a full explanation.

ENID

Either from the Anglo-Saxon meaning "fair," or from the Celtic meaning "the soul, life."

Hebrew equivalents: Chavaw, Cha'yaw, and L'vawnaw. Masculine Hebrew equivalents: Amrawm, Cha'yim, Lawvawn, Naamawn and Y'cheeayl.

ERGA

From the Hebrew meaning "yearning, hope, longing."

The exact Hebrew equivalent is Ergaw. Masculine Hebrew equivalents: Yachl'ayl and Yawchil.

ERICA, ERIKA

The feminine form of Eric meaning "ever kingly, brave, powerful," in the Teutonic and Anglo-Saxon.

Hebrew equivalents: Atawraw, Ateres, Gavreeaylaw, Geeboraw, Kleelaw, Klulaw and Malkaw. Masculine Hebrew equivalents: Amtzaw, Gavreeayl, Kasreeayl, Kisron, Melech and Zayraw.

ERIN

From the Irish meaning "peace."

Hebrew equivalents: Acheeshawlom, Margayaw, Shaananaw, Shlomis and Shulamis. Masculine Hebrew equivalents: M'shulawm, Shawlayv, Shawlom and Shlomo.

ERMA

A variant spelling of Irma. See Irma for a full explanation.

ERNA

From the Anglo-Saxon meaning "retiring, shy, reserved, peaceful."

ee as in b*ee*t; *i* as in b*i*t; *o* as in n*o*; *oi* as in v*oi*d; *u* as in r*u*de.

Hebrew equivalents: M'nuchaw, M'shulemes, Shalvaw, Shulamis and Za'yis. Masculine Hebrew equivalents: Ish-Shawlom, Shawlayv, Shlomee, Shlomo and Zaysawn.

ERNESTINE
The feminine form of Ernest meaning "serious-minded," in the Teutonic.

Hebrew equivalents: B'ruraw, Tawmawr and T'mee-maw. Masculine Hebrew equivalents: Ameetai, Amnon, Aveeshur, Bawrur and Konanyawhu.

ESSIE
A popular diminutive form of Esther. See Esther for a full explanation.

ESTA, ESTELLA, ESTELLE
Variant forms of Esther. See below for a full explanation.

ESTER, ESTHER
Esther and its many variant forms are of Persian origin meaning "a star." In the Bible Esther was the central figure in the Book of Esther. She was the cousin and adopted daughter of Mordecai, who later became the queen of King Ahasueros. Her Hebrew name was Hadassah meaning "myrtle." Esta, Essie, Ettie, Etty, Estella and Estelle are some of the variant forms. Ester is a modern spelling. Hester, and its diminutive, Hetty, are Latinized forms of Esther.

The exact Hebrew equivalent is Estayr. Masculine Hebrew equivalents: Bar-Kochvaw, Kochawv, Kochvaw, Mazawl, Orawn and Zik.

ETANA
From the Hebrew meaning "strong." Etan and Ethan are masculine forms.

The exact Hebrew equivalent is Aysawnaw. The exact masculine Hebrew equivalent is Aysawn.

Key: *a* as in f*a*ther; *ai* as in *ai*sle; *aw* as in l*aw*; *ay* as in s*ay*; *e* as in b*e*t;

ETHEL
From the Teutonic meaning "noble." In Old German *adal,* and in modern German *edel,* are words of the same origin. These gave rise to names like Adele and Alice. The Yiddish name Edel is of the same origin.

Hebrew equivalents: N'deevaw, Sawraw and Yis'r'aylaw. Masculine Hebrew equivalents: Acheerawm, Adawr, Adoneeyawhu, Nawdawv and Yisrawayl.

ETTA
A diminutive of Henrietta meaning "mistress of the house, lord, ruler."

Hebrew equivalents: Atawraw, Geeboraw, Layaw, Malkaw, Tz'feeraw and Yis'r'aylaw. Masculine Hebrew equivalents: Baal, Kasreeayl, Kisron, Melech and Rosh.

EUDICE
A modern variant spelling of Judith. See Judith for a full explanation.

EUGENIA
From the Greek meaning "well-born." Ina and Ena are diminutive forms.

Hebrew equivalents: Adeenaw, Malkaw, N'deevaw and Sawraw. Masculine Hebrew equivalents: Adeer, Awdiv, Cheerom, Nadawv and Y'honawdawv.

EUNICE
From the Greek meaning "happy victory."

Hebrew equivalents: Dafnaw and Hadasaw. Masculine Hebrew equivalents: N'tzeeach and Yatzleeach.

EVA, EVE
Eva is the German form of Eve which is derived from the Hebrew meaning "life." In the Bible, Eve, the wife of Adam, was the first woman. Evie is a pet form of Eve and Eva. Eva is sometimes used as a diminutive of Evangeline. Evita is a Spanish pet form of Eve.

The exact Hebrew equivalent is Chavaw. Masculine Hebrew equivalents: Cha'yim, Cheeyaw and Y'cheeayl.

---

ee as in b*ee*t; *i* as in b*i*t; *o* as in n*o*; *oi* as in v*oi*d; *u* as in r*u*de.

EVANGELINE

From the Greek meaning "bearer of glad tidings, a messenger."

Hebrew equivalents: Geelaw, Deetzaw, Reenaw, R'nawnaw and Seesaw. Masculine Hebrew equivalents: Sawson, Simchaw, Yawgil and Yitzchawk.

EVELYN

Either a diminutive of Eve (see Eve), or from the Celtic meaning "pleasant, good."

Hebrew equivalents: Acheenoam, Nawawmee, Shifraw, Tovaw, Yawfaw and Yawtvaw. Masculine Hebrew equivalents: Aveenoam, Ben-Tzeeyon, Naamawn, Nawam and Tuveeyaw.

EZRA

Ezra is normally a masculine name, but is used in Israel as a feminine name (with a slight change in spelling). Derived from the Hebrew meaning "help." For more information see Ezra in the masculine section.

Ezraw may be used as the feminine and masculine Hebrew equivalent.

EZRAELA, EZRAELLA, EZRELA

A feminine form similar to the masculine Ezra. Derived from the Hebrew meaning "God is my help or support."

The exact Hebrew equivalent is Ezr'aylaw. The exact masculine Hebrew equivalent is Ezraw.

FABIA

The feminine form of Fabian meaning "bean farmer," in the Greek.

Hebrew equivalents: Karmelaw, Nawvaw and Yiz'r'elaw. Masculine Hebrew equivalents: Awdawm, Karmel, Karm'lee and Yiz'r'ayl.

FAIGA

From the Anglo-Saxon meaning "the beautiful" or a Yiddish name derived from the German meaning "a bird." Feigel is a variant spelling.

Key: *a* as in f*a*ther; *ai* as in *ai*sle; *aw* as in l*aw*; *ay* as in s*ay*; *e* as in b*e*t;

Hebrew equivalents: Nofeeyaw, Shifraw, Yawfaw, Yaw-fis and Y'fayfeeyaw. Masculine Hebrew equivalents: Shapeer, Shefer, Shifron, Yawfe and Yefes. See Feigel for additional equivalents.

FAITH
From the Teutonic meaning "unswerving trust, hope." Faith, along with Hope and Charity came to be used as personal names after the Reformation.

Hebrew equivalents: Bitchaw, Amawnaw, Emunaw, Tikvaw and Tzeepeeyaw. Masculine Hebrew equivalents: Ameetai, Amnon, Bukee, Haymawn and Ne'emawn.

FALICE, FALICIA
Variant spellings of Felice. See Felice for a full explanation.

FANNIE, FANNY, FANNYE
Diminutive forms of Frances which is derived from the Teutonic meaning "free, liberal."

Hebrew equivalents: Chufshis, D'roraw, D'roris and Leed'ror. Masculine Hebrew equivalents: Aveed'ror, Chayrus, D'ror, Droree, Pesach and P'sachyaw.

FAWN
From the Latin meaning "a young deer."

Hebrew equivalents: Awfraw, A'yawlaw, A'yeles, Hertzaylaw, Hertz'leeyaw and Tzivyaw. Masculine Hebrew equivalents: Ayfer, Efron, Hertzayl, Ofer, Tzivyon and Tz'veeayl.

FAY, FAYE, FAYETTE
From the Old French meaning "fidelity."

Hebrew equivalents: Amawnaw, Bitchaw, Emunaw, Ne'-emawnaw, Ne'emenes, Tikvaw and Tzeepeeyaw. Masculine Hebrew equivalents: Ameetai, Amnon, Bukee, Haymawn and Ne'emawn.

---

ee as in b*ee*t; *i* as in b*i*t; *o* as in n*o*; *oi* as in v*oi*d; *u* as in r*u*de.

FEIGEL

A Yiddish name derived from the German meaning "a bird." Faiga is a variant form.

Hebrew equivalents: Chaseedaw, Chawglaw, Efronaw, Gozawlaw, Tzeepawrtaw and Tzeeporaw. Masculine Hebrew equivalents: Gozawl, Orayv and Tzeepor.

FELICE, FELICIA, FELECIA, FELICITY, FELISSE

From the Latin meaning "happy, fortunate." These names are derived from Felicitas, the Roman goddess of good luck. Felicia was common in 12th century England as a feminine form of Felix, which is Latin for "lucky."

Hebrew equivalents: Ashayraw, Ashayris, Awshraw, Gadaw and Mazawl. Masculine Hebrew equivalents: Maimon, Mazawl-Tov and Seemawn-Tov.

FERN

Either an Old English plant name, or from the Teutonic meaning "brave, strong." Ferdinand is the masculine form.

Hebrew equivalents: Areeayl, Kalawnis, Kanaw, Keedaw, Margawnis, Marvaw, No'is, Neta, N'teeyaw and Savyon. Masculine Hebrew equivalents: Awmotz, Narkis, Shawsil, Shawsul, Tzemach and Zoraya.

FIDELIA

From the Latin meaning "faithful."

Hebrew equivalents: Amawnaw, Bitchaw, Emunaw, Tikvaw and Tzeepeeyaw. Masculine Hebrew equivalents: Ameetai, Amnon, Bukee, Haymawn and Ne'emawn.

FLORA, FLORELLA, FLORRIE, FLORYN, FLOSSIE

Flora was the Roman goddess of flowers and springtime. For a full explanation of Flora and its variant forms see Florence.

FLOREN, FLORENCE

From the Latin meaning "flower, flowery, flourishing." In medieval times Florence was commonly used as a masculine name as well. Floren, as well as Flo, Floss and Flossie

are diminutive forms. For additional variant forms see
Flora.

Hebrew equivalents: Astayraw, Eeris, Neetzaw, Pirchaw, Pircheeyaw, Pirchis, P'reechaw, Shoshanaw and
Y'neekaw. Masculine Hebrew equivalents: Efra'yim, Neeris, Neetzawn, Pekach, Perach, P'rachyaw, Puraw, Savyon
and Shoshan.

FLOWER
A rare form of Flora and Florence first used in the
18th century. It was even more popular in its French form,
Fleur. See Flora and Florence for additional information.

FRAN, FRANCIS, FRANCINE, FRANKIE
Frances and its various forms are derived from the
Teutonic meaning "free, liberal." Frances is the feminine
form of the masculine Francis. Frances actually means
"free-woman," while Francis means "free-man." The origin
of these names dates back to the Franks, a confederacy of
German tribes who for a long time battled with the Romans
before settling permanently in Gaul, in the 5th century.
France took its name from the Franks. Fan, Fran, Francie,
Frankie and Fanny are popular diminutives.

Hebrew equivalents: Chufshis, D'roraw, D'roris, G'ulaw,
Lee-d'ror and Rawchawv. Masculine Hebrew equivalents:
Aveed'ror, Pesach, P'sachyaw, R'chavawm and R'chavyaw.

FRANCESCA
A form of Frances meaning "a little French lady." See
above for information about the origin of Frances.

FREDA, FREDDA, FREDDIE, FREDERICA, FREDYNE, FRIEDA, FRITZI
Frederica and its various forms are derived from the
Teutonic meaning "peaceful."

Hebrew equivalents: M'nuchaw, Shlomis, Shulamis and
Za'yis. Masculine Hebrew equivalents: Avshawlom, Ish-
Shawlom, Noach, Shabsai, Shawlom and Shlomo.

ee as in b*ee*t; *i* as in b*i*t; *o* as in n*o*; *oi* as in v*oi*d; *u* as in r*u*de.

FREIDA, FREIDE, FRAYDE
Either forms of Frieda and Freda (see above), or from the Yiddish meaning "joy."

Hebrew equivalents: Rawneesaw, Reenaw, Simchis, Simchonaw and Tzawhawlaw. (Frayde is sometimes used instead of a Hebrew name.) Masculine Hebrew equivalents: Aliz, Awgil, Geelon, Seesee and Yawgayl.

FRUMA
A Yiddish name meaning "pious, the pious one."

Hebrew equivalents: B'ruraw, B'ruryaw and Chaseedaw. (Fruma is popularly used instead of a Hebrew name.) Masculine Hebrew equivalents: Bawrur, Chawsid, Kadish and Y'kuseeayl.

GABI, GAVI
Pet forms of Gabriella. See Gabriella for a full explanation.

GABRIELA, GABRIELLA, GABRIELLE
Feminine forms of the masculine Gabriel meaning "God is my strength," in the Hebrew. Gabi and Gavi are pet forms. There is a superstition that if parents who have lost several children give a new baby one of these names, the baby will survive.

The exact Hebrew equivalent is Gavreeaylaw. The exact masculine Hebrew equivalent is Gavreeayl.

GADA
A current name is Israel, derived either from the Aramaic meaning "luck," or it is a feminine form of Gad. In Hebrew it is also the name of a plant.

The exact Hebrew equivalent is Gadaw. Masculine Hebrew equivalents: Gawd, Maimon, Mazawl-Tov and Seemawn-Tov.

GAFNA
From the Hebrew meaning "a vine."

The exact Hebrew equivalent is Gafnaw. The exact masculine Hebrew equivalent is Gefen.

Key: *a* as in f*a*ther; *ai* as in *ai*sle; *aw* as in l*aw*; *ay* as in s*ay*; *e* as in b*e*t;

GAIL, GALE
Diminutive forms of Abigail meaning "father's joy," in Arabic and Hebrew. See Abigail for a full explanation.

GAL, GALI, GALICE, GALIT
From the Hebrew meaning either "a mound, a hill," or "a fountain, a spring."

The exact Hebrew equivalents are Gal, Galee and Galis. Masculine Hebrew equivalents: Gilawd, Gilawdee, Givaw, Givon, Givson and Talmai.

GALYA
From the Hebrew meaning "God has redeemeed." Used as a masculine name as well.

The exact Hebrew equivalent is G'alyaw. Masculine Hebrew equivalents: G'alyaw, Eg'awl and Yig'awl.

GANA, GANICE, GANIT
From the Hebrew meaning "a garden." Ganice and Ganit also have the meaning "defender."

The exact Hebrew equivalents are Ganaw and Ganis. Masculine Hebrew equivalents: Bust'nai, Carmel, Ginson, Sh'maryawhu and Zimree.

GARNICE, GARNIT
From the Hebrew meaning "a granary."

The exact Hebrew equivalent is Garnis. Masculine Hebrew equivalent: Dawgawn.

GAVRILLA
From the Hebrew meaning "a heroine, strong."

The exact Hebrew equivalent is Gavreelaw. Masculine Hebrew equivalents: Awmotz, Gavreeayl, Gawd, Geebor, Gever and Y'chezkayl.

GAY
From the Teutonic meaning "gay, merry."

Hebrew equivalents: Aveega'yil, Bilgaw, Geelaw, Geeleeyaw and Geelis. Masculine Hebrew equivalents: Bilgai, Gil, Gil-ad, Gil-awm, Geelawn and Yitzchawk.

---

ee as in b*ee*t; *i* as in b*i*t; *o* as in n*o*; *oi* as in v*oi*d; *u* as in r*u*de.

GAYLE
A variant spelling of Gail, which, in turn, is a pet form of Abigail meaning "father's joy," in Arabic and Hebrew. See Abigail for a full explanation.

GAYORA
From the Hebrew meaning "valley of light."

The exact Hebrew equivalent is Gayoraw. Masculine Hebrew equivalents: Eleeor, Leeor, Mayeer, Or, Oree and Ureeyaw.

GAZELLA
From the Latin meaning "a gazelle, a deer."

Hebrew equivalents: A'yeles, A'yawlaw, Tzivyaw, Y'aylaw and Y'aylis. Masculine Hebrew equivalents: A'yawl, A'yawlon, Tz'vee, Tz'veeayl and Tzivyon.

GAZIT
From the Hebrew meaning "hewn stone."

The exact Hebrew equivalent is Gawzis. Masculine Hebrew equivalents: Eleetzur, Tzur, Tzureeshadai and Tzureeyaw.

GEDULA
From the Hebrew meaning "big, great, greatness."

The exact Hebrew equivalent is G'dulaw. Masculine Hebrew equivalents: G'dalyaw, G'dalyawhu and Geedayl.

GEELA
A variant spelling of Gila meaning "joy" in the Hebrew. See Gila for feminine and masculine Hebrew equivalents.

GENA
Variant spellings of Gina. See Gina for a full explanation.

GENE
Used as a feminine and masculine name. Either a diminutive of Genevieve (see Genevieve), or a form of Jean (see Jean).

Key: *a* as in f*a*ther; *ai* as in *ai*sle; *aw* as in l*aw*; *ay* as in s*ay*; *e* as in b*e*t;

GENEVIEVE

From the Celtic meaning "white wave." Some claim it is of French-German origin and equivalent to Winifred. Other authorities find its origin in two Old German words, *geno,* meaning "race," and *wefo,* meaning "woman."

Hebrew equivalents: L'vawnaw, Miryawm and Zawhawraw. Masculine Hebrew equivalents: Lawwawn, Livnee, Moshe and Peleg. See Winifred for other interpretations and equivalents.

GEORGEANNE

A combination of the Greek, George, and the Hebrew, Anne, meaning "gracious husbandman."

Hebrew equivalents: Ganaw, Chanaw and Karmelaw. Masculine Hebrew equivalents: Awdawm, Chawnawn, Karmel and Yochawnawn.

GEORGETTE, GEORGIA, GEORGIANA, GEORGINA, GEORGINE

Feminine forms of George meaning "farmer" in the Greek.

Hebrew equivalents: Ganaw, Karmelaw, Nawvaw and Sh'daymaw. Masculine Hebrew equivalents: Awdawm, Geenaw, Karmel, Karm'lee, Notaya, Shadmon and Yiz'r'ayl.

GERALDENE, GERALDINE, GERERDINE, GERRIE, GERRY

From Old High German meaning "the spear-wielder, warrior." Gerrie and Gerry are diminutive forms. The original form of these names is the masculine Gerald.

Hebrew equivalents: Chaneesaw, Cheenis, Gavreelaw, Geeboraw and Tigraw. Masculine Hebrew equivalents: Gawd, Gayraw, Gidon, Kaneeayl, Naftawlee and Yisrawayl.

GERDA

From the Old High German meaning "the protected one."

Hebrew equivalents: Ganaw, Mawgaynaw, Migdawlaw,

ee as in b*ee*t; *i* as in b*i*t; *o* as in n*o*; *oi* as in v*oi*d; *u* as in r*u*de.

Shimris and Tzeenaw. Masculine Hebrew equivalents: Mawgayn, Saadyaw, Sisree and Zimree.

GERTRUDE

From the Teutonic meaning "battlemaid, spear-strength," and having the connotation of warrior. Gert, Trudi and Trudy are pet forms.

Hebrew equivalents: Gavreelaw, Geeboraw, Tigraw and Yis'r'aylaw. Masculine Hebrew equivalents: Gawd, Gayraw, Gidon, Naftawlee and Yisrawayl.

GEULA, GEULAH

From the Hebrew meaning "redemption."

The exact Hebrew equivalent is G'ulaw. Masculine Hebrew equivalents: G'alyaw, Eg'awl and Yig'awl.

GEVIRA

From the Hebrew meaning "lady, queen."

The exact Hebrew equivalent is G'veeraw. The exact masculine Hebrew equivalent is Gever.

GEVURA

From the Hebrew meaning "strength."

The exact Hebrew equivalent is G'vuraw. Masculine Hebrew equivalents: Aveeaz, Aveecha'yil, Gavreeayl, Geebor and Gever.

GIA

A short form of Regina meaning "pure" in the Teutonic or "queen" in the Latin.

Hebrew equivalents: Atawraw, B'ruraw, Malkaw, Tz'-feeraw and Zakaw. Masculine Hebrew equivalents: Avraw-hawm, Eleemelech, Kasreeayl, Melech and Zakai.

GIBORA

From the Hebrew meaning "strong, heroine."

The exact Hebrew equivalent is Geeboraw. The exact masculine Hebrew equivalent is Geebor.

Key: *a* as in father; *ai* as in aisle; *aw* as in law; *ay* as in say; *e* as in bet;

GILA, GILAH, GILI, GILIA, GILIAH

From the Hebrew meaning "joy." Gilia means "my joy is in the Lord," or "the Lord is my joy."

The exact Hebrew equivalents are Geelaw, Geelee and Geeleeyaw. Masculine Hebrew equivalents: Awgayl, Awgil, Gil, Gil-ad, Gil-awm, Gelee and Geelon.

GILADA

From the Hebrew meaning either "my hill is my witness," or "my joy is forever." The masculine form is Gilad or Gilead.

The exact Hebrew equivalent is Gilawdaw. The exact masculine Hebrew equivalents are Gil-ad and Gilawd.

GILANA

From the Hebrew meaning "joy" or "a stage in life." A variant form of Gilat and Gilit.

The exact Hebrew equivalent is Geelawnaw. See Gilat for masculine equivalents.

GILAT, GILIT

From the Hebrew meaning "joy" or "a stage of life." Variant forms of Gilana.

The exact Hebrew equivalents are Geelas and Geelis. Masculine Hebrew equivalents: Awgayl, Awgil, Gil, Gil-ad, Gilawd, Gil-awm, Geelee and Geelon.

GILBERTA

The feminine form of Gilbert meaning "light of many," "a bright pledge," or "a sword," in the Teutonic.

Hebrew equivalents: B'heeraw, Eleeoraw, M'eeraw, Noga, Oraw, Orlee, Orlis and Zakaw. Masculine Hebrew equivalents: Barkai, Bawrawk, Eleeor, Mayeer, Shimshon, Shragaw and Zohar.

GILDA

From the Celtic meaning "servant of God," and connoting a helper.

Hebrew equivalent: Aleksandraw. Masculine Hebrew equivalents: Aleksandayr, Avdee, Malawchee and Ovadyaw.

---

ee as in b*ee*t; *i* as in b*i*t; *o* as in n*o*; *oi* as in v*oi*d; *u* as in r*u*de.

GILL

From the Old English meaning "girl." The original form of Gill is Gillian. Jill is a variant spelling. The name has become synonymous with "sweetheart," as in the expression, "Every Jack has his Jill."

Hebrew equivalents: Almaw, B'sulaw, Naaraw, and Tz'eeraw. Masculine Hebrew equivalents: Ben-Tzeeyon, Moshe, Naarai, Naaryaw and Nun.

GINA

Either a short form of Regina or from the Hebrew meaning "garden."

The exact Hebrew equivalent is Geenaw. See Ginas and Regina for additional equivalents.

GINAS, GINAT

From the Hebrew meaning "garden." These names are also used as masculine names.

The exact Hebrew equivalent is Geenas. Masculine Hebrew equivalents: Chavakuk, Geenas, Ginson, Karmel and Karm'lee.

GIMRA

From the Hebrew meaning "to ripen, fulfill, complete."

The exact Hebrew equivalent is Gimraw. Masculine Hebrew equivalents: G'maryawhu, Gomer, M'shulawm and Shlomo.

GISA, GIZA

From the Hebrew meaning "hewn or cut stone." Giza is also derived from the Teutonic meaning "a gift."

The exact Hebrew equivalent is Geezaw. Masculine Hebrew equivalents: Eleetzur, Elnawsawn, Matisyawhu, N'sanayl and Yeeshai.

GISELA, GISELLE, GIZELA

From the Teutonic, taken to mean either "light of many," "a bright pledge," or "a sword."

Hebrew equivalents: B'heeraw, M'eeraw, Noga and

Key: *a* as in f*a*ther; *ai* as in *ai*sle; *aw* as in l*aw*; *ay* as in s*ay*; *e* as in b*e*t;

Oraw. Masculine Hebrew equivalents: Ureeayl, Zerach, Z'rachyaw and Zohar.

GITA, GITEL

Derived from the Yiddish meaning "good."

The exact Hebrew equivalents are Bas-Tzeeyon, Tovaw, Tovis, Tzeeyonaw and Yawtvaw. Masculine Hebrew equivalents: Acheetuv, Ameetuv, Ben-Tzeeyon, Eleetuv, Tabai, Tuveeyaw and Tzeeyon.

GITICE, GITIT

From the Hebrew meaning "cut off," or it may be the name of a musical instrument mentioned in the Book of Psalms.

The exact Hebrew equivalent is Geetis. Masculine Hebrew equivalents: Gidon and Kotz.

GIVA, GIVONA

From the Hebrew meaning "a hill or high place."

The exact Hebrew equivalents are Givaw and Givonaw. The exact masculine Hebrew equivalents are Geva and Givon.

GLADYS

Taken by some as the Welsh form of the Latin Claudia meaning "lame." Others take it from the Celtic meaning "brilliant, splendid."

Hebrew equivalents: B'heeraw, M'eeraw, Oraw, Tz'leelee and Zawhawraw. Masculine Hebrew equivalents: Bawheer, Shimshon, Shragaw, Zerach, Z'rachyaw and Zohar.

GLENNA

The feminine form of the masculine Glenn which is derived from the Celtic meaning "a dale," or "a small secluded woody valley."

Hebrew equivalents: Ganaw, Ganis, Geenas, Geenaw and Karmeeyaw. Masculine Hebrew equivalents: Gai, Gaychazee, Ginson, Karmel and Yaaree.

ee as in b*ee*t; *i* as in b*i*t; *o* as in n*o*; *oi* as in v*oi*d; *u* as in r*u*de.

GLORA, GLORIA, GLORIANA, GLORY

From the Latin meaning "glorious," connoting one who is praiseworthy, famous.

Hebrew equivalents: Ahudaw, D'voraw, T'heelaw, Y'hudis, Yocheved and Zimraw. Masculine Hebrew equivalents: G'dalyaw, Hadar, Heelayl, Shevach and Y'hudaw.

GOLDA, GOLDARINA, GOLDIE, GOLDY

From the Teutonic meaning "golden haired."

Hebrew equivalents: D'leelaw, Ofeeraw and Zawhawvaw. Masculine Hebrew equivalents: Eleefaz, Pawz and Upawz.

GOMER

From the Hebrew meaning "to finish, complete." It is also used as a masculine name. In the Bible one Gomer was the son of Japhet (the son of Noah), and another was the wife of Hosea, the prophet.

The exact Hebrew equivalent, feminine and masculine is Gomer.

GOZALA

From the Hebrew meaning "a young bird."

The exact Hebrew equivalent is Gozawlaw. The exact masculine Hebrew equivalent is Gozawl.

GRACE

From the Latin meaning "grace." Gracie is a pet form. In Italy Grazia is a popular variant form.

Hebrew equivalents: Chanaw, Diklaw and Tawmawr. Masculine Hebrew equivalents: Elchawnawn, Chaneenaw, Chawnawn, Eetawmawr, Kalmawn and Yochawnawn.

GRETA, GRETCHEN

From the Greek meaning "a pearl." Greta is a Swedish form and Gretchen is a German variant.

Hebrew equivalents: Margawlis, P'neenaw and P'neenis. Masculine Hebrew equivalents: Dar, P'neenee and Tarshish.

Key: *a* as in father; *ai* as in aisle; *aw* as in law; *ay* as in say; *e* as in bet;

GULA
A variant spelling of Geula. See Geula for a full explanation.

GURICE, GURIT
From the Hebrew meaning "the young of an animal," and most often refers to the lion.

The exact Hebrew equivalent is Guris. Masculine Hebrew equivalents: Gur and Gur-Aryay.

GUSSIE, GUSSY
Popular short forms of Augusta. See Augusta for a full explanation.

GWEN, GWENN, GWENDALINE, GWENDOLYN, GWENNIE
From the Welsh meaning "white, fair," or "beautiful and blessed."

Hebrew equivalents: Acheenoam, Naamaw, Nawawmee and L'vawnaw. Masculine Hebrew equivalents: Aveenoam, Lawvawn, Livnee and Naamawn.

GWYN, GWYNNE
Variant forms of Gwen. See above for a full explanation.

HADARA, HADURA
From the Hebrew meaning "beautiful, ornamented," or "honored."

The exact Hebrew equivalents are Hadawraw and Haduraw. Masculine Hebrew equivalents: Hadar, Hadarawm, Hadarezer, Hawdawr and Hawdur.

HADASSAH
From the Hebrew meaning "a myrtle tree," which is the symbol of victory. In the Bible Hadassah was the Hebrew name of Esther, cousin of Mordecai. Hadassa is a modern variant spelling. See Esther for more information about Hadassah. Dasa and Dasi are diminutive forms.

The exact Hebrew equivalents are Hadaws and Hadasaw. See Esther for additional equivalents.

---

ee as in b*ee*t; *i* as in b*i*t; *o* as in n*o*; *oi* as in v*oi*d; *u* as in rude.

HAGAR

From the Hebrew meaning "emigration, forsaken, stranger." In the Bible Hagar was the concubine of Abraham, the mother of Ishmael.

The exact Hebrew equivalent is Hawgawr. Masculine Hebrew equivalents: Gayrshom, Gayrshon and Gawlyas.

HAGIA, HAGIT

From the Hebrew meaning "festive, joyous." Hagia is a masculine name in the Bible, the name of a Levite. In Israel today it is used as a feminine form. Hagit in the Bible was the wife of David, the mother of Adoniyah.

The exact Hebrew equivalents are Chageeyaw and Chagis. The exact masculine Hebrew equivalents are Chagai, Chagee and Chageeyaw.

HALEY, HALLIE, HALLY, HALIE

Feminine forms of Harold. See Harold in masculine section for full information. Hollis and Hollace are variant feminine forms.

HAMUDA

From the Hebrew meaning "desirable, precious."

The exact Hebrew equivalent is Chamudaw. Masculine Hebrew equivalents: Chawmud, Leshem, Nofach, Shovai, Yahalom and Yawkawr.

HANA, HANNAH

From the Hebrew meaning "gracious, merciful." In the Bible Hannah was the mother of Samuel, the wife of Elkanah. Before she became a mother she vowed that if she bore a son she would consecrate him to the service of God. She called her son Samuel meaning "God heard my plea." Hana is a variant spelling. The New Testament records Hannah as Anna. See Anna for additional information.

The exact Hebrew equivalent is Chanaw. Masculine Hebrew equivalents: Ameechayn, Aveechayn, Chaneeayl, Chanun, Chawnaw, Chawnawn, Chawnin, Chonayn, Chonee, Chonyo and Yochawnawn.

Key: *a* as in f*a*ther; *ai* as in *ai*sle; *aw* as in l*aw*; *ay* as in s*ay*; *e* as in b*e*t;

HANIA, HANIYA
From the Hebrew meaning "a rest place, an encampment."

The exact Hebrew equivalent is Chaneeyaw. Masculine Hebrew equivalents: Chawnaw and Tachan.

HANICE, HANIT
From the Hebrew meaning "a spear."

The exact Hebrew equivalent is Chanis. Masculine Hebrew equivalent: Kaneeayl.

HANITA
Either a diminutive form of Hannah or of Hanit. See Hannah and Hanit for a full explanation of each name.

The exact Hebrew equivalent is Chaneesaw. See Hannah and Hanit for additional equivalents.

HARMONY
From the Greek meaning "harmony, peace."

Hebrew equivalents: Margayaw, M'nuchaw, M'shulemes, Shlomis and Za'yis. Masculine Hebrew equivalents: Acheeshawlom, Mawnoach, M'shulawm, Noach, Shlomo and Zaysawn.

HARRIET, HARRIETTE, HATTIE
From the Teutonic meaning "mistress of the house, ruler, lord." Harri, Hattie, Hatty and Etta are pet forms. Harry is the masculine form of Harriet and Henrietta.

Hebrew equivalents: Atawraw, Geeboraw, Layaw, Malkaw, Tz'feeraw and Yis'r'aylaw. Masculine Hebrew equivalents: Baal, Kasreeayl, Melech, Rabaw, Rawvaw and Rosh.

HASIA, HASYA
From the Hebrew meaning "protected of the Lord."

The exact Hebrew equivalent is Chasyaw. Masculine Hebrew equivalents: Akavyaw, Akeevaw, Chetzron, Chosaw and Chupawm.

ee as in beet; i as in bit; o as in no; oi as in void; u as in rude.

HASIDA

From the Hebrew meaning "a stork." Hasida also means "pious one," in Hebrew.

The exact Hebrew equivalent is Chaseedaw. The exact Masculine Hebrew equivalent is Chawsid.

HASINA

From the Hebrew meaning "strong."

The exact Hebrew equivalent is Chaseenaw. The exact masculine Hebrew equivalent is Chawseen.

HAVA

From the Hebrew meaning "life" or "to exist." The English form of Hava is Eve.

The exact Hebrew equivalent is Chavaw .Masculine Hebrew equivalents: Chai, Cha'yim, Cheeyaw, Cheeayl and Y'cheeayl.

HAVIVA

From the Hebrew meaning "beloved."

The exact Hebrew equivalent is Chaveevaw. The exact masculine Hebrew equivalent is Chawviv.

HAYA

From the Hebrew meaning "life." A variant spelling of Chaya.

The exact Hebrew equivalent is Cha'yaw. Masculine Hebrew equivalents: Aveechai, Chai, Cha'yim, Eleechai and Y'cheeayl.

HAZEL

The Anglo-Saxon name of a tree. Some authorities relate Hazel to Aveline which is French for hazel nut. Among the ancients of northwestern Europe the wand formed from the Hazel tree was the symbol of protection and authority.

Hebrew equivalents: Mawgaynaw, Shimris, Tzeelaw and Yaakovaw. Masculine Hebrew equivalents: Awsawf, Chetzron, Eleefelet, Lot, Tachan and Yaakov.

Key: *a* as in f*a*ther; *ai* as in *ai*sle; *aw* as in l*aw*; *ay* as in s*ay*; *e* as in b*e*t;

HAZELBELLE
A combination of Hazel and Belle. See Hazel and Belle for a full information.

HEATHER
From the Anglo-Saxon meaning "a heath, a plant, a shrub."

Hebrew equivalents: K'tzeeaw, Marvaw, Neta, N'tee-yaw, Raychawnaw, Sh'seelaw and Sh'sulaw. Masculine Hebrew equivalents: Narkis, Shawsil, Shawsul, Tzemach and Zoraya.

HEDDA
From the German meaning "strife, warfare."

Hebrew equivalents: Amtzaw, Gavreeaylaw, Geeboraw and Tigraw. Masculine Hebrew equivalents: Aveecha'yil, Ben-Cha'yil, Naftawlee and Yisrawayl.

HEDIA, HEDYA
From the Hebrew meaning "the voice or echo of the Lord."

The exact Hebrew equivalent is Haydyaw. Masculine Hebrew equivalents: Amaryaw, Divree and Imree.

HEDVA
From the Hebrew meaning "joy."

The exact Hebrew equivalent is Chedvaw. Masculine Hebrew equivalents: Chusheeawm, Chusheeayl, Ditz, Semach and Simchaw.

HEDY, HETTY
Either diminutive forms of Hedda or Hester and Esther.

For feminine and masculine equivalents, see Hedda and Esther.

HEIDI
Probably a variant form of Hester and its diminutive, Hettie, both of which are derivatives of Esther. See Esther for a full explanation.

ee as in b*ee*t; *i* as in b*i*t; *o* as in n*o*; *oi* as in v*oi*d; *u* as in r*u*de.

HELAINE

A variant form of Helen meaning "light," in the Greek.
See Helen for feminine and masculine Hebrew equivalents.

HELEN, HELENA, HELENE

From the Greek meaning "light." There are many variations and short forms of Helen including Elaine, Eleanor and Ellen. In Ireland Eileen is a very popular variant form.

Hebrew equivalents: Ameeor, B'heeraw, M'eeraw, Nawhawraw, N'heeraw, Oraw, Oris, Orlee, Orlis, Ornaw, Tz'feeraw, Y'eeraw and Zawhawraw. Masculine Hebrew equivalents: Acheenayr, Barkai, Bawrekes, Mayeer, Nawheer, Nayreeyaw, N'horai, Or, Oree, Uree, Ureeayl and Z'rachyaw.

HELENMAE

A combination of Helen meaning "light," and Mae meaning "kingswoman."
See Helen and Mae for feminine and masculine Hebrew equivalents.

HEMDA

From the Hebrew meaning "desirable, precious."
The exact Hebrew equivalent is Chemdaw. Masculine Hebrew equivalents: Chamadayl, Chawmud, Chayfetz, Chemdawn and Chemed.

HENRIETTA, HENRIETTE, HETTA, HETTY

Variant forms of Harriet meaning "mistress of the house, lord, ruler," in the Teutonic.

Hebrew equivalents: Atawraw, Geeboraw, Layaw, Malkaw, Tz'feeraw and Yis'r'aylaw. Masculine Hebrew equivalents: Baal, Kasreeayl, Melech, Rabaw, Rawvaw and Rosh.

HEPHZIBAH, HEPZI, HEPZIA

From the Hebrew meaning "my desire." Hephzibah means "my desire is in her." Hephziba is a variant spelling of Hephzibah. Hepzi and Hepzia are independent names.

Key: *a* as in f*a*ther; *ai* as in *ai*sle; *aw* as in l*aw*; *ay* as in s*ay*; *e* as in b*e*t;

The exact Hebrew equivalents are Cheftzee, Cheftzee-yaw and Cheftzeebaw. The exact masculine Hebrew equivalent is Chayfetz.

HERMA
From the Teutonic meaning "beloved."

Hebrew equivalents: Ahuvaw, Chaveevaw, Cheebaw and Y'deedaw. Masculine Hebrew equivalents: Chovawv, Dawvid, Eldawd and Y'didyaw.

HERZLIA, HERZLIAH
The feminine form of Herzl. Herzl became a popular masculine personal name in honor of Theodor Herzl. See Herzl in masculine section for more information. Derived from the German and Yiddish meaning "deer." Herzliah is the name of a city in Israel.

The exact Hebrew equivalent is Hertz'leeyaw. The exact masculine Hebrew equivalent is Hertzayl.

HESTER
The Latin form of Esther meaning "star." Hetty is a pet form of Hester. See Esther for more information.

HILA, HILLA, HILLAH
From the Hebrew meaning "praise." The original form is the masculine Hillel. Hili and Hilly are diminutive forms.

The exact Hebrew equivalent is Heelaw. The exact masculine Hebrew equivalent is Heelayl.

HILARY, HILLARY
Either from the Greek meaning "cheerful," or from the Teutonic meaning "protector." Hillary is also used as a masculine name.

Hebrew equivalents: Aveega'yil, Bawtzraw, Chedvaw, Geelaw, Shimraw, Shimreeyaw, and Shimris. Masculine Hebrew equivalents: Avigdor, Awgil, Chusheeayl, Shmaryawhu, Shomayr, Simchaw and Yachmai.

HILDA, HILDERGARDE
From the Teutonic meaning "battlemaid." Hilda is also a short form of Mathilda.

ee as in b*ee*t; *i* as in b*i*t; *o* as in n*o*; *oi* as in v*oi*d; *u* as in r*u*de.

Hebrew equivalents: Almaw, Awtzmaw, Gavreelaw, Gee-boraw and Tigraw. Masculine Hebrew equivalents: Awmotz, Marwd'chai, M'dawn, Midyawn, Naftawlee and Yisrawayl.

HILLELA

The feminine form of Hillel meaning "praise" in the Hebrew.

The exact Hebrew equivalent is Heelaylaw. The exact masculine Hebrew equivalent is Heelayl.

HINDA

From the Anglo-Saxon or Yiddish meaning a "hind, a deer," and having the connotation of swiftness.

Hebrew equivalents: Awfraw, A'yeles and Tzivyaw. Masculine Hebrew equivalents: Ayfer, Boaz and Tz'vee.

HOLIDAY

From the Anglo-Saxon meaning "festive day, holiday."

Hebrew equivalents: Chageeyaw and Chagis. Masculine Hebrew equivalents: Chagai, Chagee, Simchaw and Yom-Tov.

HOLLACE, HOLLIS

Variant forms of Haley. See Haley for a full explanation.

HOLLY

From the Anglo-Saxon meaning "holy." It was also the name of a plant with red berries that was hung on the door in ancient English homes, with the hope that it would bring luck.

Hebrew equivalents: Ashayraw, Ashayris, Awshraw, Awshras and Mazawl. Masculine Hebrew equivalents: Chagai, Kadish, Mazawl-Tov, Seemawn-Tov and Y'kuseeayl.

HONEY

From the Anglo-Saxon meaning "honey."

Hebrew equivalents: Acheenoam, D'vawshaw, D'voraw, M'sukaw, Nawawmee and Tovaw. Masculine Hebrew equivalents: Aveenoam, Mawsok, Naamawn and Tuveeyaw.

Key: *a* as in f*a*ther; *ai* as in *ai*sle; *aw* as in l*aw*; *ay* as in s*ay*; *e* as in b*e*t;

HOPE

From the Anglo-Saxon meaning "trust or faith." Hope was first used as a Christian name by the 17th century Puritans who delighted in adopting abstract virtues for names. In addition to Hope—Faith, Charity, Prudence, Honour, etc., were used. Hope in Russian is "Nadezhda," from which the French created the name Nadine.

Hebrew equivalents: Emunaw, Bitchaw, Ergaw, Tocheles and Tzeepeeyaw. Masculine Hebrew equivalents: Ameetai, Amnon, Ne'emawn and Yawchil.

HORTENSE

From the Latin meaning "gardener."

Hebrew equivalents: Ganaw, Karmelaw and Nawvaw. Masculine Hebrew equivalents: Awdawm, Geenas, Karmel and Kar'mlee.

HULA

From the Hebrew meaning "to play (an instrument)."

The exact Hebrew equivalent is Chulaw. Masculine Hebrew equivalent: Yitzchawk.

HULDA

From the Hebrew meaning "a weasel." The literal meaning is "to creep, or crawl, or dig."

The exact Hebrew equivalent is Chuldaw. Masculine Hebrew equivalents: Chayled and Cheldai.

IDA

From the Greek meaning "happy" or from the Teutonic meaning "to work hard, industrious," or "a woman."

Hebrew equivalents: Aleezaw, Aveega'yil, Chawrutzaw, Deetzaw, Geelaw and S'maychaw. Masculine Hebrew equivalents: Awmayl, Simchaw, Yachdeeayl, Yawgil, Yitzchawk and Zeeruz.

IDEL, IDELLE, IDALEE, IDENA

Diminutive forms of Ida. See above. Idena may also be a compounded name derived from a combination of Ida and Dena (Dinah) ; and Idalee, a combination of Ida and Lee.

---

ee as in b*ee*t; *i* as in b*i*t; *o* as in n*o*; *oi* as in v*oi*d; *u* as in r*u*de.

IDIT

Either a variant Yiddish form of the Hebrew Y'hudis, which is Judith in English, or from the Arabic meaning "the best, choicest."

Hebrew equivalents: Eedis and Y'hudis. Masculine Hebrew equivalents: Aluf, Arzee, Erez and Uryawn.

IDRA

From the Aramaic meaning "a flag," or "a fig tree." The fig tree was symbolic of the scholar in ancient Hebrew culture.

The exact Hebrew equivalent is Idraw. Masculine Hebrew equivalents: Aluf, Arzee, Erez and Oryawn.

ILA, ILIT

Ila is a variant form of Ilit meaning "uppermost or superlative," in Aramaic.

The exact Hebrew equivalents are Eelaw and Eelis. Masculine Hebrew equivalents: Acheetuv, Aveetuv, Ben-Tzeeyon, Mishbawch and M'shubawch.

ILANA, ILANIT

From the Hebrew meaning "a tree." Elana and Elanit are variant spellings.

The exact Hebrew equivalents are Eelawnaw and Eelawnis. The exact masculine Hebrew equivalent is Eelawn.

ILENE

A variant form of Eileen and Helen meaning "light," in the Greek.

Hebrew equivalents: Eleeoraw, Leeoris, M'eeraw, N'heeraw, Oraw and Orlis. Masculine Hebrew equivalents: Eleeor, Leeor, Or, Oree and Ureeayl.

ILISA, ILISE, ILSA, ILYSE

Variant forms of Elizabeth. See Elizabeth for a full explanation.

IMMA

From the Hebrew meaning "mother." Also used as a

Key: *a* as in f*a*ther; *ai* as in *ai*sle; *aw* as in l*aw*; *ay* as in s*ay*; *e* as in b*e*t;

variant form of the Teutonic Emma meaning "the big one," or "grandmother."

The exact Hebrew equivalent is Eemaw. Masculine Hebrew equivalents: Abaw and Awvee.

IMOGEN, IMOGENE

From the Latin meaning "image, likeness."

Hebrew equivalents: Meechal and Meechawaylaw. Masculine Hebrew equivalents: Meechaw and Meechawayl.

INA

From the Latin meaning "mother."

See Imma for feminine and masculine Hebrew equivalents.

INEZ

From the Greek and Portuguese meaning "pure."

Hebrew equivalents: P'nuyaw, Zakaw, Zakeeyaw and Zakis. Masculine Hebrew equivalents: Ameezakai, Tzach, Tzachai and Zakai.

INGRID

A name very popular in Scandinavian countries. The literal meaning is "Ing's ride." In Norse mythology Ing was the god of fertility and peace.

Hebrew equivalents: Poraw, Poreeyaw, Shlomis and Shulamis. Masculine Hebrew equivalents: Efra'yim, Puraw, Shawlom and Shlomee.

IRENE, IRENA

From the Greek meaning "peace."

Hebrew equivalents: Margayaw, Rivkaw, Shaananaw, Shlomis and Shulamis. Masculine Hebrew equivalents: Avshawlom, Margoa, Margee'a, Shaanawn, Shawlom, Shlemyaw and Shlomeeayl.

IRIS

Iris is the Greek word for "rainbow." In Latin it means "faith, hope," which was the significance of the rainbow in

---

ee as in b*ee*t; *i* as in b*i*t; *o* as in n*o*; *oi* as in v*oi*d; *u* as in r*u*de.

the biblical account of the Flood, as it was in all classical mythology.

Hebrew equivalents: Emunaw, Bitchaw, Keshes and Tzeepeeyaw. Masculine Hebrew equivalents: Ameetai, Amnon, Ne'emawn and Yawchil.

IRMA
From the Teutonic meaning "maid of high degree," connoting nobility.

Hebrew equivalents: Almaw, Basyaw, Naaraw and N'deevaw. Masculine Hebrew equivalents: Adoneeyaw, Ameenawdawv, Aveehud, Nawdawv and Yisrawayl.

ISAACA
The feminine form of Isaac meaning "laughter," in the Hebrew. See Isaac in the masculine section for a full explanation.

ISABEL, ISABELE, ISABELLA, ISABELLE
Variant forms of Elisabeth meaning "God's oath," or "oath of God," in the Hebrew. See Elisabeth for additional information.

ISDORA
The feminine form of the masculine Isadore meaning "gift of Isis" in the Greek. Isis was the Egyptian moon goddess.

Hebrew equivalents: Matawnaw, Migdawnaw, N'sanyaw, Z'veedaw and Z'vudaw. Masculine Hebrew equivalents: Elnawsawn, Elzawvawd, Aveeshai, Matisyawhu, Nawsawn and Y'honawsawn.

ITA, ITTA
Either from the Celtic meaning "thirsty," or a corrupt Yiddish form of the Hebrew Y'hudis (Judith). Ita and Itta are also used as variant forms of Ida.

ITI, ITTI
From the Hebrew meaning "with me."

The exact Hebrew equivalent is Eetee. Masculine Hebrew equivalents: Eeseeayl and Eetai.

Key: *a* as in f*a*ther; *ai* as in *ai*sle; *aw* as in l*aw*; *ay* as in s*ay*; *e* as in b*e*t;

IVRIA, IVRIAH, IVRIT
Ivri is the original form by which Jews are known in the Bible, dating back to Abraham. Ivri means "from the other side (of the river Euphrates)" from which Abraham came. Ivria and Ivriah are variant forms of Ivri. Ivrit is the Hebrew word for the Hebrew language.

The exact Hebrew equivalents are Ivreeyaw and Ivris. Masculine Hebrew equivalents: Ayver and Ivree.

IVY
Ivy is a plant name derived from the Greek meaning "clinging." The clinging vine is the symbol of fruitfulness.

Hebrew equivalents: Poraw and Poreeyaw. Masculine Hebrew equivalents: Efra'yim and Puraw.

JACKIE
A diminutive form of Jacoba and Jacqueline which are, in turn, forms of Jacob. Jackie is also used as a masculine pet form.

The exact Hebrew equivalent is Yaakovaw. The exact masculine Hebrew equivalent is Yaakov.

JACOBA
The feminine form of Jacob meaning "to supplant," or "protect," in the Hebrew.

The exact Hebrew equivalent is Yaakovaw. The exact masculine Hebrew equivalent is Yaakov.

JACQUELINE, JACLYN
Variant forms of Jacoba, which is the feminine form of Jacob meaning "to supplant," or "protect," in the Hebrew.

The exact Hebrew equivalent is Yaakovaw. The exact masculine Hebrew equivalent is Yaakov.

JAEL
Either from the Hebrew meaning "mountain goat," or "to ascend," and having the connotation of height. It may also be derived from the Arabic meaning "prominent." In the Bible, Yael was the Kenite woman who slew Sisera with

ee as in b*ee*t; *i* as in b*i*t; *o* as in n*o*; *oi* as in v*oi*d; *u* as in r*u*de.

a tent-pin, in the days of Deborah. In Israel Jael is also used as a masculine name.

The exact Hebrew equivalent is Yawayl.

JAEN
From the Hebrew meaning an "ostrich."

The exact Hebrew equivalent is Yawayn. Masculine Hebrew equivalents: Gozawl and Tzeepor.

JAFFA, JAFIT
From the Hebrew meaning "beautiful, comely."

The exact Hebrew equivalents are Yawfaw and Yawfis. Masculine Hebrew equivalents: Yawfe and Yefes.

JAIME, JAIMEE, JAMIE
Feminine forms of the masculine James, which is derived from Jacob, meaning "to supplant," or "protect."

The exact Hebrew equivalent is Yardaynaw. Masculine Hebrew equivalents: Akavyaw, Akeevaw and Yaakov.

JAN, JANINA, JANNA
Variant forms of Jane. See below for a full explanation.

JANE, JANET, JANICE, JANIE, JANIS
Jane and its many variations are of Hebrew origin, akin to the masculine John and the feminine Hannah, meaning "gracious, merciful." When used as a middle name Jane is most frequently coupled with Susan and Barbara. Until the 16th century Joan was the popular feminine form of John. Jane became popular in the following centuries.

Hebrew equivalents: Chanaw and Yochawnaw. Masculine Hebrew equivalents: Amee-Chayn, Avee-Chayn, Chonee, Chonyo and Yochawnawn.

JARDENA
From the Hebrew meaning "to descend, to flow downward." The masculine counterpart is Jordan.

The exact Hebrew equivalent is Yardaynaw. Masculine Hebrew equivalents: Yardayn and Yered.

Key: *a* as in f*a*ther; *ai* as in *ai*sle; *aw* as in l*aw*; *ay* as in s*ay*; *e* as in b*e*t;

JASMINA, JASMINE
A Persian flower name, usually a flower in the olive family.

Hebrew equivalents: Yasmeen, Yasmeenaw. Masculine Hebrew equivalents: Za'yis and Zaysawn.

JEAN, JEANE, JEANINE, JEANETTE, JEANNE, JEANETTA, JEANIE, JEANNETTE, JEN, JENNIE, JENNY
Jean and its many variant spellings and forms are the feminine counterparts of John (Yochanan) and are closely related to Hannah. They are all derived from the Hebrew meaning "gracious, merciful."

Hebrew equivalents: Chanaw and Yochawnaw. Masculine Hebrew equivalents: Amee-Chayn, Avee-Chayn, Chonee, Chonyo and Yochawnawn.

JEMIMA
From the Arabic meaning "a dove." In the Bible Jemima was a daughter of Job. The Hebrew equivalent is Jonina.

Hebrew equivalents: Y'meemaw and Yoneenaw. Masculine Hebrew equivalents: Yonaw.

JEMINA
From the Hebrew meaning "right-handed."

The exact Hebrew equivalent is Y'meenaw. The exact masculine Hebrew equivalent is Yawmin.

JENNIFER
A Hebrew and Latin name meaning "graceful bearing." It is also used by the Welsh meaning "fair." Jen and Jenny are pet forms.

Hebrew equivalents: Adeevaw, Chanaw, Diklaw and Tawmawr. Masculine Hebrew equivalents: Chayn, Chonayn, Chonee, Eetawmawr, Elchawnawn and Yochawnawn.

JERI
A diminutive form of Geraldene. See Geraldene for a full explanation.

---

ee as in b*ee*t; *i* as in b*i*t; *o* as in n*o*; *oi* as in v*oi*d; *u* as in r*u*de.

JESSICA, JESSIE

From the Hebrew meaning "God's grace," or, if taken from the same root as the masculine Jesse, it has the meaning of "riches." Jessie is a pet form.

Hebrew equivalents: Bash-Shua, Chanaw, Tawmawr and Yisraw. Masculine Hebrew equivalents: Elchawnawn, Eetawmawr, Yisro and Yochawnawn.

JETHRA

A feminine form of Jethro meaning "abundance, riches," in the Hebrew.

The exact Hebrew equivalent is Yisraw. The exact masculine Hebrew equivalent is Yisro.

JEWEL

From the Old French meaning "joy."

Hebrew equivalents: Aleezaw, Deetzaw, Geelaw and Reenaw. Masculine Hebrew equivalents: Simchaw, Yachdeeayl, Yawgil and Yitzchawk.

JEZEBEL

From the Hebrew meaning "unexalted," or "impure." In the Bible Jezebel was the wife of King Ahab.

The exact Hebrew equivalent is Eezevel. There are no masculine Hebrew equivalents.

JILL

A variant form of Gill meaning "girl." See Gill for a full explanation.

JOAN, JOANN, JOANNA, JOANNE, JO-ANN, JO-ANNE, JOHANNA

A variety of names derived from the Hebrew meaning "gracious." Johanna is the feminine form of John and Jochanan. The Yiddish name Yachne, popular among Lithuanian and Polish Jews, is also a form of Jochanan.

Hebrew equivalents: Chanaw, Diklaw, Tawmawr and Yochawnaw. Masculine Hebrew equivalents: Chananayl, Chananyaw, Chawnawn and Yochawnawn.

Key: *a* as in f*a*ther; *ai* as in *ai*sle; *aw* as in l*aw*; *ay* as in s*ay*; *e* as in b*e*t;

JOCELIN, JOCELINE, JOCELYN, JOSCELINE, JOSCELIND, JOSCELYN

Forms of Justina which is the feminine form of the Latin Justin meaning "just, honest."

Hebrew equivalents: Danyaw, Dawneeaylaw, Dawnis and Tawmawr. Masculine Hebrew equivalents: Acheedawn, Acheetzedek, Ameetzedek, Aveedawn, Dawn, Dawneeayl, Tzawdok and Tzidkeeyawhu.

JOCHEBED, JOCHEVED

From the Hebrew meaning "God is glorious," or "the honor of God." In the Bible Jochebed was the wife of Amram, and the mother of Moses, Aaron and Miriam.

The exact Hebrew equivalent is Yocheved. Masculine Hebrew equivalents: Kawvud and M'chubawd.

JODETTE, JODI, JODY

Either diminutive forms of Jocelyn or from the Latin, *jocose,* meaning "happy."

Hebrew equivalents: Geelaw, Geelee, Geelawnaw, Reenaw and Ronee. Masculine Hebrew equivalents: Eleeron, Eles, Eletz, Simchai and Yachdeeayl. See Jocelin for additional equivalents.

JOELA, JOELLA, JOELLE

Feminine forms of Joel meaning "God is willing," in the Hebrew. See Joel in the masculine section for additional information.

The exact Hebrew equivalent is Yoaylaw. The exact masculine Hebrew equivalent is Yoayl.

JOHNNIE, JONNIE

Diminutives of Johanna. See Johanna for a full explanation.

JOICE, JOY, JOYCE

From the Latin meaning "happy."

Hebrew equivalents: Aleezaw, Geelaw, Reenaw, R'nawnaw and Seesaw. Masculine Hebrew equivalents: Aliz, Awgil, Geelawn, Geelee, Semach, Simchaw and Simchon.

ee as in b*ee*t; *i* as in b*i*t; *o* as in n*o*; *oi* as in v*oi*d; *u* as in r*u*de.

JONINA

From the Hebrew meaning "a dove." Jemima is the Arabic equivalent.

The exact Hebrew equivalent is Yoneenaw. The exact masculine Hebrew equivalent is Yonaw.

JONIT, JONATI

A variant spelling of Yonit and Yonati meaning "dove" in Hebrew.

The exact Hebrew equivalents are Yonawsee and Yonis. The exact masculine Hebrew equivalent is Yonaw.

JORDANA, JORDENA

Variant spelling of Jardena meaning "to descend" or "to flow downard," in the Hebrew. Jordan is the masculine form.

The exact Hebrew equivalent is Yardaynaw. The exact masculine Hebrew equivalent is Yardayn.

JOSEFA, JOSEPHA

Feminine forms of Joseph meaning "He (God) will add or increase," in the Hebrew. See Joseph in the masculine section for additional information.

The exact Hebrew equivalent is Yosayfaw and Yoseefaw. The exact masculine Hebrew equivalent is Yosayf.

JOVITA

From the Latin meaning "jovial."

Hebrew equivalents: Aveega'yil, Bilgaw, Chedvaw, Deetzaw and S'maychaw. Masculine Hebrew equivalents: Eletz, Ditz, Marnin, Mawsos, Yawgayl and Yitzchawk.

JUDITH, JUDI, JUDIE, JUDY

From the Hebrew meaning "praise." In the Bible Judith was the name of Esau's wife. It became popular, however, because of the beautiful heroine in the book of Judith (in the Apocrypha) who succeeded in beheading Holofernes, the Assyrian general. Judah is the masculine counterpart. Judi and Judy are popular diminutive forms. Eudice, Yudit, Yehudit and Yuta are variant forms of the original Hebrew.

Key: *a* as in f*a*ther; *ai* as in *ai*sle; *aw* as in l*aw*; *ay* as in s*ay*; *e* as in b*e*t;

The exact Hebrew equivalent is Y'hudis. The exact masculine Hebrew equivalent is Y'hudaw or Y'hudee.

JULE, JULES, JULIE, JULIET
Variant forms of the masculine Julius. Julia, Julian and Juliana are additional variant forms. See Julia for a full explanation.

JULIA, JULIAN, JULIANA
From the Greek meaning "soft-haired," symbolizing youth. Julian is used primarily as a masculine name. Some authorities consider Julian and Juliana to be derived from Gillian meaning "girl" (see Gill). The Roman family Julii were noted for their long hair.

Hebrew equivalents: Almaw, Aveevaw, D'leelaw, Neemaw, Tz'eeraw, Y'neekaw and Zilpaw. Masculine Hebrew equivalents: Awviv, Aylawm, S'orim and Yefes.

JUNE
From the Latin meaning "ever youthful."

Hebrew equivalents: Almaw, Aveevaw, Aveevis, Tz'eeraw, Y'neekaw and Zilpaw. Masculine Hebrew equivalents: Awviv, Aylawm, Eleenoar, Naarai, Naaryaw and Yefes.

JUSTINA, JUSTINE
The feminine form of Justin meaning "just, honest," in the Latin.

Hebrew equivalents: Danyaw, Dawneeaylaw, Dawnis, Acheetzedek, Ameetzedek, Avcedawn, Dawn, Dawneeayl, and Tawmawr. Masculine Hebrew equivalents: Acheedawn, Tzawdok and Tzidkeeyawhu.

KAILE, KAYLE
Variant form of Kelila. See Kelila for full information.

KALANIT
The name of a plant with cup-shaped, colorful flowers seen on the Israeli countryside.

The exact Hebrew equivalent is Kalawnis. Masculine Hebrew equivalents: Chavakuk, Neta, Shawsil and Tzemach.

---

ee as in b*ee*t; *i* as in b*i*t; *o* as in n*o*; *oi* as in v*oi*d; *u* as in r*u*de.

KAREN
A variant form of Katherine. Also spelled as Caren. Derived from the Greek meaning "pure, purity."

See Katherine for feminine and masculine Hebrew equivalents.

KARMA, KARMEL, KARMELA, KARMIA, KARMICE, KARMIT
From the Hebrew meaning "vineyard." Karmia means "vineyard of the Lord." Karmit is the Israeli pronunciation of Karmis. Karmel is used as a masculine as well as feminine.

Hebrew equivalents: Karmaw, Karmel, Karmeeyaw, Karmis and Karmelis. Masculine Hebrew equivalents: Karmel, Karmee, Karmeeayl and Kerem.

KARNA, KARNICE, KARNIT
From the Hebrew meaning "horn (of an animal)."

The exact Hebrew equivalents are Karnaw and Karnis. The exact masculine Hebrew equivalent is Karneeayl.

KARNIELA, KARNIELLA
From the Hebrew meaning "the horn of the Lord."

The exact Hebrew equivalent is Karneeaylaw. The exact masculine Hebrew equivalent is Karneeayl.

KAROLYN
A variant spelling of Carolyn and Caroline. See Caroline for a full explanation.

KATE, KATHIE, KATHY, KATY, KITTY
Variant diminutive forms of Katherine and Catherine. See Katherine for a full explanation.

KATHERINE, KATHRYN
Variant spellings of Catherine, derived from the Greek meaning "pure, purity."

Hebrew equivalents: B'ruraw, P'nuyaw, Zakaw, Zakis and Zakeeyaw. Masculine Hebrew equivalents: Ameezakai, Bawrur, Tzach, Tzachai and Zakai.

Key: *a* as in f*a*ther; *ai* as in *ai*sle; *aw* as in l*aw*; *ay* as in s*ay*; *e* as in b*e*t;

KATHLEEN

A variant spelling of Cathleen. Kathleen and Cathleen are the Irish forms of Katherine and Catherine. See Katherine for a full explanation.

KATRINA, KATRINE, KATRINKA

Variant forms of Katherine. In various European countries these are popular forms, as are: Katarina, Kathrina, Karina and Katya. See Katherine for a full explanation.

KAY

Either from the Greek meaning "rejoice," or a form of Katherine meaning "purity."

Hebrew equivalents: B'ruraw, Reenaw, Seesaw, Zakaw and Zakeeyaw. Masculine Hebrew equivalents: Bilgai, Bawrur, Chusheeawm, Yachdeeayl and Zakai.

KEDMA

From the Hebrew meaning "towards the east."

The exact Hebrew equivalent is Kaydmaw. The exact masculine Hebrew equivalent is Kedem.

KEFIRA

From the Hebrew meaning "a young lioness."

The exact Hebrew equivalent is K'feeraw. The exact masculine Hebrew equivalent is K'feer.

KELILA, KELULA

From the Hebrew meaning "a crown or laurel," symbolic of victory, perfection and beauty. Kaile, Kayle, Kyla and Kyle are variant forms used as Yiddish names. Kelila and Kelula are used in Israel today.

The exact Hebrew equivalents are K'leelaw and K'lulaw. The exact masculine Hebrew equivalents are Kawlil and Kawlul.

KEREN, KERYN

From the Hebrew meaning "horn (of an animal)."

The exact Hebrew equivalent is Keren. The exact masculine Hebrew equivalent is Karneeayl.

---

ee as in be*e*t; *i* as in b*i*t; *o* as in n*o*; *oi* as in v*oi*d; *u* as in r*u*de.

KERET

From the Hebrew meaning "city or settlement."

The exact Hebrew equivalent is Keres. Masculine Hebrew equivalents: Dur, D'vir, Y'shevawm, Y'shevawv, Z'vul and Z'vulun.

KESHET

From the Hebrew meaning "a bow, a rainbow."

The exact Hebrew equivalent is Keshes. Masculine Hebrew equivalents: Rawviv and Tal.

KESHISHA

From the Aramaic meaning "old or elder."

The exact Hebrew equivalent is K'sheeshaw. Masculine Hebrew equivalents: Yawshish and Y'sheeshai.

KETIFA

From the Arabic meaning "to pluck" (usually ripened fruit).

The exact Hebrew equivalent is K'teefaw. Masculine Hebrew equivalents: Gidon and Kotz.

KETZIA, KEZIA

From the Hebrew meaning "a powdered, cinnamon-like bark," hence, the secondary meaning of "fragrant." Kezia was one of the daughters of Job in the Bible.

The exact Hebrew equivalent is K'tzeeaw. Masculine Hebrew equivalents: Mawrd'chai, Mivsawm, Mor, Raychawn, Tz'ree and Yivsawm.

KIM

A contrived name made up of the first letters of Kansas, Illinois and Missouri. At one point, these three states meet.

There are no Hebrew equivalents.

KORENET

From the Hebrew meaning "to shine, to emit rays."

The exact Hebrew equivalent is Korenes. Masculine Hebrew equivalents: Karnee, Karneeayl and Kawrin.

Key: *a* as in father; *ai* as in aisle; *aw* as in law; *ay* as in say; *e* as in bet;

KYLA, KYLE
Variant forms of Kelila. See Kelila for full information.

LAILA, LAILI, LAILIE, LAYLIE
From the Hebrew meaning "nocturnal, pertaining to the night or darkness."
The exact Hebrew equivalents are Lailaw and Laylee. Masculine Hebrew equivalents: Adawr, Ashchur, Chachalyaw and Pinchaws.

LARAINE
From the Latin meaning "sea-bird."
Hebrew equivalents: A'yaw, Dawaw, Da'yaw, Tzeepawreeyaw, Tzeepawrtaw and Tzeeporaw. Masculine Hebrew equivalents: Gozawl and Tzeepor.

LARISSA
From the Latin meaning "cheerful."
Hebrew equivalents: Aveega'yil, Elzaw, Geelawnaw, Geeleeyaw, Geelis and Reenaw. Masculine Hebrew equivalents: Aliz, Geelon, Eleerawn, Elez and Yawgil.

LAURA, LAURANE, LAURE, LAUREL, LAUREN, LAURENE, LAURIE
From the Latin meaning "the laurel," which is a symbol of victory.
Hebrew equivalents: Atawraw, Dafnaw, Hadasaw and Tz'feeraw. Masculine Hebrew equivalents: Govayr, N'tzeeach and Yatzleeach.

LAURETTE, LAURETTA
Diminutive forms of Laura. See above for a full explanation.

LEA, LEAH
From the Hebrew meaning "to be weary," or from the Assyrian meaning "mistress, ruler." Lee is a popular pet form. Lia is an Italian variant, and Lea is a French variant as well as a diminutive form. In the Bible Leah was the daughter of Laban and the first of Jacob's wives.

ee as in b*ee*t; *i* as in b*i*t; *o* as in n*o*; *oi* as in v*oi*d; *u* as in r*u*de.

The exact Hebrew equivalent is Layaw. Masculine Hebrew equivalents: Aveemelech, Eleemelech, Kasreeayl, Melech and Yisrawayl.

LEANA, LEANNE, LIANA
From the Latin meaning "to bind."

Hebrew equivalents: Oganyaw and Rivkaw. Masculine Hebrew equivalents: Asir, Awnuv, Awtayr and Eesur.

LEANOR, LEANORE
Variant forms of Eleanor. See Eleanor for a full explanation.

LEATRICE
Probably a combination of Leah and Beatrice. See Leah and Beatrice for a full explanation.

LEE
Either from the Anglo-Saxon meaning "meadow-land," or a diminutive of Leah.

Hebrew equivalents: Ganaw, Geenaw, Karmel and Layaw. Masculine Hebrew equivalents: Hevel, Karmel and Karm'lee.

LEEBA
A Yiddish name, of Germanic origin, meaning "beloved." Leeba is also used in Israel, and is taken as of Hebrew origin meaning "heart."

Hebrew equivalents: Ahuvaw, Chaveevaw, Cheebaw, Leebaw and Dawveedaw. Masculine Hebrew equivalents: Bildawd, Chovawv, Dawvid, Layv and Y'didyaw.

LEILA
From the Arabic and Hebrew meaning "dark oriental beauty," or "night." Among the Persians Leilah was used as a name meaning "dark-haired." Laila, Laili, Lailie and Laylie are variant forms.

The exact Hebrew equivalent is Lailaw. Masculine Hebrew equivalents: Aveenoam, Ayfai, Chemdawn and Pinchaws. See Laila for additional equivalents.

Key: *a* as in f*a*ther; *ai* as in *ai*sle; *aw* as in l*aw*; *ay* as in s*ay*; *e* as in b*e*t;

LELA, LELIA
From the Teutonic meaning "loyal, faithful."

Hebrew equivalents: Bitchaw, Emunaw and Tikvaw. Masculine Hebrew equivalents: Ameetai, Amnon, Bukee and Haymawn.

LENA, LENNIE, LENORA, LENORE
Forms of Eleanor. See Eleanor for a full explanation. Lena is also used as a modern Israeli name derived from the Hebrew meaning "to dwell," or "lodging."

The exact Hebrew equivalent is Leenaw. Masculine Hebrew equivalents: Dur, Mawlon, Z'vul and Z'vulun.

LEOLA
From the Teutonic meaning "deer," and having the connotation of swiftness.

Hebrew equivalents: Awfraw, A'yeles, Tzivyaw, Yaalis and Y'aylaw. Masculine Hebrew equivalents: Ayfer, Boaz, Tz'vee, Tz'veeayl and Tzivyon.

LEONA, LEONARDA, LEONIE
From the Greek meaning "lion-like," and having the connotation of strength.

Hebrew equivalents: Amtzaw, Areeayl, Areeaylaw, Gavreelaw and Geeboraw. Masculine Hebrew equivalents: Aree, Areeayl, Aryay, Aveecha'yil, Gavreeayl, Kawlayv and La'yish.

LEONORE
A variant form of Eleanor. See Eleanor for a full explanation.

LEORA, LEORIT
From the Hebrew meaning "light, my light."

The exact Hebrew equivalents are Leeoraw and Leeoris. The exact masculine Hebrew equivalent is Leeor.

LERON, LERONE
From the Hebrew meaning "song is mine." In Israel it is used as a feminine and masculine name.

The exact Hebrew equivalent is Leeron.

---

ee as in b*ee*t; *i* as in b*i*t; *o* as in n*o*; *oi* as in v*oi*d; *u* as in r*u*de.

LESLEY, LESLIE
From the Anglo-Saxon meaning "meadow-lands."
Hebrew equivalents: Ganaw, Karmelaw and Nawvaw. Masculine Hebrew equivalents: Karmel, Kar'mlee and Yaaree.

LETA, LETTY
Probably forms of Elizabeth. See Elizabeth for a full explanation.

LETIFA, LETIPHA
From the Hebrew meaning "to pat, caress."
The exact Hebrew equivalent is L'teefaw. The exact masculine Hebrew equivalent is Lawtif.

LETITIA
From the Latin meaning "joy." Letty, Lettie, Tisha and Titia are pet forms.
Hebrew equivalents: Aleezaw, Elzaw, Geelaw, Geelawnaw, Leeron and Ronlee. Masculine Hebrew equivalents: Awgil, Eleerawn, Eles, Elez, Geelon, Yachdeeayl and Yitzchawk.

LEVANA, LIVANA
From the Hebrew meaning "the moon," or "white."
The exact Hebrew equivalent is L'vawnaw. The exact masculine Hebrew equivalent is Lawvawn.

LEVIA
From the Hebrew meaning "to join." The masculine form is Levi. A similar sounding name is derived from the Hebrew meaning "lioness."
The exact Hebrew equivalent is L'veeyaw. The exact masculine Hebrew equivalent is Lawvee.

LEVONA, LIVONA
From the Hebrew meaning "spice, incense," used during the sacrificial system, and so-called because of its white color. Levana, in Hebrew meaning "white," is derived from the same root as the word meaning "spice."

The exact Hebrew equivalent is L'vonaw. Masculine Hebrew equivalents: Lawvawn.

LEYLA
A variant spelling of Leila. See Leila for a full explanation.

LIA
The Italian form of Leah. See Leah for a full explanation.

LIBA
A variant spelling of Leeba. See Leeba for a full explanation.

LIBBIE, LIBBY
Diminutive forms of Elizabeth. See Elizabeth for a full explanation.

LILA, LILAC, LILAH
Flower names of Persian origin relating to the lilac flower.

The exact Hebrew equivalent is Leelawch. Masculine Hebrew equivalents: Efra'yim, Pekach, P'rachyaw and Tzemach.

LILIAN, LILLIAN, LILI, LILIBET, LILY, LILLY, LILYAN
Either Greek or Latin forms pertaining to the lily (flower), or forms derived from Elizabeth meaning "God's oath," in the Hebrew. Lilibet is a popular pet form for Queen Elizabeth. Lil and Lily, in their various forms and spellings, are diminutive forms.

Hebrew equivalents: Eleesheva, Neetzaw, Shoshanaw and Vardaw. Masculine Hebrew equivalents: Efra'yim, Pekach, P'rachyaw, Sheva and Tzemach.

LINA
Diminutive of either Carolina or Adelina. See Caroline and Adeline for an explanation of each name.

---

ee as in b*ee*t; *i* as in b*i*t; *o* as in n*o*; *oi* as in v*oi*d; *u* as in r*u*de.

LINDA

Either from the Latin and Spanish meaning "handsome, pretty," or from the Teutonic meaning "lovely or gentle maid." Some authorities maintain that Linda is derived from Old German meaning "serpent."

Hebrew equivalents: Almaw, Naamaw, Nawawmee, Rivkaw and Yawfaw. Masculine Hebrew equivalents: Chemdawn, Binyawmin, Moshe, Naarai and Nun.

LINN, LINNE

From the Welsh meaning "waterfall, lake." Lyn and Lynne are variant forms.

Hebrew equivalents: D'roraw, Mawrawsaw and Miryawm. Masculine Hebrew equivalents: Arnon, Aynawn, Aveeyawm, Moshe and Peleg.

LINNET

From the Latin meaning "flax or flaxen-haired." Linnet may also be a diminutive form of the Welsh Linn (see above).

Hebrew equivalents: Pazeeyaw, Pazis, Tz'huvaw and Z'huvaw. Masculine Hebrew equivalents: Elifaz, Pawz, Upawz and Zawhawvee.

LIORA

A variant spelling of Leora meaning "light," in the Hebrew.

See Leora for feminine and masculine equivalents.

LIRIT

A name used in Israel meaning "lyrical, musical, poetic." The original form of the word is Greek, but it is also used in Latin and French as well as Hebrew.

The exact Hebrew equivalent is Leeris. Masculine Hebrew equivalents: Ameerawn, Leeron, Yawron, Zimrawn and Z'maryaw.

LIRON, LIRONE

From the Hebrew meaning "song is mine." Leron and

Lerone are variant spellings. These names are used in Israel as masculine names as well.

The exact Hebrew equivalent is Leeron.

LISA, LITA, LIZA

Forms of Elizabeth. See Elizabeth for a full explanation.

LITAL

From the Hebrew meaning "dew (rain) is mine."

The exact Hebrew equivalent is Leetal. Masculine Hebrew equivalents: Tal, Tal-Or and Tal-Shachar.

LIVIA, LIVIYA

Livia is generally taken as a short form of Olivia meaning "olive" in Latin. In Hebrew Livia (pronounced Livyaw) means "a crown." Liviya (accent on last syllable) is from the Hebrew meaning "lioness." Liviya is also spelled Leviya and Levia.

The exact Hebrew equivalents are Livyaw and L'veeyaw. Masculine Hebrew equivalents: Aree, Gur, Gur-Aryay, Kasreeayl and Tzofar.

LIZBETH, LIZZIE, LIZZY

Diminutive forms of Elizabeth. See Elizabeth for a full explanation.

LOIS

From the Greek meaning "good, desirable."

Hebrew equivalents: Bas-Tzeeyon, Tovaw, Shifraw and Yawtvaw. Masculine Hebrew equivalents: Ben-Tzeeyon, Naamawn, Nawam and Tuveeyaw.

LOLA

A diminutive of the Spanish Carlota, related to Caroline. See Caroline for interpretation and equivalents.

LORA, LORAN, LORAINE, LORRAINE

From the Latin meaning "she who weeps, sorrowful," or from Old High German meaning "famous warrior."

Hebrew equivalents: Bas-Shua, Mawraw, Mawrawsaw,

ee as in beet; *i* as in bit; *o* as in no; *oi* as in void; *u* as in rude.

Miryawm and Tzawraw. Masculine Hebrew equivalents: Awmos, Ben-Oni, Eeyov and Onawn.

LORELEI
From the German meaning "melody, song."

Hebrew equivalents: Leeris, Leeron, Reenaw, Sheeraw and T'heelaw. Masculine Hebrew equivalents: Aharon, Anaw, Leeron, Yawron and Zemer.

LOREN
From the Latin meaning "crowned with laurel," the symbol of victory.

Hebrew equivalents: Dafnaw, Hadasaw, K'leelaw, K'lulaw and Tagaw. Masculine Hebrew equivalents: Kasreeayl, Kisron, N'tzeeach, Yatzleeach and Zayraw.

LORETTA
From the Teutonic meaning "ignorant."

The only equivalent is the feminine Hebrew Aveeshag. Euphemistically interpreted it would mean "wise, educated." Hebrew equivalents: Beenaw, Bunaw and Milkaw. Masculine Hebrew equivalents: Achbawn, Chanoch, Yawvin and Yoshaw.

LORETTE, LORI
Forms of Lora, or Loretta. See Lora or Loretta for a full explanation.

LORNA
From the Anglo-Saxon meaning "lost, forlorn, forsaken." This name was created by R. C. Blackmore in his novel *Lorna Doone* in 1869.

Hebrew equivalents: Azuvaw and Hawgawr. Masculine Hebrew equivalents: Gayrshom, Gayrshon and Yismaw.

LOTTA, LOTTIE
Diminutive forms of Charlotte. See Charlotte for a full explanation.

Key: *a* as in f*a*ther; *ai* as in *ai*sle; *aw* as in l*aw*; *ay* as in s*ay*; *e* as in b*e*t;

LOUISA, LOUISE
From the Teutonic meaning "hero or refuge of the people, warrior, prince." Lou and Louie are pet forms.

Hebrew equivalents: Gavreelaw, Sawraw, Tigraw and Yis'r'aylaw. Masculine Hebrew equivalents: Aveecha'yil, La'yish, Naftawlee, Shmaryawhu and Yisrawayl.

LOURA, LOURANA
Variant forms of Laura. Lourana is a combination of Laura and Anna. See Laura for a full explanation.

LUCETTE, LUCIA
Diminutive forms of Lucille. See below for a full explanation.

LUCILE, LUCILLE, LUCY
From the Latin meaning "light, light-bringing, daybreak." Luce is a surname derived from Lucile.

Hebrew equivalents: B'heeraw, M'eeraw, Leeoraw, Nawhawraw and Oraw. Masculine Hebrew equivalents: Mayeer, Lapeedos, Leeor, Ureeayl and Z'rachyaw.

LUELLA
A variant form of Louise. See Louise for a full explanation.

LUISA, LULA
Forms of Louise. See Louisa for a full explanation.

LULIE, LULU
From the Anglo-Saxon meaning "soothing, comforting."

Hebrew equivalents: Nechawmaw. Masculine Hebrew equivalents: M'nachaym, Nawchum and N'chemyaw.

LUNETTA
From the Latin meaning "shining one" or "the moon."

The exact Hebrew equivalent is L'vawnaw. Masculine Hebrew equivalents: Eleeor, Lawvawn, Leeor, Shragai and Shragaw.

LYDA, LYDIA
A Greek place name meaning "a maiden from Lydia."

ee as in b*ee*t; *i* as in b*i*t; *o* as in n*o*; *oi* as in v*oi*d; *u* as in r*u*de.

Hebrew equivalents: Almaw, Naaraw, Reevaw and Tz'eeraw. Masculine Hebrew equivalents: Ben, Binyawmin, Moshe and R'uvayn.

LYN, LYNN, LYNNE, LYNETTE
Variant English forms of Linn and Linnet. See Linn for a full explanation.

MABEL, MABELLA, MABELLE, MABLE
Either from the Latin meaning "my beautiful one," or from Old Irish meaning "merry." Some authorities contend that Mabel is derived from the Latin meaning "lovable."

Hebrew equivalents: Acheenoam, Aveecha'yil, Geelaw, Nawawmee and Shifraw. Masculine Hebrew equivalents: Aveenoam, Chemdawn, Nawam, Simchaw and Yawgil.

MADELAINE, MADELEINE, MADELINE, MADELON, MADELYN
Variant forms of Magdalene. See Magdalene for a full explanation. Maddie and Maddy are pet forms.

MADGE, MAGGIE
Diminutive forms of Margaret. See Margaret for a full explanation.

MAE
Either a form of Mary or a form of May. See Mary and May for a full explanation.

MAGDA, MAGDALENE MAGDALINE
From the Hebrew meaning "a high tower."

The exact Hebrew equivalent is Migdawlaw. Masculine Hebrew equivalents: Aharon, Aylee, Hawrawn, Rawm and Talmai.

MAGNOLIA
From modern Latin meaning "the big laurel tree," a symbol of victory.

Hebrew equivalents: Dafnaw, and Hadasaw. Masculine Hebrew equivalents: Matzleeach, N'tzeeach and Yatzleeach.

Key: *a* as in f*a*ther; *ai* as in *ai*sle; *aw* as in l*aw*; *ay* as in s*ay*; *e* as in b*e*t;

MAHIRA
From the Hebrew meaning "speedy, energetic."
The exact Hebrew equivalent is M'heeraw. The exact masculine Hebrew equivalents are Maharee, Mahayr and Mawheer.

MAIDA
From the Teutonic meaning "a maiden."
Hebrew equivalents: Almaw, Naaraw, Reevaw and Tz'eeraw. Masculine Hebrew equivalents: Bawchur, Naarai and Naaryaw.

MAISIE
Either a form of Miriam or a form of Margaret. See Miriam and Margaret for a full explanation.

MALINDA
From the Old English meaning "gentle." Lindy is a pet form.
Feminine Hebrew equivalents: Adeevaw, Naamaw, N'deevaw and Rawchayl. Masculine Hebrew equivalents: Awdiv, Naamawn, Nawdiv and Noam.

MALKA
From the Hebrew meaning "a queen."
The exact Hebrew equivalent is Malkaw. The exact masculine Hebrew equivalent is Melech.

MALVINA
The feminine form of Melvin meaning "servant or chief," in the Celtic. According to some authorities it is derived from the Anglo-Saxon meaning "friendly toiler," or "famous friend."
Hebrew equivalents: Atawraw, Ameesaw, Nawawmee, Malkaw and Yis'r'aylaw. Masculine Hebrew equivalents: Awmis, G'dalyaw, Maydawd, Ovadyaw, Ovayd and R'uayl.

MAMIE
A variant form of Mary, used as a pet name. See Mary for a full explanation.

ee as in b*ee*t; *i* as in b*i*t; *o* as in n*o*; *oi* as in v*oi*d; *u* as in r*u*de.

MANDY
A pet form of Amanda which is derived from the Latin meaning "to love."

Hebrew equivalents: Ahuvaw, Chaveevaw, Cheebaw, Dawveedaw and L'teefaw. Masculine Hebrew equivalents: Chemdawn, Chovawv, Dawvid and Y'didyaw.

MANETTE
A variant form of Mary. See Mary for a full explanation.

MANGENA, MANGINA
From the Hebrew meaning "song, melody."

The exact Hebrew equivalent is Mangeenaw. Masculine Hebrew equivalents: Zawmir, Zemer, Zimraw, Zimrawn and Z'maryaw.

MANUELA
A Spanish feminine form of Manuel or Emanuel which are of Hebrew origin meaning "God is with us."

The exact Hebrew equivalent is Emawnuaylaw. The exact masculine Hebrew equivalent is Emawnuayl.

MARA
A form of Mary and Miriam. See Mary and Miriam for a full explanation.

MARCELLA, MARCILEN
From the Latin meaning "brave, martial" or "a hammer." Marcilen is a variant form of Marcella which is the feminine counterpart of Mark. Mars, from which Mark is derived, was the Roman god of war.

Hebrew equivalents: Amtzaw, Awtzmaw, Gavreelaw and Tigraw. Masculine Hebrew equivalents: Gayraw, Mawrd'-chai, M'dawn, Midyawn and Naftawlee.

MARCIA, MARCIE, MARCY, MARSHA, MARSHE
Marcia and its variant forms are related to Marcella. See above for a full explanation.

Key: *a* as in f*a*ther; *ai* as in *ai*sle; *aw* as in l*aw*; *ay* as in s*ay*; *e* as in b*e*t;

MAREEA, MARENA, MARIA, MARINA, MARINNA
Variant forms of Mary. See Mary for a full explanation.

MARGALIS, MARGALIT, MARGALITH
A Hebrew name derived from the Greek meaning "pearl." Margaret is derived from the same root.

The exact Hebrew equivalent is Margawlis. Masculine Hebrew equivalents: Dar, P'neenee and Tarshish.

MARGANIT
A plant with blue, gold and red flowers that is common in Israel.

The exact Hebrew equivalent is Margawnis. Masculine Hebrew equivalents: Chavakuk, N'teea, Shawsil, Shawsul and Zoraya.

MARGARET, MARGE, MARGERY, MARGET, MARGIE, MARGO, MARGOT
From the Greek meaning either "pearl (a precious stone)," or "child of light." Marjorie is a Scottish version of Margaret and Margery is an English version. In addition to the names listed many additional variations have evolved from Margaret in quite a number of countries throughout the ages. Included are: Meg, Maggie, Madge, Mae, May, Greta, Gretchen, Margareta, Margaretta, Marguerite, Peg and Peggy. Perel, Perles, Perlman and Pearlman have become popular surnames.

Hebrew equivalents: Margawlis, P'neenaw and P'neenis. Masculine Hebrew equivalents: Dar, P'neenee and Tarshish.

MARIAN, MARIANE, MARIE, MARION
Variant forms of Mary. Marian, Mariane and Marion are compounds of Mary and Ann. Marion is used as a masculine as well as feminine name. See Mary for a full explanation.

MARILYN, MARILYNN
These names are derived from Mary, and mean "Mary's

ee as in b*ee*t; *i* as in b*i*t; *o* as in n*o*; *oi* as in v*oi*d; *u* as in r*u*de.

line," or "descendants of Mary." See Mary for a full explanation.

MARJORIE, MARJORY
Variant forms of Margery which is a form of Margaret. See Margaret for a full explanation.

MARLEEN, MARLENE
Forms of Magdalene. See Magdalene for a full explanation.

MARNI, MARNINA
Marnina is derived from the Hebrew meaning "rejoice." Marni is a pet form.

The exact Hebrew equivalent is Marneenaw. The exact masculine Hebrew equivalent is Marnin.

MARTELLE, MARTINA
Feminine forms of Martin meaning "warlike, martial," in the Latin. Martelle is used in France; Martina in England.

Hebrew equivalents: Amtzaw, Awtzmaw, Gavreeaylaw, Gavreelaw and Geeboraw. Masculine Hebrew equivalents: Ben Cha'yil, Gawd, Gid'on, Mawrd'chai, M'dawn and Midyawn.

MARTHA
From the Aramaic meaning either "sorrowful," or "mistress." Marta and Martita are pet forms.

Hebrew equivalents: Mawraw, Mawrawsaw and Miryawm. Masculine Hebrew equivalents: Aveemelech, Awmos, Eeyov, Malkawm and Melech.

MARVA
A Hebrew name used in Israel. Marva is a plant of the mint family.

The exact Hebrew equivalent is Marvaw. Masculine Hebrew equivalents: Narkis, Neta, N'teea and Tzemach.

Key: *a* as in f*a*ther; *ai* as in *ai*sle; *aw* as in l*aw*; *ay* as in s*ay*; *e* as in b*e*t;

MARY

Mary is the Greek form of Miriam which means either "sea of bitterness or sorrow," in the Hebrew, or "mistress of the sea," in Chaldaic. For almost 2,000 years Mary has been one of the most popular names, and has taken on hundreds of forms in almost every language. Among the most common foreign forms are: Marie, Marion and Manette in the French and Scotch; Maria, Marita and Mariquita in the Spanish; Mair in the Welsh; Maureen, Maura, Moya, Moira, Maire and Muire in the Irish; Marya in the Polish. Minnie is a Scottish form that was widespread in England in Victorian times. Molly and Polly are pet forms used in England and America, as are Minnie, May, Moll, Molly and Min.

The exact Hebrew equivalent is Miryawm. Masculine Hebrew equivalents: Arnon, Aveeyawm, Aynawn, Melech, Moshe and Peleg.

MARYLIN, MARYLINE

Marylin and Maryline mean "from Mary's line," or "descendants of Mary." See Miriam for a full explanation.

MASADA

From the Hebrew meaning "foundation or support."

The exact Hebrew equivalent is Masawdaw. Masculine Hebrew equivalents: Saad and Saadyaw.

MATANA

A modern Hebrew name meaning "gift."

The exact Hebrew equivalent is Matawnaw. Masculine Hebrew equivalents: Matawn, Matnai, Matanyaw, Matisyawhu and Y'honawsawn.

MATHILDA, MATILDA, MATTYE

From the Teutonic meaning "battlemaid." Maude, Mattye, Patty, Tilda, Tillie and Tilly are pet forms.

Hebrew equivalents: Almaw, Awtzmaw, Gavreelaw, Geeboraw and Tigraw. Masculine Hebrew equivalents: Mawrd'chai, M'dawn, Midyawn, Naftawlee and Yisrawayl.

ee as in b*ee*t; *i* as in b*i*t; *o* as in n*o*; *oi* as in v*oi*d; *u* as in r*u*de.

MAUD, MAUDE

These are pet forms of Mathilda used among the French. See above for a full explanation.

MAURA, MAUREEN

Both are forms of Mary used prominently in Ireland. They may also be derived from the Celtic meaning "dark." Maurella and Morena are variant forms.

Hebrew equivalents: Ayfaw, Chacheelaw, Miryawm and Tzeelaw. Masculine Hebrew equivalents: Adawr, Ayfai, Kaydawr and Pinchaws.

MAVIS

A bird-name that evolved in France from an Old English word meaning "song-thrush."

Hebrew equivalents: Droraw, Efronaw, Tzeepawreeyaw, Tzeepawrtaw and Tzeeporaw. Masculine Hebrew equivalents: Gozawl, Orayv and Tzeepor.

MAXA, MAXIME, MAXINE

Feminine forms of Max and Maximilian which are derived from the Latin meaning "great, famous."

Hebrew equivalents: G'dulaw, T'heelaw, Yawayl and Y'hudis. Masculine Hebrew equivalents: G'dalyaw, Geedayl, Heelayl, Rav and Rawvaw.

MAXIMA

From the Hebrew meaning "enchanter, diviner, miracle worker."

The exact Hebrew equivalent is Makseemaw. The exact masculine Hebrew equivalent is Makseem.

MAY

Either from the Teutonic referring to the month of May, or it has the meaning of "a maiden," or "springtime," and carries the connotation of youth. It may also be derived from the Old English meaning "a flower" (daisy). Or, it may be a contraction of Mary.

Hebrew equivalents: Almaw, Miryawm, Naaraw, Neet-

Key: *a* as in f*a*ther; *ai* as in *ai*sle; *aw* as in l*aw*; *ay* as in s*ay*; *e* as in b*e*t;

zaw and Shoshanaw. Masculine Hebrew equivalents: Aylawm, Efra'yim, Pekach, P'rachyaw and Yefes.

MAZAL
From the Hebrew meaning "a star." In the popular sense it has the meaning of "good luck."

The exact Hebrew equivalent is Mazawl. The exact masculine Hebrew equivalent is Mazawl-Tov.

MEHIRA
From the Hebrew meaning "speedy, energetic."

The exact Hebrew equivalent is M'heeraw. The exact masculine Hebrew equivalent is Mawheer.

MEIRA
From the Hebrew meaning "light."

The exact Hebrew equivalent is M'eeraw. The exact masculine Hebrew equivalent is Mayeer.

MELANIE
From the Greek meaning "black, dark in appearance." Mel and Melly are sometimes used as pet forms.

Hebrew equivalents: Ayfaw, Chacheelaw and Tzeelaw. Masculine Hebrew equivalents: Adawr, Ayfai, Kaydawr and Pinchaws.

MELBA, MELVA, MELVINA
Variant feminine forms of the masculine Melvin, derived from the Celtic meaning "servant or chief," or from the Anglo-Saxon meaning "friendly toiler," or "famous friend."

Hebrew equivalents: Ameesaw, Atawraw, Malkaw, T'heelaw and Y'hudis. Masculine Hebrew equivalents: Awmis, G'dalyaw, Heelayl, Ovadyaw and Y'hudaw.

MELINDA
From the Greek meaning "gentle." Linda, Lindy and Mindy are diminutive forms.

Hebrew equivalents: Adeevaw, N'deevaw, Naamaw, Nawawmee and Rawchayl. Masculine Hebrew equivalents: Awdiv, Naamawn and Nawdiv.

ee as in b*ee*t; *i* as in b*i*t; *o* as in n*o*; *oi* as in v*oi*d; *u* as in r*u*de.

MELISSA

From the Greek meaning "bee, honey," and having the connotation of sweet, pleasant, good. Millicent, Millie, Missie, Lissa and Lisse are variant forms.

Hebrew equivalents: D'vawshaw, D'voraw, M'sukaw and Nawawmee. Masculine Hebrew equivalents: Ben-Tzeeyon and Tuveeyaw.

MELODY

From the Greek meaning "a melody, a song."

Hebrew equivalents: Leeron, Mangeenaw, Reenaw, Sheeraw, Sheerlee and Yawronaw. Masculine Hebrew equivalents: Ameerawn, Ameershawr, Yawron, Zimrawn and Z'maryaw.

MENORA, MENORAH

A modern Israeli name derived from the Hebrew meaning "a candelabrum."

The exact Hebrew equivalent is M'noraw. Masculine Hebrew equivalents: Mayeer, Nawhor, Nawhur, Nuri, Nureeayl and Nureeyaw.

MERCEDES

From the Latin meaning "mercy, pity." Used also as a masculine name.

Hebrew equivalents: Nechawmaw and Ruchawmaw. Masculine Hebrew equivalents: Chawnin, Rachamawn and Rachmeeayl.

MEREDITH

From the Celtic meaning "protector of the sea." Used primarily as a masculine name.

Hebrew equivalents: Bawtzraw, Chasyaw, Chosaw, Magaynaw and Migdawlaw. Masculine Hebrew equivalents: Mawgayn, Mivtach, Mivtachyawhu and Lotawn.

MERI

From the Hebrew meaning "rebellious," and having the connotation of "bitterness," which has led some authorities

Key: *a* as in f*a*ther; *ai* as in *ai*sle; *aw* as in l*aw*; *ay* as in s*ay*; *e* as in b*e*t;

to the contention that Meri is synonymous with Miriam and Mary.

The exact Hebrew equivalent is Meree. Masculine Hebrew equivalents: Mardus, Mawrd'chai, M'rawree, Nimrod and Rosh.

MERLE

From the Latin and French meaning "a bird" (blackbird).

Hebrew equivalents: Dawaw, Da'yaw, Chawglaw and Tzeeporaw. Masculine Hebrew equivalents: Orayv and Tzeepor.

MERRIE, MERRIELLE

From the Anglo-Saxon meaning "joyous, pleasant."

Hebrew equivalents: Aleezaw, Aveega'yil, Reenaw, R'nawnaw, Simchonaw and S'maychaw. Masculine Hebrew equivalents: Awshayr, Geelon, Marnin, Mawsos and Simchaw.

MERYL, MERRIL, MERRYL

Either a variant form of Muriel or Merle. See Muriel and Merle for a full explanation.

METUKA

From the Hebrew meaning "sweet."

The exact Hebrew equivalent is M'sukaw. The exact masculine Hebrew cquivalent is Mawsok.

MIA

A modern Israeli name derived from Michaela meaning "who is like God?" in the Hebrew.

The exact Hebrew equivalents are Meeyaw and Meechawaylaw. The exact Masculine Hebrew equivalent is Meechawayl.

MICHAELA

The feminine form of Michael meaning "who is like God?" in the Hebrew.

---

ee as in b*ee*t; *i* as in b*i*t; *o* as in n*o*; *oi* as in v*oi*d; *u* as in r*u*de.

The exact Hebrew equivalent is Meechawaylaw. The exact masculine Hebrew equivalent is Meechawayl.

MICHAELANN
A combination of Michael and Ann. See Michael and Ann for interpretation and equivalents.

MICHAL, MICHEL, MICHELE, MICHELLE
A contracted form of the masculine Michael meaning "who is like God?" in the Hebrew. In the Bible Michal was the daughter of King Saul whom David married.

The exact Hebrew equivalent is Meechal. Masculine Hebrew equivalents: Meechaw and Meechawayl.

MIGDALA
From the Hebrew meaning "fortress, tower."

The exact Hebrew equivalent is Migdawlaw. Masculine Hebrew equivalents: Mawgayn, Maygayn, Mivtach and Mivtachyawhu.

MIGDANA
From the Hebrew meaning "gift."

The exact Hebrew equivalent is Migdawnaw. Masculine Hebrew equivalents: Magdeeayl, Matanyaw, Matisyawhu, Meged and N'sanayl.

MIGNON
From the French meaning "delicate, graceful, petite."

Hebrew equivalents: Adeevaw, Chanaw, Chaneesaw, Dovayvaw and Yochawnaw. Masculine Hebrew equivalents: Ameechayn, Chanaw, Chawnawn, Chonayn and Yochawnawn.

MILDRED
From the Teutonic meaning "gentle of speech," or "gentle counselor," and having the connotation of wisdom. Millie and Milly are popular pet forms.

Hebrew equivalents: Ameeraw, Bunaw, D'voraw, Milkaw and Neevaw. Masculine Hebrew equivalents: Achbawn, Chachmonee, Dovayv, Omer, Utz, Yawvin and Yoshaw.

Key: *a* as in f*a*ther; *ai* as in *ai*sle; *aw* as in l*aw*; *ay* as in s*ay*; *e* as in b*e*t;

MILI

A modern Israeli name meaning "who is for me " or a form of Millie, which is the diminutive form of Millicent.

The exact Hebrew equivalent is Meelee. See below for additional equivalents.

MILLICENT, MILLIE, MILLY

Either from the Latin meaning "sweet singer," or from the Teutonic meaning "strength." Millie and Milly, which are diminutives of Millicent, are also diminutives of Mildred. Molly and Mandy are also used as pet forms of Millicent. In 10th century France, Melisande was extremely popular as a variant form of Millicent.

Hebrew equivalents: Amtzaw, Gavreelaw, N'eemaw, Neevaw, Reenaw, Sheeraw and T'heelaw. Masculine Hebrew equivalents: Aharon, Anaw, Amatzyaw, Avrawm, Binyawmin and Dovayv.

MIMI

From the Teutonic meaning "martial," or a pet form of Miriam.

For feminine and masculine Hebrew equivalents see Millicent and Miriam.

MINDY

Either a pet form of Melinda of Mildred. See Melinda and Mildred for a full explanation.

MINERVA

The Roman goddess of wisdom.

Hebrew equivalents: Beenaw, Bunaw and Milkaw. Masculine Hebrew equivalents: Chachmonee, Utz, Yawvin and Yoshaw.

MINNA, MINETTE

Diminutive forms of Wilhelmina meaning "ruler or warrior," in the Teutonic.

Hebrew equivalents: Amtzaw, Awtzmaw, Gavreeaylaw, Geeboraw, Malkaw and Yis'r'aylaw. Masculine Hebrew

ee as in beet; i as in bit; o as in no; oi as in void; u as in rude.

equivalents: Areeayl, Gavreeayl, Geebor, Melech and Yis-rawayl.

MINNIE
Either a pet form of Miriam or derived from the Scotch meaning "mother."

The exact Hebrew equivalent is Eemaw or Miryawm. Masculine Hebrew equivalents: Abaw, Avrawhawm and Moshe.

MINTA
From the Greek meaning "the mint" (an aromatic leaf).

Hebrew equivalents: K'tzeeaw and Tz'ruyaw. Masculine Hebrew equivalents: Mivsawm and Yivsawm.

MIRANDA
From the Latin meaning "the admirable or adored one."

Hebrew equivalents: Achsaw, Adeenaw, Awdaw, Hadawraw, Hadawris and Sawraw. Masculine Hebrew equivalents: Adeeayl, Hawdar, Hod, Hodeeyaw, M'udawn and Y'ho'yawdawn.

MIRIAM
Either from the Hebrew meaning "sea of bitterness, sorrow," or from the Chaldaic meaning "mistress of the sea." Mary is the most popular name that has developed from Miriam which, in turn, has been the source of a large variety of other names. In the Bible Miriam was the sister of Moses and Aaron.

The exact Hebrew equivalent is Miryawm. Masculine Hebrew equivalents: Arnon, Aveeyawm, Aynawn, Melech, Moshe and Peleg.

MIRA, MIRI, MIRIT
Popular short forms of Miriam used in Israel. See Miriam for a full explanation.

Meeraw, Meeree and Meeris are the exact feminine Hebrew equivalents: See Miriam for additional equivalents.

Key: *a* as in f*a*ther; *ai* as in *ai*sle; *aw* as in l*aw*; *ay* as in s*ay*; *e* as in b*e*t;

MISSIE
A modern American name meaning "young girl."

The exact Hebrew equivalent is Naaraw. Masculine Hebrew equivalents: Naarai, Naaree and Naaryaw.

MITZPA, MITZPAH, MIZPA, MIZPAH
From the Hebrew meaning "a tower or observation post."

The exact Hebrew equivalent is Mitzpaw. Masculine Hebrew quivalents: Armonee, Bachan, Chazawyaw, Chazeeayl, Chozai and Migdawl.

MOLLIE, MOLLY, MOLLYE
Variant diminutive forms of Miriam. See Miriam for a full explanation.

MONA, MONICA, MONIQUE
Either from the Greek meaning "alone," or from Late Latin meaning "the advisor." Saint Monica, the mother of Saint Augustine, was revered for her saintliness which gave to the name a connotation of "purity."

Hebrew equivalents: Milkaw, Rawchayl and Zakaw. Masculine Hebrew equivalents: Eflawl, Pawlawl and Zakai.

MORASHA
From the Hebrew meaning "inheritance."

The exact Hebrew equivalent is Morawshaw. The exact Hebrew equivalent is Morawsh.

MORIAH, MORICE, MORIEL, MORIT
From the Hebrew meaning "teacher." Moriah, and Moriel mean "God is my teacher." In the Bible Moriah is the name of the montain where Abraham prepared to sacrifice his son, Isaac.

The exact Hebrew equivalents are Moreeyaw, Moreeayl and Moris. Masculine Hebrew equivalents: Aharon, Chanoch, Likchee, Rabee, Tanaw and Yoraw.

ee as in b*ee*t; *i* as in b*i*t; *o* as in n*o*; *oi* as in v*oi*d; *u* as in r*u*de.

MORNA

From the Celtic meaning "soft, gentle, beloved." Myrna is a variant form.

Hebrew equivalents: Adeevaw, Ahuvaw, Chaveevaw, Cheebaw, Dawveedaw and Y'deedaw. Masculine Hebrew equivalents: Awhud, Awhuv, Chavivayl, Dawvid, Nawdiv and Yakir.

MORRISA

The feminine form of Morris, derived either from the Latin meaning "moorish, dark-skinned," or from the Gaelic meaning "great warrior."

Hebrew equivalents: Amtzaw, Awtzmaw, Ayfaw, Chacheelaw, Gavreelaw, Geeboraw and Tzeelaw. Masculine Hebrew equivalents: Adawr, Ayfai, Chawm, Dawvid, Gad, Mawrd'chai, M'dawn and Pinchaws.

MURIEL

Either the feminine of the Greek Myron meaning "fragrant" (see Myron in masculine section for equivalents), or from Middle English meaning "merry."

Hebrew equivalents: Aleezaw, Marneenaw, Mazawl, R'nawnaw and S'maychaw. Masculine Hebrew equivalents: Marnin, Mawzawl-Tov, Sawson, Simchaw, Yachdeeayl and Yitzchawk.

MYRA, MYRNA

From the Greek and Arabic meaning "myrrh," hence the connotation of bitter and sorrowful. Myrna may also be either a short form of Miranda meaning "a girl to be admired," in the Latin, or a form of Morna meaning "soft, gentle, beloved," in the Celtic.

Hebrew equivalents: Mawraw, Mawrawsaw, Miryawm and Tzawraw. Masculine Hebrew equivalents: Awmos and Eeyov. See Morna for additional equivalents.

MYRTLE

From the Persian meaning a "tree or shrub." The myrtle tree was the symbol of victory.

Key: *a* as in f*a*ther; *ai* as in *ai*sle; *aw* as in l*aw*; *ay* as in s*ay*; *e* as in b*e*t;

Hebrew equivalents: Dafnaw and Hadasaw. Masculine Hebrew equivalents: N'tzeeach and Yatzleeach.

NAAMA, NAAMAH
From the Hebrew meaning "pleasant, beautiful."
The exact Hebrew equivalent is Naamaw. The exact masculine Hebrew equivalent is Naamawn.

NAAMANA
From the Hebrew meaning "pleasant."
The exact Hebrew equivalent is Naamawnaw. The exact masculine Hebrew equivalent is Naamawn.

NAAMIT
The Hebrew name of an ostrich-like bird.
The exact Hebrew equivalent is Naamis. Masculine Hebrew equivalents: Gozawl and Tzeepor.

NADA, NADINE
From the Slavic meaning "hope." Nadine is an English and French form.
Hebrew equivalents: Bitchaw, Emunaw, Ergaw, Tikva, Tocheles and Tzeepeeyaw. Masculine Hebrew equivalents: Ameesawn, Ameetai, Amnon and Yawchil.

NAGIDA
From the Hebrew meaning "ruler, wealthy or prosperous."
The exact Hebrew equivalent is N'gcedaw. The exact masculine Hebrew equivalent is Nawgid.

NAN, NANA, NANETTE, NANNA
Diminutive forms of Nancy which is a variant form of Anna and Hannah. See below for a full explanation.

NANCY
A form of Hannah which is derived from the Hebrew meaning "gracious."
The exact Hebrew equivalent is Chanaw. Masculine Hebrew equivalents: Chawnawn, Chonayn and Yochawnawn.

ee as in b*ee*t; *i* as in b*i*t; *o* as in n*o*; *oi* as in v*oi*d; *u* as in r*u*de.

NAOMI

From the Hebrew meaning "beautiful, pleasant, delightful." In the Bible Naomi was the mother-in-law of Ruth, a Moabitess who converted to Judaism.

The exact Hebrew equivalent is Nawawmee. Masculine Hebrew equivalents: Naam, Naamawn, Nawam, Naweem, Noam and Tuveeyaw.

NASIA, NASYA

From the Hebrew meaning "miracle of the Lord."

The exact Hebrew equivalent is Nasyaw. The exact masculine Hebrew equivalents are Nays, Neesee and Neeseem.

NATALIE, NATHALIE

From the Latin meaning "Christmas child," or "lively, vivacious."

Hebrew equivalents: Chavaw, Cha'yaw and T'cheeyaw. Masculine Hebrew equivalents: Amrawm, Cha'yim, Cheeyaw and Y'cheeayl.

NATANIA, NATHANIA

The feminine form of Nathan meaning "he gave." Natania and Nathania mean "a gift of God."

The exact Hebrew equivalent is N'sanyaw. Masculine Hebrew equivalents: N'sanayl, Nawsawn and Y'honawsawn.

NATANIELLA, NATANIELLE, NATHANIELLA, NATHANIELLE

Feminine forms of Nathan and Nathaniel which are derived from the Hebrew and mean "gift of God."

The exact Hebrew equivalent is Nechawmaw. Masculine Hebrew equivalents: N'sanyaw, Nawsawn and Y'honawsawn.

NAAVA, NAVA, NAVIT

From the Hebrew meaning "beautiful, pleasant."

The exact Hebrew equivalents are Acheenoam, Nawvaw and Nawvis. Masculine Hebrew equivalents: Naamawn, Naw'e, Nawim, Nawos and Ne-h'dawr.

Key: *a* as in f*a*ther; *ai* as in *ai*sle; *aw* as in l*aw*; *ay* as in s*ay*; *e* as in b*e*t;

NECHAMA, NEHAMA
A Hebraic name meaning "comfort."

The exact Hebrew equivalent is N'chawmaw. Masculine Hebrew equivalents: M'nachaym, Nawchum and N'chemyaw.

NEDIVA
From the Hebrew meaning "noble, generous."

The exact Hebrew equivalent is N'deevaw. The exact masculine Hebrew equivalent is Nawdiv.

NEGINA
From the Hebrew meaning "song, melody, tune."

The exact Hebrew equivalent is N'geenaw. Masculine Hebrew equivalents: Aveeshar, Ameerawn, Ameeron, Ameeshawr, Ronayn, Zemer and Z'maryaw.

NEHORA
From the Aramaic meaning "light."

The exact Hebrew equivalent is N'horaw. Masculine Hebrew equivalents: Nawhir, Nawhor, Nawhur and N'horai.

NELL, NELLIE
Diminutive forms of Eleanor and Helen meaning "light," in the Greek.

See Nehora for feminine and masculine Hebrew equivalents.

NEMA, NIMA
From the Hebrew meaning "a thread, a hair."

The exact Hebrew equivalent is Neemaw. Masculine Hebrew equivalent: S'orim.

NETA, NETTA, NETIA
From the Hebrew meaning "a plant, a shrub." Neta is also used as a masculine name in Israel.

The exact Hebrew equivalents are Neta and N'teeyaw. The exact masculine Hebrew equivalents are Neta and N'teea.

---

ee as in b*ee*t; *i* as in b*i*t; *o* as in n*o*; *oi* as in v*oi*d; *u* as in r*u*de.

NETANIA, NETANYA, NETHANIA

From the Hebrew meaning "gift of God." These are variant spellings of Natania and Nathania.

The exact Hebrew equivalent is N'sanyaw. Masculine Hebrew equivalents: N'sanayl, Nawsawn and Y'honawsawn.

NETTIE, NETTY

A pet form of Antonia and also of Janet. See Antonia and Janet for a full explanation.

NICOLA, NICOLE, NICOLLE, NICOLETTE

Feminine forms of Nicolas and Nicholas which are derived from the Greek meaning "victory of the people." Bernice, Berenice and Colette are variant forms.

Hebrew equivalents: Dafnaw, Hadasaw, Nitzchaw and Nitzcheeyaw. Masculine Hebrew equivalents: Govayr, Matzleeach, N'tzeeach, Yatzleeach and Yitzlawch.

NINA

Either a French form of Anne (from Nanine), or from the Spanish meaning a "young girl." Some authorities believe Nina is of Babylonian origin meaning "goddess of the deep waters." There is also a Hebrew name Nina meaning "granddaughter" or "great-granddaughter."

Hebrew equivalents: Almaw, Miryawm and Neenaw. Masculine Hebrew equivalents: Aveeyawm, Naarai, Naaree, Naaryaw and Nin.

NIREL

Derived from the Hebrew and meaning either "a cultivated field," or "light of God." Nirel is also used as a masculine name in Israel.

The exact Hebrew equivalent is Nirayl.

NIRICE, NIRIT

A plant found in Israel that blooms annually, and has yellow flowers.

The exact Hebrew equivalent is Neeris. Masculine Hebrew equivalents: Neer, Neerawm, Neerayl, Neereeayl and Neereeyaw.

Key: *a* as in f*a*ther; *ai* as in *ai*sle; *aw* as in l*aw*; *ay* as in s*ay*; *e* as in b*e*t;

NITA

A diminutive form of Anita which, in turn, is derived from Hannah meaning "gracious," in Hebrew.

The exact Hebrew equivalent is Chanaw. Masculine Hebrew equivalents: Chananayl, Chananayaw, Chawnawn, Cheenawn and Yochawnawn.

NITZA, NITZANA, NIZANA

From the Hebrew meaning the "bud of a flower."

The exact Hebrew equivalents are Neetzaw and Neetzawnaw. The exact masculine Hebrew equivalent is Neetzawn.

NIXIE

From German meaning "a water sprite." In Teutonic mythology a Nixie was half-girl and half-fish. Nixie is also used as a pet form of Berenice. In recent times it has been adopted as a masculine name.

Hebrew equivalents: B'ayris, Galvaw, Dawleeyaw, Dawlis, Meechal and Miryawm. Masculine Hebrew equivalents: Aynawn, B'ayree, Bayree, Peleg, Yawvawl and Yuval.

NOEL, NOELLE

Noel is more commonly used as a masculine name. These names are French for "Christmas," and are closely related in origin to Natalie.

See Natalie for feminine and masculine equivalents.

NOFIA, NOPHIA

From the Hebrew meaning "beautiful panorama," or "God's beautiful landscape."

The exact Hebrew equivalent is Nofeeyaw. Masculine Hebrew equivalents: Nawve, Naw'e, Noy, Yaw'e and Yawfe.

NOGA

From the Hebrew meaning "morning light, shining." Noga is also used as a masculine name in Israel.

The exact Hebrew equivalent is Noga. Masculine Hebrew equivalents: Aveeshachar, Noga, Tzafreer, Tzafreeree and Tzofar.

ee as in b*ee*t; *i* as in b*i*t; *o* as in n*o*; *oi* as in v*oi*d; *u* as in r*u*de.

NORA, NORAH, NOREEN

From the Latin meaning "honor, respect." The original form of Nora is Honoria, which was widely used in England in the Middle Ages. It was later shortened to Honora and Honor. Noreen is a variant form that has been popular in Ireland for several centuries. Nora is sometimes considered a diminutive form of Leonora and Eleanor.

Hebrew equivalents: Asalyaw, Efrawsaw, Haduraw, K'vudaw, N'deevaw and Nichbawdaw. Masculine Hebrew equivalents: Aveenawdav, Hadar, Hawdur, M'chubawd, Nawdawv, Y'horawm and Yirmeeyawhu.

NORMA

From the Latin meaning "exact to the pattern, normal, peaceful."

Hebrew equivalents: Margayaw, M'nuchaw, M'shulemes and Shaananaw. Masculine Hebrew equivalents: Margee'a, Margo'a, Shaanawn, Shlemyaw, Shlomee and Shlomeeayl.

NOYA

From the Hebrew meaning "beautiful, ornamented."

The exact Hebrew equivalent is Noya. Masculine Hebrew equivalents: Nawos, Naw'e and Nawve.

NURICE, NURIT, NURITA

Names of plants, common in Israel, having red and yellow flowers.

The exact Hebrew equivalents are Nureesaw and Nuris. Masculine Hebrew equivalents: Nur, Nuree, Nureeayl and Nureeyaw.

ODEDA

From the Hebrew meaning "strong, courageous."

The exact Hebrew equivalent is Odaydaw. The exact masculine Hebrew equivalent is Odayd.

ODELIA

Either from the Hebrew meaning "I will praise God," or from the German meaning "noble, rich." Odette is a French variant form of the German.

Key: *a* as in f*a*ther; *ai* as in *ai*sle; *aw* as in l*aw*; *ay* as in s*ay*; *e* as in b*e*t;

The exact Hebrew equivalent is Odel'yaw. Masculine Hebrew equivalents: Heelayl, Hunaw, Y'halelayl and Y'hudaw.

ODERA
From the Hebrew meaning "plough."

The exact Hebrew equivalent is Odayraw. Masculine Hebrew equivalents: Neer, Neerayl, Neereeyaw, Talmai and Yawnir.

OLGA
An old Russian name, derived from Old Norse and popular in Russia and Scandinavian countries, meaning either "holy," or "peace." Some authorities relate Olga to Oliver meaning "olive," the symbol of peace.

Hebrew equivalents: Chageeyaw, Chagis, Shlomis, Shulamis and Za'yis. Masculine Hebrew equivalents: Chagai, Shlomee, Shlomo and Zaysawn.

OLIVE, OLIVIA
From the Latin meaning "olive," the symbol of peace. Among the many variant and diminutive forms which are offshoots of Olive the most popular are Olivia, Olivette, Livia, Nola, Nollie and Livy.

Hebrew equivalents: M'nuchaw, M'shulemes, Shlomis, Shulamis and Za'yis. Masculine Hebrew equivalents: Shlomee, Shlomo and Zaysawn.

OONA
An Old Irish name which is a variant form of the Latin Una meanin "the one." Ona, Onnie and Unity are variant English forms.

Hebrew equivalent: Reeshonaw. Masculine Hebrew equivalent: Rosh.

OPHELIA
From the Greek meaning "a serpent." Shakespeare made this name a synonym for "sorrow."

ee as in b*ee*t; *i* as in b*i*t; *o* as in n*o*; *oi* as in v*oi*d; *u* as in r*u*de.

Hebrew equivalents: Mawraw, Mawrawsaw, Miryawm and Tzawraw. Masculine Hebrew equivalents: Awmos, Ben-Onee, Nachshon, Nawchawsh and Onawn.

OPHIRA
From the Hebrew meaning "gold."

The exact Hebrew equivalent is Ofeeraw. The exact masculine Hebrew equivalent is Ofeer.

ORA, ORAH, ORIT
From the Hebrew meaning "light." Ora is also taken from the Latin meaning "gold."

The exact Hebrew equivalents are Oraw and Oris. Masculine Hebrew equivalents: Or, Oree and Oron.

ORALEE, ORLEE, ORLY
From the Hebrew meaning "light," or "light is mine."

The exact Hebrew equivalents are Oraw-lee and Orlee. Masculine Hebrew equivalents: Or, Oree and Oron.

ORLICE, ORLIT
From the Hebrew meaning "light."

The exact Hebrew equivalent is Orlis. Masculine Hebrew equivalents: Or, Oree and Oron.

ORNA
From the Hebrew meaning either "let there be light," or "a fir or cedar tree."

The exact Hebrew equivalent is Ornaw. Masculine Hebrew equivalents: Or, Oren and Oron.

ORNICE, ORNIT
From the Hebrew meaning "a fir or cedar tree."

The exact Hebrew equivalent is Ornis. The exact masculine Hebrew equivalent is Oren.

PALOMA
A Spanish name derived from the Latin meaning "dove."

Hebrew equivalents: Y'meemaw, Yonawsee and Yoneenaw. The masculine Hebrew equivalent is Yonaw.

Key: *a* as in f*a*ther; *ai* as in *ai*sle; *aw* as in l*aw*; *ay* as in s*ay*; *e* as in b*e*t;

PAMELA

Pamela is a coined name which has been interpreted to be a derivative of the Greek and Anglo-Saxon meaning "the loved one," or "all sweetness" or "dark brunette." Pam is a popular diminutive.

Hebrew equivalents: Ayfaw, Cheebaw, Dawveedaw, Nawawmee and Y'deedaw. Masculine Hebrew equivalents: Bildawd, Dawvid, Kaydawr and Pinchaws.

PANSY

An English flower name derived from the French and having the connotation of "growth, flourishing." The literal French meaning is "to think or consider." Shakespeare uses the phrase: "Pansies for thought."

Hebrew equivalents: Neetzaw and Shoshanaw. Masculine Hebrew equivalents: Efra'yim, Pekach, P'rachyaw and Tzemach.

PAT, PATTI, PATTY

Diminutive forms of Patricia. See below for a full explanation.

PATRICIA, PATRICE

The feminine form of Patrick, derived from the Latin meaning "a patrician," or "one of noble descent." Pat, Patsy, Patti and Patty are pet forms. Patrice is a variant form.

Hebrew equivalents: N'deevaw, Sawraw and Yis'r'aylaw. Masculine Hebrew equivalents: Aveenawdawv, Chcerom, Nawdawv, Nawdiv and Yisrawayl.

PATSY

A diminutive form of Patricia. See above for a full explanation.

PAULA

Paula is the feminine form of Paul meaning "small," in the Latin. Paola is a Spanish variant and Pavla is a Russian form.

Hebrew equivalents: D'leelaw and K'tanaw. Masculine

ee as in b*ee*t; *i* as in b*i*t; *o* as in n*o*; *oi* as in v*oi*d; *u* as in r*u*de.

Hebrew equivalents: Kawtawn, Tzuawr, Vawfsee and Z'ay-raw.

PAULETTE, PAULINE
Diminutive French forms of Paula. See above for a full explanation.

PAZ, PAZA, PAZIA, PAZICE, PAZIT
Various names derived from the Hebrew, all meaning "gold." Paz is also used as a masculine name.

The exact Hebrew equivalents are Pawz, Pazaw, Pazeeyaw and Pazis. Masculine Hebrew equivalents: Pawz, and Pazee.

PEARL
From the Latin meaning "pearl." Pearl is sometimes used as a pet form for Margaret which is the Greek for "pearl."

Hebrew equivalents: Margawlis, P'neenaw, S'gulaw and Tz'feeraw. Masculine Hebrew equivalents: Shoham, Shovai and Yawkawr.

PEG, PEGGIE, PEGGY
Diminutive forms of Margaret or Pearl meaning "pearl" in Latin.

See Pearl for feminine and masculine Hebrew equivalents.

PENELOPE, PENNEY, PENNIE, PENNY
From the Greek meaning "a worker in cloth, a weaver, or silent worker." Penney, Pennie and Penny are pet forms.

Hebrew equivalents: Amalyaw, Charutzaw and Z'reezaw. Masculine Hebrew equivalents: Awmayl, Bashaw, Ovadyaw and Ovayd.

PENINA, PENINIT
From the Hebrew meaning "coral or pearl." Penny is a pet form.

The exact Hebrew equivalents are P'neenaw and P'neenis. Masculine Hebrew equivalents: Shoham, Shovai and Yawkawr.

PHEBE, PHOEBE

From the Greek meaning "bright, shining one." Among the Greeks Phoebus was the sun god, and Phoebe, the moon goddess.

Hebrew equivalents: B'heeraw, M'eeraw, Oraw, Oris, Orlee and Tz'feeraw. Masculine Hebrew equivalents: Avnayr, Bawrawk, Feivel (in Yiddish), Mayeer, Shimshon, Shragaw and Yawir.

PHILIPPA

The feminine form of Philip, derived from the Greek meaning "lover of horses." Pippa is a diminutive Italian form.

See Philip in masculine section for Hebrew equivalents.

PHYLLIS

From the Greek meaning "little leaf, green bough," and having the connotation of growth, flourishing. Phillis is a modern spelling.

Hebrew equivalents: Neetzaw, Shoshanaw, Vardaw and Y'neekaw. Masculine Hebrew equivalents: Chavakuk, Efra'yim, Pekach and Puraw.

PIUTA

A Hebrew form of the Greek word for "poet, poetry."

The exact Hebrew equivalent is Peeyutaw. Masculine Hebrew equivalents: Zawmir, Zemer and Zimrawn.

POLLY

Polly is a variant form of Molly. Molly was, at one time, a popular form of Mary. Mary is the Greek form of Miriam.

See Miriam for a full explanation.

PORA, PORIA

From the Hebrew meaning "fruitful."

The exact Hebrew equivalents are Poraw and Poreeyaw.

ee as in b*ee*t; *i* as in b*i*t; *o* as in n*o*; *oi* as in v*oi*d; *u* as in r*u*de.

Masculine Hebrew equivalents: Efra'yim, Poraws and Puraw.

PORTIA

Derived from Porcii, an ancient Roman clan. Made famous by Shakespeare through his girl-attorney in the *Merchant of Venice,* who pleaded, "The quality of mercy is not strained." Because women lawyers are called "Portias," the connotation of lawyer, counsellor or helper is given to this name.

Hebrew equivalents: Beenaw, Bunaw, and Milkaw. Masculine Hebrew equivalents: Avee'ezer, Eflawl, Pawlawl and Utz.

PRISCILLA

From the Latin meaning "ancient, old," and having the connotation of long life. Pris, Prissie and Prissy are pet forms.

Hebrew equivalents: Bilhaw, Chavaw, Cha'yaw and Z'kaynaw. Masculine Hebrew equivalents: Altayr, Kadmeeayl, Shnayor, Y'seeshai and Zawkayn.

QUEENIE

Usually, a nickname for Regina meaning "queen," in Latin. Queenie is used in England as an independent name. Queena is a variant form.

Hebrew equivalent: Malkaw. Masculine Hebrew equivalent: Melech.

RACHEL, RACHELLE, RAHEL

From the Hebrew meaning "a ewe," the symbol of purity and gentility. In the Bible Rachel was the wife of Jacob and the sister of Leah. Joseph and Benjamin were Jacob's two sons with Rachel. Rachelle and Rahel are modern spellings. Rae and Ray are popular diminutive forms. Raquel is a Spanish variant form.

The exact Hebrew equivalent is Rawchayl. Masculine Hebrew equivalents: Ameezakai, Aveeshur, Awdiv and Zakai.

RAE, RAY, RAYE
Either diminutive forms of Rachel or from the Celtic meaning "grace, gracious."
See Rachel and Hannah for feminine and masculine equivalents.

RAIZEL, RAYZEL, RAZIL
Yiddish forms of Rose or Rosa. See Rose for a full explanation.

RAMA
A Hebrew name derived from the ruby-colored, precious stone mentioned in the Bible. It also has the meaning of "lofty, exalted."
The exact Hebrew equivalent is Rawmaw. Masculine Hebrew equivalents: Rawm, Yawkawr and Yakir.

RAMONA
A short form of the Teutonic Raymonda meaning "peace," or "protection."
Hebrew equivalents: Bawtzraw, Efraws, Shlomis, Shulamis and Teeraw. Masculine Hebrew equivalents: Avigdor, Shawlom, Shlomo and Shmaryawhu.

RANDI
A short form of the masculine Randall which is a variant form of Randolph meaning "helper, advisor." Randy is popular as a masculine name.
Hebrew equivalents: Aleksandraw, Beenaw, Bunaw, Milkaw and Saadaw. Masculine Hebrew equivalents: Azaryaw, Azreeayl, Elee-ezer and Saadyaw.

RANICE, RANIT, RANITA
From the Hebrew meaning "joy or song."
The exact Hebrew equivalents are Rawnis and Rawneesaw. Masculine Hebrew equivalents: Marnin, Mawsos, Seesee, Simchaw, Simchonee and Yawgil.

RAOUL
A variant form of Randolph and Ralph meaning "ad-

ee as in b*ee*t; *i* as in b*i*t; *o* as in n*o*; *oi* as in v*oi*d; *u* as in r*u*de.

visor, helper," in the Teutonic. Raoul is used more often as a masculine name.

Hebrew equivalents: Aleksandraw, Beenaw, Bunaw, Milkaw and Saadaw. Masculine Hebrew equivalents: Azaryaw, Azreeayl, Elee-ezer and Saadyaw.

RAPHAELA
The feminine form of Raphael meaning "God has healed," in the Hebrew.

The exact Hebrew equivalent is R'fawaylaw. The exact masculine Hebrew equivalent is R'fawayl.

RAYNA, REYNA
From the Yiddish meaning "pure, clean."

Hebrew equivalents: B'ruraw, P'nuyaw, Zakaw, Zakeeyaw and Zakis. Masculine Hebrew equivalents: Ameezakai, Bawrur, Tzach, Tzachai and Zakai.

RAZ, RAZI, RAZIA, RAZIAH, RAZIELA
Variant forms derived from the Aramaic meaning "secret." Razia, Raziah and Raziela mean "secret of the Lord." Raz and Razi are also used as masculine names.

The exact Hebrew equivalents are Rawz, Rawzee, Rawzeeyaw and Rawzeeaylaw. Masculine Hebrew equivalents: Rawz, Rawzee and Rawzeeayl.

RAZILEE, RAZILI
From the Aramaic and Hebrew meaning "my secret."

The exact Hebrew equivalent is Rawzeelee. Masculine Hebrew equivalents: Rawz, Rawzee and Rawzeeayl.

REBA
From the Hebrew meaning "a young girl." Reba is also used as a diminutive form of Rebecca. Reva is a variant spelling.

The exact Hebrew equivalent is Reevaw. Masculine Hebrew equivalents: Bawchur, Naamawn, Naarai and Naaryaw.

Key: *a* as in f*a*ther; *ai* as in *ai*sle; *aw* as in l*aw*; *ay* as in s*ay*; *e* as in b*e*t;

REBECCA, REBEKAH

Rebecca and its short form Reba are from the Hebrew and Arabic meaning "to tie, to bind." Fattened animals were tied and prepared for slaughtering, hence the figurative meanings of beautiful, voluptuous, desirable. Beautiful Rebecca in the biblical narrative was the wife of Isaac and the mother of Jacob and Esau. Reba is a pet form, as are Beckie, and Becky. In some versions of the Bible Rebecca is spelled Rebekah.

The exact Hebrew equivalent is Rivkaw. Masculine Hebrew equivalents: Chemdawn, Naamawn, Raanawn and Yoayl.

REDA, REITHA

Variant forms of Rita. See Rita for a full explanation.

REGINA

Either from the Teutonic meaning "pure," or from the Latin meaning "queen." Among the more popular variant and diminutive forms are: Raina, Reina, Rani, Rayna and Gina.

Hebrew equivalents: Atawraw, B'ruraw, Malkaw, Tz'feeraw and Zakaw. Masculine Hebrew equivalents: Avrawhawm, Eleemelech, Kasreeayl and Yisrawayl.

RENA, REENA

Either a form of Regina or Serena (see Regina and Serena for an explanation of these names), or a Hebraic name meaning "joy," or "song." Rina is a variant spelling.

The exact Hebrew equivalent is Reenaw. Masculine Hebrew equivalents: Aharon, Awshayr, Ranayn, Rawnee, Yachdeeayl and Yawgil.

RENANA, RENANIT

From the Hebrew meaning "joy or song."

The exact Hebrew equivalents are R'nawnaw and R'nawnis. Masculine Hebrew equivalents: Gawd, Ranayn, Rawnee, Reenaw and Yawgil.

---

ee as in b*ee*t; *i* as in b*i*t; *o* as in n*o*; *oi* as in v*oi*d; *u* as in r*u*de.

RENATA
From the Latin meaning "to be born again," similar to Rene. See below.

RENE, RENEE
From the Latin meaning "to be born again," or "to be renewed." Rennie and Renata are variant forms.

Hebrew equivalents: Chavaw, Cha'yaw and T'cheeyaw. Masculine Hebrew equivalents: Cha'yim, Cheeyaw and Y'cheeayl.

REUBENA, REUVENA
Feminine forms of Reuben derived from the Hebrew and meaning "behold a son."

The exact Hebrew equivalent is R'uvaynaw. The exact masculine Hebrew equivalent is R'uvayn.

REVA
A variant spelling of Reba. See Reba for a full explanation.

REXANA
The feminine form of Rex meaning "king" in the Latin.

Hebrew equivalents: Atawraw, Malkaw and Tz'feeraw. Masculine Hebrew equivalents: Aveemelech, Eleemelech, Malkawm and Melech.

RHEA
From the Greek meaning "protector of cities," or "a poppy" (flower).

Hebrew equivalents: Mawgaynaw, Shimris and Tzeelaw. Masculine Hebrew equivalents: Armonee, Chetzron, R'fawayl and Sisree.

RHETA
Either a variant spelling for Rita or from the Greek meaning "one who speaks well."

Hebrew equivalents: Ameeraw, D'voraw and Neevaw. Masculine Hebrew equivalents: Amaryawhu, Dovayv, Imree, Niv, and Yawniv. See Rita for additional equivalents.

Key: *a* as in father; *ai* as in aisle; *aw* as in law; *ay* as in say; *e* as in bet;

RHODA, RHODE
From the Greek meaning "a flower" (rose). Rhoda became popular through its Latin form Rosa. Its English variant form, Rose, is the most common. See Rose for additional information.

RHONA, RHONDA, RHONNIE
A combination of Rose and Anna. See Rose and Anna for a full explanation of each name. Rona is a variant spelling.

RICA, RICARDA
Feminine forms of Richard. Ricarda is an Italian form. Rica is a pet form of Ricarda and is also used as a diminutive of Patricia and Roberta. See each name independently for more information.

RICKA, RICKI, RICKY
Diminutive forms of either Patricia, Roberta, or the masculine, Richard. See each name separately for more information.

RICKMA, RIKMA
From the Hebrew meaning "a woven product."
The exact Hebrew equivalent is Rikmaw. The exact masculine Hebrew equivalent is Rekem.

RIMONA
From the Hebrew meaning "a pomegranate."
The exact Hebrew equivalent is Reemonaw. The exact masculine Hebrew equivalent is Reemon.

RINA
A variant spelling of Rena meaning "joy," in the Hebrew.
See Rena for feminine and masculine equivalents.

RISHONA
From the Hebrew meaning "first."
The exact Hebrew equivalent is Reeshonaw. The exact masculine Hebrew equivalent is Rosh.

ee as in b*ee*t; *i* as in b*i*t; *o* as in n*o*; *oi* as in v*oi*d; *u* as in r*u*de.

RITA

From the Sanskrit meaning "brave," or "honest." Some authorities contend that it is a short form of Marguerita meaning "pearl," in the Greek. Rheta is a variant spelling.

Hebrew equivalents: Ameetzaw, Gavreeaylaw, Geeboraw, Margawlis, P'neenaw and P'neenis. Masculine Hebrew equivalents: Amatzyaw, Awmotz, Gavreeayl, Geebor, P'neenee and Tarshish.

RIVKA

The Hebraic spelling of Rebecca. See Rebecca for a full explanation.

ROANNA, ROANNE

A combination name consisting of Rosa and Anne. See Rose and Anne for a full explanation.

ROBERTA

Roberta is the feminine form of Robert derived from the Teutonic and meaning "bright or famous counsel."

Hebrew equivalents: Aleksandraw, Ezr'aylaw, Milkaw, Saadaw and Y'hudis. Masculine Hebrew equivalents: Azreeayl, Elee-ezer, Ezraw, Heelayl and Saadyaw.

ROBIN, ROBYN

Diminutive forms of Roberta. See above for a full explanation.

ROCHELLE, ROCHETTE

French forms of the Latin meaning "a little rock." Rochella is a variant English form.

Hebrew equivalents: Ritzpaw, Tzurayl, Tzuris and Tzureeyaw. Masculine Hebrew equivalents: Acheetzur, Aveetzur, Avneeayl, Tzuree and Tzureeshadai.

ROMA, ROMIA, ROMICE, ROMIT

From the Hebrew meaning "height, lofty, exalted."

The exact Hebrew equivalents are Romaw, Romeeyaw and Romis. Masculine Hebrew equivalents: Rabaw, Rav, Rawvaw, Rom, Romaym and Rosh.

Key: *a* as in f*a*ther; *ai* as in *ai*sle; *aw* as in l*aw*; *ay* as in s*ay*; *e* as in b*e*t;

RONA, RONI, RONIA, RONICE, RONIT
From the Hebrew meaning "joy."

The exact Hebrew equivalents are Ronaw, Ronee, Ronee-yaw and Ronis. Masculine Hebrew equivalents: Ron, Ronayl, Ronayn, Ronee and Ronlee.

RONALDA
The feminine form of Ronald, derived from the Teutonic and meaning "mighty, powerful ruler."

Hebrew equivalents: Atawraw, Gavreeaylaw, Geeboraw, Malkaw and Yis'r'aylaw. Masculine Hebrew equivalents: Barzeelai, Gavreeayl, Kasreeayl, Melech, Rawzin, Rozayn and Yisrawayl.

RONNI, RONNIE, RONNY
Feminine diminutive forms of Ronald and its feminine counterpart, Ronalda, meaning "mighty ruler," in the Teutonic.

See Ronalda for feminine and masculine Hebrew equivalents.

RONLI
From the Hebrew meaning "joy is mine."

The exact Hebrew equivalent is Ronlee. Masculine Hebrew equivalents: Ron and Ronee.

ROSA
A popular Italian form of Rose. See Rose for a full explanation.

ROSABEL
A variant form of Rose meaning "beautiful rose." See Rose for a full explanation.

ROSALIE
A variant form of Rose popular in Germany and America. See Rose for a full explanation.

ROSALIND, ROSALINDA, ROSALYN, ROSELYN, ROSLYN
From the Latin meaning "beautiful rose." Rosalinda is a Spanish variant form.

ee as in b*ee*t; *i* as in b*i*t; *o* as in n*o*; *oi* as in v*oi*d; *u* as in r*u*de.

Hebrew equivalents: Raananaw, Rivkaw, Shawron and Shoshanaw. Masculine Hebrew equivalents: Efra'yim, P'rachyaw, Puraw and Raanawn.

ROSANNE
A combination of Rose and Anne. See Rose and Anne for an explanation of each name.

ROSE
Rose is the English form of the Latin Rosa, meaning a "flower" (the rose), and has the connotation of growth, flourishing. Rosette, Rosina and Rosita are French, Italian and Spanish diminutives, respectively. Among the other many variant and pet forms of Rose are: Rosena, Rosalie, Rosella, Rozina, Rosie, Rozy, Rhoda and Rosaleen.

Hebrew equivalents: Shawron, Shoshanaw, and Vardaw. Masculine Hebrew equivalents: Efra'yim, Pekach, P'rachyaw and Puraw.

ROSELOTTE
A combination of Rose and Lotte. See Rose and Lotte for an explanation of each name.

ROSEMARY
A combination of Rose and Mary. This name was also used as the name of a plant and was derived from the Latin meaning "dew of the sea." In Shakespeare's time the medicine made from the plant was believed to refresh the memory. Ophelia, in *Hamlet,* says: "There's Rosemary, that's for remembrance; pray, love, remember." See Rose and Mary for more information about each name.

ROXANE, ROXANNE
From the Persian meaning "dawn," or "brilliant light." Roxy is a popular diminutive form.

Hebrew equivalents: Barkawis, Bas-Shachar, Shacharis, Tzafraw, Tzafreeraw and Tzafreeris. Masculine Hebrew equivalents: Aveeshachar, Ben-Shachar, Shacharyaw, Tzafreer and Tzafreeree.

Key: *a* as in f*a*ther; *ai* as in *ai*sle; *aw* as in l*aw*; *ay* as in s*ay*; *e* as in b*e*t;

RUBY

A French-Latin name meaning "precious stone." It is used as a masculine and feminine name. In England and Scotland Ruby was also used as a nickname for Roberta and Robina which are feminine forms of Robert.

Hebrew equivalents: Margawlis, P'neenaw, S'gulaw and Tz'feeraw. Masculine Hebrew equivalents: Shoham, Shovai and Yawkawr.

RUDELLE

From the Old High German meaning "the famous one."

Hebrew equivalents: T'heelaw, Yawayl, Y'hudis and Zimraw. Masculine Hebrew equivalents: Heelayl, Shevach, Shim'ee, Y'hudaw and Yishbach.

RUTH

A name first possessed by the biblical character whose loyalty to her mother-in-law, Naomi, won for her the admiration of all peoples, and one of the most popular of modern names. It is derived from the Hebrew and Syriac meaning "friendship." Ruthie is a common pet form.

The exact Hebrew equivalent is Rus. Masculine Hebrew equivalents: Dawvid, Raya, Rayee, Regem and R'uayl.

SAADA

From the Hebrew meaning "support, help."

The exact Hebrew equivalent is Saadaw. The exact masculine Hebrew equivalent is Saadyaw.

SABINA

The feminine form of the Latin Sabin meaning "of the Sabines." The Sabines were an ancient Italian people who conquered the Romans in 290 B.C.

There are no Hebrew equivalents for this name.

SABRA

The Hebrew name for a native born Israeli. From the Hebrew meaning "thorny cactus." Used primarily as a feminine name, but occasionally as a masculine name.

ee as in b*ee*t; *i* as in b*i*t; *o* as in n*o*; *oi* as in v*oi*d; *u* as in r*u*de.

SABRINA
A diminutive form of Sabra. See Sabra for a full explanation.

SACHA
A variant form of Alexandra used in Russia. The masculine form is Sascha. See Alexander and Alexandra for a full explanation.

SADI, SADIE, SADYE
Sadi and Sadye are modern spellings of Sadie which is a pet form of Sarah. See Sarah for a full explanation. Sadie was once popular among Roman Catholics, having been used as a pet form of Mercedes meaning "Mary of the Mercies."

SAHARA
From the Aramaic and Hebrew meaning "moon."

The exact Hebrew equivalent is Saharaw. Masculine Hebrew equivalents: Chodesh and Yerach.

SALLIE, SALLY
Variant forms of Sarah. See Sarah for a full explanation.

SALOME
From the Hebrew meaning "peaceful." In history, Salome Alexandra was the ruler of Judea from 76-67 B.C.E. She was succeeded by her husband Alexander Yannai. A sister of King Herod was also named Salome.

The exact Hebrew equivalents are Shlomis and Shlomtzeeyon. Masculine Hebrew equivalents: Ish-Shawlom, Shawlom, Shlomee and Shlomo.

SAMANTHA
From the Aramaic meaning "the listener." A biblical name revived in the latter part of the 19th century by the popular book, *Samantha Among the Brethren.*

Hebrew equivalents: Kashuvaw and Shimonaw. Masculine Hebrew equivalents: Aveeshawmaw, Eleeshawmaw, Shimee, Shimon and Yaazanyaw.

Key: *a* as in f*a*ther; *ai* as in *ai*sle; *aw* as in l*aw*; *ay* as in s*ay*; *e* as in b*e*t;

SAMARA
From the Hebrew meaning "a guardian."
The exact Hebrew equivalent is Shomronaw. Masculine Hebrew equivalents: Shimrai, Shimree and Shimron.

SAMUELA
The feminine form of Samuel meaning "God has heard," or "His name is God," or "God has appointed." See Samuel in masculine section for more information.

SANDRA, SANDY
Forms of Alexandra. See Alexandra for a full explanation.

SAPIR, SAPIRA
From the Hebrew meaning "a sapphire, a precious stone." Sapir is also used as a masculine name.
The exact Hebrew equivalents are Sapeer and Sapeeraw. Masculine Hebrew equivalents: Sapeer, Segel and Yakeer.

SARA, SARAH, SARAI, SARETTE, SARI, SARITA
Sarah, first of the matriarchs and wife of Abraham, is derived from the Hebrew meaning "princess, noble." Her name in the Bible was originally Sarai and later changed to Sarah. She and Abraham were the parents of Isaac. Among Jews the name was always popular, but among Christians it was rarely used before the Reformation. Sally and Sadie are pet forms of Sarah. Sarita is a diminutive form, as are Sari, Sarette and Sarita.
The exact Hebrew equivalent is Sawraw. Masculine Hebrew equivalents: Aveehud, Cheerawm, Nawdawv and Yisrawayl.

SARAN, SARANN, SARANNE
A combination of Sarah and Ann. See Sarah and Ann for a full explanation of each name.

SARENE, SARINA, SARINE
Variant forms of Sarah. See Sarah for a full explanation.

ee as in b*ee*t; *i* as in b*i*t; *o* as in n*o*; *oi* as in v*oi*d; *u* as in r*u*de.

SARICE

From the Hebrew meaning "a ruler, a princess."

The exact Hebrew equivalent is Sawris. Masculine Hebrew equivalents: Aveehud, Cheerawm, Nawdawv and Yisrawayl.

SAUNDRA

A variant spelling of Sandra which is a diminutive form of Alexandra. See Alexandra for a full explanation.

SCARLET, SCARLETT

A Middle English name meaning "a deep red color."

Hebrew equivalent: Puaw. Masculine Hebrew equivalents: Admon, Almog, Gunee and Tzochar.

SEEMA, SEMA

From the Greek meaning "sprout." A name related to Cyma.

Hebrew equivalents: Neetzaw, Pirchaw, P'reechaw, Shoshanaw and Tifrawchaw. Masculine Hebrew equivalents: Efra'yim, Neetzan, Savyon, Shoshan and Tzemach.

SELA

From the Greek and Hebrew meaning "a rock." Also used as a masculine name.

The exact Hebrew equivalent is Sela.

SELDA

Either from the Anglo-Saxon meaning "precious, rare," or from Middle English meaning "booth, hut," and having the connotation of protection.

Hebrew equivalents: Awdaw, Chamudaw, Sapeeraw, S'gulaw and Y'kawraw. Masculine Hebrew equivalents: Bawhat, Leshem, Nofach, Sapir, Yahalom and Yakir.

SELINA

From the Greek meaning "moon." This name was used by the Greeks for the moon goddess, along with Phoebe and Cynthia. The Romans called the moon goddess Diana.

Hebrew equivalents: Chodesh, L'vawnaw and Saharaw.

Masculine Hebrew equivalents: Yerach. See Phoebe for additional equivalents.

SELMA

From the Celtic meaning "fair."

Hebrew equivalents: L'vawnaw, Naamaw and Raananaw. Masculine Hebrew equivalents: Lawvawn, Livnee and Raanawn.

SERENA

From the Latin meaning either "peaceful," or "light, fair, cheerful."

Hebrew equivalents: Acheenoam, L'vawnaw, M'eeraw, Shlomis and Shulamis. Masculine Hebrew equivalents: Aveenoam, Lawvawn, Mayeer, Shawlom and Shlomee.

SHAINA, SHAINE, SHAYNA, SHAYNE

From the Yiddish meaning "beautiful."

Hebrew equivalents: Adeenaw, Nawawmee, Rivkaw and Shifraw. Masculine Hebrew equivalents: Aveenoam, Chemdawn, Naamawn and Raanawn.

SHALGIA

From the Hebrew meaning "snow, snow-white." In Israel it is the name of a plant with white flowers.

The exact Hebrew equivalent is Shalgeeyaw. Masculine Hebrew equivalents: Lawvawn and Livnee.

SHANE, SHANIE

Variant spelling of Shaina. See Shaina for a full explanation.

SHARI

Probably a diminutive form of Sharon. See below for a full explanation.

SHARON

A name for a variety of roses found abundantly in Israel. King Solomon sang of the Roses of Sharon in the Song of Songs in the Bible.

The exact Hebrew equivalent is Shawron. Chavatzeles-

ee as in b*ee*t; *i* as in b*i*t; *o* as in n*o*; *oi* as in v*oi*d; *u* as in r*u*de.

Hashawron is a modern Israeli equivalent. Shawron is also used as a masculine name in Israel.

SHEBA
A diminutive of Bathsheba. See Bathsheba for a full explanation.

SHEILA, SHEILAH, SHEILLA, SHIELA
These names are variant forms of Cecelia and Celia introduced into Ireland by the earlest Englishmen. See Cecelia for a full explanation.

SHENA, SHEENA
A Gaelic form of Jane. See Jane for a full explanation.

SHERRY
A variant form of Caesrina which is the feminine form of the Latin Caesar meaning "king," hence Sherry and means "queen." Sheryl and Cheryl are forms of the same name.

Hebrew equivalents: Malkaw. Masculine Hebrew equivalent: Melech.

SHERYL
A form of Sherry, also spelled Cheryl. See above for a full explanation.

SHIFRA
From the Hebrew meaning "beautiful."

The exact Hebrew equivalent is Shifraw. Masculine Hebrew equivalents: Shapir and Shefer.

SHIMRA, SHIMRIA, SHIMRIT
From the Hebrew meaning "to guard, conserve."

The exact Hebrew equivalents are Shimraw, Shimreeyaw and Shimris. Masculine Hebrew equivalents: Shemer, Shimree, Sh'maryaw and Sh'maryawhu.

SHIRA, SHIRAH, SHIRI
From the Hebrew meaning "song." Shiri means "my song."

Key: *a* as in f*a*ther; *ai* as in *ai*sle; *aw* as in l*aw*; *ay* as in s*ay*; *e* as in b*e*t;

The exact Hebrew equivalents are Sheeraw and Sheeree. Masculine Hebrew equivalents: Ron, Ronayl, Ronayn, Ronee and Ronlee.

SHIRLEE
Either a fanciful spelling of Shirley (see below) or from the Hebrew meaning "song is mine."

The exact Hebrew equivalent is Sheerlee. Masculine Hebrew equivalents: Ron, Ronayl, Ronayn, Ronee and Ronlee.

SHIRLEY
From the Old English meaning "from the white meadow." Shirl is often used as a pet form.

Hebrew equivalents: Ganaw, Karmelaw, L'vawnaw, Nawvaw and Shalgeeyaw. Masculine Hebrew equivalents: Geenas, Hevel, Karmel, Lawvawn and Yaraw.

SHOSHAN, SHOSHANA, SHOSHANAH
From the Hebrew meaning "a lily" or "a rose." Shoshan is also used as a masculine name in Israel.

The exact Hebrew equivalents are Shoshawn or Shoshanaw. The exact masculine Hebrew equivalent is Shoshawn.

SHULAMIT, SHULAMITH
From the Hebrew meaning "peaceful." Salome is the Greek form. See Salome for more information.

The exact Hebrew equivalent is Shulamis. Masculine Hebrew equivalents: Shawlom and Shlomo.

SIBYL
From the Greek meaning "counsel of God," or "wise woman." Sibelle, Sibbie and Sevilla are variant forms.

Hebrew equivalents: Beenaw, Bunaw and Milkaw. Masculine Hebrew equivalents: Achbawn, Chachmonee, Utz and Yoshaw.

SIMA
From the Aramaic meaning "a treasure."

ee as in beet; *i* as in bit; *o* as in no; *oi* as in void; *u* as in rude.

The exact Hebrew equivalent is Seemaw. Masculine Hebrew equivalents: Hunaw, Matmon, Michmawn and Segel.

SIMAJEAN
A combination of Sima and Jean. See each name for a full explanation.

SIMEONA, SIMONA, SIMONE
Feminine forms of the masculine Simeon and Simon meaning "to hear," or "to be heard," in the Hebrew.

The exact Hebrew equivalent is Shimonaw. Masculine Hebrew equivalent is Shimon.

SINDY
A fanciful spelling of Cindy. Cindy and Sindy are pet forms of Cynthia. See Cynthia for a full explanation.

SISS, SISSIE, SISSY
Pet forms of Cecelia. See Cecelia for a full explanation.

SIVANA
The feminine form of the masculine Sivan. Sivan is the ninth month after the Jewish New Year, corresponding to May-June. In the Zodiac its sign is Gemini ("twins").

The exact Hebrew equivalent is Seevawnaw. The exact masculine Hebrew equivalent is Seevawn.

SIVIA, SIVYA
From the Hebrew meaning "a deer." It is also spelled Civia and Tzivya.

The exact Hebrew equivalent is Tzivyaw. The exact masculine Hebrew equivalent is Tz'vee.

SONDRA
A variant spelling of Saundra which is a form of Alexandra. See Alexandra for a full explanation.

SONIA, SONJA, SONYA
Variant Slavic and Russian forms of Sophia. See below for a full explanation.

Key: *a* as in f*a*ther; *ai* as in *ai*sle; *aw* as in l*aw*; *ay* as in s*ay*; *e* as in b*e*t;

SOPHIA, SOPHIE
From the Greek meaning "wisdom, wise one." Sonia, Sonja and Sonya are variant forms.

Hebrew equivalents: Beenaw, Bunaw, Chawchmaw, Milkaw and Tusheeyaw. Masculine Hebrew equivalents: Achbawn, Chachmonee, Chanoch, Haskayl, Utz and Yoshaw.

SORALE, SORALIE, SOROLIE
Variant diminutive forms of Sarah. See Sarah for a full explanation.

STACEY, STACY
A form of Anastasia, derived from the Greek meaning "resurrection, revival." These names are also used as masculine forms.

Hebrew equivalents: Chavaw, Cha'yaw, Cheeyusaw, T'cheeyaw and Y'cheeaylaw. Masculine Hebrew equivalents: Ameechai, Bar-Yochawee, Chai, Cha'yim and Y'cheeayl.

STEFANA, STEFANIA, STEPHANIA
Variant spellings of Stefanie. See below for a full explanation.

STEFANIE, STEFENIE, STEPHANIE, STEPHENIE
Feminine forms of the masculine Steven and Stephen. Derived from the Greek meaning "crown, ruler."

Hebrew equivalents: Atawraw, Malkaw, T'zfeeraw and Yis'r'aylaw. Masculine Hebrew equivalents: Eleemelech, Kasreeayl, Melech and Yisrawayl.

STEVANA, STEVENA
Variant forms of Stefanie. See above for a full explanation.

STELLA
From the Latin meaning "star." Esther is the Persian form of Stella.

The exact Hebrew equivalent is Estayr. Masculine Hebrew equivalents: Bar-Kochvaw, Kochawv and Kochvaw.

---

ee as in b*ee*t; *i* as in b*i*t; *o* as in n*o*; *oi* as in v*oi*d; *u* as in r*u*de.

SUE, SUSIE
Popular diminutive forms of Susan. See below for a full explanation.

SUSAN
From the Hebrew meaning "a rose or lily." Many variant forms of Susan have developed over the centuries, particularly as diminutives. Most popular are: Sue, Suzie, Suzy, Sukie, Sukey, Susanne, Susette and Suzette.

The exact Hebrew equivalents are Shoshan and Shoshanaw. The exact masculine Hebrew equivalent is Shoshawn.

SUSANNE, SUZANNE, SUZETTE
Variant forms of Susan. Suzette is a French diminutive form. See above for a full explanation.

SYBIL
A variant spelling of Sibyl. See Sibyl for a full explanation.

SYDELLE
A variant form of Sydney which is the feminine form of Sidney. See Sydney below. Sydelle has been used as a form of Sadie which, in turn, is derived from Sarah. See Sadie, Sarah and Sidney for more information about the origin of these names.

SYDNEY
The feminine form of the masculine Sidney. Sid and Syd are popular diminutive forms. See Sidney in the masculine section for a full explanation.

SYLVIA
From the Latin meaning "forest," or "one who dwells in in the woods." Sylvan is the original masculine form.

Hebrew equivalents: Ganaw, Karmelaw and Nawvaw. Masculine Hebrew equivalents: Karmel, Kar'mlee and Yaraw.

Key: *a* as in f*a*ther; *ai* as in *ai*sle; *aw* as in l*aw*; *ay* as in s*ay*; *e* as in b*e*t;

SYMA
A form of Sema and Cyma. See Seema and Cyma for more information.

TAGA
From the Aramaic and Arabic meaning "a crown."

The exact Hebrew equivalent is Tagaw. Masculine Hebrew equivalents: Kasreeayl, Kisron, Melech and Zayraw.

TAL, TALIA, TALYA
From the Hebrew meaning "dew." Talia and Talya mean "the dew of heaven," and also "a young lamb," in Aramaic.

The exact Hebrew equivalents are Tal and Talyaw. Masculine Hebrew equivalents: Leetal, Talor and Tal-Shachar.

TALMA, TALMICE, TALMIT
From the Hebrew meaning "mound, hill."

The exact Hebrew equivalents are Talmaw and Talmis. Masculine Hebrew equivalents: Geva, Harayl and Talmai.

TALMOR
From the Hebrew meaning "heaped or sprinkled with myrrh (spice), perfumed."

The exact Hebrew equivalent is Talmor. Masculine Hebrew equivalents: Mivsawm, Mor, Raychawn and Yivsawm.

TALOR, TALORA
From the Hebrew meaning "dew of the morning."

The exact Hebrew equivalents are Talor and Taloraw. Masculine Hebrew equivalents: Leetal, Talor and Tal-Shachar.

TAMAR, TAMARAH
From the Hebrew meaning "a palm tree," and having the connotation of upright, righteous, graceful.

The exact Hebrew equivalent is Tawmawr. Masculine Hebrew equivalents: Ameetai, Amnon, Dekel, Eetawmawr, Tawmir, Tzawdok and Yochawnawn.

---

ee as in be*et*; *i* as in b*i*t; *o* as in n*o*; *oi* as in v*oi*d; *u* as in r*u*de.

TAMARA

From the East Indian meaning "spice," or from the Hebrew meaning "palm tree," equivalent to Tamar.

Hebrew equivalents: Bawsmaw and K'tzeeaw. Masculine Hebrew equivalents: Mivsawm, Mor and Yivsawm.

TAMI, TAMMY

Feminine forms of Thomas. See Thomas in masculine section for a full explanation.

TARA

Either a French name derived from the Arabic meaning "a measurement," or from the Aramaic meaning "to throw or carry."

Hebrew equivalent: T'rumaw. Masculine Hebrew equivalent: Yoraw.

TELI

From the Aramaic and Hebrew meaning "a lamb."

The exact Hebrew equivalent is T'lee. The exact masculine Hebrew equivalent is Talyaw.

TEMIMA

A Hebraic name meaning "whole, honest."

The exact Hebrew equivalent is T'meemaw. Masculine Hebrew equivalents: Ameetai, Amnon, Eetawmawr and Konanyawhu.

TEMIRA

From the Hebrew meaning "tall."

The exact Hebrew equivalent is T'meeraw. Masculine Hebrew equivalents: Eetawmawr and Tawmir.

TERESA

A variant spelling of Theresa. See Theresa for a full explanation.

TERI

Pet forms of Teresa and Theresa. See Theresa for a full explanation.

Key: *a* as in *father*; *ai* as in *aisle*; *aw* as in *law*; *ay* as in *say*; *e* as in *bet*;

TERUMA
From the Hebrew meaning "an offering, a gift."
The exact Hebrew equivalent is T'rumaw. Masculine Hebrew equivalents: Matanyaw, Matawn, Matnai, N'sanayl and Tesher.

TESHURA
From the Hebrew meaning "a gift."
The exact Hebrew equivalent is T'shuraw. Masculine Hebrew equivalents: Matanyaw, Matawn, Matisyawhu, Nawsawn, Tesher and Y'honawsawn.

THALIA
From the Greek meaning "luxurious, flourishing."
Hebrew equivalents: Astayraw, Astayreeyaw, Pirchaw, Pirchis, Tifrachas and Tifrawchaw. Masculine Hebrew equivalents: Efra'yim, Neetzawn, Perach, Puraw and Tzemach.

THEA
A short form of Althea. It is also the name of a goddess in Greek mythology. See Althea for more information.

THELMA
From the Greek meaning "a nursling, infant," and having the connotation of youth.
Hebrew equivalents: Almaw, Aveevaw, Sh'seelaw, Tz'eeraw, Y'neekaw and Zilpaw. Masculine Hebrew equivalents: Aylawm, Bichree, Kawtawn and Yefes.

THEODORA
Feminine form of Theodore. See Theodore in masculine section for interpretation and equivalents.

THERESA, THERESE
From the Greek meaning "a harvester, a farmer." Teresa is a variant spelling used in Italy and Spain. Tracey and Tracy are variant English forms. Among the pet forms that have developed over the centuries are: Tess, Tessa and Terry. Teri and Terri are modern spellings.

---

ee as in b*ee*t; *i* as in b*i*t; *o* as in n*o*; *oi* as in v*oi*d; *u* as in r*u*de.

Hebrew equivalents: Ganaw, Karmelaw and Nawvaw. Masculine Hebrew equivalents: Awdawm, Karmel, Karm'lee and Yiz'r'ayl.

TILLA
A variant form of Tillie. See Tillie for a full explanation.

TILLAMAE
A combination of Tilla and Mae. See Tilla and Mae for a full explanation.

TILLIE, TILLY
Either from Mathilda, or from the Latin meaning "graceful linden tree."

Hebrew equivalents: Eelawnaw, Hadasaw and Tirzaw. Masculine Hebrew equivalents: Aylaw, Oren and Miklos. See Mathilda for additional equivalents.

TIMORA
From the Hebrew meaning "tall" (like the palm tree).

The exact Hebrew equivalent is Teemoraw. Masculine Hebrew equivalents: Eetawmawr and Tawmir.

TINA
Like Ina, Tina is a suffix meaning "pertaining to." It is also a diminutive form of names like Christina and Bettina. See Christina and Bettina for a full explanation of each name.

TIRA
A Hebraic name meaning "encampment, enclosure," and having the connotation of protection.

The exact Hebrew equivalent is Teeraw. Masculine Hebrew equivalents: Akeevaw, Chosaw, Lot, Tachan and Yaakov.

TIRZA
A Hebraic name meaning either a "cypress tree," or "willing, desirable." In the Bible (Book of Kings) the city Tirzah was the capital of Samaria.

Key: *a* as in father; *ai* as in aisle; *aw* as in law; *ay* as in say; *e* as in bet;

The exact Hebrew eqivalent is Tirtzaw. Masculine Hebrew equivalents: Aylaw, Yoawv and Yoayl.

TITANIA
From the Greek meaning "the great one."
Hebrew equivalents: Asalyaw, G'dulaw and Rawchawv. Masculine Hebrew equivalents: G'dalyaw, Geedayl, Rabaw, Rav, Rawvaw and R'chavyaw.

TIVONA
From the Hebrew meaning "a lover of nature."
The exact Hebrew equivalent is Tivonaw. The exact Masculine Hebrew equivalent is Tivon.

TOBA, TOBELLE, TOBY
Toby and its forms are either from the Hebrew meaning "good," or from the Yiddish meaning "dove."
Hebrew equivalents: Tovaw, Tzeeyona, Yawtvaw, Y'meemaw and Yoneenaw. Masculine Hebrew equivalents: Acheetuv, Ben-Tzeeyon, Tuveeyaw and Yonaw.

TOBIT
From the Hebrew meaning "good." In the Apocrypha Tobit is the name of a book, the hero of which is the blind Tobit who dispatches his son Tobias to Persia to collect a debt. Tobit is also mentioned several times in the Bible where it is a masculine name. In Israel today it is used in both forms.
The exact feminine and masculine Hebrew equivalent is Tovis.

TONI, TONIA
Diminutive forms of Antoinette derived from the Greek and Latin, and meaning "of high esteem, revered."
Hebrew equivalents: Asalyaw, Ahudaw, Malkaw, Odelyaw, Shawvchaw and Tishbawchaw. Masculine Hebrew equivalents: Adoneeyaw, Ameenawdawv, G'dalyaw, Heelayl, M'hulawl and Yishbach.

---

ee as in b*ee*t; *i* as in b*i*t; *o* as in n*o*; *oi* as in v*oi*d; *u* as in r*u*de.

TOVA, TOVAH
From the Hebrew meaning "good."

The exact Hebrew equivalent is Tovaw. Masculine Hebrew equivalents: Acheetuv, Aveetuv, Tuveeyaw and Yawtvaw.

TRACY
From the Anglo-Saxon meaning "brave." Used as a masculine name as well. Tracy may also be a pet form of Theresa (see Theresa).

TRINA
A short form of Katrina which is derived from Catherine. See Catherine or Katherine for a full explanation.

TRUDI, TRUDY
Popular pet forms of Gertrude. See Gertrude for a full explanation.

UNA
From the Latin meaning "the one." Oona is a popular Irish variant form. Ona and Unity are also forms of Una.

Hebrew equivalents: L'veeyaw and Reeshonaw. Masculine Hebrew equivalents: Chever, Chevron and Layvee.

URICE, URIT
From the Hebrew meaning "light."

The exact Hebrew equivalent is Uris. Masculine Hebrew equivalents: Uree and Ureeyaw.

URSALA
From the Latin meaning "a bear."

Hebrew equivalent: Dubaw. Masculine Hebrew equivalents: Dov and Dubee.

VALERIE
From the Latin meaning "strong."

Hebrew equivalents: Amtzaw, Areeayl, Gavreelaw and Geeboraw. Masculine Hebrew equivalents: Aree, Barzeelai, Gever and Yoawsh.

Key: *a* as in f*a*ther; *ai* as in *ai*sle; *aw* as in l*aw*; *ay* as in s*ay*; *e* as in b*e*t;

VANESSA
From the Greek meaning "a butterfly."
There are no Hebrew equivalents.

VARDA, VARDICE, VARDIS, VARDIT
From the Hebrew meaning "a rose."
The exact Hebrew equivalents are Vardaw and Vardis.
Masculine Hebrew equivalents: Shoshawn and Vered.

VARDIA, VARDINA
From the Hebrew meaning "a rose."
The exact Hebrew equivalents are Vardeeyaw and Vardeenaw. Masculine Hebrew equivalents: Shoshawn and Vered.

VEDA
From the Sanscrit meaning "sacred understanding."
The Veda is the sacred Writings of the Hindus.
Hebrew equivalents: Beenaw, Bunaw and Tusheeyaw.
Masculine Hebrew equivalents Achbawn, Chanoch, Haskayl, Yawvin and Yoshaw.

VERA
Either from the Latin meaning "truth," or from the Russian meaning "faith."
Hebrew equivalents: Amawnaw, Bitchaw, Emunaw, Ne'emawnaw, Ne'emenes and Tikvaw. Masculine Hebrew equivalents: Ameesawn, Ameetai, Amnon and Ne'emawn.

VERED
From the Hebrew meaning "a rose." In Israel Vered is used as a feminine and masculine name.
The exact Hebrew equivalent is Vered.

VERENA, VERINA
From the Latin meaning "one who venerates God," or "respect, praise, or sacred wisdom."
Hebrew equivalents: D'voraw, T'heelaw, Tusheeyaw, Y'udis and Zimraw. Masculine Hebrew equivalents: Ach-

ee as in b*ee*t; *i* as in b*i*t; *o* as in n*o*; *oi* as in v*oi*d; *u* as in r*u*de.

bawn, Chanoch, G'dalyaw, Haskayl, Hodeeyaw, M'halalayl and Y'hudaw.

VERNA
A form of either Verena, Verne or Veronica. See each name for a full explanation.

VERNE
From the Latin meaning "spring-like." Literally it means "to grow green."

Hebrew equivalent: Yarkonaw. Masculine Hebrew equivalent: Yarkon.

VERONICA
Either a form of Berenice meaning "bringer of victory," (see Berenice) or from the Latin meaning "truthful, faithful." Nicky is a pet form.

Hebrew equivalents: Bitchaw, Emunaw and Tikvaw. Masculine Hebrew equivalents: Ameetai, Amnon, Bukee and Haymawn.

VICI, VICKI, VICKY
Diminutive forms of Victoria. See below for a full explanation.

VICTORIA
From the Latin meaning "victorious." Victoria is the feminine form of Victor. Vicki and Vicky are popular pet forms.

Hebrew equivalents: Dafnaw, Hadasaw, Nitzchaw and Nitzchis. Masculine Hebrew equivalents: Govayr, Matzleeach, N'tzeeach and Yatzleeach.

VIDA
Either a form of Vita or a short form of Davida. See Vita and Davida for a full explanation.

VIOLA, VIOLET
Flower names of Latin origin, having the connotation of modest, graceful, or flourishing.

Key: *a* as in f*a*ther; *ai* as in *ai*sle; *aw* as in l*aw*; *ay* as in s*ay*; *e* as in b*e*t;

Hebrew equivalents: Neetzaw, Shoshanaw, Tawmawr and Vardaw. Masculine Hebrew equivalents: Efra'yim, Pekach, P'rachyaw and Puraw.

VIRGILIA
The Latin form of Virginia. See below for a full explanation.

VIRGINIA
From the Latin meaning "virgin, pure," or "a maiden." Virginia is a feminine form of the masculine Latin name, Virgil, meaning "unbloomed, unmarried." Ginny and Virgie are pet forms.

Hebrew equivalents: B'ruraw, B'sulaw, Diklaw, Rawchayl, Tawmawr and Zakaw. Masculine Hebrew equivalents: Ameetai, Amnon, Eetawmawr, Konanyawhu, Yesher and Y'shurun.

VITA
From the Latin meaning "life, animated." Vivian, Vivien and Vyvyan are variant forms.

Hebrew equivalents: Chavaw, Chayaw and T'cheeyaw. Masculine Hebrew equivalents: Ameechai, Amrawm, Cha'yim, Cheeyaw and Y'cheeayl.

VIVIAN, VIVIANA, VIVIEN, VYVYAN
Variant forms of Vita. See above for a full explanation. Viviana appears as a name in 12th century England and is probably a combination of Vivian and Anna.

WALDA
The feminine form of Waldo. From Old High German meaning "to rule."

Hebrew equivalents: Atawraw, Malkaw, N'deevaw and Sawraw. Masculine Hebrew equivalents: Elrawd, Malkeeayl, Malkeeyaw, Melech and Yisrawayl.

WANDA
A form of Wandis. From the Teutonic meaning "wanderer."

ee as in b*ee*t; *i* as in b*i*t; *o* as in n*o*; *oi* as in v*oi*d; *u* as in r*u*de.

Hebrew equivalent: Aveeshag. Masculine Hebrew equivalents: Gawlyas and Yawglee.

WENDEY, WENDI, WENDY
Either diminutive form of Genevieve or Gwendaline. See Genevieve and Gwendaline for a full explanation.

WILHELMINA
Wilhelmina and its short forms are from the Teutonic meaning "warrior," and "leader of many, ruler." Among the many pet forms of Wilhelmina are: Mimi, Minnette, Wilmot, Mina, Minna, Helma, Willa, Willene, Wilmena and Wilma.

Hebrew equivalents: Amtzaw, Awtzmaw, Gavreeaylaw, Geeboraw, Malkaw and Yis'r'aylaw. Masculine Hebrew equivalents: Gavreeayl, Mawrd'chai, M'dawn, Melech and Yisrawayl.

WILLA, WILLENE, WILMA
Pet forms of Wilhelmina. See above for a full explanation.

WINIFRED
From the Teutonic meaning "friend of peace." Win, Wyn, Winnie, Freda and Frieda are pet forms.

Hebrew equivalents: M'nuchaw, M'shulemes, Shlomis and Shulamis. Masculine Hebrew equivalents: Avshawlom, Shalum, Shawlayv, Shawlom and Shlomo.

WYNNE, WYNETTE
Short forms of Gwendaline. See Gwendaline for a full explanation.

XENA
From the Greek meaning either "great," or "stranger." Hebrew equivalents: Asalyaw, Aveeshag and G'dulaw. Masculine Hebrew equivalents: Geedayl, G'dalyawhu, Rav, Rawvaw and Yawglee.

YAALIT, YAEL, YAELA, YAELLA
Variant spellings of Jael. See Jael for a full explanation.

Key: *a* as in f*a*ther; *ai* as in *ai*sle; *aw* as in l*aw*; *ay* as in s*ay*; *e* as in b*e*t;

YAFFA, YAFIT

From the Hebrew meaning "beautiful."

The exact Hebrew equivalents are **Yawfaw and Yawfis.** Masculine Hebrew equivalent: **Yawfe.**

YAKIRA

From the Hebrew meaning "valuable, precious."

The exact Hebrew equivalent is **Yakeeraw.** The exact masculine Hebrew equivalent is **Yakir.**

YARDENA

The feminine Hebraic name for Jordan. See Jordan in the masculine section for a full explanation.

YARKONA

The feminine form of the masculine Yarkon. From the Hebrew meaning "green." A bird with golden-green feathers, called Yarkona, is found in southern Israel.

The exact Hebrew equivalent is **Yarkonaw.** The exact masculine Hebrew equivalent is **Yarkon.**

YATVA

From the Hebrew meaning "good."

The exact Hebrew equivalent is **Yawtvaw.** Masculine Hebrew equivalents: **Ameetuv, Eleetuv, Maytiv, Tov** and **Tovee.**

YEDIDA, YEDIDAH

From the Hebrew meaning "friend, beloved."

The exact Hebrew equivalent is **Y'deedaw.** The exact masculine Hebrew equivalent is **Y'didyaw.**

YEHIELA, YEHIELLA

Feminine forms of Yehiel of Jehiel. From the Hebrew meaning "may God live."

The exact Hebrew equivalent is **Y'cheeaylaw.** The exact masculine Hebrew equivalent is **Y'cheeayl.**

YEHUDIT, YUDIT, YUTA

The Hebrew name for Judith. In the Bible Yehudit

ee as in b*ee*t; *i* as in b*i*t; *o* as in n*o*; *oi* as in v*oi*d; *u* as in r*u*de.

appears only once, as the wife of Esau. Yudit and Yuta are abbreviated forms. See Judith for more information.

YEIRA
From the Hebrew meaning "light."
The exact Hebrew equivalent is Y'eeraw. The exact masculine Hebrew equivalent is Yawir.

YEMIMA
A variant Hebraic form of Jemima meaning "dove," in the Arabic. In the Bible Jemima was a daughter of Job.
The exact Hebrew equivalent is Y'meemaw. The exact masculine Hebrew equivalent is Yonaw.

YEMINA
From the Hebrew meaning "right hand," and signifying "strength."
The exact Hebrew equivalent is Y'meenaw. The exact masculine Hebrew equivalent is Yawmin.

YESHISHA
From the Hebrew meaning "old."
The exact Hebrew equivalent is Y'sheeshaw. Masculine Hebrew equivalents: Yawshish, Y'sheeshai and Zawkayn.

YETTA
A diminutive form of Henrietta. See Henrietta for a full explanation.

YIGAALA, YIGALA
From the Hebrew meaning "to redeem."
The exact Hebrew equivalent is Y'gawawlaw. Masculine Hebrew equivalents: Eg'awl, G'alyaw, Goayl and Yeegaw-ayl.

YOCHEBED, YOCHEVED, YOHEVED
Hebraic spellings of Jochebed. See Jochebed for a full explanation.

YONA, YONINA, YONIT, YONITA
Various forms of Hebrew meaning "dove." These names

Key: *a* as in f*a*ther; *ai* as in *ai*sle; *aw* as in l*aw*; *ay* as in s*ay*; *e* as in b*e*t;

are also spelled Jona, Jonina and Jonati. Yona is used primarily as a masculine name (see Jonah).

The exact Hebrew equivalents are Yonaw, Yoneenaw and Yonis. The exact masculine Hebrew equivalent is Yonaw.

YOSIFA, YOSEFA
Variant spellings of Josepha, the feminine form of Joseph, which is derived from the Hebrew, and means "he will add."

The exact Hebrew equivalent is Yoseefaw. The exact masculine Hebrew equivalent is Yosayf.

YOVELA
From the Hebrew meaning "jubilee or rejoicing."

The exact Hebrew equivalent is Yovaylaw. Masculine Hebrew equivalents: Yachdeeayl, Yovayl and Yitzchak.

YVETTE, YVONNE
Derived from the French masculine name, Yves, meaning "the archer." Some authorities maintain that Yves is the equivalent of the Welsh Evan which is a form of John. See John for more information.

ZAKA, ZAKIA, ZAKIT
From the Hebrew meaning "bright, pure, clear."

The exact Hebrew equivalents are Zakaw, Zakeeyaw and Zakis. The exact masculine Hebrew equivalent is Zakai.

ZARA, ZORA
Variant forms of Sarah. Zora is also Arabic for "dawn." In Hebrew Zara also has the meaning of "stranger."

Hebrew equivalents: Aveeshag, Hawgawr, Sawraw, Shacharis and Tz'feeraw. Masculine Hebrew equivalents: Ben-Shachar, Gawlyas, Gayrshon and Sh'charyaw.

ZARIZA, ZERIZA
A Hebraic name meaning "industrious."

The exact Hebrew equivalent is Z'reezaw. Masculine Hebrew equivalents: Arnon, Yawziz and Zeezaw.

---

ee as in b*ee*t; *i* as in b*i*t; *o* as in n*o*; *oi* as in v*oi*d; *u* as in r*u*de.

ZAYIT
From the Hebrew meaning "olive." Also used as a masculine name.

The exact Hebrew equivalent is Za'yis.

ZEHARA, ZEHARI
From the Hebrew meaning "to shine, light, brightness."

The exact Hebrew equivalents are Zawhawraw and Zawhawree. Masculine Hebrew equivalents: Z'haryaw and Zohar.

ZEHAVA, ZEHAVI, ZEHAVIT, ZEHUVA
A Hebraic name meaning "golden." Zehavi is also used as a masculine name.

The exact Hebrew equivalents are Zawhawvaw, Zawhawvee, Z'hawvis and Z'huvaw. Masculine Hebrew equivalents: Eleefaz, Pawz, Upawz and Zawhawvee.

ZEHIRA
From the Hebrew meaning "guarded, protected."

The exact Hebrew equivalent is Z'heeraw. Masculine Hebrew equivalents: Chosaw, Eleefelet, Sisree, Tzilsai and Yaakov.

ZELDA
A variant spelling of Selda. See Selda for a full explanation.

ZEMIRA, ZEMORA
From the Hebrew meaning "a branch."

The exact Hebrew equivalent is Z'meeraw and Z'moraw. Masculine Hebrew equivalents: Naytzer and Sawrig.

ZENA
A variant spelling of Xena. See Xena for a full explanation.

ZETA, ZETANA
From the Hebrew meaning "an olive."

The exact Hebrew equivalents are Zaysaw and Zaysawnaw. Masculine Hebrew equivalent: Za'yis.

Key: *a* as in f*a*ther; *ai* as in *ai*sle; *aw* as in l*aw*; *ay* as in s*ay*; *e* as in b*e*t;

ZEVA

The feminine form of Zev or Ze'ev meaning "a wolf" in Hebrew.

The exact Hebrew equivalent is Z'ayvaw. The exact masculine Hebrew equivalent is Z'ayv.

ZEVIDA, ZEVUDA

From the Hebrew meaning "a gift."

The exact Hebrew equivalents are Z'veedaw and Z'vudaw. Masculine Hebrew equivalents: Zavdee, Zavdeeayl and Z'vadyaw.

ZEVULA

From the Hebrew meaning "a dwelling place," or "a palace."

The exact Hebrew equivalent is Z'vulaw. The exact masculine Hebrew equivalents are Z'vul and Z'vulun.

ZILA, ZILLA, ZILI, ZILLI

From the Hebrew meaning "a shadow."

The exact Hebrew equivalents are Tzeelaw and Tzeelee. Masculine Hebrew equivalents: Hertzayl and Tzilsai.

ZIMRA

From the Hebrew meaning either "a branch of choice fruits," or "song of praise."

The exact Hebrew equivalent is Zimraw. Masculine Hebrew equivalents: Naytzer, Sawrig, Y'hudaw, Zimrawn, and Z'maryaw.

ZIMRIA, ZIMRIAH

From the Hebrew meaning "sing or song."

The exact Hebrew equivalent is Zimreeyaw. Masculine Hebrew equivalents: Zawmir, Zemer, Zimrawn and Z'maryaw.

ee as in b*ee*t; *i* as in b*i*t; *o* as in n*o*; *oi* as in v*oi*d; *u* as in r*u*de.

ZIONA

A Hebraic name meaning "excellent."

The exact Hebrew equivalent is Tzeeyonaw. Masculine Hebrew equivalents: Aveetuv, Ben-Tzeeyon, Tuveeyaw and Yawtvaw.

ZIPPORAH

A Hebraic name meaning "a bird." In the Bible Zipporah was the wife of Moses and the daughter of Jethro.

The exact Hebrew equivalent is Tzeeporaw. Masculine Hebrew equivalents: Orayv and Tzeepor.

ZIRA

From the Hebrew meaning "an arena."

The exact Hebrew equivalent is Zeeraw. Masculine Hebrew equivalents: Mo'adyaw, No'adyaw and No'awd.

ZITA

A diminutive form of Theresa. See Theresa for a full explanation.

ZIVA, ZIVIT

From the Hebrew meaning "brightness, splendor."

Hebrew equivalents: Zeevaw and Zeevis. Masculine Hebrew equivalents: Bawhir, Zerach, Zohar and Z'rachyaw.

ZOE

From the Greek meaning "life." In a third century translation of the Bible by Alexandrian Jews, Eve (Chavah), meaning "life," is translated as Zoe.

Hebrew equivalents: Chavaw, Cha'yaw and Y'cheeaylaw. Masculine Hebrew equivalents: Chai, Cha'yim, Y'cheeawm and Y'cheeayl.

ZOHAR

A Hebraic name meaning "light, brilliance." Used also as a masculine name.

The exact Hebrew equivalent is Zohar.

Key: *a* as in f*a*ther; *ai* as in *ai*sle; *aw* as in l*aw*; *ay* as in s*ay*; *e* as in b*e*t;

ZOHERET
From the Hebrew meaning "she shines."

The exact Hebrew equivalent is Zoheres. Masculine Hebrew equivalents: Bawrawk, Mayeer, Zerach, Zohar and Z'rachyaw.

ZORA
See Zara for a full explanation.

ee as in b*ee*t; *i* as in b*i*t; *o* as in n*o*; *oi* as in v*oi*d; *u* as in r*u*de.

APPENDICES

The History and Development of Personal Names

THE HISTORY AND DEVELOPMENT
OF PERSONAL NAMES

In 1924, Robert Lynd wrote an article in the *New Statesman* entitled "Names," in which he described the results of a poll taken in England to decide the ten most popular girls' names. The result of 628,000 votes cast seemed to astonish him. He was actually annoyed with the results and expressed his disapproval with great vehemence.

The poll showed that the ten most popular girls' names were: Phyllis, Grace, Elsie, Barbara, Patience, Prudence, Jane, Susan, Priscilla and Matilda.

Robert Lynd seemed to be under the impression that the name makes the person. He was convinced that a person with a better sounding name would have a better chance of success in life. If he had his choice, his list would begin with Mary, Ann and Elizabeth. He goes on to say that "there never has been a man of genius called Ebenezer Fudge," and that you can tell a poet from a plumber merely by his name.

Judaism agrees with Mr. Lynd in only one respect. From biblical days onward, the name was always considered of extreme importance—although the choice of a name, and the final determination of whether a name will bring success or not, nice sounding or not, is purely subjective.

IN THE BEGINNING

To our earliest ancestors, and for many centuries thereafter, the name was of tremendous significance. As names were bestowed, the meaning of the name was the prime consideration in its selection. In the first pages of the Bible, when Adam was alone and God sought a companion for him, the narrative explains that every beast of the field and fowl of the heavens was brought before him to see which name he would choose.

Oddly enough, the task of choosing a mate is also coupled with that of naming the creatures. One biblical commentator resolves the strange cohesion by asserting that "the name would reflect the impression produced in his (Adam's) mind by each creature, and would indicate whether he regarded it as a fit companion for himself."

This example, early in the pages of the Bible, is characteristic of the attitude of our ancestors with regard to the name. The name was an important part of their lives and carried with it profound meaning. The name was more than just a word. It was a whole world—a world of ideas and experiences, a world of hopes and aspirations.

This significance, which was attributed to the name, is further emphasized very often throughout our biblical history in the changes that were made in the names of Abraham (from Abram), Sarah (from Sarai), Jacob (to Israel), Joshua (from Hosea), Gideon (to Jerubaal), Zedekiah (from Mattaniah) and Jehoiakim (from Eliakim); changes which were made to honor or glorify a person's newly acquired position or to predict the role of the individual in the future.

An analysis of the types of names employed in the Bible reveals even more concretely that every appellation attached to an individual had significance—a significance which is evident only as we understand the meaning of the name.

Biblical names can be broken down into the following categories:

1. Names describing a characteristic of the person, or

peculiarity of the body, e.g. Laban meaning white; Korah meaning bald; Harim meaning flat nosed.

2. Names influenced by experiences in the life of parents or child, e.g. Moses—"because I *drew him out* of the water (Ex. 2:10); Eve—"because she was the mother of all *living*" (Gen. 3:20).

34. Names of animals, e.g. Deborah meaning a bee, Jonah meaning a dove, Hulda meaning weasel. These names may have been adopted for a variety of reasons. Either the child's appearance resembled the animal, or perhaps the parents loved the animal, or the child may have been born in a locality where the animal was common.

4. Names of plants and flowers, e.g. Susan meaning rose, Tamar meaning palm. Perhaps the same reasons as for animal names would apply.

5. Theophoric names with God's name either as the prefix or suffix, e.g. Jehoiakim meaning "God will establish," or Isaiah meaning "salvation of the Lord."

6. Conditions or experiences of mankind or the nation, e.g. Noah—"and he called his name Noah, saying: 'This same shall *comfort* us in our work and in the toil of our hands, which cometh from the ground which the Lord hath cursed'" (Gen. 5:29), or Peleg—"in his days was the earth *divided*" (Gen. 10:25).

7. Names which express hope for the future or a desired condition, e.g. Joseph: "*may the Lord add* to me another son" (Gen. 30:24).

RELATION OF SUPERSTITION TO MEANING OF NAME

Superstitions which have developed in the course of the history of the world are perhaps the best indications of the influence and power of the name and the importance of its meaning, for they reveal the inner thoughts—the hopes and fears of the peoples who believed in them. Above all they reveal the close relationship that it was assumed existed between the name and the actual person. A person's name was to regarded and treated with the utmost reverence. It was a very real thing that dared not be abused or misused lest harm befall the person whose name was so treated. In their thinking, there was no difference between abuse of one's body and one's name. The same harm that the body might suffer through physical mistreatment could befall the body through mistreatment of the name.

Many queer and interesting customs developed as a result of this belief. Foremost among them were the customs of concealing and changing names in order that the evil spirit would not be enabled to harm the person through his name. If the name were camouflaged the spirit would not recognize the person and, hence, his safety was assured. As a result, we find in studying the practices among some of the tribes of the East Indies, South Africa, Central Australia and New Guinea that nicknames and secret names were commonly used instead of the person's real name. It was considered that this substitute name had nothing in common with the person to whom it referred. It was bad manners to ask anyone his name, for that would be inviting danger, since it was believed to be harmful for a person to pronounce his own name. You might ask someone else, but never the person himself.

Other tribes went even further. In addition to the personal name, the child was given a secret name which was known only to the immediate family or close friends. For the name to become known to members outside of the close tribal group was considered dangerous. Should a stranger even ask his name, they would either refuse outright to tell or pretend to have forgotten. This procedure was common to many tribes in uncivilized parts of the world and still persists to this day. At the christening of a Christian Eskimo, as has been observed in Greenland, it is not uncommon for the mother to answer the minister's question as to the child's name with *Naluvara*—"I don't know."

In *The Eskimos,* by Kaj Kirket-Smith, describing his observations among the primitive people of Greenland, Arctic Canada and Alaska, many of these superstitions are graphically portrayed. To these primitive people, the most important ceremony in the life of a person is the naming of a new child. The name, to them, is much like a person. When a person dies the name continues to live, wandering about helplessly until it is taken up and bestowed upon a child who, along with the name, inherits the qualities of the deceased. At birth, they claim, the child cries because it wants a name. That the name is important and holy to them is evidenced from the fact that "until the naming has been performed, no one will mention the name of the deceased person, but refer to him only by innuendoes and indefinite phrases. If the name is a common word in the language, it must be dropped, at any rate for a time, and it is this circumstance more than anything else that has given the East Greenland dialect its peculiar vocabulary."

Similar superstitious practices with regard to the change of name as a protective measure are to be found among many groups in various parts of the world today. Chinese parents, who fear that their new-born child will die, give him as his first name (milk name) at the age of one month, a contemptible appelation. Thus, it is not uncommon to hear of a Chinese baby called "Dust-Pan," or "That Dog," or "The Stupid," or "The Flea." It is hoped that the evil spirit will be deceived by considering the child unworthy of being bothered with. In some parts of the Orient the same objective was achieved by calling a new-born Jewish child in whose family several people have died "Vechai"—"May he live."

Although most of these primitive customs appear queer and outlandish to us, they are by no means completely foreign to Judaism. It is true that although we never went quite as far as other groups did, we do find that a great deal of superstitious practice has engulfed the Hebrew name in the course of history.

From talmudic times to this very day we find the same ideas prevailing among Jews with regard to the identification of the individual with his name. The Talmud records (Rosh Hashanah 16b) : "Four things can abrogate the decree (fate) of man and they are: charity, supplication, change of name and change of action."

The statement of the 13th century rabbi, Moses of Coucy, is typical of the general subscription to the idea that the spirits will be deceived by a change of name. He states that the person who changes his name is actually declaring to the angel looking for him: "I am not the person you are seeking. I am not the one who committed the sins you charge me with."

In Poland, when several people have died in a family, the new-born baby was given a name which was never uttered, much the same as the tribal practice mentioned above. But, in addition, the Yiddish or Hebrew appelative was bestowed upon the child, such as Alte or Alter, meaning another or old one, Chaim meaning life, Zaida meaning grandfather, or Zekeine, meaning old man. This was their way of deceiving the angel of death who, when he came to visit his victim, would be baffled by not finding his subject but "another," or he would find an "old man" instead of the child. Lauterbach explains that "the angel of death will thus find before him not only a person against whom he has no warrant, but one whose name declares that he must continue to live, grow old, and become a grandfather."

This practice of misleading the angel of death by changing or giving a new name in addition to the old one is current among us even today. It is not uncommon for a sick man, in a critical condition, to be given a new name which would suggest long life or health, and thus deceive the spirits charged with taking the invalid's life. The practice and the names adopted, vary with different communities and countries.

This, in brief, is an account of the attitude of our predecessors, ancient and modern, Jewish and non-Jewish, towards the name. It was an important matter, and was often, in their thinking, the key to life and death. We, of course, do not view the name in this same light, although many have retained, and are still guided by, these primitive superstitious motivations. That the name is still considered

of great importance to the overwhelming majority of us
is evidenced by the common phenomenon of conferences and
meetings, often resulting in quarrels and lasting feuds, that
some families will engage in over the selection of a name
for a newly born child. But the significance with which our
ancestors regarded the name has been lost to us, and we
now find that the status of the name, especially in the
relationship of the Hebrew to the secular (English), is
confused.

NAME CONFUSION

Enough pertinent material to fill a sizeable volume
might be gathered to demonstrate how confusing are the
names that we assume for ourselves and bestow upon our
children. It is a confusion that becomes more intensified
with the passage of time, and is evidenced not only in the
relationship of the Hebrew to the secular name, but within
the Hebrew name itself. What name may we or may we
not choose? What name should we or should we not choose?
What is the proper English name for a particular Hebrew
name, and what Hebrew name is suitable for a certain
English name?

NAMING AFTER ANCESTORS

Although neither dictated by history nor demanded by
Jewish law, the custom of naming an offspring after a
relative in order to perpetuate his memory has by now
reached almost universal acceptance. There were times in
our history when such a practice was the established norm,
and there were times when it was condemned. The con-
spicuous absence throughout the entire Bible of relatives
bearing a common name is a certain indication of the attitude of our earliest ancestors. With the exception of Gen.
11:2, 26 and I Chron. 7:20 and 5:35, 36, no other example of
a grandfather and a grandson with the same name is to be
found. Only a limited number of similar relationships are

to be found between other relatives (Cf. I Chron. 6:2-14; 3:5 and 6:7).

Most scholars date the beginning of this practice, of naming after relatives, as of the 6th century B.C.E. There is evidence from the Elphantine Papyri to prove that the practice was in vogue among Egyptian Jews in the 5th century, although the German scholar Low maintains that the Jews derived this custom from the Greeks, a century later. Leopold Zunz, in his book, *Namen der Juden*, likewise links the custom with this same period when he says that the custom of naming a boy after his father or relative began in the time of the Seleucides. Among the High Priests we find that names like Jochanan and Simon are repeated, and that a bit later, among the Maccabees of the 2nd century, it was even more common. In the first century B.C.E., the custom of naming after living and dead relatives was prevalent, as is evidenced from Hillel's family in which only four different names were used (Hillel, Simon, Gamaliel and Judah) in fourteen generations (500 years). This practice, which was well established in talmudic times, persisted in post-talmudic (after 500 C.E.) and later times. We do find, however, that in the 12th century an outstanding personality like Judah the Pious stated in his testament that none of his descendants shall be called by his name, Judah, or by his father's name, Samuel.

SEPHARDIC PRACTICE

The Sephardic Jews (Italian, Portuguese, French, North African, and others of Eastern countries) of these centuries were less superstitious than their fellow Ashkenazic brethren and did not hesitate to name their offspring after living grandparents, and occasionally, though infrequently, even parents. This was true among illustrious men like Judah Halevi, whose grandson was also named Judah; Rabbi Isaiah ben Elijah de Trani, whose maternal grandfather's name was Isaiah; and Nahmanides, whose grandson had the same name as his maternal grandfather, Jonah (Girondi).

This practice of naming after living ancestors is deeply rooted in the life of the Sephardic Jew, and is not peculiar to any particular period. It is still current today in Sephardic countries, as is revealed by the following typical case of a Sephardic family living in Oran, Algeria, North Africa:

Solomon Moni Kessous and Marie Rose Albaz (maiden name) Kessous are the heads of an old family of the city. In Algeria, the Jews of that country having been under the dominion of the French for many decades, it is customary for the Jews to adopt a French name in addition to the Hebrew. Hence, Moni and Rose are the French names of the father and mother respectively. When a person has a middle name, at times the Jewish name is the first name and the French name is the middle name, and at times the reverse is true. There is no accepted order. A Hebrew equivalent is chosen for only the Jewish name. In this case the Hebrew name of Solomon Moni is Sh'lomo and that of Marie Rose, Miryawm.

Seven children resulted from the marriage of Solomon and Marie: Louisette, Jeanette, Lulu, Rachel Helene, Marcelle, Robert and Caroline. All but Robert (Shmuayl in Hebrew), who was named after his father's father, are married, and all but Caroline, who is named after her paternal grandmother, have children.

Louisette married Jacques and their offspring include: Marise, Henri Leon (Leon being the name of Jacques' brother), Jean Solomon (Solomon being the name of Louisette's father), Paul, Henri (name of Jacques' father), and Francis.

Jeanette married Pierre and their offspring include: Marie Rose (exact name of Jeanette's mother), and Annie (Estayr, in Hebrew, being the name of Pierre's mother).

Lulu (Sawraw in Hebrew and named after her father's sister) married a Catholic and their child's name is Jean Charles. He is not named after anyone as the daughter has been disinherited (although the families exchange visits).

Rachel Helene (named after the sister of her mother) is married to Abraham Hartman, an American soldier whom she met in 1942. Their first child is named Solomon Jean (Solomon being the name of Rachel's father).

Marcelle married Gaston and their only child is Nicol Marie (Marie being the first name of Marcelle's mother).

In every case listed above, in which the children are named after a relative, (oftentimes it is an aunt or an uncle as well as a grandparent), the relative is still living. Some of the children are not named for anyone in particular.

ASHKENAZIC PRACTICE

Ashkenazic Jews, with but very few exceptions, will not name a child after a living relative. An incident that occurred when the child of the soldier mentioned above was born, illustrates the pointed contrast between the Sephardic and Ashkenazic practice very vividly. The girl's family suggested that perhaps the soldier would like to name the boy after his father. The soldier wired home relaying this message. The reply received from the soldier's father in America expressed amazement, and ended with the words (which we might naturally have expected), "I am not dead yet!"

The reasons for the divergent practices among Jews of various centuries is speculative, although most probably steeped in the superstitious beliefs of the day. Primarily, it was due to the fact that Ashkenazim identified the name more closely with the soul than did the Sephardim. They felt that it was dangerous to name the child after any person, living or dead, for fear that it would rob the living of his full life and would upset the spirit of the dead. At any rate, we find today that we are left with a definite custom (which is not law, but in the minds of most Jews is as binding as law), that bids us refrain from naming after living relatives, but that impels parents to name their children after a deceased relative.

PROBLEM OF NAMING TODAY

There was no problem in connection with naming after a relative, as long as *only* the Hebrew name was used. For then, if the child was to be named after the grandparent whose Hebrew name was Avrawhawm (Abraham), he was called Avrawhawm. The difficulty arose with the widespread usage of both a Hebrew and secular name. It was intensified, even more, in relatively recent times, when Jews sought a "modern" or "fancy" English (secular) name for the child. Prior to the past few decades, a child to be named after a grandmother whose secular name was Sarah, and whose Hebrew name was Sawrah, was called by exactly these two names. Today, however, the Hebrew Sawraw would be accepted and used, but Sarah, in most cases, would be changed to practically any other name.

And so it was at this point, where a secular and a Hebrew name had to be given, that the problem which resulted in the present day confusion really had its inception. (The term confusion is accurate in this connection, for when complete arbitrariness exists and the person suggesting a name has no guide or rule other than his own inclination, the results cannot be other than confusing.) Were the old custom of having only one name—a religious name, still our practice, or were we all willing to disregard the names of our relatives as the basis for the present name, the recommended procedure would be simple. Biblical names or names steeped in Jewish tradition and culture, past and present, would be strongly urged.

This approach has been employed by many Jews in the past and is being employed today. Many have taken the Hebrew names which are euphoniously appealing and have transliterated them into English. Thus, names such as Ruvane, Shira, Rena, Zehava and Ranana are currently being used as both the Hebrew and English name. (In Israel, today, to some extent the reverse process has taken place. The secular name has been converted into a Hebrew name by many of the Jews who have recently arrived from Europe. It is, therefore, not surprising to find, as we read the personal notices in Israeli newspapers, names like Dora, Leon, Kurt, Victoria, Hugo, Minna and Harry transliterated into Hebrew characters.) But as matters stand today, the

established practice is that of naming after relatives, on
the one hand, and at the same time to search for a more
modern name which is usually derived from any one of a
number of languages other than Hebrew.

POSSIBLE SOLUTIONS — BIBLICAL NAMES

Were the chief name source of the past to become our
source once again, the confusion that reigns today would
be overcome in short order. It would be a magnificent com-
pliment to our Jewish social sense, no less than to our
aesthetic sense, were we willing to desist from the niceties
of the times and return to biblical names when we decide
upon the nomenclature of our children. Biblical names are
beautiful, and compare favorably with the best of the modern names that we find concocted daily. They possess
strength and warmth, charm and beauty.

The history of the biblical name it should, however, be
noted, is like the history of all other things. It was and is
subject to admiration and repulsion; avidity to the point
of acceptance, and distaste to the point of scorn. The history
of the biblical name is replete with examples that bear out
this polarity of attitudes and is as true of Christian life as
it is of Jewish life.

SOME HISTORY OF BIBLICAL NAMES IN POST-
BIBLICAL TIMES

The fluctuation in the general popularity of biblical and
religious names has a very interesting history. Biblical
names were not very much in use in the early centuries of
the common era. Among Jews, because of the custom of
naming after relatives, which most probably began in the
Greek period when foreign names were much more common than biblical names, scriptural names were never per-
mitted to blossom forth to any degree. Even during the
talmudic period, in the first five centuries of the Common
Era, a paucity of biblical names is to be found. Of the
innumerable names mentioned in the Talmud, we find that

not one rabbi is named Abraham, Moses, or David, and, with the exception of Jeremiah, Zechariah, Obadiah, Isaiah, Jonah and Nahum, the name of no other prophet is mentioned. The most frequently occurring biblical names in the Talmud are: Judah (33 times), Simeon (92), Joshua (84), Isaac (80) and Elazar (70).

Christians, in their early period of existence, either abandoned their biblical names or simply refrained from adopting them, probably because of their prejudice against Jews. This former tendency is noticeable in the pages of the New Testament as characters give up their Old Testament names and a personality like Simon bar Jonah becomes Peter, and Saul of Tarsus becomes Paul.

Throughout the ages, of course, many Christians have borne Old Testament names. This was so, however, not because of any special admiration for its characters but, primarily, because they were being named after saints or church fathers who had borne these names. Bardsley in his book, *English Surnames,* describes the early Christian attitude when he writes, "The reverence of the despised Jew for Abraham prevented this from becoming acceptable to Christians, but Isaac's sacrifice was too popular a story not to leave an impression."

Earliest Christians used names associated with mythological culture and pagan cults such as, Phoebe, Olympius and Jovianus, despite the fact that they disbelieved in them. Even the influence exerted by the Bishop of Seville in the 7th century through his *Etymologiae,* in which he points out the significance of biblical names, failed to carry too much weight with the masses. Because of anti-Semitic feeling, widespread adoption was curtailed until the tenth century. And even then the process was a slow one. In a list of names that comes down to us from the 11th century, the majority are Celtic and Anglo Saxon, and only two are biblical.

Among the Jews of England, however, at about this time, an opposite tendency existed. Scriptural names were extremely popular. Of the 748 names used in England in the 12th century, as found in the Pipe Rolls (English records) the favorite ones were biblical. Isaac led the list with 59; Josce, i.e. Joseph, 55; Abraham 49; Benedict (Latinized form of Berachyaw) 49; Jacob 40; and Mosse and Moss, i.e. Moses, 38.

Not too much is known about the Jews of China, but four stones with inscriptions have been found in the now defunct community at Kaifeng in northern China. These stones which record some of the history of the Jews of the community are dated 1489, 1512, 1663 and 1679. The following 10 personal names—all biblical—are recorded on these tablets. They are: Aaron, Abraham, Adam, Ezra, Isaac, Jacob, Joshua, Moses, Israel and Noah. In the 1663 inscription we find the following names recorded: Ben Israel, Ben Josef, Ben Aron, Ben Moshe, Ben Jehoshua and Abraham ben Israel. The names Bas Adam and Bas Israel are found as feminine names.

Prior to the 16th century, names most popularly used by Christians, especially among the northern European nations including France and England, were of Teutonic, Celtic and Slavic origin. Names like Arnold, Alfred and Charles were the most common, with scriptural names occupying a very insignificant place.

It was not until the period of the Reformation that biblical names were eagerly adopted. In the 16th and 17th centuries, as a reaction to church dogmatism and policy, a sudden burst of enthusiasm in favor of scriptural names took place. Puritan England, in particular, preferred Old Testament names to the others which they said "savoured of Papacy and Paganism." Many Puritan extremists, even as late as the 18th and 19th centuries, went so far as to take obscure and ugly names, or even an entire phrase from Scripture. Ernest Weekley in his book, *Jack and Jill*, reports that at the beginning of the present century there lived in Norfolk a family of four—two sisters and two brothers, with the names: Asenoth Zaphnathpaaneah, Kezia Jemima Kerenhappukh, Maher Shalal Hashbaz and Arphad Absolom Alexander Habakkuk William. And Bardsley points out, that Camden mentions as existing in his own day, appellations such as: Free-gift, Reformation, Earth, Dust, Ashes, Delivery, Morefruit, Tribulation, The Lord Is Near, More Trial, Discipline, Joy Again, etc. . . . One person chose the name, If-Christ-had-not-died-for-you-you-had-been-damned-Barebones, but his acquaintances becoming weary of its length, retained only the last part, Damned-Barebones. The more sober type of Puritan was satisfied, in addition to Old Testament names, with the simplest names derived from abstract virtues, such as: Perseverance, Faith, Hope, Humility, Charity and Repentance.

The Quakers, like the Puritans, preferred Old Testament names and despised the nomenclature of the New Testament. The life of John Bunyan epitomizes the conflict between the Quakers and Puritans and their opponents. In his younger days Bunyan was an antagonist of the Quakers. For this reason we find the names of his children to be Mary, John, Thomas and Elizabeth—all but the last, pure New Testament names. By the time of his second marriage his whole philosophy had changed. He no longer was an opponent of the Quakers and, on the other hand, became thoroughly and intensely opposed to the church and its bishops. His children by his second wife were Joseph and Sara—Old Testament figures.

It might be added, as Weekley remarks jestingly, that the pious names did not immunize the Puritans from sin. Gamliel Parsey, a famous highwayman was hanged in 1605, and Salvation Yeo, according to his mother, "swore terribly in his speech."

STATE OF BIBLICAL NAMES IN MODERN TIMES

But with the coming of the French Revolution there came a revulsion against biblical names. The legislature strictly forbade the introduction of names not already in use. As is true of all periods of public excitement, the fashion in names was greatly influenced by the times, and the people turned to the most famous Greek and Roman republican heroes for their names.

The antipathy toward scriptural names grew with the passage of time and is still in evidence as two recent polls of masculine names reveal. The first poll conducted by Simon Newton, and reported in the 1921 World Almanac, reveals that out of 100,000 names examined, five of the leading fifteen were biblical (two Old Testament and three New Testament). In the 1929 Almanac a study of 400,000 names reveals four biblical names among the most popular (one Old Testament and three New Testament). John, James and Joseph appear in both lists.

As compared with the rapid rate of decrease in the usage of biblical names evidenced in these two studies, the two surveys conducted by the author (see chapter on Statistics and Trends) reveal a similarly sad state. Although much more limited in scope than the above two, they are comprehensive enough to at least indicate the tendency of the times. Only two names of biblical origin are to be found among the leading fifteen of Survey No. 1, and of these two, only one, David, is taken from the Old Testament. The other, Paul, is a New Testament character. The second survey reveals that only four biblical names are to be found among the leading fifteen names of the new generation (two from the new Testament) and four among the parent generation. The biblical names of the new generation include: Michael, David, Stephen and Peter while the names of the parent generation consist of Ruth, Joseph, David and Samuel. The tendency today, as indicated in a limited 1966 survey conducted by the author (see Survey No. 3), may indicate a return to biblical names. Of the ten most popular boys' names six are biblical. These are: David, Michael, Andrew, Steven, Jonathan and Mark (or Marc). Of the ten most popular girls' names five are of biblical origin. These are: Lisa, Susan, Beth, Debra and Elizabeth. Lisa and Beth are forms of Elizabeth, and Debra is a variant form of Deborah.

ASSONANCE AND TRANSLATION METHODS OF CHOOSING NAMES

In the past, in addition to choosing directly from Scripture, two additional procedures were employed in the selection of the Hebrew and secular name. One was that of selection a secular name on the basis of similarity in sound with the Hebrew name. The other sought to make the two conform in meaning. As early as the third century B.C.E. when Greek became the vernacular of the Jews in various countries, many Jews assumed Greek names which corresponded with the Hebrew only in assonance. Menachem became Menelaus; Joshua became Jason; and Eliakim became Aleimus. The Greek New Testament contains many names, later adopted by Jews, which are hellenized forms of the Hebrew. Prominent among them are: Elas for Elijah, Jonas for Jonah, Jeremias for Jeremiah, Anna for Hannah, Elizabeth for Elisheba and Lazarus for Eleazar.

On the other hand, in this same period many Greek and Latin names were adopted by translating the Hebrew into Greek. Tobiah became Agathou, both meaning "good"; Nathaniel became Theodotion, both meaning "God given"; Uri became Phoebus, both meaning "light"; and Zadok became Justus, both meaning "justice."

These same procedures were employed throughout the centuries. In medieval Normandy and England (the first English Jews came from the northern part of France in 1066), many examples of Hebrew names translated into French were to be found. Cha'yim meaning "life," became Vive; Gamleeayl meaning "God has rewarded," became Dieulecresse, as did Solomon and G'dalyaw; Obadiah meaning "servant of the Lord," became Serfdeu; Jonathan meaning "gift of God," became Deudone; Elchawnawn meaning "God is gracious," became Deodatus. B'rachyaw Nakdawn, one of the greatest literary figures in medieval Judiasm, became known as Benedict le Puncteur. Among Italian Jewry this practice was common too, as is seen in the name Menahem which became Tranquillus.

MERITS AND DEMERITS OF BOTH METHODS

Having more or less rejected scriptural names, it remains with us to decide which of these two methods we shall choose to follow. As we have seen, historically there is a basis for the use of either. And although it is the purpose of this volume to indicate the value and encourage the use of the translation method, it must, in all fairness, be pointed out that in both methods good and bad features are to be found.

The assonance method, it has been pointed out, is valuable in that, although the original name is different from the present one, at least it has the sound in common. It is an emotional tie with the past and serves as a reminder of that which went before. The validity of this contention is borne out by changes that have occurred in surnames. When a person changes his surname, very often his desire (unfortunately) is to forget his original name. Yet, even in these cases, the new name will begin with the first letter of the old, as in the case of Goldberg who changed his name to Gorman.

To the discredit of the translation method the valid objection has been made that in very many cases the exact etymology of a name is only a matter of conjecture. The original meaning has been lost and, as such, translating that which may be inaccurate is of little value. Yet, it is believed, that although this difficulty is a very real one, it has been overcome, to some extent, by listing in the name sections more than one etymology of a name when it exists, and leaving it to the discretion of the reader to make his choice.

But even more to recommend the translation method and discourage the use of the assonance method are the large number of short-comings of the latter which will be pointed out in the pages to come. The translation method *aims,* at least, at being scientific, and makes use of the etymologic knowledge that we possess to date. It is an attempt to normalize, as well as harmonize, the English name in relation to the Hebrew. In very many cases, as an examination of the name lists will reveal, a deliberate attempt has been made, wherever possible, to incorporate translated names that bear a similar sound. However, where that has proven impossible, the more scientific method of translating was alone employed.

The cause of much of the confusion in the naming process may be attributed to the unconscious and widespread adoption of the assonance method. Although it is true that the etymology of many names is doubtful, it is also true that most are very well known. Yet, no conscious effort has been made in the recent past by any individual or group to encourage the translation method, even in these cases. Although a case may be built for the assonance method upon its psychological merits, the advantages it has to offer, are more than offset by the confusion that it has helped to create.

SUPERIORITY OF TRANSLATION METHOD

With a conscious adoption of the translation method, we can hope to avoid many of the far-fetched, and often silly results that we witness today in connection with naming after relatives. The case of a girl named Judith who was named after her grandfather Joseph, is a case in point, and merely one example out of hundreds that might be cited. What connection is there between Judith and Joseph? With the exception of the common first letter "J," they are as far apart as two names could be etymologically. Judith means "praise God," while Joseph means "He (God) will add." If it is letters or sounds in common that we seek, Joan or Joyce would be more fitting. If an appropriate feminine name, to *really* carry on the memory of Joseph was sought, Josepha or Josephine might easily have been chosen.

Survey No. 1 (See: Statistics and Trends) reveals further the confusing results produced by the assonance method. A long list of misnomers has been found in the relationship of many Hebrew names to their supposed English equivalents. Many of them have been so long in use that they are taken for granted as the appropriate equivalent. The following are some of the most popular misnomers:

Using Cha'yim (life) for Hyman (dweller on heights), or Herman and Herbert (warrior).

Using Moshe (drawn out or saved or child) for Morris (dark complexion or great warrior), Morton (related to the moor), Melvin (servant or chief) or Milton (mill town).

Using Avrawhawm (father of a multitude) for Albert (all bright), Arnold (eagle chief or honorable), or Alvin (beloved by all). Using Efra'yim (fruitful) for Fred or Frederic (peaceful ruler) or Frank (free).

Using Dawvid (beloved) for Donald (chief or ruler).

Using Z'ayv (wolf) for William (warrior).

Using Tz'vee (deer) for Harold (warrior), or Harry (home ruler).

Using Chanaw (grace) for Helen (light).

Using Yitzchawk (he will laugh) or Yisrawayl (wrestle with God, or prince of God) for Irvin, Irving or Irwin (beautiful, fair).

Using Malkaw (queen) for Molly (bitter water) or Mildred (gentle counselor).

Using Pesach (skip over) for Paul (small).

Using Sawraw (princess) for Shirley (white meadow).

This is, by no means, the entire list of misnomers that might be pointed to.

Even if we should choose to agree for the moment with those who maintain that assonance is a legitimate gauge by which to select a corresponding Hebrew or English name, there are a number of instances appearing in our survey that would definitely rule it out. We might concede that inasmuch as Cha'yim has so long been applied to Hyman, as have Moshe to Morris and Avrawhawm to Albert, that they be accepted. The nature of language is such that a word becomes part of a language by virtue of prolonged usage, even when it is proven to be based upon an invalid premise. However, what excuse could there be for calling Samuel, Shawul, or Joel, Yosayf, or Joseph, Y'hudaw, when perfectly beautiful and *exact* Hebrew names appear for them in Scripture? Yet, from the point of view of assonance, these names should be, and unfortunately are, looked upon with favor.

The majority of the names encountered, however, do not fall into this category. Most of them have not become fixed by usage, and afford very little rhyme, and still less reason, for their selection.

Let us take a typical Hebrew name that appeared in our survey—Baruch, and we shall see how haphazard is our present practice of naming. The following names all had Baruch for their Hebrew equivalent: Bernard (18 times), Bertram (4), Barry (4), Burton (3), Robert (3), and Benjamin, Barnet, Benson, Bertrem, Bert, Bruce, and Brian once each. Few, if any of these, have been fixed by usage but appear merely because of the common "B" sound.

It is also quite common to find names in which there is neither a correlation in meaning nor in sound, such as: Barry and Robert which appear for Meechawayl; Harvey and Larry which appear for Mawr'dchai; Joseph and Fred which appear for Matisyawhu; and Barbara and Carol which appear for D'voraw. These are but a few examples chosen at random. The inference that may be drawn is that the Hebrew name is an afterthought in our name selection process. We generally select an English name according to our likes, and then append the Hebrew name of a deceased ancestor regardless of correlation.

A typical case which exemplifies the workings of the modern mind is seen in the name Freddie Marlene which was given to a new-born girl. The child was named after two grandfathers, Fishel and Melech. The "F" for Fishel was the starting point in the search for an English name which led to Freddie. Marlene was chosen because it had an "M" in common with Melech. It was thus considered that the child was named after her grandparents!

In the sphere of English names our self-deception is equally marked. The case of John Barton, who was named after Joseph Benjamin, is merely one out of the hundreds of thousands who deceive themselves into believing that they are naming their child after a relative when they select a name beginning with the first letter of the name of the deceased. John and Joseph, as well as Barton and Benjamin, are as distant as day is from night. Like day and night they meet only at the extremes, but their essence is completely different. Two names may have a first letter or last letter in common, yet remain completely foreign to one another.

The importance of an awareness of the etymology and meaning of the name, and the confusion and haphazardness which have resulted because of a lack of it, is even more forcefully illustrated from a further hurried glance at some of our biblical names. Many odd and amusing results have developed because of our ignorance of the definition of these names. Out of the confusion have arisen two unwarranted developments: (1) the adoption by Jews of many Christian religious names, and (2) the shying away from names originally regarded as wholesome for Jews, but now reserved for Christians only.

If we were to study the name Sidney, for example, we would find that it is of Teutonic derivation, from St. Denys. How many are the rabbis who are "namewards" of the patron saint! And how many of our daughters are named Natalie, meaning "Christmas child," or Dolores, meaning "sorrow of the mother of our Lord." And Noel, meaning "Christmas," is not uncommon to Jewish boys. An examination of names of recently born Jewish children reveals that names of definitely Christian origin are quite common: Peter, Stephen, Patricia, Anthony, Mark, Thomas, Andrew, Paul and Paula appear many times in the lists. It seems almost as though many of these strictly Christian religious names have become exclusively Jewish appellations. There is hardly a doubt that Sidney and Natalie (Nathalie) are more common to Jewish people than to Christians. Paul and Paula are used as frequently by Jews as by Christians, and Stephen (Steven) has become very popular.

At the other extreme we find that many names which we think of as belonging to Christians only, are actually either Jewish names of long standing or forms of ancient Jewish nomenclature. The average person, upon seeing a Jew with the name John, will look upon him warily. John, to him, is not a name which a Jew should carry. Only the aristocratic or social climbers would choose such a name. The average Jew will reason that way. But as a matter of fact, John is immeasurably closer to Jewish tradition than the more common Henry or Louis or Robert. John is but a form of the very old, and once common, Johanan. It was a name carried by many important Jewish notables—political leaders and scholars alike: Johanan (John) Hyrcanus and Johanan ben Zaccai, to mention but two. At least 52 different persons are to be found in the Talmud by the name of Johanan. James, which is but the English form of Jacob, and Mary, the Greek form of Miriam, are in the same category. Because we have forgotten the meaning and significance of the names we use, we have mistakenly encouraged the use of some names, and avoided others.

But undoubtedly, as suggested earlier, the most sorry feature of modern tendencies revealed in our name study is reflected in the ever diminishing position that the religious (or biblical) name occupies. For, it may very well be that it is through the name that a man gives to his child that his religious convictions are revealed. Hence, the name becomes a barometer of our religious life.

CHIEF SOURCES OF PERSONAL NAMES

Inasmuch as we are to give special attention to the derivation and definition of names, it is well that we consider the method by which these names (and especially the more modern ones) came into active use. It is necessary that we acquire this background, for it is only in this way that many of the strange names (all of them in current use) become intelligible and meaningful. The source of almost every name appearing in the lists that follow is the birth columns of newspapers and school rolls. The classification that is to follow is a general one and as such it will deal with English and Hebrew names as a unit.

The groups fall under the following headings: Patronymics; Telescoped Names; Apheresis, Apocopation and Diminutives; Agglutination or Combinations; Sex Switches; Spelling; Personalities and Places. This is followed by a general category entitled Odds and Ends and includes brief pieces on: Names Derived From Days and Months of the Year and Holidays; Numeral Names; Names in Jest; Maiden Names; Invented Names; and Inversions.

PATRONYMICS

A chief source from which many of our personal names are derived is included under the heading of patronymics. A patronymic is a name derived from an ancestor, or more specifically, a name formed from one's father's name. It occupied a very important position in the history of the surname and, at the same time, played a significant role in the naming of children in early times.

The surname is a comparatively recent innovation as far as Jews are concerned. Until the 18th and 19th centuries most Jews used only first names. Thereafter, they were forced to adopt surnames in most European countries. Many had voluntarily taken on a family name especially in Spain, Portugal and Italy. But in Germany, Austria, France and Russia legislation was passed requiring them to adopt family names. Austria was first among such nations, during the 1785-1787 period. In the Kingdom of Westphalia on March 3, 1808, it was decreed that all Jews adopt surnames within three months. On July 20, 1808, Napoleon issued a similar decree for his empire. March 11, 1812, saw Prussia order the adoption of family names by all Jews, as did 1821 in Poland; 1833 in the part of Prussia called Posen; 1844 in Russia; and 1845 in other parts of the Prussian Kingdom. Christians had adopted surnames centuries earlier.

But prior to the formal adoption of surnames it was

the patronymic that served the same purpose. As the population increased it became necessary to differentiate between people, especially in legal documents, where confusion could have serious consequences.

The earliest Hebrews coped with the problem by inserting the Hebrew word "ben," meaning son, between the child's name and the father's name, e.g. Moses ben Amram (Moses the son of Amram). Very often the Aramic patronymic, "bar," was used, as in the name of Bar Kochba (the son of Kochba), leader of Jewry in the 2nd century C.E. In practically every country where Jews lived they made use of the local patronymic. In Arabic speaking countries it was "ibn," e.g. Solomon ibn Ezra. In Spain it was "en." In France and Angevin England it was fil, e.g. Abraham fil Rabi.

Every language had its patronymic. In some it was used as a prefix, in others as a suffix. The following are some of the more common ones which may be recognized in many surnames in use today. In the course of time it was through a combination of personal name and patronymic that many of our surnames were created:

Scandinavians added "son," e.g. Johnson (son of John).

Norman-French added "fitz," e.g. Fitzgerald (son of Gerald).

Welsh added "Ap," or "Ab," e.g. ApEvan (son of Evan), also the suffix "s" as in Davis or Ewards (son of David or Edward).

Gaelic added "Mc," or "M," e.g. McDonald (son of Donald).

Irish added "Mc," or "O," e.g. O'Donald (son of Donald).

Anglo Saxons added "ing," e.g. Cidding (son of Cidda).

Spaniards added "ez," e.g. Rodriquez (son of Rodrigo).

Basques added "ana," or "ena," e.g. Lorenzana (son of Lorenzo).

Germans added "sohn," e.g. Mendelsohn (son of Mendel).

Danish added "sen," e.g. Andersen (son of Andrew).

Dutch added "zen," e.g. Janzen (son of Jan [John]).

Slavonic races added "vich," "wicz," "itch," "witz," "ski," "sky," "off," "eff," e.g. Rabinovich, Itzkowitz, Rubinoff, etc.

Greeks added "ides," e.g. Maimonides, Gersonides, Platonides.

Offhand it may seem that the discussion of patronymics is out of place here. But many personal names cannot be properly understood without some knowledge of patronymics. The name Barry, for example, is probably a form of Parry, from the Welsh ApHarry or AbHarry, meaning the son of Harry. Benzecry is a combination of Ben and Zechariah. Benson is probably a corruption of Ben Zion, and Benroy of Ben Aryeh.

Then, of course, it is of immeasurable help in ascertaining the meaning of personal names which were formerly surnames. When Davis or Harris, for example, appear as personal names we can immediately tell, if we are familiar with patronymics, that the surname mean David's son, or Harry's son. This is a growing tendency today. For just as we have witnessed throughout the ages personal names being converted into surnames, so is it evident that the reverse process is taking place before our very eyes. More and more are surnames being adopted as personal names, and especially in the case of the mother's maiden name (See section on Maiden Names for further discussion and illustrations.) These newer names that we encounter as personals are often better understood in the light of the patronymic or metronymic (maternal name).

TELESCOPED NAMES

Many new names are the result of telescoping or contracting one or two names into shorter forms than they were originally. It is a common feature of languages, as when the "v" in "over" is dropped and "o'er" results. Grammatically, it is termed elision. It is very noticeable in patronymics as when Ben Zachariah becomes Benzecry,

Ben Zion becomes Benson, or the son of David becomes Davis. But it is even more noticeable in other names, and can very well constitute a group of its own. A vivid example is that of a John Cromwell, who lived in the middle of the 17th century, and who named his son Ben-Oni-Jamin. Actually the name is a compromise between Benjamin and Benoni. The biblical Benjamin was called Benoni by his mother and Benjamin by his father (Genesis 35:18).

At the time when Jews selected names to be used in their civic relations they resorted on occasions to the procedure of telescoping. The sacred or Hebrew names were often contracted, and a secular one formed. Thus came about the names Lezer, originally Eliezer; Sender, originally Alexander; Mann or Mannes, originally Menahem.

A very interesting example of a telescoped name in its purest form is to be found in one of the case histories of the psychiatrist Karl Menninger in his volume, *The Human Mind*. One of his patients had a strong feeling that she must name her new baby Constandine, a name which she had never heard of before. Upon analysis it was discovered that the name, when broken down, described her character and career. She was not constant (from which the first part of the name was derived), she suffered from an obsession that her husband was in love with another woman (Nadine, a girl's name, and the symbol of the other love) and, to overcome her disturbed, sleepless nights, she had become addicted to a sleep-producing drug, codeine. All these she wove unconsciously into a new name for her baby.

Another form of telescoped names is the result of scribal errors which occur in the recording of names. Lin, for example, is most probably a misspelling of Lion. The result is a telescoped name, and the process purely accidental. (See section on spelling for a discussion of scribal errors.)

Other examples among modern names that have been the result of the telescoping procedure include: Banet from Barnett; Bennet or Benet from Benedict; Bernice from Berenice; Debra from Deborah; Hattie from Harriette;

Hetta from Henrietta; Joan from Johanna; Karen from Katherine; and Reba from Rebecca.

A form of telescoped names that might be added, although of a slightly different nature, are those in which the first letter of a person's and/or his parents' names (sometimes his title too) were joined into one, making a new name. A modern example of this procedure is to be found in the name, Pia, daughter of actress Ingrid Bergman and Dr. Peter Aron Lindstrom; Pia being composed of the first letters of the personal names of the parents.

Another recent name, formed in this fashion, was the product of the imagination of a soldier who combined the letters "V" for Victory, "E" for England, "R" for Russia and "A" for America and named his daughter Vera.

In the Middle Ages the names of outstanding personalities, in particular, were telescoped by combining the first letters of title and name. Thus, Rabbi Moses ben Maimon became R(A)MB(A)M and Rabbi David Kimchi became R(A)D(A)K.

APHERESIS, APOCOPATION AND DIMINUTIVES

Another source of new names, somewhat similar to the category we discussed under Telescoped Names may be grouped under the headings of Apheresis, Apocopation and Diminutives. This group differs from telescoped names more in form than in content. They both result in a shorter name. It is only a question of how the new name acquired its abbreviated form. As we have seen in the previous section, telescoped names normally are contractions of longer names. A letter or series of letters is dropped from the old name and, after a slight alteration or modification of the shortened form, a new name results. When Menahem became Mann or Mannes, not only were letters dropped, but some were added and inverted as well. In this new grouping a shortened name is the result of dropping a few letters, but, with the exception of the diminutive, never the addition of any. Another difference lies in the position of the letters that were dropped. In telescoped names they may be dropped from any part of the name. In the category under discussion, letters are dropped either from the beginning or at the end of the name. They are rarely plucked out of the middle.

Apheresis consists of dropping an unaccented syllable or letter from the beginning of a word. It is usually a natural process, and develops, imperceptibly, in the course of time. It is the process by which the word "mend" devolved from "amend," or "squire," from "esquire." Some of the more common names that are the result of Apheresis are: Lena, originally Helena; Gail, originally Abigail; Tony, originally Antony; Tilda, originally Matilda; Anna, originally Hannah; Lenore, originally Elenore; Beth, originally Elisabeth; Nora, originally Eleanora; Adrian, originally Hadrian; Zak, originally Isaac; and Drew, originally Andrew.

There are times, however, when the new name is not so easily identifiable. Gilbert Doane in his book, *Searching For Your Ancestors,* describes a name that required several years of searching before it could be identified. He found on a tombstone inscription, "Diah Sherwood, Died April 24, 1853 in his 90th year—A soldier of the revolution." On another tombstone next to it he found: "Jayhannah, wife of Dyer Sherwood, died May 22, 1833 in her 67th year." Through the land records, he finally identified Dyer (the "r" was due to the New England pronunciation of vowel-ending words) with Diah, and found that the name was originally the biblical Jedediah. Other names of biblical origin that have so been formed are: Manuel from Emanuel; Shaya from Yeshaya; Akim from Jehoiakim; Hiel from Ahiel; and Hiram from Ahiram.

Apocopation is the reverse of Apheresis. It consists of dropping the last letter or syllable of a word. Many of our present day names have so been formed: Will was originally William; Elisa, originally Elisabeth; Ada, originally Adaline; Eva originally Evangeline; Bert, originally Bertram; Nicol, originally Nicolas; Jose, originally Joseph; Lazar, originally Lazarus.

Diminutives are a further development of the apocopated name. After dropping a letter or syllable it usually took a "y," or "ie," or "ette," ending which gave it the familiar touch, as in the case of Katy or Kathy from Katherine; Willy from William; Georgie from George; Tillie from Tilda or Matilda; Benny or Benjy from Benjamin; Essie from Esther; Claudette from Claudia; Rosette from Rose, etc. In many instances the apocopated form became the diminutive as in the case of Will from William; Fran from Frances, etc.

The origin of many names remains unintelligible unless we can recognize the diminutive endings of the different languages from which they are derived which have had an influence upon the English language. The diminutive endings of the old Anglo-Saxons included: "kin, cock, ot, and et." The "ot" and "et" prevailed as diminutives from the 12th to the 15th centuries to an even greater extent than did the "y" and "ie" in the 19th and 20th centuries. Thus were derived, for example, names like: Elliot (dim. of Ellis or Elias); Colin (dim. of Nicol); Robin (dim. of Robert); Hancock (dim. of Hans). Among the Norman-French the "en" and "on" were popular diminutives. Among the Italians the number of diminutives employed was large. Some of the most popular are: ina (also in Latin) ella, etta and ucco (fem. sing.); ino, ello, etto and uccio (masc. sing.); ine, elle, ette and ucce (fem. pl.); and ini, elli, etti and ucci (masc. pl.). Although the diminutives of other languages might be recorded here, only the above are included, for it is these that have most influenced the English diminutive, as can be seen in names like Rochelle, Rosetta, Rosette, Carolina, etc.

In many cases of the diminutive, the actual name that it refers to, unless specifically stated, cannot always be ascertained. The diminutive Bert might be a form of Albert,

Adelbert, Bertram, Bertran, Bertrand, Robert, Alberta, Roberta or any number of other names. Jeff is most likely a diminutive of Jeffrey, but it might possibly be a form of Joseph—the "o" and "s" having been dropped. Any number of instances of the above difficulty might be culled from a study of our name lists.

AGGLUTINATION OR COMBINATIONS

Combining two originally independent names into one is characteristic of many names today. These names resemble, to some extent, telescoped names and double names, but are different from both. The telescoped name is the result of elision, while our present category rarely loses its identity to that extent. Usually, not more than the last letter of the first name is dropped. Double names, on the other hand, are two independent names that remain completely independent.

A modern example of a combination is to be found in the name Jerrilyn—the daughter of George Jessel and Lois Andrews (Jessel's ex-wife). Jerrilyn is a combination of the names of Lois' aunt, Geraldine, (the diminutive form Jerry being used in which the "J" is substituted for "G"), and her mother Lynn. Other modern examples of combinations are: Annalee, Clarabella, Georgeanne, Harrianne, Mabella, Marian, Marianna, Marianne, Roselotte, Roxanne, Sallyann, Suellen and Suzanne.

SEX SWITCHES

The practice of interchanging names between the sexes in an old one. The Bible contains many examples of names common to both sexes. Athaliah was the daughter of Ahab and Jezebel in the Book of Kings, while in Chronicles it is a masculine name. Ayfaw is the concubine of Caleb in one place and a masculine name in another. Shlomith appears as both masculine and feminine, as do Tzivyaw, Bilgaw, Chubaw, Noga, Chupaw, Gomer, Bunaw, Beenaw, Aveeyaw, Awfraw, Reenaw, Chaveelaw and Simchaw. Among the early Normans every name was free to be used by either sex, thus Druetta and Williametta became feminine names by simply adding an "a" to the original masculine form. During the 18th century in the army lists, the names Lucy, Ann, and Caroline are to be found recorded as boys' names. Today, more than ever do we find male names and female names shared by the opposite sex.

In a list of army casualties in *The New York Times* on August 10, 1943, there appeared two men named Patsy: Patsy Natale, Jr. and Patsy Demarco. Vivian, also spelled Vyvyan, is occasionally used by men as are Carol, Dorris, Carrol and Evelyn. A number of outstanding personalities are to be found today with names that are characteristically feminine. The famous polar explorer Richard Evelyn Byrd, noted author Evelyn Waugh, and Representative Clare Hoffman of Michigan are typical examples of this group.

But it is among women's names that we find a vast number of newly converted masculine names. In many instances the feminine name is so long established and accepted that we do not even realize that it had its origin in a masculine name. Among the group the following are prominent: Alexandra and Alexandria from Alexander; Charlotte and Charleene from Charles; Davi, Davida and Davita from David; Erica from Eric; Frederica from Frederic; Georgia, Georgine and Georgette from George; Harriet and Harri from Harry; Henrietta, Henri and Henria from Henry; Herma and Hermine from Herman; Horatia (daughter of Horatio "Lord" Nelson and Lady Hamilton) from Horatio; Isaaca from Isaac; Josepha and Josephine from Joseph; Lou, Louise and Louisa from Louis (the wife of Herbert Hoover was Lou Henry Hoover); Roberta from Robert; Stephanie from Stephan; and Willa and Willene from Will or William. Other less common feminine names of masculine origin are: Alexis, Alwyn, Barnetta, Cary, Ellys, Franklyne, Freddie, Herberta, Jamie, Joelle, Merril, Merrill, Meryl, Raymonde, Roye, Simona, Simonne and Toni.

The recorded death in *The New York Times* of May

1939, of Alfreda Ernestine Alberta, is an example of a woman who went all the way, as is even more so the case of a Negro who entered an army judge advocate's office to make out a will, and gave as his wife's maiden name, William Henry Miller. Richard Shattuck, authoress of *The Half Hunted Saloon,* is another striking example.

The birth columns of recent years present us with current and striking examples of sex switches which are of interest:

Gail *Henry* used as a feminine name and George *Henry* as a masculine.

Leslie Ellen used as a feminine name and *Leslie* Warren as a masculine.

Joanne *Sydney* used as a feminine name and *Sydney* as a masculine.

Judith *Terry* used as a feminine name and *Terry* as a masculine.

Jane *Lee* used as a feminine name and *Lee* Alan as a masculine.

Norma *Alva* used as a feminine name and Charles *Alva* as a masculine.

Meredith Joan used as feminine name and *Meredith* as a masculine.

Allen Jane used as a feminine name and *Allen* as a masculine.

Adrian Beth used as a feminine name and *Adrian* as a masculine.

Some of the other names used indiscriminately by both sexes are: Barrie, Bert, Beryl, Billy, Bobby, Buddy, Connie, Daryl, Frankie, Ira, Jean, Kay, Lesley, Lynn, Marion, Michel, Noel, Ruby, Sonny, Teddy and Toby.

Among Hebrew names we find a similar trend, although to a lesser extent. Some names which were originally bisexual (see biblical names listed above), have clung to one sex for many centuries, and were eventually considered belonging exclusively to that sex. Such is the history of

Tzivyaw, which is taken today as a feminine, and Simchaw, taken as masculine. Others which were originally of one sex were taken over wholly by the opposite sex. Such is the case of B'rawchaw (originally a member of King David's band), but today considered only as a feminine name, and Yente (originally a talmudic masculine name), today regarded as a purely feminine form. Among Israeli names we find sex switches occurring by the addition or deletion of a letter from a name. Thus, the masculine name Yizra'ayl became Yiz'r'elaw, Yardayn became Yardaynaw, and Yisrawayl became Yisr'aylaw. Also, names such as Z'meeraw and Y'saraylaw (revocalized), which were originally masculine biblical names, have become outright feminine names.

SPELLING

A change in the spelling of names accounts for a great number of new ones. The old name is easily recognizable inasmuch as the change is usually a substitution of one vowel for another, or the addition of a letter. Again it is the feminine sex which is responsible for a majority of such changes. The most common characteristic of this new fad is substituting a "y" for an "i," or adding an "e." Fannye is no longer Fannie and Mollye is no longer Mollie. Likewise Sadie has become Sadye, Edith has become Edyth or Edythe (a double change), and Shirley has become Shirlee, Shirlie or Sherle. Sarah and Hannah have dropped the "h" and become Sara and Hanna. Esther can now be found as Ester and sometimes as Esta or Estee.

Among the many feminine names that have, because of a new spelling, made their appearance of late, are the following familiar ones: Rosalin, Rosaline, Rosalyn, Roselyn, Roslyn, Roslyne and Rosylin from Rosalind; Debra and Dobra from Deborah; Karolyn and Carolyn from Caroline; Alyce and Alyse from Alice; Gale from Gail; Arlyne from Arline; Arleyne from Arlene; Lilyan from Lilian, Elane and Elayne from Elaine; Ilene and Iline from Eileen; Ethyl and Ethyle from Ethel; Janis from Janice; Jayne from Jane; Madeline, Madelon, Madelyn, Madelyne, and Madlyn from Madeleine; Marilin and Marylin from Marilyn; and Vyvyan and Vivien from Vivian.

Changes in spelling also account for a large number of new masculine names. Prominent among these are: Allan, Alyn, Allyn and Allen from Alan; Frederic, Fredric and Fredrick from Frederick; Irwin, Erwin, Irving and Irvine from Irvin; Isidore, Isador and Isadore from Isidor; Laurance, Laurence, Lawrance, and Lorence from Lawrence; Maury, Morey and Morry from Morris; Murry from Murray; and Mervyn from Mervin.

In earlier times many new names arose not because of intentional changes in spelling, as the above illustrates, but because of the ignorance and indifference of the people. The illustration given earlier of Diah being confused with Dyer, is a case in point. People were wont to spell the name as they heard it and took no pains to spell it correctly. For this reason, corruptions in spelling as Alys or Ellis for Alice, Febe for Phoebe, Joll for Joel, are often to be found.

Indifference has also been the cause for a great many of the new names; the indifference primarily of the clerk recording the name of the newborn or of newlyweds. Through carelessness "t's" were not crossed and "i's" were not dotted which resulted in the mistaking of the "t" for an "l" and the "i" for an "e." It isn't strange to find, therefore, that Merrel was originally Merritt. Many record keepers sometimes neglected to get the name of one of the parties at a marriage and recorded, as Doane observed in one Connecticut marriage, John Boyghton married "I Dono Who."

Misspelling because of ignorance and indifference has been a source of confusion to those who seek the derivation of the name. Many names cannot be accurately defined because of the new spelling, and must often be guessed at or inferred as originally bearing a different spelling. The name Banett appears among modern personal names and its derivation is a mystery unless we assume that it became

Banett through a misspelling due to the application of the phonetic spelling, or because of carelessness. It may have been originally Barnett and have become Banett somewhere in New England where the middle "r" is slurred over, or the "r" may have been omitted through the carelessness of the recorder and retained by the owner in its new form, since it already appeared as such in legal documents.

A natural cause of new spelling of names can be traced to the influence of foreign languages upon the English. Many of our names, and especially the biblical ones, assumed new forms as they travelled from country to country and were adjusted to the dialects and aesthetic language tastes of the environment in which they sojourned. Thus, John became Jean in French, Joannes in Latin, Joao in Portuguese, Johan in Swedish, Janos in Hungarian, Hans or Johannes in German, Juan in Spanish, Giovanni in Italian, Ivan in Russian, Jan in Dutch and Polish, and Yanez in Slovenian. Jacob became James in English, Jacques in French, Giacomo or Giacobbe in Italian, Jacobus in Latin, Jocobo in Spanish, and Jakob in German, Danish, Hungarian, Polish and Swedish. Michael became Michel in French, Mihaly in Hungarian, Michele in Italian, Miguel in Portuguese and Spanish, Michal in Polish, Michail in Russian and Mikael in Swedish. Joseph became Jozsef in Hungarian and Polish, Giussepe in Italian, Josephus in Latin, and Jose in Portuguese and Spanish. Mary (originally Miriam in Hebrew) became Marie in French and Danish, Maria in Dutch, German, Italian, Portuguese, Spanish, Swedish, Hungarian and Latin, and Marya in Polish. The source of many names currently used by Americans can be found among the above mentioned names as well as many other similar examples that might have been cited.

PERSONALITIES

A very common name source for modern as well as ancient names has been the personal or surname of an outstanding personality who has achieved prominence either in world history or in local environment.

When Alexander the Great entered Palestine, according to the legend, all Jewish boys born in that year were named Alexander in his honor. The names of kings and queens, priests and church leaders have throughout the centuries been adopted by the loyal and devout.

Hugh, originally spelled Hew, became a popular name in England after the middle of the 13th century. It developed as a result of an unjustified (and later proved unfounded) charge, that the child, Hugh of Lincoln, was murdered by Jews for religious reasons. Hugh became an infant-martyr and was canonized by the church. The popularity of the name grew and was widely adopted not only as a personal name, but surnames such as Huet, Hutchins, Higgin, Hewet and Hughes developed from it.

Many Catholics are named after the saint on whose day or in whose month the birth takes place. A boy born in March may be named after Saint Joseph, while one born on March 17th, after Saint Patrick. Others are named after one or both of the sponsors who, according to Catholic church law, are required to be present at the baptism. Louis Adamic in his *The Native's Return,* tells of his uncle Yanez who was named after his patron saint, John the Baptist (Yanez being the Slovenian form of John). Protestants will sometimes choose a famous or well-liked minister as a namesake. There can hardly be a doubt that the name of Luther Martin, a delegate from Maryland to the Constitutional Convention in Philadelphia, was influenced by Martin Luther. In *Get Thee Behind Me,* the author, Hartzell Spence, tells that he was named after Bishop Hartzell. Freddy Fitzsimmons, the well known baseball player, whose middle name is Landis, was named after Fred Landis the brother of Judge Landis. Fred Landis was a prominent midwestern evangelist and a friend of Fitzsimmon's father. Many Jewish boys have been named after Theodor Herzl, the founder of modern Zionism. Julius Caeser, Napoleon, George Washington and Abraham Lincoln are but few of the better known personalities who have so influenced the nomenclature of their own and later times, that not only were their first names adopted, but their surnames were converted into personal names as well.

PLACES

Another significant group of modern names is an outgrowth of place names. It is quite common to find many surnames to have been originally a local name, e.g. Berlin, English, Englander, etc. Many personal names are likewise traceable to localities in various countries. Florence, the Italian city, has long been a favorite personal name. Burton is a local name from Burton in Leicestershire, England. Bruce is a Scottish name of Norman origin. Robert de Bruys came to England with William the Conqueror in 1066 from Bruys or Brieux in Normandy. Murray, acocrding to one opinion, is a name adopted from the Scottish county of Moray.

The Bible contains many instances of personal names which are found at an earlier period to have been place names although according to some scholars they are eponyms. Efraws, the place where Rachel died and was buried, appears again in Chronicles as the name of Caleb's wife. Today it is commonly used as a feminine name in Palestine. Beer Sheba is a local name in Genesis and a masculine name in Samuel. Awfraw is a city in which part of the tribe of Benjamin lived in the Book of Joshua, while in Chronicles it is a masculine name. Ur is a local place name in Genesis and a masculine name in Chronicles.

Many of the more recent Israeli personal names have been taken from towns and cities, e.g. Y'shurum, Shomronaw, Eeyunaw, Karmelaw and Sharon.

More recent place names adopted from the American scene are to be observed in the nomenclature of many personalities. Judge Kenesaw Mountain Landis, brother of the evangelist, Fred Landis, mentioned above is an excellent example of a name drawn from a place. Kenesaw Landis was the first of his family born after the Civil War (November 20, 1866), and was the son of a veteran medical officer of that war. Dr. Landis, who was wounded while performing an amputation during the battle of Kenesaw Mountain, named his son after that engagement. Myrna Loy, the actress, was named after the whistle stop Myrna, which intrigued her father. Portland Hoffa, the radio comedienne and wife of Fred Allen, was named after Portland, Oregon. Florida Edwards is the name of a radio actress. Tallulah Bankhead, the actress, was named after her grandmother who in turn was named after Tallulah Falls in Georgia. The feminine name, Philadelphia, is of great interest since it belonged to a member of the Levy family, prominent on the American-Jewish scene, at the close of the 18th century.

ODDS AND ENDS

Many of our present day names are derived from sources which are odd. Each subdivision in itself would not seem to contain a group large enough to be worthy of special attention. But the various subdivisions taken as a whole, constitute a substantial number of names. It is to these, sometimes rarely heard of names, that we turn our attention for a moment.

DAYS, MONTHS, AND HOLIDAYS

In the course of history we find that a great many of the days of the week, months of the year, and holidays have constituted a source of personal names as well as surnames. Monday (spelled Munday), Tuesday (Dienstag, in German) and Saturday were long used as names. Friday, the famous character in *Robinson Crusoe,* is well known to all. Likewise many of the months of the year have been used as surnames and, even to a greater extent, as personal names. Augustus (August) and Julia (July) were especially common in Roman days. May and June are very popular forenames today. April, a name given by actress June Havoc to her daughter, is also occasionally encountered. Howard Fast in his book, *Patrick Henry and the*

Frigate's Keel, records the name of January Fernandez, a Portuguese who participated in the breaking of the British blockade in 1812. November and April are also used as surnames as is January (Lois January—a radio entertainer). From the Hebrew calendar the months of Nisan, Awv (Ab), and Adar have been appropriated for use as personals. One rabbi, the father of twelve sons, is reported to have named each son after a different Hebrew month.

Among the Holy Days that are of Hebrew origin, Sabbatai (Sabbath) and Pesach (Passover) have been adopted, and are very popular Hebrew names to this day. We also find the name of the Pentecost holiday appropriated by Pentecostes, a servant of King Henry VII. In fact, the Hebrew term for holiday—Yom Tov, is commonly used by Jews as a personal name. It also might be noted that it was customary during the Middle Ages to name boys who were circumcized on Purim, Mordecai (in honor of the hero of the holiday), and those born on Tish'aw B'Awv, Menachem. (Tish'aw B'awv, or the ninth day of the month Awv (Ab) is a fast day commemorating the destruction of the Temple in Jerusalem. The prophetic portion read on the Sabbath following the fast day is from Isaiah 40 in which the prophet comforts Israel. Menachem means "comforter.") Children born on Yom Kippur were sometimes called Rachamim (mercy). Among the Jews of Eastern Europe a son born on Chanukah was usually called by the name of the holiday. Among the Christian holidays, Easter and Christmas have long served as sources for forenames. Easter is commonly used and can be found as a character in Lillian Smith's novel *Strange Fruit,* and Christ and Christmas are the backbone of names such as Chris, Christopher, Christine and Noel.

During World War II America looked forward anxiously to the day of victory. The day of victory in Europe was designated as V-E day. In commemoration of the occasion, one parent named his daughter *Victoria E*thel. Others, likewise, bestowed the name Victoria upon their daughters during that period of victory over Germany and Japan.

NUMERAL NAMES

Numbers are another source that were used a great deal in the past and in some rare instances today. The Romans were the first to take numeral names. Among the more common are: Quintus (5), Octavius (8), and Septimus (7). Among recent Tripolitan Jews in North Africa, Hmessa and Hammus, meaning five, are used as feminine and masculine personal names respectively. There was recently a family in Michigan by the surname Stickaway who named their three boys: One, Two and Three, and their three girls: First, Second and Third. One of the rare present day examples of a number being used as a personal name made its appearance recently in the case of a young rabbi who, having difficulty finding a satisfactory Hebrew name for his first daughter, decided to name her Reeshonaw (first). Ten is used as a masculine name in the novel *Strange Fruit*.

It is interesting to note that the Puritans, and especially the Quakers, refrained from using the names of months, and substituted numbers in their place. They felt that inasmuch as most months had names of pagan origin it would be best not to use them. For this reason we find, as we study some of the official records and tombstone engravings of the 17th century, that months are referred to by numbers rather than name. January referred to as 1, February as 2, etc.

NAMES IN JEST

In another category would appear names that seem to have been given merely to be amusing. A name of this type appeared in Leonard Lyon's column, "The Lion's Den." In it he reports that "Bill Lear, president of the radio company, Lear Avia, and his wife named their new daughter "Chrystal Chanda Lear (chandalier)."

The original names suggested for Walter Winchell's second child would have applied perfectly to this category had they been accepted. Charles Fisher in his book, *The Columnist* reports that Winchell's wife wanted to call the child Reid (read) Winchell if it were a boy, while he preferred Sue Winchell in the event that the offspring were a girl. Ben Bernie, who at the time was carrying on a pre-arranged feud with Winchell, suggested the name Lynch Winchell. In the end the boy was named Walter Jr. But Winchell's daughter, who was born some nine years earlier, was named Walda, and was undoubtedly so named because it sounded very much like Walter. No doubt the author of these names had his tongue in his cheek at the moment of inspiration.

The Broadway publicist, Spencer Hare, was in a jesting mood, it would seem, when he named his daughter Hedda Hare. Especially does it seem that this was the case from recent reports that if he should have another daughter he would call her Lotta Hare and if a boy, Noah Hare.

An amazing collection of names which seem to be of this nature appears in the Dewey Genealogy which lists the following names in one family: Armenius Philadelphus, Almira Melpomena, Pleiades Arastareus, Victor Millenius, Octavia Ammonia and Encyclopedia Brittannica.

MAIDEN NAMES

Use of the mother's maiden name is sometimes a source of names that appear for the first time. Gouverneur Morris, United States Minister to France from 1791-1794, and earlier a member of the Committee on Style that drafted the Constitution, got his first name in that way. Reed Gresham Landis, son of baseball commissioner Kenesaw M. Landis and a major in the first World War, can trace his first name to his mother's maiden name (Winifred Reed). Dr. Henry Sloane Coffin, a former president of Union Theological Seminary in New York, received his middle name from his mother whose maiden name was Euphemia Sloane.

The practice is not peculiar to any one type or group. The birth columns of almost any newspaper will attest to the fact of its growing usage by the average American family. Becker, Bloom, Borker, Hut, Geller, Jacobs, Lewis,

Miller, Paris, Sultan and Waldman are but a few of the many found in the recent columns of *The New York Times*.

INVENTED NAMES

Every now and then we happen across names that are completely original and the figment of the imagination of an author or some other individual. A typical example (which is also an example of a telescoped name) of very recent date was related by a native Hawaiian, a soldier in the United States Army, who expected a child very soon. If it were a boy he planned to name it William Jr. If it were to be a girl, his wife, May had decided to name her Mayliam —a combination of May and the last four letters of William. Many more cases of this type are to be found frequently within the average family, examples of which are to be found among the above categories, as well as in the literary products of our best known authors. A few of the outstanding classic examples include: Zephalinda and Gay, invented by Alexander Pope; Vanessa, which is in reality a combination forged out of the name of Esther Vanhorurigh, coined by Jonathan Swift; and Pamela coined by Sidney in his *Arcadia*.

INVERSIONS

A sub-group of the invented name might be termed inversions. Many new names have come about through the process of rejuggling the syllables of a name, or by joining two or more syllables that have individual meanings. In olden times it was quite common for a new name to make an appearance by the use of this simple procedure. Nathaniel and Elnathan consist of the same syllables and have the same meaning. Theodora and Dorothea, likewise, are the same name except for the inverted order. Although this practice is not too common today (except in the case of Caroline that became Linn Carol), it is worthy of mention because it is not unlikely that someday this may become a popular method of arriving at novel names.

STATISTICS AND TRENDS

In the past 24 years the author has undertaken three surveys. The first was conducted in 1942, and entailed a sampling of 5200 names—2600 English and 2600 Hebrew. The information was supplied on a questionnaire sent to the heads of 49 different schools in 38 cities in 13 states from the east coast as far west as Minnesota.

The second survey was conducted over a period of two years, and consisted of an analysis of the names of 9,658 children and parents reported in the birth columns of the *New York Times,* from August 1943 to August 1945. The names of the parents were also analyzed, and a fascinating study of comparison and contrast between the parent generation and the new generation resulted.

A third, very limited, survey was conducted in 1966, over a six-month period. This survey analyzed 583 names that appeared in the *New York Times* birth columns. As in Survey No. 2, a study was also made of the names of the parents of the newborn children.

The names in the first survey are wholly Jewish. In the second and third surveys no attempt was made at omitting names that were not Jewish for two reasons. Firstly, because in many cases it is impossible to tell from a name (family or personal) whether or not it belongs to a Jewish person. Secondly, since the overwhelming majority of names in the columns were definitely Jewish (perhaps 80-90%), the net result was not substantially affected by the small percentage belonging to non-Jews.

MOST POPULAR HEBREW NAMES (Survey No. 1)

Moshe was the most popular of all Hebrew names, occurring as the name of different individuals 102 times. In six cases, the corresponding English name was of the same meaning as the Hebrew name, while in 96 cases the choice of the English equivalent of Moshe was, quite evidently, based upon a similarity in sound (both began with the "M" sound). Thirty different English names were used as equivalents for Moshe. Approximately the same proportions governed the other leading names in the survey. The following were the most popular Hebrew names:

Cha'yim, Avrawhawm, Yitzchawk, Yaakov, R'uvayn, Dawvid, Tz'vee, Yosayf and Shmuayl led the list of masculine names, while Sawraw, Miryawm, Chanaw, Cha'yim, Estayr, Layaw, Rawchayl, D'voraw, Y'hudis and Rivkaw led the list of feminine names.

MOST POPULAR FIRST NAMES (Survey No. 1)

The following are the ten leading names, and the number of times each occurred:

Masculine names: Robert 72; Stanley 49; Howard 38; David 37; Donald 36; Martin 35; Harold 33; Bernard 32; Edward 31; Richard 31.

Feminine names: Ruth 27; Barbara 21; Shirley 19; Marilyn 16; Elaine 13; Judith 12; Harriet 11; Phyllis 11; Edith 10; Eleanor 10.

MOST POPULAR FIRST NAMES (Survey No. 2)

The following were the ten most popular names found in Survey No. 2. The first number after the name indicates how many times the name appeared; the second number, in parentheses, indicates how often this same name appeared as the first name of the parent.

Masculine names: Michael 173(9), Robert 153(46), Richard 151(25), David 132(73), Alan 123(13), Stephen 105(2), Peter 86(2), Jeffrey 74(0), Steven 73(2), and Mark 67(6).

Feminine names: Ellen 174(0), Susan 171(2), Jane 152(12), Ann 141(9), Barbara 109(11), Carol 88(7), Joan 77(13), Nancy 77(1), Linda 74(0), and Judith 72(5).

The leading masculine names of the parents found in the above survey were: Irving 100, Harry 94, Joseph 79,

Sidney 75, Arthur 74, David 73, Harold 73, Samuel 66, Herbert 64, and Milton 63.

Feminine names of the parent generation that led the list were: Ruth 125, Dorothy 63, Shirley 61, Helen 47, Florence 40, Doris 39, Muriel 39, Beatrice 35, Lillian 35, and Frances 34.

MOST POPULAR DOUBLE NAMES (Survey No. 2)

The following is a list of the most common children's double names. All double names with a frequency of five and over are listed. Names of different spelling, but of close kinship in origin and sound are grouped together.

Judith Ann 17, Judith Anne 2; Susan Jane 15; Barbara Ann 13; Ellen Sue 10; Jane Ellen 10; Richard Alan 8, Richard Allen 3, Richard Allan 2; Patricia Ann 8, Patricia Anne 2; Alan Michael 8; Michael David 8; Michael Jay 8; Nancy Sue 8; Michael Alan 7, Michael Allen 2; Carol Ann 7; Peter Michael 7; Barbara Jane 6; Nancy Ellen 6; Robert Michael 6.

MOST POPULAR FIRST NAMES (Survey No. 3)

Of the 583 personal names analyzed in Survey No. 3, 244 were masculine and 339 were feminine. The number after the name refers to the number of times the names appeared.

Masculine names: David 46, Michael 30, Andrew 22, Steven 21, Jonathan 19, Robert 16, Richard 15, Jeffrey 14, Mark (or Marc) 14, and Gary 11.

Feminine names: Lisa 19, Jill 16, Susan 14, Beth 13, Amy 13, Debra 12, Elizabeth 12, Nancy 12, Ellen 10, and Jennifer 10.

The names Robin and Leslie, used interchangeably as masculine and feminine names, each appeared six times.

In analyzing the most popular first names of the parents of the above mentioned, the following led the list:

Masculine names: Robert 40, Michael 29, Richard 26,

Alan 23, Howard 19, Martin 16, Edward 14, Stanley 14, Paul 13, and Harvey 11.

Feminine names: Barbara 24, Carol 17, Joan 17, Susan 17, Ellen 16, Jane 13, Linda 12, Judith 11, Sandra 10, and Nancy 10.

The most popular masculine middle names discovered in Survey No. 3 were: Mark (or Marc) 23, Scott 21, David 16, Andrew 15, and Alan (or Allan and Allen) 13). The most popular feminine middle names were Ann (or Anne) 32, Beth 32, Lynn 30, Sue (or Susan) 24, Ellen 14, and Robin 13.

ANALYSIS OF MIDDLE NAMES

The fact that Ann, Ellen, Alan, Mark, Scott and David are among the most popular middle names is not an accident. The tendency in the use of middle names seems to point to two distinct practices. The first consists of employing, in a good number of cases, middle names that begin with a vowel. The fact that twenty-two of the forty-six most popular double names in Survey No. 2 have a middle name beginning with a vowel is evidence of this tendency. The second practice is that of using a short middle name, usually of one or two syllables. The list of fifty most popular middle names reveals that only in one case does a middle name have more than two syllables (Barbara—with three). Thirty-two have two syllables, and eighteen have one syllable (nine of the eighteen are among the first eighteen on the list). This practice, which has proven to be the common one, is, in reality, but another illustration of an old principle of rhetoric (which people sense unconsciously): that the shorter word in a combination of word follows the longer. Both this practice, as well as that of using a name beginning with a vowel for a middle name, make for better and easier pronunciation and euphony.

The facts and figures with regard to middle names are interesting. Of the 4207 children's names examined in Survey No. 2, more than half (2875) used a double name: 1368 masculine and 1507 feminine. Among the parent generation a total of only 78 employed double names: 48 masculine and 30 feminine. This is striking evidence of the growing popularity of the use of double names today as compared with earlier generations.

NAME VARIETY

All three surveys reveal that there exists a greater variety of English feminine names than masculine names. The evidence is most striking in Survey Number 2, where among a total of 4207 children's names (2039 masculine and 2168 feminine) there are 557 different feminine names, as against 411 masculine. Among the parents' 5451 names (3124 masculine and 2327 feminine) there are 413 feminine to 382 masculine. This latter fact makes the evidence all the more conclusive, because, although there was a sampling of 797 more masculine than feminine names (because the birth notice often omits the mother's first name), there still was a greater variety of feminine names.

Another striking fact is that although there were 1244 more parents' than children's names recorded in the birth columns, there is a greater variety (213) of children's names. The reason for this is undoubtedly that many new spellings have been invented for names originally spelled only one way. There are, today, no less than five ways of spelling Lawrence; four ways of spelling Isidor; and at least six ways of spelling Lynne.

With regard to Hebrew names the case is reversed. There is a preponderance of masculine names and a paucity of feminine names. Survey Number 1 reveals that of 184 different Hebrew names, 123 are masculine and 61 feminine.

Taken as a whole it is surprising to note how few Hebrew names exist in contrast to secular names—a ratio of 1 to 2.5.

BIBLICAL NAMES

In Survey Number 1, 105 of the 184 Hebrew names are from the Old Testament while only 66 of the 439 English equivalents are taken from that source (61% to 15%). Of the ten leading masculine English names only one is from the Old Testament and of a similar number of feminine names only two are biblical names.

In Survey Number 2, of the leading six names of both generations (masculine and feminine), three of the younger generation's are taken from the Old Testament (two masculine and one feminine), while of the parent generation, five (four masculine and one feminine) are from the Bible.

In survey Number 3, of the leading ten masculine names six are biblical and among the feminine ten most popular names five are from the Bible. Lisa and Beth, which are among the top ten, are diminutive forms of Elizabeth. Debra is a varient spelling of Deborah. Of the masculine names, three are from the Old Testament, and all five of the feminine names are from the Old Testament.

Masculine Hebrew
Name Index

אֲדוֹרָם	אֲבִישַׁי	אָבִים	א
אָדִיב	אֲבִישָׁלוֹם	אֲבִימָאֵל	אַבָּא
אַדִּיר	אֲבִישָׁמָע	אֲבִימִי	אַבְגָה
אָדָם	אֲבִישֶׁר	אֲבִימֶלֶךְ	אַבְדִימִי
אַדְמוֹן	אֲבִישֻׂר	אֲבִימָן	אַבָּהוּ
אַדְעָה	אֲבִיתַּגָּר	אֲבִימַעַץ	אֲבוּיָה
אַדְנִיקָם	אֶבְיָתָר	אָבִין	אַבְטַלְיוֹן
אֲדְנִירָם	אִבֶּן	אֲבִינָא	אָבִי
אַדָּר	אַבְנֵר	אֲבִינָדָב	אֲבִיאוֹר
אַדְרָם	אַבְנִיאֵל	אֲבִי־נָעִים	אֲבִיאוּר
אַהֲבָה	אִבְצָן	אֲבִינֹעַם	אֲבִיאֵל
אֹהַד	אַבְרָהָם	אֲבִיכֵר	אֲבִיאָסָף
אָהוּב	אַבְרִיאֵל	אֲבִיסָמָךְ	אָבִיב
אֲהוּבְיָה	אֲבְרֵךְ	אֲבְיָסָף	אֲבִיגְדוֹר
אֲהוּבְעַם	אַבְרָם	אֲבִיעַד	אֲבִידוֹר
אֵהוּד	אַבְשִׁי	אֲבִיעֵז	אֲבִידָן
אֵהוּד	אַבְשָׁלוֹם	אֲבִיעֶזֶר	אֲבִידָע
אֹהֶל	אָגָא	אֲבִיעֶזְרִי	אֲבִידְרוֹר
אָהֳלִי	אַגַּאי	אֲבִימֶלֶט	אֲבִיָּה
אָהֳלִיאָב	אֶגְאָל	אֲבִיצֶדֶק	אֲבִיהוּ
אַהֲרֹן	אָגוּר	אֲבִיצוּר	אֲבִיהוּא
אוּאֵל	אָגִיל	אֲבִיקָם	אֲבִיהוּד
אוֹבִיל	אָגֵל	אֲבִיקָר	אֲבִיחַי
אוּד	אֶגְרוֹן	אַבִּיר	אֲבִי־חַי
אוּדִי	אַגְרִיפַּס	אֲבִירִי	אֲבִיחַיִל
אוֹהַד	אַדָּא	אֲבִירָם	אֲבִי־חֵן
אוֹהַד	אַדְבְּאֵל	אֲבִישׁוּעַ	אֲבִיטוּב
אוּזָל	אִדּוֹ	אֲבִישׁוּר	אֲבִיטַל
אֱוִי	אֲדוֹנִים	אֲבִישַׁחַר	אַבָּיֵי

אַהֲרוֹן	אֲחִילוּד	אֲדָנִיָהוּ	אוֹכָל
אַחְרָח	אֲחִימוֹת	אֶזְרָח	אוֹלָם
אַחַרְחֵל	אֲחִימֶלֶךְ	אַחָא	אוֹמָר
אָטֵר	אֲחִימָן	אַחְאָב	אוֹן
אַיָה	אֲחִימַעַץ	אַחַאי	אוֹנָם
אִיּוֹב	אֲחִין	אַחְבָּן	אוֹנָן
אִי-כָבוֹד	אֲחִינָדָב	אֵהוּד	אוֹפָז
אַיָּל	אֲחִיכַעַם	אֵהוֹח	אוֹפִיר
אַיָל	אֲחִיכֶר	אֲחוֹמִי	אוֹפָר
אֱיָל	אֲחִיסָמָךְ	אָחָז	אוּר
אַיָּלוֹן	אֲחִיעֶזֶר	אַחְזַי	אוֹר
אֵילוֹן	אֲחִיעָם	אֲחַזְיָה	אוֹרוֹן
אִילָן	אֲחִיפֶלֶט	אֲחַזְיָהוּ	אוֹר-חַיִּים
אַיָּיר	אֲחִיצֶדֶק	אֲחֻזָּם	אוּרִי
אִיָּרִי	אֲחִיצוּר	אָחִי	אוֹרִי
אִיסוּר	אֲחִיקַם	אָחִי	אוּרִיאֵל
אִיסִי	אֲחִיקָר	אָחִי	אוֹרִיָה
אִיעֶזֶר	אֲחִירַם	אֲחִיאָב	אוֹרִיָּהוּ
אִיקָא	אֲחִירַע	אֲחִיאָם	אוּרִיוֹן
אִישׁ-בֹּשֶׁת	אֲחִישׁוּר	אֲחִיאָסָף	אוּרְדָן
אִישׁ-הוֹד	אֲחִישַׁחַר	אֲחִי-דוֹד	אוֹרֶן
אִישׁ-חַיִל	אֲחִישַׁי	אֲחִידָן	אוֹרֶן
אִישׁ-שֵׂכֶל	אֲחִישָׁלוֹם	אֲחִידָע	אוֹרְנִי
אִיתַּאי	אֲחִישָׂר	אֲחִיָה	אוֹשַׁעְיָא
אִיתִּי	אֲחִישַׁר	אֲחִיָהוּ	אוֹשֶׁר
אִיתַּי	אֲחִיתֹפֶל	אֲחִיהוּד	אוֹשְׁרִי
אִיתִיאֵל	אַחְלָב	אָחִיו	אָזְבַּי
אִיתָם	אַחְלַי	אֲחִיחוּד	אָזְנִי
אִיתָמָר	אַחַר	אֲחִיטוּב	אֲזַנְיָה

אֵיתָן
אֵלָא
אֶלְדָד
אֶלְדָּעָה
אֶלְגָּבִישׁ
אֵלָה
אֱלִיל
אַלּוֹן
אַלּוֹן
אַלּוּף
אֶלְזָבָד
אֶלְחָנָן
אֵלִי
אֱלִיאָב
אֱלִיאוֹר
אֱלִיאֵל
אֶלְיָסָף
אֱלִיאָתָה
אֱלִידָד
אֶלְיָדָע
אֵלִיָּה
אֵלִיָּהוּ
אֱלִיהוּא
אֱלִיהוּד
אֱלִיחַי
אֱלִי חֹרֶף
אֱלִיטוּב
אֱלִימוֹר
אֱלִימֶלֶךְ

אֱלִינָתָן
אֶלְיָסָף
אֱלִיעַד
אֱלִיעֶזֶר
אֱלִיעֵינַי
אֱלִיעָם
אֱלִיעַז
אֱלִיפָל
אֱלִיפֶלֶט
אֱלִיצוּר
אֱלִיצֶדֶק
אֱלִיצוּ
אֱלִיצוּר
אֱלִיצָפָן
אֶלְיָקִים
אֶלְיָקִים
אֱלִירָם
אֱלִירָן
אֶלְיָשׁוּב
אֱלִישׁוּעַ
אֶלְיָשִׁיב
אֱלִישָׁמָע
אֱלִישָׁע
אֱלִישָׁפָט
אֲלֶכְּסַנְדֶּר
אַלְמוּג
אַלְמוֹדָד
אֶלְעַם
אֶלְנָקָם

אֶלְנָתָן
אֶלְעָאי
אֶלְעָד
אֶלְצָדָה
אֶלְעוּזַי
אֶלְעָזָר
אֶלְעָזְרִי
אֶלְעָשָׂה
אֶלְפַּעַל
אֶלְצָפָן
אֶלְקוֹשׁ
אֶלְקָנָה
אֶלְרָאִי
אֶלְרָד
אֶלְתָּר
אָמוֹן
אָמוֹץ
אַמִּי
אֲמֵימַר
אֲמִיגוֹן
אַמִיץ
אָמִיר
אֲמִישַׁי
אֲמִיתַי
אֲמִיתָן
אֹמָן
אַמְנוֹן
אֹמֶץ
אִמְצִי

אֲמַצְיָה
אֲמַצְיָהוּ
אֹמֶר
אָמֵר
אִמְרִי
אֲמַרְיָה
אֲמַרְיָהוּ
אָמָרֶט
אֲמִתַּי
אֲמִתָּן
אֱנוֹשׁ
אֲנִיעָם
אָסָא
אַסִי
אַסִיר
אַסְנָה
אָסָף
אֵאוּד
אָפְלָל
אֶפְרַיִם
אֶפְרָת
אֶצְבּוֹן
אָצֵל
אֲצַלְיָהוּ
אֹצֶם
אֹצֶד
אַרְאֵל
אַרְאֵלִי
אַרְגָּמָן

בֶּן-טוֹבִים	בָּחוּר	אֲשַׂרְאֵל	אָרְד
בֶּן-יִשַׁי	בַּחְיָא	אֲשַׂרְאֵלָה	אַרְדּוֹן
בָּנִי	בְּחִיאֵל	אֶשְׂרִי	אֶרֶז
בֻּנִּי	בְּחַיֵּי	אֲשַׂרְיָאֵל	אַרְזָא
בְּנָיָה	בָּחִיר	אֶתְאֵל	אַרְזִי
בְּנָיָהוּ	בַּחַן	אִתַּי	אֲרִי
בִּנְיָמִין	בֶּטַח	אִתִּיאֵל	אֲרִיאָב
בִּנְיָמִין-זְאֵב	בִּינָה	אֶתְנִי	אֲרִיאֵל
בֶּן-עֶזְרָה	בִּיתָן	אֲתַנְיָה	אַרְיֵה
בֶּן-עַמִּי	בְּכוֹר	אֶתְנָן	אַרְיוֹךְ
בֶּן עָשׂוֹר	בֶּכֶר	ב	אַרְמוֹן
בִּנְצִי	בִּכְרִי	בְּאָרָה	אַרְמוֹנִי
בֶּן צִיּוֹן	בִּלְגָּה	בְּאֵרִי	אַרְמְנִי
בֶּן-שַׁחַר	בִּלְגַּי	בָּבָא	אֹרֶן
בֶּן-שֵׁם	בִּלְדַּד	בֵּבַי	אֶרֶן
בֹּעַז	בִּלְהָן	בַּג-בַּג	אַרְנוֹן
בַּעַל	בַּלְעוּר	בִּגְוַי	אַרְנִי
בַּעֲנָה	בָּלָק	בְּדֹלַח	אָרְנָן
בַּעְשָׂא	בִּלְשָׁן	בַּקְּעַ	אַרְנָן
בְּצַלְאֵל	בֵּן	בָּהִיר	אַרְצִי
בֶּצֶר	בֶּן-אוֹנִי	בּוּגִי	אֶשְׁבֵּל
בִּצְרוֹן	בֶּן-בָּרוּךְ	בּוּז	אֶשְׁבָּן
בַּקְבּוּק	בֶּן-גּוּרִיוֹן	בּוּזִי	אַשְׁבֵּעַ
בַּקְבּוּקְיָה	בֶּן גֶּבֶר	בּוֹחֵר	אֶשֶׂד
בֻּקִּי	בֶּן חוּר	בּוּסְתְּנַאי	אַשְׁחוּר
בֶּרֶד	בֶּן-חַיִל	בּוּנָה	אָשִׂי
בָּרוּךְ	בֶּן-חָנָן	בּוּעִי	אֶשְׁכּוֹל
בָּרוּר	בֶּן-חֶסֶד	בָּזֵק	אֶשֶׁל
בְּרוֹשׁ	בֶּן-טוֹב	בֶּזֶק	אָשֵׁר

גְּלִילִי	גּוּרִי	גַּבְרִיאֵל	בַּרְזִילַי
גָּלְיַת	גּוּרִיאֵל	גְּבַרְיָה	בֵּרִי
גָּלָל	גּוּרְיוֹן	גְּבַרְעָם	בַּר-יוֹחָאִי
גִּלְעָד	גָּזֵז	גְּבַתּוֹן	בָּרִיחַ
גָּמוּל	גְּחָזִי	גָּד	בְּרִיעָה
גַּמְלָא	גֵּיא	גַּדָּא	בַּר-כּוֹכְבָא
גַּמְלִי	גַּחַם	גָּדוֹל	בַּדְכָּאֵל
גַּמְלִיאֵל	גַּחַר	גָּדוֹר	בְּרָכָה
גֹּמֶר	גִּידֵל	גָּדִי	בְּרֶכְיָה
גְּמַרְיָה	גִּידִי	גַּדִּי	בְּרֶכְיָהוּ
גְּמַרְיָהוּ	גִּיּוֹרָא	גַּדִיאֵל	בִּרְעָם
גִּנְתּוֹן	גִּיּוֹרָה	גָּדֵל	בָּרָק
גַּעַל	גִּיל	גִּדְלָה	בַּרְקָאי
גֶּפֶן	גִּיל-אוֹן	גְּדַלְיָה	בָּרֶקֶת
גָּפְנִיָה	גִּילַאי	גְּדַלְיָהוּ	בְּשׂוֹר
גֵּרָא	גִּילוֹן	גְּדַלְתִּי	בְּשַׁלֵם
גֵּרְיוֹן	גִּילִי	גִּדְעוֹן	בְּתוּאֵל
גֵּרְשׁוֹם	גִּיל-לִי	גִּדְעוֹנִי	בְּתֵירָא
גֵּרְשׁוֹן	גִּילָן	גּוֹאֵל	ג
גְּשׁוּר	גִּיל-עַד	גּוֹבֵר	גְּאוּאֵל
גִּתַּי	גִּילְעָד	גּוֹג	גְּאַלְיָה
גֶּתֶר	גִּיל-עָם	גּוֹזָל	גְּבוֹר
ד	גִּילְעָם	גּוֹזָן	גַּבִּי
דְּאָג	גִּיַּת	גּוֹלָן	גַּבְּי
דֹּב	גִּישָׁן	גּוּנִי	גֶּבַע
דְּבִיר	גִּיתִּי	גּוֹגֵן	גִּבְעָא
דִּבְרִי	גַּל	גּוּר	גִּבְעוֹל
דָּגוּל	גַּלִּי	גּוּר-אֲרִי	גִּבְעוֹן
דִּגְלַאי	גָּלִיל	גּוּר-אַרְיֵה	גֶּבֶּר

דָּגָן
דָּדָן
דּוֹבֵב
דּוּבִי
דָּוִד
דּוֹדוֹ
דּוֹדַי
דּוּר
דּוֹר
דּוֹרוֹן
דּוֹרוֹנִי
דּוֹתָן
דִּיבּוֹן
דִּידִי
דִּיכַאי
דִּיץ
דְּלָיָה
דְּלָיָהוּ
דַּלְפוֹן
דָּמָא
דָּן
דָּנִי
דָּנִיאֵל
דָּנִיעָם
דְּעוּאֵל
דָּפִי
דֶּקֶל
דִּקְלָה
דֶּקֶר

דַּר
דָּרוֹם
דְּרוֹר
דְּרוֹרִי
דַּרְיָוֶשׁ
דָּתָן
ה
הַאי
הֶבֶל
הָדוּר
הֲדַר
הָדָר
הֲדַרְעֶזֶר
הֲדַרְעָם
הוֹד
הוֹדִיָה
הוּנָא
הוּרְקָנוּס
הוֹשָׁמָע
הוֹשֵׁעַ
הוֹשַׁעְיָה
הוֹתִיר
הֵימָן
הֵלָא
הִלֵּל
הֶלֶם
הִלָּן
הַמְנוּנָא
הִצִלְיָהוּ

הַרְאֵל
הַרְדּוֹף
הָרוּם
הָרָן
הֶרְצֵל
הַשְׂכֵּל
ו
וֶלֶס
וַעְיָה
וָפְסִי
וֶרֶד
וַרְדִּימוֹן
וַרְדִּיעוֹן
וּשְׁנִי
ז
זְאֵב
זְאֵבִי
זָבָד
זַבְדִּי
זַבְדִּיאֵל
זְבַדְיָה
זְבַדְיָהוּ
זָבוּד
זְבוּל
זְבוּלֻן
זֶבַח
זִבְחֲיָה
זָבִיד
זְבִינָא

זַכַּבִּי
זָהוּר
זֹהַר
זְהַרְיָה
זוֹהֵר
זוּטְרָא
זוּמָא
זוֹרֵחַ
זוֹרֵעַ
זָזָא
זִיו
זִיוִי
זִיָן
זִיזָא
זִיזָה
זִיכְרוֹנִי
זִינָא
זִיעַ
זִיף
זִיפָה
זִיק
זִירָא
זִירוּז
זַיִת
זֵיתָן
זַכַּאי
זַפּוּר
זַכַּי
זֶכֶר

חִלְקִיָּה	חֲזִיאֵל	חֲבָיָה	זִכְרִי
חִלְקִיָּהוּ	חֲזָיָה	חֲבַקִּיק	זְכַרְיָה
חָם	חִזְקִי	חֶבֶר	זְכַרְיָהוּ
חָמָא	חִזְקִיָּה	חֶבְרוֹן	זַלְמָן
חֶמֶד	חִזְקִיָּהוּ	חָגָב	זָמָה
חֲמַדְאֵל	חַי	חַגִּי	זְמִינָא
חֲמַדְיָה	חִיָּא	חַגִּי	זָמִיר
חֶמְדָּן	חִיאֵל	חַגִּיָּה	זְמִירָה
חַמּוּאֵל	חִיָּא	חֲדַד	זֶמֶר
חָמוּד	חַיִּים	חוֹבָב	זִמְרָא
חָמוּל	חַיִל	חוֹבָב	זִמְרִי
חֵן	חִירָה	חוֹזַי	זִמְרִיָּה
חֵן־מֶלֶךְ	חִירוֹם	חֲוִילָה	זִמְרָן
חָנָא	חִירָם	חוֹמִי	זְעֵירָא
חָנָה	חֲכִינַאי	חוֹנִי	דִּפְרוֹן
חָנוֹךְ	חֲכַלְיָה	חוֹנְיוֹ	זָקוּף
חַנּוּן	חַכְמוֹנִי	חוֹנֵן	זָקִיף
חָנוּן	חֵלֶב	חוּסָה	זָקֵן
חֲנִיאֵל	חֶלְבּוֹ	חוּפָם	זְרוּבָּבֶל
חָנִין	חֶלֶד	חוּצְפִּית	זֶרַח
חֲנִינָא	חֶלְדַּי	חוּר	זְרַחְיָה
חֲנֻכָּה	חַלּוֹן	חוּרִי	זֶתֶל
חֲנַמְאֵל	חֶלֶף	חוּרִי	ח
חָקָן	חַלְפּוֹן	חוּרַף	חֹבָב
חָקָן	חֲלִפְתָּא	חוּשַׁי	חֹבָּה
חֲנַנְאֵל	חֵלֶץ	חוּשִׁיאֵל	חָבִיב
חֲנָנִי	חַלְצוֹן	חוּשִׁיעָם	חֲבִיבָאֵל
חֲנַנְיָה	חֵלֶק	חוֹתָם	חֲבִיבְיָה
חֲנַנְיָהוּ	חֶלְקִי	חֲדָאֵל	חֲבִיבְעָם

חֲשׁוּבָה	חָנָתוּן	רַאֲזַנְיָה	וְדָיָה
חַשְׁמוֹן	חֶסֶד	יַאֲזַנְיָהוּ	יָדִין
חַשְׁמוֹנַאי	חִסְדָּא	יָאִיר	יְדִיעֵאל
חֵתַת	חִסְדַּאי	יֹאשִׁיָה	יָדָע
ט	חַסְדָּאֵל	יֹאשִׁיָהוּ	יְדַעְיָה
טַבַּאי	חֲסַדְיָה	וְבוֹרֶךְ	יָהָב
טַבְאֵל	חִסָּה	וִבְחָר	יֵהוּא
טֶבַח	חָסוּד	יָבִין	יְהוֹאָחָז
טָבִי	חָסוֹן	יָבֵל	יְהוֹאָשׁ
טִבְעוֹן	חָסִיד	יַבְנְאֵל	יְהוּדָה
טַבָּעוֹת	חָסִין	יַבְנִיאֵל	יְהוּדִי
טוֹב	חֹסֶן	יִבְנְיָה	יְהוֹזָבָד
טוֹבִי	חָפָּה	יְבֶרֶכְיָהוּ	יְהוֹחָנָן
טוֹבִיָה	חָפְנִי	יָבֵשׁ	יְהוֹיָדָע
טוֹבִיָה	חֵפֶץ	יִבְשָׂם	יְהוֹיָכִין
טוֹבִיָהוּ	חֵפֶר	יִגְאָל	יְהוֹיָקִים
טוֹדְרוֹס	תַצְפִּית	יִגְאָל	יְהוֹיָרִיב
טַל	חֶצְרוֹן	יָגֵב	יְהוֹנָדָב
טַל-אוֹר	חֶצְרַי	יִגְדֹּל	יְהוֹנָתָן
טַל-שַׁחַר	חָרוּץ	יִגְדַּלְיָהוּ	יְהוֹסֵף
טָלוֹר	חָרִים	יָגִיל	יְהוֹצָדָק
טַלְיָא	חָרִיף	יָגֵל	יְהוֹרָם
טֶלֶם	חֶרְמוֹן	גַּגְלִי	יְהוֹשֻׁעַ
טַלְמוֹן	חַרְסוּם	יָדוֹ	יְהוֹשָׁפָט
טָמִיר	חָרֵף	יָדוֹן	יָהֵל
טֶנֶא	חֶרֶשׁ	יַדּוּעַ	יְהַלֶלְאֵל
י	חֲשַׁבְיָה	יְדוּתוּן	יַהֲלֹם
יָאֶה	חֲשַׁבְיָהוּ	יָדִיד	יוֹאָב
יָאוּשׁ	חָשׁוּב	יְדִידְיָה	יוֹאָח

יַעְרִי	זָכִין	יוֹצָדָק	יוֹאָחָז
יַעֲשִׂיאֵל	זְכָרְיָה	יוֹקִים	יוֹאֵל
יִפְדְיָה	זְכַרְיָהוּ	יוֹרָה	יוֹאָשׁ
זָפֶה	זָלוֹן	יוֹרָם	יוֹב
זָפִיעַ	זְמוּאֵל	יוֹעָה	יוֹבָב
יַפְלֵט	זָמִין	יוֹשַׁבְיָה	יוּבָל
זַפְנֶה	יִמְלָה	יוֹשָׁפָט	יוֹגֵב
יִפְרָח	זָמֶלֶךְ	יוֹשֵׁר	יוּדָן
יִפְרַחְעָם	יִמְנָה	יוֹתָם	יוֹזָבָד
יֶפֶת	יִמְנָע	יִזְהָר	יוֹחָא
יִפְתָּח	יַנַאי	זָזִיז	יוֹחָאִי
יִפְתַּח-אֵל	יָנוּב	יִזְרָח	יוֹחַאי
יִצְהָר	יָנוֹחַ	יִזְרַחְיָה	יוֹחָנָן
יִצְחָק	יָנוֹן	יִזְרְעָאל	יוֹיָדָע
יִצְלָח	יָנִיב	יַחְדִּיאֵל	יוּכַל
יִצְלִיחַ	יָעִיר	יְחֶזְקֵאל	יוֹם-טוֹב
יִצְמָח	יִסְמַכְיָהוּ	יְחִידְקִיָּהוּ	יוֹנָדָב
יֶצֶר	יַעְבֵּץ	יִתְלָא	יוֹנָה
יִצְרִי	יָעוֹז	יְחִיאָב	יוֹנָתָן
זָקוּם	יָעוּץ	יְחִיאָח	יוּסִי
זְקוּתִיאֵל	יַעֲזִיאֵל	יְחִיאֵל	יוֹסֵי
זִקְטָן	יַעֲזִיָּהוּ	יְחִיאֵלִי	יוֹסִיאֵל
זָקִים	יַעְזֵר	יִחְיָה	יוֹסִיפוֹס
זָקִיר	יָעִיר	יְחֻזֶּה	יוֹסֵף
זִקְמְיָה	יָעִישׁ	יָחִיל	יוֹסִיפְיָה
זִקְמְעָם	יַעַל	יָחִיעָם	יוֹעָד
זָקֶּר	זָעֵל	יַחְלְאֵל	יוֹעֶז
זֶרֶד	יַעֲקֹב	יַחְמַי	יוֹעֶזֶר
יַרְדֵּן	יַעֲרָה	זָחָן	יוֹעָשׁ

זְרוּתָם	יָשֵׁן	כְּלוּבַי	לוּד
זָרוֹן	יִשְׁמַעְיָהוּ	כָּלוּל	לוּז
זָרוּם	יִשְׁעִי	כְּלִירוֹן	לוּחֵשׁ
זֶרַח	יְשַׁעְיָה	כָּלִיל	לוֹט
זרֹחָם	יְשַׁעְיָהוּ	כָּנְיָהוּ	לוֹטָן
זְרַחְמִיאֵל	יִשְׁפָּה	כָּנַנְיָהוּ	לֵוִי
זָרִיב	יִשְׁפָּן	כְּנַעֲכָה	לֵוִיטַס
זִרְזָה	יָשָׁר	כִּסְלוֹן	לוֹתָם
יִרְמְיָה	יֶשֶׁר	כְּפִיר	לַחְמִי
יִרְמְיָהוּ	יִשְׂרָאֵל	כֶּרֶם	לָטִיף
יִרְקוֹן	יִשְׂרְאֵלָה	כַּדְמִי	לִי
יֶשֶׁבְאָב	יְשֻׁרוּן	כַּדְמִיאֵל	לִיאָב
זְשֵׁבָב	יִשָּׂשכָר	כַּרְמֶל	לִיאוֹן
יִשְׁבָּח	יִתְמָה	כַּרְמְלִי	לִי-אוֹן
יִשְׁבַּח	יַתְנִיאֵל	כֶּתֶר	לִיאוֹר
יָשָׁבְעָם	יֶתֶר	כִּתְרוֹן	לֵיב
יָשׁוּב	יִתְרוֹ	כַּתְרִיאֵל	לִיהוּא
יִשְׁוָה	יִתְרָן	**ל**	לִיעַד
יִשְׁוִי	**פ**	לְאוּמִי	לִיפְמַן
יֶשׁוּעַ	כָּבוֹד	לָאוֹר	לִירוֹן
יְשׁוּעָה	כַּדּוּרִי	לָאוֹר	לַיִשׁ
יְשׁוּרִין	כָּהֲנָא	לֵב	לְמוּאֵל
יִשְׂחָק	כּוֹכָב	לָבִיא	לַעְדָּה
יֶשִׁי	כּוֹכְבָא	לָבָן	לַעְדָּן
יָשִׁישׁ	כּוֹגֵן	לִבְכָה	לַפִּיד
יָשִׁישׁ	כּוֹרֶשׁ	לְבָנָה	לַפִּידוֹת
יְשִׁישַׁי	כּוּשׁ	לְבָנוֹן	לִקְחִי
יִשְׁמָעֵאל	כָּלֵב	לִבְכִי	לָקִישׁ
יִשְׁמַעְיָה	כָּלוּב	לִבְנַת	לֶשֶׁם

מְנִי	מִיקִי	מוֹצָא	מ
מִנְיָמִין	מֵירוֹן	מוּקִי	מָאוֹר
מְנַשֶּׁה	מִישָׁאֵל	מוּקִיר	מֵאִיר
מִסְפָּר	מֵישָׁע	מוֹר	מְאִירִי
מַעְדִי	מֵישָׁר	מוֹרָשׁ	מֵאָנִי
מַעֲדִיָה	מִיכְבָּד	מוּשִׁי	מְאַשֵּׁר
מְעָדָן	מַכַּבִּי	מוֹשֵׁע	מְבוֹרָךְ
מָעוֹז	מָכִיר	מַזָל-טוֹב	מִבְחָר
מָעוֹן	מִכְלוֹל	מָחוֹל	מִבְטָח
מַעֲזְיָה	מִכְלָל	מְחוֹגָן	מִבְטַחְיָהוּ
מְעַצָּר	מִכְמָן	מָחוֹגָן	מִבְדָּךְ
מָעִי	מִכְרִי	מָחִיר	מִבְשָׂם
מַעֲיָן	מַלְאָכִי	מַחֲלוֹן	מִבְשָׂר
מַעֲכָה	מִלָּבֵב	מַחְלִי	מֶגֶד
מַעַץ	מַלּוּךְ	מַחֲסֶה	מַגְדִּיאֵל
מַעֲשִׂי	מַלּוּכִי	מַחְסֵיָה	מֵגֵן
מַעֲשֵׂיָה	מְלַטְיָה	מַחַת	מָגֵן
מְפִיבשֶׁת	מֵלִיץ	מַטְרִי	מִדָּן
מֵפִים	מֶלֶךְ	מַטְמוֹן	מָדִי
מִקְדָח	מַלְכִּיאֵל	מֵידָד	מִדְיָן
מִצְהָל	מַלְכִּיָה	מֵי-זָהָב	מְהֻדָּר
מַצְלִיחַ	מַלְכִּי-צֶדֶק	מִיחָס	מָהִיר
מִקְלוֹת	מַלְכִּירָם	מֵיטָב	מַהֲלָל
מִקְנֵיָהוּ	מַלְכִּירָם	מֵיטִיב	מְהַלַלְאֵל
מַקְסִים	מַלְכִּישׁוּעַ	מִיכָאֵל	מַהֵר
מֹר	מַלְכָּם	מִיכָה	מַהֲרִי
מַרְגּוֹעַ	מִגְדָּל	מִיכָיָה	מוֹלִיד
מַרְגִּיעַ	מָנוֹחַ	מִיכָיָהוּ	מוּמִי
מֶרֶד	מְנַחֵם	מַיְמוֹן	מוֹעַדְיָה

מָרְדְּכַי	מְתוּשָׁאֵל	נָדָב	נָחוּם
מָרוֹם	מְתוּשֶׁלַח	נְדַבְיָה	נַחוּם
מָרוֹם	מַתִּי	נָדִיב	נָחוּנָא
מֵרוֹן	מַתְיָא	נִדְרִי	נְחוּנְיָה
מָרוֹן	מַתִּתְיָה	נֶהְדָּר	נָחוֹר
מָרְדָּה	מַתָּן	נָהוֹר	נַחֲלִיאֵל
מָרְמָה	מַתְּנַי	נָהוּר	נַחַם
מַרְנִין	מַתַּנְיָה	נְהוֹרַאי	נֶחְמָד
מַרְפֵּא	מַתַּנְיָהוּ	נָהִיר	נַחְמִיאֵל
מֶרֶץ	מַתִּתְיָה	נוֹגַהּ	נֶחֶמְיָה
מְרָרִי	מַתִּתְיָהוּ	נוֹדָע	נַחְמָן
מְשֻׁבָּח	**נ**	נוֹחָה	נַחֲמָנִי
מְשֻׁבָּח	נֶאְדָּר	נֹחַם	נֵחָן
מֹשֶׁה	נָאָה	נוֹטֵעַ	נַחְרַי
מְשׁוֹבָב	נָאוָה	נוֹטֵר	נָחָשׁ
מְשׁוּלָם	נָאוֹר	נוּי	נַחְשׁוֹן
מָטוֹשׁ	נְאוֹרַאי	נִין	נַחַת
מָשִׁיחַ	נָאוֹת	נוֹעָד	נְטִיעַ
מַשְׂכִּיל	נֶאֱמָן	נוֹעַדְיָה	נֶטַע
מִשְׁלָם	נֶאֱצָל	נוֹעָז	נְעִירוֹן
מְשֻׁלָּם	נָבוֹן	נוֹעָם	נְטְרוֹנַאי
מְשֶׁלֶמְיָה	נָבוֹת	נוֹצֵר	נִיב
מִשְׁמַנָּה	נִבְחָר	נוּר	נִילִי
מִשְׁמָע	נֶבָט	נוּרִי	יִין
מִשְׁמָר	נְבָיוֹת	נוּרִיאֵל	נִיסָן
מִשְׁעָן	נָבָל	נוּרְיָה	נִיצָן
מִשְׁעָן	נֶגֶב	נוּרִיָּה	נִיר
מָתוּן	נֹגַהּ	נֹחַ	נִירְאֵל
מָתוֹק	נָגִיב	נַחְבִּי	נִירְיָה

נִירְעָם	גֶּצֶר	סוֹמֵר	עַבְדִּיאֵל
נִכְבָּד	נַקְדִּימוֹן	סִינָן	עֹבַדְיָה
נָכוֹן	נִקְנוֹר	סִימוֹן	עֵבֶר
נִלְבָּב	גֵּר	סִימָן־טוֹב	עִבְרִי
כְּמוּאֵל	נַרְדִּימוֹן	סִינַי	עֶגְלוֹן
נָמִיר	גֵּרִי	סִיסִי	עִדּוֹ
נָמֵר	גֵּרְיָה	סִירָא	עִדּוֹא
נִמְרוֹד	גֵּרְיָהוּ	סִיסְרָא	עַדִי
נִמְשִׁי	נֵרְלִי	סֶלֶד	עֲדִיאֵל
נֵס	נָשִׂיא	סַלּוּ	עֲדָיָה
נֵס	נַרְקִיס	סָלוּא	עָדִין
נִסִי	נִמְאוֹ	סַלּוּא	עֲדִינָא
נִסִים	נָתִיב	סֶלַע	עֲדִינוֹ
נָעִים	נָתָן	סְמַכְיָהוּ	עָדִיף
נַעַם	נְתַנְאֵל	סִנְדֶּר	עֵדֶן
נָעַם	נְתַנְיָה	סָעַד	עֵדֶר
נֹעַם	נְתַנְיָהוּ	סְעַדְיָה	עֶדֶר
נַעֲמָן	ס	סַעַר	עַדְרִיאֵל
נַעֲרִי	סָבָא	סְפַי	עוֹבֵד
נַעֲרַי	סָבָא	סַפִּיר	עוֹבַדְיָה
נְעַרְיָה	סַבְיוֹן	סַפְרָא	עוֹדֵד
נְעַרְיָה	סְבִירָם	סְפֶרֶת	עוֹדִי
נֶפֶג	סַבְכַּי	סֶרֶד	עוֹז
נֹפֶךְ	סַבְתָּא	סִתְרִי	עֻז
נַפְתָּלִי	סֶגֶל	ע	עֻזִּי
נֵצַח	סוֹדִי	ע״ב	עוּדִנָה
נִצְחִי	סוֹמֶךְ	עֶבֶד	עוֹז־צִיּוֹן
נָצִיחַ	סוּסִי	עַבְדּוֹן	עוֹזֶר
נִצָּן	סוֹעֵד	עַבְדִּי	עוּלָא

עָמֵל	עָמוֹק	עֲזַרְיָהוּ	עוֹפֶר
עָמָל	עַמִּי	עֲזְרִיקָם	עוּץ
עַמָּנוּאֵל	עַמִּיאוֹר	עָטוּר	עוֹרֵב
אֲמַסְיָה	עַמִּיאֵל	עָטִיר	עַז
עֹמֶר	עַמִּידוֹר	עֶטֶר	עֹז
עַמְרוֹן	עַמִּידָן	עִיבָל	עֻזָּא
עָמְרִי	עַמִּיהוּד	עִידָן	עֻזַּאי
עַמְרָם	עַמִּיזָבָד	עִילַי	עַזְבּוּק
עֲמָשָׂא	עַמִּיזַכַּי	עֵילָם	עַזְגָּד
עֲמָשִׂי	עַמִּיחוּר	עִינָן	עֻזּוּז
עֵנָב	עַמִּיחַי	עֵיפָה	עֻזָּז
עֵנָה	עַמִּיחֵן	עֵיפַי	עֲזַזְיָהוּ
עָנוֹב	עַמִּיטוֹב	עִיר	עֻזִּי
עָנִי	עַמִּינָדָב	עִירָא	עֻזִּי
עֲנָיָה	עַמִּיעַד	עִירָד	עֲזִיאֵל
עָנָן	עַמִּיעַז	עִירוּ	עֻזִּיאֵל
עֲנָנִי	עַמִּיעֶזֶר	עִירָם	עֻזִּיָה
עֲנָנְיָה	עַמִּיצֶדֶק	עִירָן	עֻזִּיָהוּ
עֶגֶר	עַמִּי צוּר	עֶלָא	עֲזִיז
עֲנָת	עַמִּיקָם	עֶלְבּוֹן	עֲזִיזָא
עֹפֶר	עַמִּיקַר	עֵלֶז	עַזָּן
עֵפֶר	עָמִיר	עֵלִי	עֵזֶר
עָפְרָה	עַמִּירָם	עָלִיז	עֶזֶר
עֶפְרוֹן	עַמִּירָן	עָלִיס	עֶזְרָא
עָפְרִי	עֲמִירָן	עָלִיץ	עֲזַרְאֵל
עֶצְיוֹן	עֲמִישַׁי	עֶלֶס	עֶזְרָה
עֶצְיוֹנִי	עַמִּישַׁדַּי	עֶלֶץ	עֶזְרִי
עֹצֶם	עֲמִישָׁר	עַמְדִּיאֵל	עַזְרִיאֵל
עַצְמוֹן	עָמִית	עָמוֹס	עֲזַרְיָה

צִבְיוֹן	פְּנוּאֵל	פָּדוֹן	עַקַבְיָא
צָדוֹק	פִּנְחָס	פְּדָיָה	עַקְבְּנָה
צַדִּיק	פְּנִיאֵל	פְּדָיָהוּ	עָקוּב
צִדְקִיאֵל	פָּנִין	פְּדִיוֹם	עֲקִיבָא
צִדְקִיָּה	פֶּסַח	פְּדָת	עֵקֶר
צִדְקִיָּהוּ	פֶּסַח	פּוּאָה	עֶקְרוֹן
צָהֹוב	פְּסַחְיָא	פֻּוָה	עִקֵּשׁ
צַהַל	פְּסַחְיָה	פּוּט	עֲקַשְׁיָא
צוּבְבָה	פַּפָּא	פּוּטִיאֵל	עֵר
צוּעָר	פַּפּוּס	פּוּרָה	עֲרָד
צוּף	פֶּקַח	פּוּרָת	עֵרִי
צוֹפַי	פְּקַחְיָה	פָּז	עֶרֶךְ
צוֹפַר	פָּרָה	פַּזִּי	עַרְמוֹן
צוּר	פְּרוּדָא	פִּינְחָס	עַרָן
צוּרִי	פָּרוּחַ	פִּיתוֹן	עֵרָן
צוּרִיאֵל	פֶּרַח	פֶּלֶא	עֲשָׂהאֵל
צוּרִישַׁדָּי	פַּרְחִי	פְּלָאיָה	עֲשִׂיאֵל
צַח	פְּרִידָא	פֶּלֶג	עֲשָׂיָה
צַחַי	פְּרַחְיָה	פִּלְדָּשׁ	עֶשֶׁק
צַחַר	פֶּרֶץ	פַּלּוּא	עַתִּי
צַחַר	פֶּרֶשׁ	פֶּלֶט	עֲתָיָה
צְחַרְיָה	פַּשְׁחוּר	פַּלְטִי	עֲתְלִי
צִיּוֹן	פְּתוּאֵל	פַּלְטִי	עֲתַלְיָה
צַלְאֵל	פְּתַחְיָה	פַּלְטִיאֵל	עָתְנִי
צְלָתַי	**צ**	פְּלַטְיָה	עָתְנִיאֵל
צַלְמוֹן	צְבָבָה	פְּלָיָה	**פ**
צֶלֶךְ	צְבִי	פָּלָל	פַּגְעִיאֵל
צְלָפְחָד	צִבְיָא	פְּלַלְיָה	פְּדַהְאֵל
צֶלֶק	צְבִיאֵל	פֶּלֶת	פְּדָהצוּר

רָחִים	רָבָא	קִיבִי	צְלָתַר
רַחַם	רַבָּה	קַיִן	צֶמַח
רַחֲמִיאֵל	רַבִּי	קֵינָן	צָמְרִי
רַחֲמִים	רָבִיב	קִישׁ	צְפוֹ
רַחֲמָן	רָבִיד	קִישִׁי	צְפוֹר
רִיבִי	רַבִּינָא	קָלוֹנִימוּס	צְפִי
רֵיחָן	רֶגֶם	קָלִי	צְפַנְיָה
רִימוֹן	רַדִּי	קֶלְיָה	צְפַנְיָהוּ
רֶכָּב	רֹאִי	קַלְמָן	צְפִרִית
רָם	רוֹזֵן	קְמוּאֵל	צְפְרִיר
רִמּוֹן	רוֹם	קְמְחִי	צְפְרִירִי
רָמִי	רוֹמֵם	קְנַז	צְרוֹר
רָמֵי	רוֹן	קְנִיאֵל	צְרִי
רַמְיָה	רוֹנְאֵל	קַפָּרָא	צֶרֶת
רְמַלְיָהוּ	רוֹנִי	קְבַח	ק
רֹן	רֹנִי	קָרֵחַ	קָדִישׁ
רָנָה	רוֹנֵן	קָרְחָה	קֶדֶם
רָנִי	רוֹנְלִי	קָרִיב	קֶדְמָה
רַנֶּן	רוֹעִי	קָרִין	קַדְמִיאֵל
רַע	רוֹתֵם	קָרְדִּי	קֶדָר
רֵעִי	רָז	קַרְנִיאֵל	קֹדֶת
רְעוּאֵל	רָזִי	ר	קוֹבִי
רֵעִי	רָזִיאֵל	רָאָה	קֹהֶלֶת
רְעֶלְיָה	רְחַבְיָה	רְאוּבֵן	קוּדֶלֶת
רַעֲמְיָה	רְחַבְיָהוּ	רֹאִי	קוֹלַיָה
רַעֲנָן	רְחַבְעָם	רְאָיָה	קוֹץ
רְפָא	רְחוֹב	רָאָם	קוֹרֵא
רְפָּה	רָחוּם	רֹאשׁ	קוּשָׁיָהוּ
רְפָאֵל	רְחוּם	רַב	קָטָן

שַׁלְמַי	שְׂעֹרֵי	שָׂגֵב	דָּפוּא
שַׁלְמִי	שַׁי	שָׂגוּב	רֶפַח
שְׁלֶמְיָה	עֵיאוּל	שַׂגִּיא	רְפָר
שֶׁלֶמְיָהוּ	שִׂיאוֹן	שְׂדֵיאוּר	רָפִי
שַׁלְמָן	שִׂיאֵל	שַׁדְמוֹן	רְפָיָה
שֶׁלֶף	שִׁילָא	שֹׁהַם	רִמְרֹם
שָׁלֵשׁ	שִׁימוֹן	שָׁוֵא	רָצוֹן
שַׁלְתִּיאֵל	שִׁימִי	שׁוּבָאֵל	רִצִין
שֵׁם	שִׁישָׁא	שׁוֹבָב	רֶקַח
שְׁמָא	שִׁישִׁי	שׁוֹבִי	רֶקֶם
שַׁמַּאי	שֶׁכֶם	שׁוֹבָל	רֶשֶׁף
שְׁמוּאֵל	שַׂכְנָא	שׁוֹבֵק	רֹתֶם
שָׁמוּעַ	שְׁכַנְיָה	שׁוֹחַ	ש
שֶׁמַח	שְׁכַנְיָהוּ	נְּוֹחָה	שָׁאוּל
שִׂמְחָה	שָׂכָר	שׁוֹתָם	שְׁאַלְתִּיאֵל
שִׂמְחוֹן	שֵׁלָה	שׁוּמָה	שַׁאֲנָן
שִׂמְחִי	שֶׁלֶו	שׁוֹמֵר	שְׁאָר־יָשׁוּב
שֵׁם־טוֹב	שָׁלוֹם	שׁוּנִי	שֵׁבָא
שִׁמְחוֹנִי	שַׁלּוּם	שׁוּעַ	שְׁבוּאֵל
שַׁמַּי	שְׁלוֹמִי	שׁוֹעָל	שֶׁבַח
שָׁמִיר	שְׁלוֹמִיאֵל	שׁוּר	שֹׁבִי
שַׂמְלָה	שְׁלוֹמִית	שׁוּשָׁן	שְׁבָנָה
שֶׁמַע	שַׁלּוּן	שׁוֹשָׁן	שְׁבַנָא
שָׁמָע	שַׁלְתִּי	שׁוּתֶלַח	שְׁבַנְיָה
שִׁמְעוֹן	שָׁלֵם	שַׁחַף	שֶׁבַע
שִׁמְעִי	שַׁלְמָה	שַׁחַר	שֶׁבֶר
שְׁמַעְיָה	שְׁלֹמֹה	שַׁחֲרָיָה	שַׁבְּתַי
שְׁמַעְיָהוּ	שַׁלְמוֹן	שַׁחֲרַיִם	שָׁבִיט
שֶׁמֶר	שַׁלְמוֹנִי	שָׂטָה	שָׁגָא

תַּחַן	שָׂרוּג	שִׁמְרוֹן
תַּחַשׁ	שָׂרוֹן	שִׁמְרִי
תַּחַת	שָׂרִי	שִׂמְרִי
תִּילוֹן	שַׂרִיאֵל	שְׁמַרְיָה
תֵּימָן	שָׂרִיג	שְׁמַרְיָהוּ
תֵּימָנִי	שְׂרָיָה	שְׁמַרְעָם
תֵּל־חַי	שְׂרָיָה	שִׁמְשׁוֹן
תֶּלֶם	שְׂרָיָהוּ	שִׁמְשַׁי
תַּלְמִי	שִׂרְיוֹן	שֹׁנִי
תַּלְמַי	שִׂרְיָן	שָׁנִי
תָּם	שְׂרִירָא	שְׁנֵיאוֹר
תָּמוּז	שְׂרָלִי	שְׁעַרְיָה
תֶּמַח	שֶׁרֶשׁ	שְׂעֹרִים
תָּמוּר	שָׂשׁוֹן	שָׁפָט
תָּמִיר	שֵׁשָׁן	שְׁפַטְיָה
תְּנָא	שָׁשַׁק	שְׁפַטְיָהוּ
תַּנְחוּם	שֵׁשֶׁת	שִׁפְטָן
תַּנְחוּמָא	שֵׁת	שַׁפִּיר
תִּקְוָה	שָׁתוּל	שָׁפָם
תַּרְדִּיוֹן	שָׁתִיל	שָׁפָן
תֶּרַח	שֶׁתֶל	שֶׁפַע
תַּרְיָא	ת	שֶׁקֶר
תַּרְשִׁישׁ	תְּאֹם	שִׁפְרוֹן
תֶּשֶׁר	תָּבוֹר	שַׁפְרִיר
	תִּדְהָר	שָׁקֵד
	תַּדְמוֹר	שִׁקְמוֹן
	תּוֹלָע	שָׁקְמוֹן
	תּוֹמֶר	שְׂרַגָּא
	תַּחְכְּמֹנִי	שְׂרַגָּאִי

Feminine Hebrew
Name Index

אַמִיצָה	אַיֶּלָה	אַהֲרוֹנִית	א
אַמִירָה	אִילוֹנָה	אוֹדְיָה	אֲבוּקָה
אֲמָנָה	אִילָנָה	אַוִירִית	אַבְטַלְיָה
אָמְנָה	אַיֶּלֶת	אוֹדֶלְיָה	אַבִּי
אַמְצוּ	אַיֶּלֶת	אוֹפִירָה	אֲבִיאֵלָה
אֲמִיתָה אֲמִיתָה	אַיֶּלֶת־הַשַּׁחַר	אוֹפֶר	אֲבִיבָה
אָסְנָת	אִילִית	אוֹפְנָת	אֲבִיבִי
אֶסְתֵּר	אִילָנִית	אוֹצָרָה	אֲבִיבִית
אֶסְתֵּרָה	אִידִיס	אוֹרָה	אֲבִיגְדוֹרָה
אֶסְתֵּרִיָה	אִידְרִית	אוּרִיאֵלָה	אֲבִיגַיִל
אֲפֵקָה	אֵיתָנָה	אוֹרִית	אֲבִיָּה
אַפְרוֹדִית	אֵלָה	אוֹרִית	אֲבִיחַיִל
אֶפְרָת	אֵלוֹנָה	אוֹרְלִי	אֲבִי־יוֹנָה
אֶפְרָתָה	אֵלוֹנָה	אוֹר־לִי	אֲבִיעֵל
אֶרְאֵלָה	אַלוּפָה	אוֹרְלִית	אֲבִירָה
אַרְבֵּל	אֶלִיאוֹרָה	אוֹרְנָה	אֲבִירָמָה
אַרְדָה	אֵלָנָה	אוֹרְנִית	אֲבִישַׁג
אַרְדּוֹנָה	אֵלְיָה	אוֹרְנִית	אַדְוָה
אַרְזָה	אֵלִינוֹעַר	אוֹשָׁה	אֲדִיבָה
אַרְזָה	אֵלִיכֶּר	אוֹשְׁרָה	אַדִירָה
אַרְזִית	אֵלִימוֹר	אוֹשְׁרִיָה	אַדְרָה
אֲרִיאֵל	אֵלִיעֶזְרָה	אוֹשֶׁרֶת	אַדֶּרֶת
אֲרִיאֵלָה	אֵלִיעֶנָה	אַחֲנָה	אַהֲבָה
אַרְמוֹנָה	אֱלִישֶׁבַע	אֲחוּזָה	אֲהוּבָה
אַרְנָה	אַלֶכְּסַנְדְרָה	אֲחִינֹעַם	אֲהוּדָה
אַרְנוֹנָה	אַלְמָה	אִידִית	אָהֳלָה
אָרְנִי	אִמָּא	אַיָה	אָהֳלִיאָב
אַרְנִינָה	אִמָּה	אִינָה	אָהֳלִיבָה
אָרְנִית	אֱמוּנָה	אִיזֶבֶל	אַהֲרוֹנָה

אָרְבַת	בְּכוּרָה	בַּת גְּלִים	גְּדֵרָה
אֶרֶץ	בְּכוֹרָה	בַּת-חֵן	גּוֹאֶלֶת
אֲשָׁנָה	בְּכָרָה	בַּת-עַמִּי	גּוֹזָלָה
אֶשְׁדָה	בְּכוּרָה	בַּת-צִיּוֹן	גּוֹלְדָה
אַשְׂרָה	בְּכִירָה	בַּת-שֶׁבַע	גּוֹלְדָה מְאִירָה
אֲשֵׁרִית	בִּלְהָה	בַּת-שׁוּעַ	גּוֹלְדִי
אָשְׁרַת	בַּלְפוּרְיָה	בַּת-שַׁחַר	גּוּרִית
אַתִּי	בִּנְיָמִינָה	בַּת-שֵׁם	גִּזָּה
אִתִּיל	בְּעוּלָה	בְּתוּאֵל	גָּזִית
אֶתְנָה	בָּצְרָה	בְּתוּלָה	גִּיאָה
ב	בִּקְעָה	בַּתְיָה	גִּיאוֹרָה
בְּאֵרִית	בַּקָּרָה	בִּתְיָה	גִּיוֹרָה
בְּבָה	בָּרָה	ג	גִּיוֹרֶת
בַּבָּה	בְּרוּכָה	גְּאוּלָה	גִּילָה
בְּבָתִי	בֵּרוֹנִיקָה	גְּאָלָה	גִּילִי
בַּהַט	בְּרוּרָה	גְּאַלְיָה	גִּילְיָה
בְּהִירָה	בְּרוּרְיָה	גְּבוּרָה	גִּילִית
בּוּנָה	בְּרוֹשָׁה	גַּבִּי	גִּילְנָה
בּוֹנָה	בְּרָכָה	גְּבִירָה	גִּילַת
בּוֹשֶׂמֶת	בַּרְקָאִית	גִּבְעָה	גִּיתָּה
בּוֹשְׂמַת	בָּרֶקֶת	גְּבְעוּלָה	גִּיתִּית
בְּחוּרָה	בָּרְקַת	גְּבְעוֹנָה	גִּינָה
בְּחִירָה	בְּשׂוֹרָה	גַּבְרִיאֵלָה	גִּינַת
בִּטְחָה	בָּשְׂמָה	גַּבְרִיאֵלָה	גַּל
בִּינָה	בָּשְׂמַת	גַּבַּת	גַּלִּי
בִּירָה	בַּת-אֵל	גַּדָּה	גַּלְיָה
בִּירָנָה	בְּתוּאֵל	גְּדוּלָה	גַּלִילָה
בִּירָנִית	בְּתוּאֵלָה	גַּדִּית	גַּלִילְיָה
בִּיתָנְיָה	בְּתוּאֵלִי	גִּדְעוֹנָה	גַּלִיכָה

גָּלִית
גִּלְעָדָה
גְּמוּלָה
גְּמַלְיָאֵלָה
גְּמַלְיָאֵלִית
גֹּמֶר
גִּמְרָה
גִּנָּה
גִּנָּה
גַּנִּית
גֶּפֶן
גַּפְנָה
גְּרוּשָׁה
גָּרְנָה
גַּרְנִית
גֵּרְשׁוֹנָה
גַּת
גִּתָּה
גִּתִּית

ד

דָּאָה
דַּבָּה
דְּבוֹרָה
דְּבִירָה
דִּבְלָה
דִּבְלָתָה
דָּבְרַת
דָּבְשָׁה
דְּגוּלָה

דָּגְנִיָּה
דַּגְנִית
דּוֹרִית
דָּוִידָה
דּוֹבְבָה
דּוֹבֶבֶת
דּוּבָה
דּוֹדָה
דּוֹרוֹנָה
דּוֹרוֹנִית
דּוֹרִית
דִּיבוֹנָה
דַּיָּה
דִּימוֹנָה
דִּינָה
דִּינָר
דִּיצָה
דִּיקְלָה
דַּלָּה
דַּלְיָה
דְּלִיָה
דְּלִילָה
דָּלִית
דָּנָה
דָּנִיאֵלָה
דַּנְיָה
דָּנִית
דַּסִּי
דֵּעָה

דַּעַת
דַּפְנָה
דַּפְנִית
דְּקֶלָה
דְּקֵלִית
דְּרוֹמִית
דְּרוֹרָה
דְּרוֹרִית
דַּתְיָה

ה

הָגָר
הַדּוּרָה
הֶדְיָה
הֲדַס
הֲדַסָּה
הֲדַר
הֲדָרָה
הֲדָרִית
הוֹדִיָּה
הִילָה
הִילִי
הִלָּה
הִלֵּלָה
הִלְנָה
הַנִּימָה
הַצְלָחָה
הַרְאֵלָה
הַרְדְּפָנָה
הֶרְצְלָה

הֶרְצֵלְיָה

ו

וֶרֶד
וַרְדָּה
וַרְדִּיָה
וַרְדִּינָה
וַרְדִּית

ז

זְאֵבָה
זְבוּדָה
זְבוּלָה
זְבִידָה
זָהֲבָה
זְהֵבָה
זְהָבִי
זְהָבִית
זְהוּבָה
זְהוֹרִית
זְהִירָה
זְהֶרָה
זְהוּבִית
זֹהַר
זְהֵרִי
זוֹהַר
זוֹהֲרָה
זוֹהֶרֶת
זוּרַחַת
זִינָה
זִיוִית

ט	חֲבַצֶּלֶת הַשָּׁרוֹן חֶמְדִּיָה	זִיוָנִית
טוֹבָה	חִבַּת צִיּוֹן חֲמִידָה	זִיכְרוֹנִי
טוֹבִית	חַגִּיָה חֲמוּטַל	זִירָה
טוּבִית	חַגִּית חֲמָנִיָּה	זַיִת
טִירָה	חָגְלָה חֵן	זֵיתָה
טַל	חֶדְוָה חַנָּה	זֵיתָנָה
טַל-אוֹר	חֹדֶשׁ חִנָּה	זַכָּה
טַל-אוֹרָה	חֲדָשָׁה חֲנוּכָּה	זַכּוֹת
טָלָה	חַוָּה חֲנוּנָה	זַכִּיָּה
טַלּוֹרָה	חוּלְדָּה חַנִּיָּה	זַפִּית
טַלְיָה	חוּלָה חֲנִית	זִכְרוֹנָה
טְלִילָה	חוּמָה חֲנִּית	זְכַרְיָה
טַלִּי	חוּמִי חֲנִיתָא	זְכַרִינִי
טַלְלִית	חוֹסָה חֲנִיתָה	זִלְפָּה
טָלָל	חוּפְשִׁית חׇכְנִית	זְמוֹרָה
טַל-לִי	חוֹרְשִׁית חֲסוּדָה	זְמִירָה
טַלְלִי	חֶדְוֹנָה חֲסִידָה	זִמְרָה
טַלְמוֹנָה	חַיָּה חֲסִיָּה	זִמְרִיָּה
טַלְמוֹנִית	חִיּוּתָה חֲסִיכָה	זְפִירָה
טַלְמוֹר	חַיּוּתָה חֶפְצִי	זִפְרָה
טְמִידָה	חַיֵּי-שָׂרָה חֶפְצִי-בָּה	זִפְרוֹנָה
טְעִימָה	חֵיָּמָה חֶפְצִיָּה	זְקוּפָה
טִבְעוֹנָה	חִילָה חֶצְרוֹנָה	זְקִיפָה
טַפַּת	חֲכִילָה חֲרוּצָה	זְקֵנָה
טָרָה	חֶלְאָה חֵרוּת	זְרִיזָה
י	חֶלְדָּה חֲרוּתָה	ח
יָאָה	חֲלִי-לָה חֶרְמוֹנָה	חִבָּה
יָאִירָה	חֶלְקַת חַשְׁמוֹנָה	חֲבִיבָה
יַבְנְאֵלָה	חֶמְדָּה חַשְׁמוֹנִית	חֲבַצֶּלֶת

ל	יְרִיעוֹת	בַלָתָּא	יְגָאֵלָה
לֵאָה	יַרְקוֹנָה	יָמֹה	יְדִידָה
לְאוּמָה	יִשְׁוָה	יְמִימָה	יְהָבָה
לְאָמָה	יְשׁוּעָה	יְמִינָה	יְהוּדִית
לִבָּה	יְשִׁיבָה	יִמְנָה	יְהוֹעֶדֶן
לִבּוֹנָה	יְשִׁישָׁה	יָנוֹחָה	יְהוֹשֶׁבַע
לְבִיא	יְשָׁנָה	יֶגְטֶה	יְהוֹשַׁבְעַת
לְבִיאָה	יִשְׁעָה	יִסְכָּה	יָהֵל
לִבְנָה	יִשְׂרָאֵלָה	יַסְמִין	יָהֱלִי
לִבְנָה	יִשְׂרְאֵלִית	יַסְמִינָה	יַהֲלוֹמָה
לִבְנֶה	יְשָׂרָה	יְנִיקָה	יַהֲלוֹמִית
לִבְנָת	כ	יָעֵל	יוֹאֵלָה
לוּנָה	כְּבוּדָה	יְעֵלָה	יוֹאֵלִית
לֵוִנָה	כּוֹכָבָה	יְעֵלִית	יוֹבֶלָה
לְטִיפָה	כּוֹכָבִית	יַעֲלִית	יוֹדִית
לִי	כּוֹכֶבֶת	יָעֵן	יוֹחָנָה
לִיאוֹר	כָּזְבִּי	יַעֲקֹבָה	יוֹעֵד
לִיאוֹרָה	כְּלוּלָה	יַעְרָה	יוֹכֶבֶד
לִיאוֹרִית	כְּלִילָה	יָעֵה	יוֹנָה
לִיאַת	כְּלָנִית	יְמְהַמִיָּה	יוֹנִינָה
לִידְרוֹר	כַּנָּה	יָפִית	יוֹנִית
לִיָה	כִּנֶּרֶת	יִפְעָה	יוֹנָתִי
לִיהִיא	כַּסְפִּית	יִפְעַת	יוֹסִיפָה
לִיהִי	כְּפִירָה	יַקִּירָה	יוֹסְפָה
לִידָה	כַּרְמָה	יְקָרָה	יִזְרְעֶאלָה
לִיעַל	כַּרְמִיָה	יִקְרַת	יְחֶזְקֵאלָה
לִילָה	כַּרְמִית	יַרְדֵּנָה	יְחִיאֵלָה
לִילָה	כַּרְמְלָה	יָרוֹכָה	יָטְבָה
לִילִי	כַּרְמְלִית	ירוּשָׁה	יָטְבָתָה

מַרְגָנִית	מַלְכָּה	מוֹרִית	לִילִי
מַרְגֵעָה	מַלְכִּית	מוֹרָשָׁה	לִילָךְ
מַרְדוּת	מִנְגִינָה	מוֹשָׁעָה	לִילִית
מָרָה	מָנֶה	מַזְהִירָה	לִימוֹר
מַרְוָה	מְנוּחָה	מַזָל	לִינָה
מְרוֹמָה	מְנוֹדָה	מַחְלָה	לִינִית
מֶרְחָבָה	מִנְחָה	מַחֲלַת	לִידוֹן
מֶרְחַבְיָה	מָנַחַת	מַטְמוֹנָה	לִידַז
מְרִי	מְנַחְמָה	מִיָה	לִידִית
מִרְיָם	מְנַחְמִיָה	מִיטַל	לִידָן
מֶרְיַת	מַסָדָה	מִיכָאֵלָה	לִיתַג
מַרְנִינָה	מְעוּזָה	מִיכַיְהוּ	מ
מִרְצָה	מְעוֹנָה	מִיכַל	מְאוֹרָה
מִרְדַּת	מַעְיָן	מִילִי	מְאִירָה
מֶרְתָה	מַעְיָנָה	מִילְכָּה	מַאֲרָה
מַשְׂאַת	מַעֲכָה	מִינָה	מִבְטַחַת
מִשְׂבָּחָה	מַעֲנִית	מִיפַעַת	מְבֹרֶכֶת
מִשְׂבַּחַת	מִפְרָחָה	מֵירָב	מַגְדָה
מַשְׂכִּיָה	מִפְרַחַת	מִירָה	מִגְדָלָה
מַשְׂכִּית	מִצָדָה	מִירִי	מִגְדָנָה
מְשֻׁלֶמֶת	מִצְהָלָה	מִירִית	מַגֵנָה
מִשְׂמֶרֶת	מַצְהֶלֶת	מַכַּבִּית	מָגִינָה
מַשְׂעֵנָה	מַצִילָה	מִכְבָּדָה	מְדִינָה
מְתוּקָה	מַצְלִיחָה	מַלְבֶּבֶת	מְהִירָה
מַתְיָה	מִצְפָּה	מַלְבִּינָה	מוֹלֶדֶת
מַתְכֹּנֶת	מַקְסִימָה	מִלִי	מוֹפַעַת
מַתָּנָה	מֹר	מַלְיָה	מוֹר
מִתְעַלָה	מֶרָב	מַלְאָךְ	מוֹרִיאֵל
מַתָּת	מַרְגָלִית	מַלְכָּה	מוֹרִיָה

ג	נוׄטֵרָה	נִימָה	גְצָנָה
נָאָה	נוׄטֶרֶת	נִיעָה	גְצָנִית
גְאַדְרָה	נוׄזָה	נִיצָה	גְצְרָה
גְאַדֶּרֶת	כָוִית	נִצְחִיָה	נִרְדָּה
נָאוָה	נוׄעַדָה	נִיצָנָה	גֵרָה
נָאוׄרָה	נוׄעַדְיָה	גִירְאֵל	נֵרְלִי
נָאֱמָנָה	נוׄעָה	נִירִית	נַרְקִיסָה
נָאֱמֶנֶת	נוׄעֶזָּה	נִירָה	נְתִיבָה
נֶאֱצָלָה	נוׄפִיָה	נִכְבְּדָה	נְתִיעָנָה
נֶאֱצֶלֶת	נוׄפֶר	נְכוׄחָה	נְתַעֲנָה
נְבוׄנָה	נוׄצֶרֶת	נְכוׄנָה	נְתַנְאֵלָה
נִבְחָרָה	נוּרִית	נִלְבְּבָה	ס
נִבְחֶרֶת	נוּרִיתָה	נִלְבֶּבֶת	סַבְיוׄן
נְבִיאָה	נְזִירָה	נְמֵרָה	סַבְיוׄנָה
כֹגַּה	נְזִירְיָה	נָסָה	סְבִירָה
נְגִידָה	נָחָה	נַסְיָה	סַבְלָנוּת
נְגִינָה	גֶחָה	נְסִיכָה	סַבְרִיגָה
נְדִיבָה	נַחֲלָה	נׄעָה	סְגוּלָה
נַדִין	נַחֲלַת	נְעִימָה	סְגֻלָה
נֶהְדָּרָה	נֶחָמָה	נֹעַם	סְגֻלָה
נֶהְדֶּרֶת	נְחָשְׁתָּא	נַעֲמָה	סְגַלְיָה
נְהוׄרָה	נַחַת	נָעֳמִי	סִגְלִית
נְהוּדְרָה	נְטִיעָה	נַעֲמִית	סַהֲרָה
נְהִירָה	נֶטַע	נַעֲמָנָה	סִיגְלִית
נֶהְדָּרָה	נְטָעָה	נַעֲרָה	סִיגְלָה
נוׄאִית	נִיבָה	נַמְשִׁיָה	סִיגָלְיָה
נוׄגַּה	נִיגָה	נִצָה	סִידוׄנָה
נוׄגַהַת	נִילִי	נִצְחָה	סִיוָנָה
נָוֶה	נִילִית	נִצְחִיָה	סִימָה

סִימוֹנָה	עֲדִיָה	עִילִית	עֲנָגָה
סֶלָה	עֲדִיָה	עִיפָּה	עֲנוּפָה
סַלְחָה	עֲדִיָה	עִירָא	עֲנָפָה
סְלִילָה	עֲדִינָה	עִירִית	עֲנָת
סְמָדַר	עֲדִיפָּה	עַכְסָה	עֲנָוָה
סְמִירָה	עֲדִית	עָלָה	עֵינָא
סְנָאִית	עֲדִית	עֲלוּמָה	עֲסִיסָה
סַנָה	עֶדְנָה	עֲלוּמִית	עָפְרָה
סְנוּנִית	עוֹגַנְיָה	עֶלְדָה	עָפְרָה
סַנְסַנָה	עוֹדְדָה	עַלְיָה	עָפְרוֹנָה
סַעֲדָה	עוֹדְרָה	עֲלִיזָה	עָפְרִית
סְסְגּוֹנָא	עוֹמֶר	עֶלְיָנָא	עֶצְיוֹנָה
סַפָּה	עוֹמְרִית	עֲלִיסָה	עָצְמָה
סֶפַח	עוֹפְרָה	עֲלִיצָה	עַצְמוֹנָה
סַפִּיר	עוֹפְרָה	עֲלִית	עָרְגָה
סַפִּירָה	עוֹפְרִית	עַלְמָה	עַרְמוֹנָה
סַפִּירִית	עַזָה	עֶלְסָה	עַרְמוֹנִית
סֶרַח	עֲזוּבָה	עֶלְצָה	עָרְפָּה
סַרִינָה	עֲזִידָה	עֲמוּמָה	עֲשִׁירָה
ע	עֲזִית	עֲמִיאוֹר	עֶשְׂרוֹנִית
עֶבְרוֹנָה	עֶזְרָאֵלָה	עֲמִירָה	עֲתִידָה
עִבְרִיָה	עֶזְרָה	עֲמִיתָה	עֲתִירָה
עִבְרִית	עֲזְרִיאֵלָה	עֲמַלְיָה	עָתְנָה
עִבְרִיתָה	עֲזְרִיאֵלָה	עַמְנוּאֵלָה	עֲתַלְיָה
עֶגְלָה	עֲטוּרָה	עָמְרָה	עֲטָרָה
עֶגְלָה	עֲטִירָה	עָמְרִי	עֲטֶרֶת
עָדָה	עֲטָרָה	עָמְרִית	פ
עֲדִי	עֲטֶרֶת	עֲנָבָה	פְּדָנִיָה
עֲדִיאֵלָה	עִידִית	עֵנָב	פְּדוּת

פּוֹדָה	צֶהֲלָה	צִפְרָה	קֶשֶׁת
פּוֹעָה	צְהוּבָה	צַפְרָא	**ר**
פּוּרָה	צוּבָה	צִפְרָה	רָאָה
פּוּרַחַת	צוּפִי	צִפְרִיָה	רְאוּבֵנָה
פּוּרְיָה	צוּפִיָה	צִפְרִירָה	רְאוּבַת
פָּז	צוֹפִית	צַפְרִירִית	רְאוּמָה
פָּזָה	צוּר-אֵל	אֶפְרָתָה	רְאוּמִי
פַּזְיָה	צוּרְיָה	צָרָה	רְאָמָה
פַּזִית	צוּרִית	צְרוּיָה	רִאשׁוֹנָה
פְּעֻדָה	צֶחָה	צְרוּעָה	רְבִיבָה
פֻּנָּה	צְחוֹרָה	**ק**	רַבִּיעֵל
פִּיוּטָה	צְחוֹרִית	קָדָד	רַבִּינָה
פִּירְתָּה	צִיוֹנָה	קֶדְמָה	רִבְקָה
פִּירְחִיָּה	צִילָה	קוֹרֶגֶת	רוּחָמָה
פְּנִינָה	צִילִי	קְטוּרָה	רְוִיאֵל
פְּנִינִית	צִינָה	קְטִיפָה	רַוִית
פְּנִנָּה	צִלָּה	קְטָעָה	רוֹמָה
פְּסִיָה	צִלְחָה	קָמָה	רוּמָה
פְּרוּמָה	צָלִיל	קְצִיָה	רוֹמִיָה
פֶּרַח	צְלִילָה	קְצִיעָה	רוּמִיָה
פִּרְחָה	צְלִילִי	קַרְנִיָה	רוּמִית
פִּרְחִית	צְלֶלְפּוֹנִי	קֶרֶן	רוֹמֵמָה
פְּרִיחָה	צַמֶּרֶת	קֶרֶן הַפּוּךְ	רוּמִמִית
פִּרְחִיָה	צְעָדָה	קַרְנָה	רוֹן
צ	צְעִירָה	קַרְנִי	רוֹנָה
צְאֵלָה	צְפוֹנָה	קַרְנִיאֵלָה	רוֹנִי
צִבְיָה	צִפּוֹרָה	קֶרֶת	רוֹנִיָה
צִבְיָה	צִפִּיָה	קַשׁוּבָה	רוּנִית
צְדָקָה	צְפִירָה	קְשִׁישָׁה	רוֹנְלִי

שְׁלָמִית	שׁוּלָה	דְּנָנָה	רוּת
שְׁמוּאֵלָה	שׁוֹמְרָה	רָנָנִית	רוּתִי
שִׂמְחָה	שׁוּלַמִית	רַנַת	רוּתָם
שִׂמְחוֹנָה	שׁוֹמְרוֹנָה	רְכַתְיָה	רָז
שִׂמְחִית	שׁוֹמְרִית	רְעוּמָה	רָזִי
שִׁמְעוֹנָה	שׁוּנִית	רַעְיָה	רָזִיאֵלָה
שִׁמְעַת	שׁוּנַמִית	רַעֲנָנָה	רָזִנָה
שָׁמְרָה	שׁוּעָא	רְפָאֵלָה	רָזִינָה
שָׁמְרִיָה	שׁוּרָה	רְפוּאָה	רָזִילִי
שָׁמְרִית	שׁוֹשָׁן	רֹלִי	רָחָב
שִׁמְשׁוֹנָה	שׁוֹשָׁנָה	רִצְפָּה	רָחֵל
שַׁפִּירָה	שׁוֹתֵלָה	רִקְמָה	רְחָמָה
שִׁפְעָה	שׁוֹתֶלֶת	רַקֶפֶת	רִיבָה
שִׁפְרָה	שְׁחוֹרָה	רִשְׁפָּה	רִיבִי
שַׁפְרִירָה	שַׁחַר	רִשְׁפּוֹנָה	רֵיחָנָה
שְׁקֵדָה	שַׁחֲרִית	רֶתֶם	רֵייזֶעל
שַׁקְמָה	שְׁטוּה	**ש**	רֵייזְל
שִׁקְמוֹנָה	שִׂיאוֹנָה	שְׁאָגָה	רִימוֹנָה
שָׂרָה	שִׂירָאֵל	שְׁאוּלָה	רִמוֹנָה
שָׂרָה	שִׁירָה	שְׁאִיתָה	דִינָה
שָׂרוֹן	שִׁירִי	שַׁאֲנָנָה	דִינַת
שָׂרוֹנָה	שִׁירְלִי	שְׁאֵרָה	רָמָה
שָׂרוֹנִית	שַׁלְגִיָה	שְׁבוֹלֶת	רִמּוֹן
שֶׂרַח	שַׁלְגִית	שָׁבְתָה	רְמַזְיָה
שָׂרַי	שַׁלְהֶבֶת	שְׁבִיבִיָה	רָמִית
שָׂרִיד	שַׁלְוָה	שִׁבֹּלֶת	רֹנָה
שְׁרִיטָה	שְׁלוֹמִית	שֶׁבַע	רְנָה
שְׁרִית	שְׁלוֹמְצִיוֹן	שִׁדְמָה	רָנִית
שְׁרִיתָה	שַׁלְמָה	שִׂדְרָה	רְנִיתָה

תִּמְנָע	שַׂרִינָה
תָּמָר	שְׁתוּלָה
תֹּמֶר	שְׁתִילָה
תִּמְרָה	**ת**
תְּנוּבָה	תְּאוֹרָה
תְּנִיר	תְּבוּנָה
תִּפְאָרָה	תְּבוֹרָה
תִּפְאֶרֶת	תַּגָּה
תַּפּוּחַ	תִּגְרָה
תִּפְרָחָה	תָּהָל
תִּפְרַחַת	תְּהִילָה
תִּקְוָה	תּוֹחֶלֶת
תְּקוּמָה	תּוֹמִי
תְּרוּמָה	תּוֹמֶר
תְּרוּפָה	תּוּשִׁיָה
תִּרְזָה	תְּחִיָה
תִּרְצָה	תִּימוֹרָה
תַּרְשִׁישָׁה	תִּירִי
תְּשְׁבָּחָה	תְּכוּנָה
תִּשְׁבַּחַת	תִּכְלָה
תְּשׁוּעָה	תַּלְמָה
תְּשׁוּרָה	תַּלְמִית
	תַּמָּה
	תְּמוּרָה
	תְּמוֹרָה
	תְּמִי
	תְּמִימָה
	תְּמִירָה
	תִּמְנָה

Transliterated Index of Masculine and Feminine Hebrew Names

MASCULINE NAMES

Abaw 1, 2, 155, 200, 227, 260
Abawhu 155
Abeer 26, 141, 156, 165, 168, 180
Abeeree 3, 141, 156, 165, 180
Abir see Abeer
Achaw 10, 26
Achazyaw 68
Achbawn 23, 41, 63, 176, 178, 246, 258, 289, 291, 299
Acheedawn 233, 235
Achee-melech 28, 37, 63, 95
Acheenayr 138, 222
Acheenoam 105
Acheerawn 2, 9, 170, 203
Acheeshawlom 219
Acheetuv 159, 180, 190, 215, 297, 298
Acheetzedek 233
Acheetzur 115, 134, 144, 280
Adawr 36, 39, 40, 90, 97, 103, 157, 161, 180, 188, 203, 239, 254, 225, 262
Adeeayl 157, 158, 195, 260
Adeer 5, 41, 156, 170, 193, 203
Adir see Adeer
Admon 5, 53, 122, 124, 286
Adoneeyaw 6, 9, 20, 37, 38, 64, 157, 158, 161, 166, 170, 228, 297
Adoneeyawhu 158, 203
Aharon 1, 11, 14, 28, 31, 66, 69, 95, 102, 110, 129, 133, 136, 138, 159, 161, 165, 166, 168, 182, 191, 195, 199, 246, 259, 261, 277
Ahuveeyaw 159, 163
Akavyaw 219, 230
Akeevaw 6, 82, 219, 230, 296
Aleksandyr 8, 33, 117, 118, 161, 213
Alis 160, 162, 200
Alitz 160, 162
Aliz 160, 162, 200, 208, 233, 239
Almog 53, 122, 124, 286
Almon 8
Alon 9, 162, 173
Altayr 9, 173
Aluf 162, 226
Amaryaw 164, 175, 190, 197, 198, 221
Amaryawhu 19, 278
Amatzyaw 46, 50, 259, 280
Amee 10
Ameead 40, 195
Ameeayl 10, 38
Ameechai 33, 291, 301

Ameechayn 31, 218, 230, 231, 258
Ameedawn 192
Ameenawdawv 2, 9, 31, 48, 157, 166, 228, 297
Ameerawn 110, 166, 195, 199, 244, 256, 265
Ameeron 110, 265
Ameesawn 163, 201, 263, 299
Ameeshawr 18, 195, 199, 256, 265
Ameetai 11, 13, 46, 47, 58, 122, 159, 163, 164, 182, 185, 201, 202, 205, 206, 225, 228, 241, 263, 293, 294, 299, 300, 301
Ameetuv 215, 303
Ameetz see Amitz
Ameetzedek 233
Ameezakai 181, 227, 236, 274, 276
Amir see Awmir
Amitz 156
Amnon 11, 47, 58, 81, 159, 163, 182, 185, 201, 202, 205, 206, 225, 228, 241, 263, 293, 294, 299, 300, 301
Amrawm 11, 201, 264, 301
Amtzaw 201
Anaw 110, 166, 182, 195, 199, 246, 259
Arayl 12, 32, 166, 167
Araylee 166, 167
Aree 32, 80, 87, 89, 241, 245, 298
Areeawv 32
Areeayl 32, 87, 89, 168, 241, 260
Ardon 12
Armon 13, 15, 143, 167, 179
Armonee 13, 47, 82, 143, 172, 179, 261, 278
Arnon 14, 41, 46, 91, 100, 102, 104, 105, 164, 168, 194, 244, 253, 260, 305
Aryay 12, 13, 57, 62, 80, 87, 98, 167, 241
Arzee 167, 168, 169, 226
Aseeayl 15
Ashchur 40, 188, 239
Asir 15, 240
Atzmon 168
Avdee 85, 93, 111, 113, 134, 135, 213
Aveeayl 3, 155
Avee-az 212
Avee-chai 220
Avee-cha'yil 8, 12, 13, 14, 46, 48, 54, 62, 90, 113, 122, 182, 199, 212, 221, 241, 247
Avee-chayn 165, 218, 230, 231

Aveedawn 16, 192, 233
Aveedor 16, 69, 194
Avee-dror 51, 205, 207
Avee-ezer 120, 274
Aveehu 155
Aveehud 5, 157, 228, 285, 286
Avee-melech 21, 34, 87, 113, 120, 121, 123, 135, 178, 240, 252, 278
Aveenawdawv 12, 38, 110, 113, 114, 199, 268, 271
Avee-noam 17, 21, 69, 83, 84, 105, 136, 155, 158, 176, 177, 195, 196, 204, 217, 224, 240, 248, 287
Aveerawm 156, 170
Avee-shachar 189, 267, 282
Aveeshai 58, 71, 194, 195, 202, 228
Avee-shawmaw 284
Avee-shawr 18, 265
Avee-shur 47, 274
Avee-tal 17, 156
Avee-tuv 190, 298, 308
Avee-tzur 33, 115, 134, 280
Aveeyaw 155
Aveeyawm 28, 29, 41, 95, 100, 102, 104, 105, 128, 129, 144, 158, 244, 253, 260, 266
Avigdor 8, 16, 42, 58, 63, 66, 68, 87, 88, 119, 129, 132, 134, 135, 223, 275
Avnayr 3, 5, 17, 85, 91, 177, 187, 273
Avneeayl 17, 33, 115, 134, 144, 280
Avrawhawm 2, 4, 13, 15, 34, 62, 64, 135, 140, 156, 212, 260, 277
Avrawm 4, 259
Avshawlom 4, 7, 8, 51, 54, 57, 62, 69, 93, 125, 132, 161, 207, 227, 302
Avuyaw 155
Awch 144
Awdaw 53, 100
Awdawm 5, 40, 41, 49, 54, 86, 97, 102, 104, 108, 122, 204, 211, 225, 296
Awdiv 5, 156, 158, 170, 193, 203, 255, 274
Awdon 6
Awfree 184
Awgayl 213
Awgil 66, 137, 155, 208, 213, 223, 233, 242
Awhud 192, 262
Awhuv 159, 163, 165, 262
Awmayl 163, 164, 200, 225, 272
Awmir 102, 164, 166
Awmis 98, 131, 144, 164, 249, 255
Awmos 11, 193, 246, 252, 262, 270
Awmotz 50, 98, 141, 164, 165, 206, 209, 223, 280

Awmree 112
Awnuv 240
Awsaw 14, 61, 74, 162
Awsawayl 15
Awsawf 220
Awshayr 15, 19, 21, 42, 50, 127, 175, 176, 200, 257, 277
Awsneeayl 26, 107, 165, 180
Awtayr 240
Awvee 2, 16, 80, 172, 198, 235
Awznee 114
A'yawl 65, 172, 193, 210
Ayfai 26, 97, 103, 180, 188, 240, 254, 255, 262
Ayfaw 66
Ayfer 31, 117, 159, 184, 185, 205, 224, 241
Aylaw 4, 15, 45, 89, 175, 198, 296, 297
Aylawm 80, 162, 163, 198, 235, 255, 295
Aylee 43, 161, 170
Ayleeyawhu 44
Aynawn 34, 39, 41, 91, 100, 128, 129, 144, 158, 194, 244, 253, 260, 267
Aysawn 48, 107, 168, 202
Ayver 229
Az 173, 183
Azai 173
Azanyaw 32
Azawn 173
Azaryaw 28, 117, 118, 275, 276
Azreeayl 17, 117, 118, 121, 275, 276, 280

Baal 45, 51, 82, 178, 203, 219, 222
Bachan 261
Bahawt 177
Balfur 18, 174
Barkai 56, 175, 213, 222
Bar-Kochvaw 169, 183, 202, 291
Baruch see Bawruch
Bar-Yochawee 33, 291
Barzeelai 21, 23, 25, 26, 62, 119, 120, 180, 182, 281, 298
Bashaw 163, 272
Bawchir 33, 174
Bawchur 163, 178, 185, 249, 276
Bawhat 286
Bawheer 145, 175, 176, 177, 191, 215, 308
Bawhir see Bawheer
Bawrawk 18, 23, 56, 91, 175, 176, 185, 213, 273, 309
Bawrawm 18
Bawrekes 175, 222
Bawruch 19, 20, 21, 41, 42, 50, 127, 175, 176, 200

Key: *a* as in f*a*ther; *ai* as in *ai*sle; *aw* as in l*aw*; *ay* as in s*ay*; *e* as in b*e*t;

ee as in b*ee*t; *i* as in b*i*t; *o* as in n*o*; *oi* as in v*oi*d; *u* as in *ru*de.

Churee 40
Chuseeayl 66, 137
Chusheeawm 221, 237
Chusheeayl 221, 223

Dar 35, 216, 251
Dawgawn 34, 186, 209
Dawn 35, 81, 188, 192, 233
Dawnee 35
Dawneeayl 35, 38, 81, 188, 192, 233
Daryawvesh 36
Dawsawn 57, 165, 189
Dawvid 10, 18, 21, 23, 26, 35, 36,
    42, 45, 86, 91, 101, 103, 127, 131,
    160, 183, 189, 192, 195, 223, 240,
    250, 262, 271, 283
Deedee 38
Deenai 189
Dekel 36, 192, 293
Diklaw 192
Ditz 137, 192, 221, 234
Divree 19, 190, 221
D'lawyaw 187
Doayg 7
Dodee 36, 42, 86, 91
Dodo 38, 192
Doodai 192
Dor 38, 194
Doron 39, 58, 193, 194
Doronee 193, 194
Dosawn 39, 189
Dov 14, 20, 23, 39, 113, 194, 298
Dovayv 39, 164, 190, 200, 258, 259,
    278
D'ror 37, 191, 205
D'roree 37, 191, 205
D'uayl 38, 83
Dubee 113, 298
Dur 40, 58, 63, 108, 238, 241
D'vir 37, 61, 84, 133, 238

Eelawn 45, 140, 145
Eemawnuayl 146, 200, 250
Eeseesayl 171, 228
Eesur 240
Eetai 71, 131, 228
Eetawmawr 72, 81, 182, 192, 216,
    231, 232, 293, 294, 296, 301
Eeyov 76, 175, 178, 193, 246, 252,
    262
Eflawl 8, 120, 161, 261, 274
Efraws 42, 196
Efra'yim 12, 37, 42, 63, 132, 146,
    169, 179, 186, 207, 227, 229, 243,
    255, 271, 273, 274, 282, 286, 295,
    301
Efron 65, 184, 193, 196, 205
Egawl 209, 212, 304
Eglon 143

Elawzawr 5, 43
Elchawnawn 165, 216, 231, 232
Eldawd 10, 42, 45, 86, 91, 127, 160,
    165, 184, 223
Eleedawd 35
Elee-ezer 5, 33, 43, 117, 118, 121,
    275, 276, 280
Eleefaz 16, 171, 216, 244, 306
Eleefelet 8, 47, 82, 164, 220, 306
Eleehu 44
Eleemelech 28, 32, 33, 87, 95, 120,
    123, 135, 212, 240, 277, 278, 291
Eleenawsawn 161, 194
Eleenoar 235
Eleeor 56, 91, 138, 198, 210, 213,
    226, 247
Eleepelet 8, 82, 164, 220, 306
Eleerawm 156
Eleerawn 239, 242
Eleeron 233
Eleeshaw 44, 124
Eleeshawmaw 284
Eleeshua 124
Eleetuv 215, 303
Eleetzawfawn 164
Eleetzur 9, 96, 134, 210, 214
Eleefaz 163
Eles 160, 162, 200, 233, 242
Eletz 160, 162, 200, 233, 234
Elez 155, 239, 242
Elkawnaw 45, 51, 82
Elnawsawn 58, 71, 138, 161, 194,
    196, 214, 228
Elrawd 37, 45, 301
Eltzawfawn 8
Elyawdaw 83
Elyawkum 134
Elzawvawd 71, 161, 194, 228
Erez 45, 167, 168, 169, 226
Eshkol 47
Eved 127, 181
Ezraw 5, 33, 49, 120, 121, 181, 204,
    280
Ezree 49

Feivel 273

Gabee 51, 52
Gadeeayl 52, 175
Gai 34, 57, 127, 185, 187, 215
Gal 52, 102, 194
Galee 52, 102, 194
G'alyaw 209, 212, 304
Gavreeayl 12, 26, 41, 52, 57, 119,
    120, 180, 183, 187, 201, 208, 209,
    212, 241, 260, 280, 281, 302
Gamleeayl 53
Gawd 8, 29, 41, 48, 52, 54, 59, 61,
    91, 94, 101, 103, 113, 144, 208,
    209, 211, 212, 252, 262, 277

Key: *a* as in father; *ai* as in aisle; *aw* as in law; *ay* as in say; *e* as in bet;

Gawlyas 47, 57, 142, 173, 174, 218, 302, 305
Gaychazee 34, 57, 60, 185, 187, 215
Gayraw 25, 41, 48, 54, 59, 60, 61, 122, 211, 212, 250
Gayrshom 47, 55, 142, 143, 174, 218, 246
Gayrshon 47, 55, 142, 143, 173, 174, 218, 246, 305
G'dalyaw 12, 23, 30, 45, 53, 55, 92, 97, 98, 100, 121, 166, 200, 210, 216, 249, 254, 297, 300
G'dalyawhu 53, 170, 210, 302
Geebor 8, 28, 30, 48, 55, 57, 59, 61, 183, 209, 212, 260, 280
Geedayl 92, 97, 200, 210, 254, 297, 302
Geedee 55
Geelawn 155, 209, 233
Geelee 55, 213, 233
Geelon 155, 208, 213, 239, 242, 257
Geenas 53, 54, 58, 63, 73, 214, 225, 289
Geenaw 68, 142, 211
Geeoraw 80
Geetai 56
Geetee 56
Gefen 37, 208
Geva 66, 215, 293
Gever 41, 141, 180, 183, 187, 209, 212, 298
G'fanyaw 54
Gidon 29, 31, 41, 48, 54, 55, 59, 60, 94, 101, 103, 113, 116, 131, 185, 211, 212, 215, 238, 252
Gil 55, 137, 155, 200, 209, 213
Gilad 209, 213
Gilawd 56, 209, 213
Gilawdee 56, 209
Gil-awm 209, 213
Gil-lee 200
Ginson 53, 56, 57, 73, 209, 214, 215
Givaw 95, 209
Givon 31, 34, 57, 66, 69, 166, 187, 209, 215
Givson 31, 209
G'maryawhu 214
Goayl 57, 304
Gomer 214, 216
Govayr 32, 58, 86, 108, 141, 176, 188, 239, 266, 300
Gozawl 53, 58, 160, 171, 179, 189, 206, 216, 230, 239, 254, 263
Gunee 53, 59, 122, 124, 286
Gur 59, 80, 217, 245
Gur-Aryay 217, 245
Guree 59, 80
Gureeayl 59
Guryon 60

Guy 60
G'varawm 183
G'varyaw 183, 187

Hadar 60, 136, 139, 157, 216, 217, 268
Hadarawm 136, 139, 217
Hadarezer 136, 139, 217
Harayl 61, 66, 69, 102, 194, 293
Haskayl 33, 63, 64, 68, 291, 299, 300
Hawdawr 60, 217, 260
Hawdur 136, 139, 157, 217, 268
Hawrawn 14, 95, 102
Haymawn 46, 58, 64, 69, 146, 163, 185, 205, 206, 241, 300
Heelaw 122
Heelayl 12, 23, 30, 45, 55, 66, 85, 97, 100, 121, 122, 166, 200, 216, 223, 254, 269, 280, 283, 297
Helem 62, 64
Hersh 65
Hertzayl 62, 65, 205, 223, 307
Hevel 2, 66, 164, 171, 240, 289
Hod 67, 158, 260
Hodeeyaw 67, 158, 260, 300
Hoseer 6, 29, 42, 60, 113, 158, 160, 189
Hosha'yaw 124
Hunaw 6, 29, 42, 60, 64, 113, 120, 158, 160, 169, 175, 189, 269, 290

Ibn 92
Imree 19, 164, 190, 197, 221, 278
Ish-Cha'yil 29, 30, 54, 59, 91, 94, 123, 124
Ish-Hod 2, 113, 156, 193
Ish-Sechel 23
Ish-Shawlom 51, 57, 62, 69, 184, 202, 207, 284
Ivree 229

Kadish 7, 55, 61, 84, 116, 170, 208, 224
Kadmeeayl 7, 9, 11, 43, 81, 127
Kalmawn 31, 81, 216
Kaneeayl 74, 82, 113, 211, 219
Karmee 181, 236
Karmeeayl 181, 236
Karmel 24, 26, 28, 31, 37, 49, 51, 53, 54, 57, 66, 73, 86, 88, 100, 102, 108, 117, 123, 128, 131, 135, 142, 145, 178, 181, 204, 209, 211, 214, 215, 225, 236, 240, 289, 292, 296
Karm'lee 24, 26, 28, 40, 49, 51, 53, 54, 88, 102, 108, 117, 123, 131, 132, 135, 142, 178, 181, 204, 211, 214, 225, 240, 292, 296
Karmeeayl 28

ee as in b*ee*t; *i* as in b*i*t; *o* as in n*o*; *oi* as in v*oi*d; *u* as in r*u*de.

Karnee 238
Karneeayl 181, 182, 236, 237, 238
Kasreeayl 19, 21, 28, 30, 32, 33, 34,
   37, 38, 46, 51, 62, 63, 65, 82, 87,
   119, 120, 123, 135, 140, 144, 169,
   201, 203, 212, 219, 222, 240, 245,
   246, 277, 281, 291, 293
Kawdosh 133
Kawrin 238
Kawtawn 91, 114, 272, 295
Kawlayv 26, 27, 28, 30, 31, 50, 54,
   95, 116, 136, 165, 182, 241
Kawlil 81, 237
Kawlul 237
Kawvud 233
Kaydmaw 7, 178
Kaydawr 37, 39, 40, 66, 90, 97, 103,
   180, 254, 255, 271
Ka'yin 45
Kaynawn 45
Kedem 11, 43, 83, 173, 237
Keevee 84
Kerem 181, 236
Keren 181, 182
K'feer 32, 237
K'fir   see K'feer
Kisron 84, 135, 169, 201, 203, 246,
   293
Klonimos 82
Kochav   see Kochawv
Kochawv 151, 169, 183, 202, 291
Kochvaw 151, 169, 183, 202, 291
Kohayn 31, 116
Koheles 31
Konanyawhu 47, 182, 185, 202, 294,
   301
Konayn 134
Korach 27, 61
Koresh 29,, 34, 67, 183, 185
Kotz 215, 238
Kush 26, 32, 180

Lapeedos 85, 172, 181, 247
Lapid 41, 172
Lawtif 242
Lawvawn 7, 10, 24, 25, 40, 85, 91,
   143, 179, 181, 191, 201, 211, 217,
   242, 243, 247, 287, 289
Lawvee 81, 86, 87, 89, 242
La'yish 62, 87, 89, 90, 141, 199, 241,
   247
Layv 88, 240
Layvee 89, 298
Leeor 87, 210, 226, 241, 247
Leeron 89, 110, 195, 244, 246
Leetal 293
Leshem 88, 177, 218, 286
Likchee 261

Livnee 10, 24, 25, 40, 179, 211, 217,
   287
Lot 47, 220, 296
Lotawn 47, 90, 164, 256
Luz 45, 172
L'vawnon 40

Ma'a'yawn 41
Magdeeayl 54, 105, 136, 193, 195,
   258
Maharee 185, 249
Mahayr 185, 249
Maimon 93, 206, 208
Maksim 131, 254
Malawch 166
Malawchee 28, 85, 93, 127, 136, 165,
   166, 181, 213
Malkawm 46, 95, 120, 135, 252, 278
Malkeeayl 33, 45, 142, 301
Malkeerawm 45, 140
Malkeetzedek 45
Malkeeyaw 301
Maluchee 85
Mardus 257
Margeea 227, 268
Margoa 51, 57, 227, 268
Marnin 95, 234, 251, 257, 262, 275
Marpay 74, 162
Maskeel   see Maskil
Maskil 41, 68, 83, 95
Masyaw 96
Matan   see Matawn
Matanyaw 58, 92, 138, 193, 253,
   258, 295
Matanyawhu   see Matanyaw
Matawn 58, 92, 193, 194, 253, 295
Matee 96
Matisyaw   see Matisyawhu
Matisyawhu 58, 71, 92, 96, 138,
   193, 194, 214, 228, 253, 258, 295
Matmon 96, 120, 290
Matnai 193, 253, 295
Matzleeach 86, 248, 266, 300
Mawgayn 92, 212, 256, 258
Mawheer 92, 185, 200, 249, 255
Mawhir   see Mawheer
Mawlon 241
Mawnoach 57, 112, 219
Mawon 9, 20, 104
Mawrd'chai 14, 25, 29, 48, 60, 92,
   94, 101, 103, 113, 116, 224, 238,
   250, 252, 257, 262, 302
Mawrom 66, 102, 166
Mawsok 96, 105, 136, 224, 257
Mawsos 234, 257, 275
Maydawd 42, 95, 98, 144, 249
Mayeer 11, 23, 27, 29, 49, 56, 85,
   91, 97, 98, 110, 116, 121, 139,

Key: *a* as in f*a*ther; *ai* as in *ai*sle; *aw* as in l*aw*; *ay* as in s*ay*; *e* as in b*e*t;

ee as in b*ee*t; *i* as in b*i*t; *o* as in n*o*; *oi* as in v*oi*d; *u* as in r*u*de.

Neta 235, 252, 265
Netzach 10, 40, 195
N'horai 222, 265
Nilbawv 86, 91, 163
Nimrod 257
Nin 266
Nir 109, 266, 269
Nirayl 109, 266, 269
Nireeayl 109, 266
Nireeyaw 109, 266, 269
Nisim see Neesim
Nitron 62
Nitzchee 40, 195
Niv 109, 164, 190, 278
Nivchawr 33, 174
Noach 109, 112, 207, 219
Noadyaw 308
Noam 42, 110, 144, 195, 249, 264
Noawd 308
Noawz 180
Nodaw 110
Nofach 177, 218, 286
Noga 110, 267
Notaya 54, 86, 211
Notayr 42
Notzar 62
Notzayr 40
Noy 111, 165, 267
N'sanayl 54, 71, 107, 138, 161, 196,
    214, 258, 264, 266, 295
N'sanyaw 264
N'teea 251, 252, 265
N'tzeeach 32, 86, 108, 132, 141, 176,
    188, 203, 239, 246, 248, 266, 300
Nun 50, 167, 214, 244
Nur 41, 111, 172, 268
Nuree 41, 111, 172, 181, 256, 268
Nureeayl 41, 111, 172, 256, 268
Nureeyaw 111, 172, 256, 268
N'vawt 68

Odayd 268
Ofer 65, 112, 193, 205
Ofeer see Ofir
Ofir 270
Ohad 159
Ohayd 159, 192
Omer 190, 197, 258
On 12
Onawn 12, 246, 270
Or 197, 210, 222, 226, 270
Orawn 151, 169, 202
Orayv 25, 34, 53, 160, 171, 179, 186,
    189, 206, 254, 257, 308
Or-Cha'yim 171
Oree 210, 222, 226, 270
Oren 4, 15, 89, 112, 167, 168, 169,
    270, 296
Oron 197, 270

Ovadyaw 28, 62, 85, 93, 98, 111,
    112, 113, 127, 163, 164, 181, 213,
    249, 255, 272
Ovayd 40, 62, 85, 93, 98, 100, 111,
    113, 127, 134, 135, 163, 164, 181,
    249, 272
Oz 173

Paltee 114
Palteeayl 114
Pawlawl 120, 125, 261, 274
Pawsayach 31, 185
Pawz 171, 216, 244, 272, 306
Pazee 272
Pekach 33, 63, 175, 186, 207, 243,
    255, 271, 273, 282, 301
Peleg 34, 39, 89, 91, 100, 102, 104,
    105, 128, 129, 144, 211, 244, 253,
    260, 267
Perach 179, 207, 295
Peresh 116, 123
Peretz 115
Pesach 27, 51, 115, 205, 207
Piltai 114
Pinchaws 26, 37, 40, 66, 90, 97,
    103, 107, 116, 180, 188, 239, 240,
    254, 255, 262, 271
P'neenee 115, 216, 251, 280
Poraws 63, 132, 146, 274
P'rachyaw 63, 179, 186, 197, 207,
    243, 255, 271, 282, 301
P'rudaw 53
P'sachyaw 16, 51, 205, 207
Puraw 37, 63, 132, 146, 169, 179,
    207, 227, 229, 273, 274, 282, 295,
    301

Raanawn 21, 69, 84, 117, 155, 158,
    177, 179, 277, 287
Rabaw 73, 97, 121, 178, 200, 219,
    222, 280, 297
Rabee 36, 261
Rachamawn 256
Rachmeeayl 185, 256
Ranayn 118, 277
Rav 62, 73, 92, 97, 98, 178, 280,
    297, 302
Rawfaw 74, 162
Rawfu 74, 162
Rawm 69, 275
Rawnee 277
Rawnon 118
Rawvaw 15, 20, 62, 73, 92, 97, 98,
    121, 144, 200, 219, 222, 254, 280,
    297, 302
Rawvid 118
Rawviv 118, 238
Rawz 119, 276

Key: *a* as in f*a*ther; *ai* as in *ai*sle; *aw* as in l*aw*; *ay* as in s*ay*; *e* as in b*e*t;

ee as in b*ee*t; *i* as in b*i*t; *o* as in n*o*; *oi* as in v*oi*d; *u* as in r*u*de.

Key: *a* as in f*a*ther; *ai* as in *ai*sle; *aw* as in l*aw*; *ay* as in s*ay*; *e* as in b*e*t;

ee as in b*ee*t; *i* as in b*i*t; *o* as in n*o*; *oi* as in v*oi*d; *u* as in r*u*de.

FEMININE NAMES

Abeeree 17
Abeeraw 3, 11, 17, 26, 130, 156, 168, 170, 180
Acheenoam 7, 17, 21, 69, 83, 84, 96, 105, 136, 155, 158, 176, 195, 204, 217, 224, 248, 264, 287
Acheeshawlom 201
Achsaw 260
Achuzaw 82
Adee 118, 157
Adeeayl 158
Adeeaylaw 157
Adeenaw 21, 69, 73, 98, 118, 155, 156, 157, 158, 196, 203, 260, **287**
Adeeraw 5, 6, 55, 158, 168, 180, 193
Adeevaw 5, 31, 41, 61, 67, 158, 193, 231, 249, 255, 258, 262
Adeeyaw 118
Aderes 157
Adis 196
Advaw 158
Agawlaw 143
Ahadaw 163
Aharonaw 1, 159
Aharonis 1, 159
Ahavaw 10, 45, 159, **163**
Ahudaw 10, 121, 159, 163, 166, 216, 297
Ahuvaw 10, 26, 36, 71, 86, 91, 102, 119, 127, 131, 144, 146, 159, 160, 165, 183, 184, 195, 223, 240, 250, 262
Aleesaw 133, 200
Aleetzaw 133
Aleeyaw 161
Aleezaw 50, 70, 74, 83, 137, 160, 162, 196, 199, 200, 225, 232, 233, 242, 257, 262
Aleksandraw 6, 8, 28, 33, 44, 70, 79, 85, 93, 113, 117, 118, 121, 125, 161, 180, 213, 275, 276, 280
Almaw 80, 162, 167, 185, 214, **224**, 228, 235, 244, 248, 249, 253, 266, 295
Alonaw 4, 9, 13, 45, 162
Alufaw 33, 34, 45, 62, 76, 83, 162
Alumaw 162, 174, 185
Alumis 162, 174
Amalyaw 163, 272
Amawnaw 11, 64, 163, 205, 206, 299
Ameeor 10, 139, 141, 222
Ameeraw 19, 39, 109, 164, 258, 278

Ameesaw 71, 95, 99, 119, 131, **144**, 164, 249, 255
Ameetzaw 3, 52, 55, 59, 61, 62, **113**, 124, 130, 134, 141, 164, 165, 168, 180, 280
Amtzaw 4, 5, 8, 12, 21, 22, 28, 29, 30, 48, 50, 59, 61, 81, 92, 94, 98, 100, 102, 103, 106, 107, 113, 114, 116, 120, 144, 165, 182, 241, 250, 259, 262, 298, 302
Araylaw 136, 165
Ardaw 12
Ardonaw **12**
Areeayl 4, 8, 12, 13, 14, 21, 22, 23, 27, 28, 29 30, 32, 50, 52, 59, 60, 62, 81, 86, 88, 98, 107, 120, 144, 166, 179, 182, 206, 241, 298
Areeaylaw 12, 13, 14, 30, 32, 43, 44, 59, 60, 81, 86, 87, 90, 166, 241
Areezaw 45, 112, 167
Arelaw 166
Armonaw 13, 112, 143, 167, 172
Armonis 167
Arnaw 45
Arnee see Awrnee
Arneenaw 168
Arneenis 168
Arnis 45, 167
Arnonaw 14, 168
Arnonis 168
Arzaw 15, 112, 168
Arzis 169
Asalyaw 53, 67, 92, 97, 126, 149, 166, 170, 200, 268, 297, 302
Aseedaw 170
Aseesaw 169
Ashayraw 15, 53, 71, 176, 206, **224**
Ashayris 206, 224
Asheeraw 15, 29, 35, 120, 158, 160, 169, 189
Astayraw 207, 295
Astayreeyaw 295
Atawraw 4, 13, 21, 29, 37, 38, 45, 46, 62, 65, 82, 84, 87, 95, 99, 100, 119, 120, 121, 123, 126, 135, 140, 141, 169, 201, 203, 212, 219, 222, 239, 249, 255, 277, 278, 281, 301
Ateeraw 170
Ateres 135, 141, 169, 201
Aturaw 81, 82, 84, 170
Avee 148, 171
Aveeaylaw 2, 3, 4, 44, 148, 155

409

Key: *a* as in father; *ai* as in *ai*sle; *aw* as in law; *ay* as in say; *e* as in bet;

ee as in b*ee*t; *i* as in b*i*t; *o* as in n*o*; *oi* as in v*oi*d; *u* as in r*u*de.

Key: *a* as in f*a*ther; *ai* as in *ai*sle; *aw* as in l*aw*; *ay* as in s*ay*; *e* as in b*e*t;

ee as in b**ee**t; *i* as in b**i**t; *o* as in n**o**; *oi* as in v**oi**d; *u* as in r**u**de.

Mawgaynaw 6, 8, 46, 47, 59, 72, 73, 83, 92, 111, 112, 130, 132, 142, 164, 211, 220, 256, 278
Mawraw 91, 100, 102, 104, 105, 193, 194, 245, 252, 262, 270
Mawrawsaw 39, 95, 100, 102, 104, 105, 130, 144, 244, 245, 252, 262, 270
Mayeeraw see M'eeraw
Mazal see Mazawl
Mazawl 48, 93, 98, 151, 206, 224, 255, 262
Mazheeraw 98
Meechal 34, 38, 41, 100, 101, 227, 258, 267
Meechawaylaw 101, 227, 257, 258
Meelee 259
Meeraw 79, 260
M'eeraw 1, 3, 5, 12, 18, 27, 29, 34, 50, 56, 85, 91, 98, 110, 116, 121, 130, 133, 141, 143, 153, 176, 177, 183, 184, 186, 187, 191, 197, 213, 214, 215, 247, 255, 260, 273, 287
M'eeree see M'eeraw
M'eeris 260
Meeyaw 257
Meree 257
M'heeraw 92, 185, 249, 255
Migdawlaw 8, 13, 31, 42, 46, 72, 73, 87, 95, 129, 130, 172, 211, 248, 256, 258
Migdawnaw 38, 54, 58, 71, 77, 92, 96, 107, 138, 192, 193, 194, 196, 228, 258
Milkaw 6, 8, 33, 41, 43, 44, 49, 63, 70, 79, 93, 117, 118, 120, 121, 246, 258, 259, 261, 274, 275, 276, 280, 289, 291
Minchaw 58, 76, 77, 96, 107, 193, 194
Miryawm 14, 28, 34, 39, 41, 45, 62, 89, 91, 95, 100, 102, 104, 105, 128, 130, 144, 193, 194, 211, 244, 246, 252, 253, 254, 262, 266, 267, 270
Mitzpaw 261
M'labeves 163
M'nachaymaw 99
M'nachaymeeyaw
   see M'nachaymaw
M'noraw 256
M'nuchaw 4, 51, 54, 57, 62, 69, 94, 109, 143, 202, 207, 219, 268, 269, 302
M'onaw 9, 20, 58, 63
M'oraw 98
Morawshaw 261
Moreeayl 36, 149, 261
Moreeaw 36, 149, 261
Moris 36, 149, 261

Moshawaw 44, 49, 79, 104, 114, 124
M'romaw 66, 166
M'shulemes 94, 109, 112, 128, 143, 184, 202, 219, 268, 269, 302
M'sukaw 96, 98, 105, 136, 195, 224, 256, 257
M'tzawdaw 172
M'shulemes 57, 62
M'voreches 20

Naamaw 7, 17, 69, 105, 110, 111, 119, 136, 144, 180, 194, 217, 244, 249, 255, 263, 287
Naamawnaw 105, 263
Naamis 110, 263
Naaraw 92, 167, 185, 214, 228, 248, 249, 254, 261
Nachas 109
Nafsheeyaw 29
Nasyaw 264
Nawawmee 7, 17, 25, 83, 84, 96, 98, 105, 110, 111, 119, 136, 138, 144, 179, 180, 194, 196, 204, 217, 224, 244, 248, 255, 256, 265, 271, 287
Nawchaw 109
Nawdin 145
Nawvaw 24, 26, 49, 53, 54, 88, 98, 102, 104, 108, 242, 264, 289, 292, 296
Nawvis 83, 84, 109, 265
Nayrlee 17
N'chawmaw see Nechawmaw
N'deevaw 2, 5, 6, 9, 34, 37, 41, 48, 76, 105, 110, 114, 142, 156, 157, 161, 170, 193, 199, 203, 228, 249, 255, 264, 268, 271, 301
Nechaw 109
Nechawmaw 100, 106, 108, 247, 256, 264, 265
Ne'edawraw 2, 6, 9, 156, 157, 193, 199
Neelee 108
N'eemaw 1, 73, 80, 166, 195, 199, 235, 259, 265
Ne'emawnaw 11, 64, 205, 299
Ne'emenes 205, 299
Neenaw 266
Neereeayl see Nirayl
Neeris 179, 266
Neetzaw 12, 42, 63, 115, 132, 179, 186, 197, 207, 243, 255, 267, 271, 273, 286, 301
Neetzawnaw 115, 267
Neevaw 19, 39, 109, 200, 258, 259, 278
Neta 206, 221, 265
N'geedaw 15, 29, 35, 106, 158, 160, 189, 263

Key: *a* as in father; *ai* as in *ai*sle; *aw* as in law; *ay* as in say; *e* as in bet;

ee as in b*ee*t; *i* as in b*i*t; *o* as in n*o*; *oi* as in v*oi*d; *u* as in r*u*de.

R'nawnaw 70, 74, 200, 204, 233, 257, 262, 277
R'nawnis 277
Roaw 68
Rofee 14, 61, 74, 118, 162
Romaw 75, 148, 149, 280
Romaymaw 75
Romeeyaw 75, 148, 149, 280
Romis 75, 280
Rom'mis 75
Ronaw 200, 281
Ronee 133, 233, 281
Roneeyaw 118, 133, 281
Ronis 118, 281
Ronlee 146, 242, 281
Ruchawmaw 100, 106, 108, 185, 256
Rus, 18, 24, 26, 41, 45, 89, 127, 131, 144, 195, 283
R'uvas 120
R'uvaynaw 68, 120, 278
R'veevaw 118

Saadaw 18, 28, 43, 85, 93, 124, 275, 276, 280, 283
Saharaw 186, 284, 286
Sapeer 285
Sapeeraw 126, 285, 286
Sapeeris 126
Sapir   see Sapeer
Savyon 206
Sawrai   see Sawraw
Sawraw 2, 6, 12, 14, 26, 30, 41, 62, 67, 83, 90, 110, 114, 121, 126, 140, 149, 156, 157, 161, 170, 180, 193, 199, 203, 247, 271, 285, 301, 305
Sawrid 114
Sawris 286
Seemaw 152, 290
Seesaw 50, 70, 133, 200, 204, 233, 237
Seevawnaw 133, 139, 290
Sela 286
S'gulaw 53, 74, 82, 120, 123, 126, 127, 152, 272, 283, 286
Shaanawnaw 51, 129, 201, 227, 268
Shachar 171
Shachareeyaw 187
Shacharis 171, 187, 282, 305
Shafreeraw 108
Shalgeeyaw 61, 287, 289
Shalgis 61
Shalheves 41, 111, 181
Shalvaw 202
Shapeeraw 137
Shawron 282, 287
Shawulaw 126
Shawvchaw 166, 297
Sh'choraw 97, 116

Sh'daymaw 40, 54, 86, 100, 102, 108, 211
Sh'eefaw 66, 164
Sheeraw 1, 19, 73, 110, 118, 122, 182, 246, 256, 259, 289
Sheeree 89, 122, 195, 199, 289
Sheerlee   see Shirlee
Shifraw 7, 21, 23, 83, 129, 155, 159, 176, 204, 205, 245, 248, 287, 288
Shikmaw 33
Shikmonaw 33
Shimaws 32, 70, 114, 129
Shimonaw 32, 70, 114, 129, 133, 290
Shimraw 40, 42, 47, 223, 288
Shimreeyaw 40, 42, 47, 223, 288
Shimris 8, 16, 40, 42, 62, 63, 66, 68, 69, 79, 83, 87, 88, 129, 132, 153, 164, 212, 220, 223, 278, 288
Shimshonaw 34, 50, 73, 116, 125, 284
Shirlee 19, 89, 110, 122, 195, 199, 256, 289
Sh'kaydaw 33
Sh'lomis 4, 51, 54, 57, 62, 69, 80, 94, 109, 112, 119, 128, 132, 143, 161, 184, 201, 207, 219, 227, 269, 275, 284, 287, 302
Sh'lomtzeeyon 284
Shmuaylaw 70, 125, 128, 129
Shomayraw 62, 69
Shomronaw 285
Shoshanaw 131, 179, 186, 197, 207, 243, 255, 271, 273, 282, 286, 289, 292, 301
Shoshawn 131, 289, 292
Sh'seelaw 221, 295
Sh'sulaw 221
Shulamis 4, 7, 8, 51, 54, 57, 62, 69, 80, 94, 109, 112, 119, 125, 128, 132, 134, 143, 161, 184, 201, 202, 207, 227, 269, 275, 287, 289, 302
Simchaw 132
Simchis 208
Simchonaw 118, 137, 208, 257
S'maychaw 132, 225, 234, 257, 262
S'nunis 160, 179

Tachan 219
Tagaw 135, 246, 293
Tal 136, 293
Talmaw 20, 31, 34, 56, 66, 69, 95, 102, 137, 166, 293
Talmis 20, 34, 40, 56, 66, 69, 95, 102, 137, 187, 293
Talmor 293
Tal-or 293
Taloraw 137, 293
Talyaw 136, 137, 159, 293
Tamaw 46, 64, 185

Key: *a* as in f*a*ther; *ai* as in *ai*sle; *aw* as in l*aw*; *ay* as in s*ay*; *e* as in b*e*t;

ee as in b*ee*t; *i* as in b*i*t; *o* as in n*o*; *oi* as in v*oi*d; *u* as in r*u*de.